"For neither the first nor, surely, the last time, Ken Hersh has given others a valuable gift: a stunningly candid account of the challenges he's confronted—happily and successfully in the main but painfully and failingly at times—as his remarkable life has unfolded. Few in his or any generation have struck a better balance than Ken in doing both well and good. This brutally honest memoir teaches us not only how but why."

— **DAVID SALEM,** senior advisor to the Investment Fund for Foundations

"Ken Hersh sees and then seizes opportunities. His book could accurately be called *The Art of Possibility* or *The Art of the Deal*. To use Faulkner's words, Ken has weathered professional and personal storms and not just endured but prevailed."

— **TALMAGE BOSTON,** lawyer and historian

PRAISE FOR
THE FASTEST TORTOISE

"I have long admired Ken Hersh's business skills and now admire his literary skills as well. A first-rate read about a compelling life story. I cannot recommend it too highly."

—**DAVID M. RUBENSTEIN,** cofounder of the Carlyle Group, host of *The David Rubenstein Show*, and author of *How to Lead* and *How to Invest*

"We always look at successful people and wonder what special qualities they had to bring them success. In *The Fastest Tortoise*, Ken Hersh lays out a charming, funny, and human story of how he rose to the pinnacle of success in America. In addition to the many totally readable life lessons, the most important one is that nice guys can finish first."

—**BILL BROWDER,** author of *Red Notice* and *Freezing Order*

"Ken Hersh has a knack for storytelling. His career spans building a $20 billion private equity firm to heading a presidential center on an academic campus. But he is much more than a latter-day Forrest Gump—he is a teacher. *The Fastest Tortoise* should be required reading in every graduate business school, but the stories are so entertaining—and enlightening—that the everyday reader will not be able to put it down. A true delight to read!"

—**ROBERT W. JORDAN,** diplomat in residence at Southern Methodist University and former U.S. ambassador to Saudi Arabia

"By any measure, Ken Hersh has led a rich, purposeful life—from Dallas middle-class youth to Ivy League aspirant, to builder of a private equity firm with billions in capital, and then to CEO of a presidential think tank. Along the way, Ken has become a foremost expert on leadership. Thankfully, the 'fastest tortoise' has come out of his shell to share the considerable wisdom he has gathered on his journey. As he says, he has 'a story to tell.' This absorbing, highly readable book more than proves it."

—**MARK K. UPDEGROVE,** president and CEO of the LBJ Foundation and author of *Incomparable Grace: JFK in the Presidency*

THE

FASTEST
TORTOISE

THE
FASTEST
TORTOISE

WINNING IN INDUSTRIES
I KNEW NOTHING ABOUT

A LIFE SPENT FIGURING IT OUT

KEN HERSH

IN CONVERSATION WITH STEVE FIFFER

GREENLEAF
BOOK GROUP PRESS

All the author's proceeds from this book will be donated to medical research focused on eradicating heart disease and mental illness.

Published by Greenleaf Book Group Press
Austin, Texas
www.gbgpress.com

Distributed by Greenleaf Book Group

For ordering information or special discounts for bulk purchases, please contact Greenleaf Book Group at PO Box 91869, Austin, TX 78709, 512.891.6100.

Design and composition by Greenleaf Book Group and Sheila Parr
Cover design by Greenleaf Book Group and Sheila Parr
Cover image © iStockphoto / lvcandy

Publisher's Cataloging-in-Publication data is available.

Print ISBN: 979-8-88645-037-8

eBook ISBN: 979-8-88645-038-5

To offset the number of trees consumed in the printing of our books, Greenleaf donates a portion of the proceeds from each printing to the Arbor Day Foundation. Greenleaf Book Group has replaced over 50,000 trees since 2007.

Printed in the United States of America on acid-free paper

23 24 25 26 27 28 29 30   10 9 8 7 6 5 4 3 2 1

First Edition

*To all my colleagues, friends, and supporters who have driven
me to keep putting one foot in front of the other*

IN LIFE, THERE IS NO NEUTRAL OR REVERSE.
ONLY FORWARD.

CONTENTS

A STORY TO TELL

L IFE IS A SERIES of historical accidents.

Lucky for me, I am accident-prone.

Having reached this point in life, I am often asked for my secrets, like I'm some modern-day Yoda. People want to hear some learning, leadership, or life lessons, as if I have followed some scripted action plan designed at an earlier point in my life. While paying it forward is a concept that should never get old, I often wonder how this "admissions mistake" has wisdom others seek out. I had mentors who imparted lessons and I feel like I have built on those. If those who come behind me build on that foundation, I will be an even happier camper.

I have been fortunate in many ways to have had opportunities present themselves to me. While it may appear that my resume-building path was a series of logical steps, it sure didn't feel that way at the time. However, as good fortune would have it, here I am. Good luck and hard work put me in a position where people seem interested in hearing what I have to say. I have no shortage of places where I get to express my opinion, be it from my perch as CEO of a major presidential think tank, as a private investor who has had the luxury of working with some of the most skilled investors of our time, or as a participant in some of the leading intellectual forums in the world.

I have no idea where my self-confidence came from. Maybe my mother didn't breastfeed me long enough when I was an infant. (Frankly, to this day, I have no idea if she breastfed me at all!) I have spent countless hours trying to roll back the clock to find some seminal event that defined everything that came after. But I cannot find it. Instead, I've come to accept that I have been shaped by my experiences and I'll leave it at that.

Building a private equity firm in one industry in one town that went from a start-up to over $20 billion of capital has a way of attracting some attention. It couldn't have been my good looks. Along the way, I was never shy about sharing my opinions regarding investing or the energy business whenever asked. Heck, I was just flattered that someone cared enough to listen.

Since coming on board to lead the George W. Bush Presidential Center in 2016, I continue to share my views with whoever will listen. But the table has also been turned. In my role as CEO, I have had the opportunity and privilege to meet many global dignitaries and to interview leaders such as Amazon's Jeff Bezos, Carlyle's David Rubenstein, former ambassador Nikki Haley, comedian Jay Leno, businessman and philanthropist Michael Milken, Chobani founder and CEO Hamdi Ulukaya, former secretary of state Henry Kissinger, and former secretary of defense Jim Mattis, among others. Those conversations, I hope, offered insight into what makes the person tick as much as what he or she has accomplished. They were each incredible learning experiences for me as well.

Amid this work, colleagues encouraged me to share the tales and takeaways from my exposure to both the private and public sectors. One Dallas friend, former U.S. ambassador to Saudi Arabia (2001–2003) Bob Jordan, suggested I contact the writer with whom he had worked on his fascinating memoir, *Desert Diplomat*. Steve Fiffer, I learned, had also collaborated on the memoirs of former secretary of state Jim Baker and the Southern Poverty Law Center's founder, Morris Dees.

After a simple Google search, I was sufficiently intimidated. I had to work up the strength to propose to Steve that I write something with him. Steve is a prolific author and one heck of a writer. His personal story is even more intimidating: A high school wrestling accident was supposed to leave him paralyzed for the remainder of his life, but he wouldn't take no for an answer, and he dedicated himself to an excruciating rehabilitation regimen that ultimately and miraculously landed him on two feet again. That would have been inspirational enough, but some twenty-five years later, he was hit by a car while walking across the street, which ultimately caused him to return to the wheelchair. Despite his physical setbacks, however, he remained an optimistic voice on the pages of his seventeen books, numerous screenplays, and a plethora of articles about business, sports, and his personal journey. He is an American literary treasure.

Even though I went to Princeton and Steve went to Yale and our politics are, nicely put, rather different, Steve and I immediately hit it off. I was encouraged when he agreed with my friends and family that I had a story to tell and insights to share. Thus began more than twenty lengthy conversations ranging from one to two hours—usually in the early hours of weekend mornings. When we finally finished and discussed how we might structure a book, we decided on the unconventional Q&A format that follows. *The Fastest Tortoise* is, like my interviews at the Bush Center, a freewheeling, extended, and purposeful conversation.

In putting the book together, I have tried my best to describe accurately the important events and individuals in my life and build that tale around some key observations that, in hindsight, form quite the glossary of my life's lessons. I have highlighted many of the "Ken-isms" that seem to have found their way into my everyday vocabulary. I have also relied on public and private documents and articles as well as conversations with those with whom I've worked. If any facts prove to be "alternative," please know this was not our intent.

Of course, over time some memories fade. I do feel confident that these pages paint an accurate picture. Most likely there are many memories that are repressed, many that would, no doubt, make me second-guess some of the conclusions here. If I ever dig those out of my dusty attic, I will present them in a volume two, with full redaction of the tales told here. (Caution: Do not hold your breath waiting for that one.)

As I worked on this tome, the planet was gripped by the COVID-19 pandemic. This situation tested just about every aspect of society—from family dynamics to corporate organizations to societal constructs themselves. This was a confluence of events that had seemed relegated to the history books. The post–World War II order was something whose origins we studied and whose structure we enjoyed. I have a feeling that the next fifty years will be shaped by the next few.

Closer to home, my circumstance was no exception. Since the onset of the COVID-19 pandemic, my world was rocked as well. In 2020, my personal situation experienced volatility that culminated in an end to my thirty-year marriage to the woman I loved, while some simple discomfort in my chest one October morning quickly evolved into a full-fledged reconstruction of my heart. Amid the drafts of this work, my personal evolution continued, and I found myself no longer writing in the past tense. I have come to realize that moving forward requires a lot of tenacity and a strong sense of optimism.

After passing the baton at my investment firm to the next generation of executives, my sights widened, allowing me to flex some intellectual muscles that I had only barely developed. But more important, in entering my second career I've been energized by the exposure to a dynamic group of exceptionally talented young professionals knee-deep in trying to figure out some of the most pressing issues of the day.

In this future-focused context, leadership traits are more important than ever. But leadership is not something that is demonstrated by just a few individuals. Everyone demonstrates aspects of leadership, whether it be at the kitchen table, during sidewalk conversations, in the communities with which we engage, or within the organizations in which we are members.

As a young capitalist, I thought leadership was relatively easy. To navigate uncertainty, I'd think through the decision tree of choices, evaluate the relative costs and benefits, and pick the best route. I had studied managing through uncertainty. In the volatile energy industry, uncertainty was the norm, and I navigated those waters relatively well. While the future was uncertain, the range of outcomes was not.

That was true throughout the economy. Leaders who could navigate well through uncertainty succeeded. Those who could not failed.

Today, that challenge has changed. This era is one of artificial intelligence, machine learning, manipulating human DNA, distributed blockchain networks, lightning-fast global connectivity, and the coming quantum computers with speeds one hundred million times faster than today's versions. In this era, a leader's challenge is not just navigating through uncertainty but also managing through the *unknowable*.

Relying on the past to be predictive will be less useful. There is no simple decision tree to draw when the choices and outcomes cannot be defined. We only have who we are to lean on. The characteristics that define our personal cores will guide us, whether we like it or not. Unfortunately, that personal core isn't something that we just acquire. It is the accumulation of experiences—some intentional, some accidental. As is often said, life is what happens while we're busy making other plans.

Without a script, moving forward is a straightforward exercise. Just be your best self and remain true to your values.

My simple goal here is to share the stories of my journey. Some stories may provide inspiration; others may incentivize you to change course. At a minimum, my hope is that they will inspire you to reflect. Contrary to conventional wisdom, leadership is not that complicated. Leaders are optimistic and present a clear vision. Leaders have only one gear—forward. There is no reverse.

As you read about my journey, let your mind wander as you look toward your horizon.

Ken Hersh
February 2023

ARE YOU KIDDING ME?

I HAVE A CONFESSION TO make to Ken. I'm not really interested in how the shareholders in the Mesa deal were compensated, or the particulars of his firm's sale to Barclays, or the specific arrangement Ken made with the Carlyle Group. Moreover, unlike Ken, I am not a compassionate conservative who believes in small government and thinks it was wise to pull out of the Paris Agreement. Au contraire, although Ken would hand me my lunch if we debated our differences, I am a flaming liberal, capital-G Government, *oui oui* Paris Agreement guy.

So why, you might ask, did I spend a good portion of the last two years working with Ken on this book?

It's a good question, and one that several friends have asked me over the course of this project. They know that in the past—because of ideological differences—I have turned down the opportunity to collaborate with both a former secretary of defense and a member of one of the wealthiest, most influential conservative dynasties in the country. "Are you kidding me? Life's too short," I've explained. "I couldn't look myself or my family in the mirror if I helped give voice to their stories."

While "How could you do it?" may be a good question, it is one I've never asked myself after my first conversation with Ken. We hit it off immediately—he's a *mensch*—and it was clear that he wasn't pushing an agenda, trying to justify some controversial past deeds, or attempting to puff himself up for family and friends. He was just a guy with an interesting story to tell and an intriguing philosophy about how to live life, run a business, shepherd a not-for-profit, give back to the community, and relate to others.

It did not hurt that much of this philosophy was expressed through colorful but meaningful maxims such as the title of this book or "Yellow lights don't turn green" or "Create a foxhole and fill it" or "Be uncomfortable." It also didn't hurt that I had previously had wonderful experiences collaborating with two Republicans from the Lone Star State—former U.S. ambassador to Saudi Arabia Bob Jordan (who put Ken in touch with me) and former secretary of state James A. Baker III. What all three of these successful Texans had in common was that they felt comfortable in their own skin and didn't mind being asked tough questions. All are fine writers in their own right, as well—a most helpful skill when you're working as a team.

What I gathered quickly from that first conversation with Ken was that this was going to be a book about a fascinating journey taken by someone who is smart and funny, a good storyteller with an eye for detail, a guy who has a strong sense of self but does not take himself too seriously, a fellow who learns from his failures as much as his successes and is willing to be honest about both. In short, it was apparent from the beginning that this would be the story of a guy you like so well that you don't mind if occasionally, you're confused by the details of certain transactions.

As for those transactions, while I personally may not have been captivated by the particulars, I was fully engaged in the *processes* by which those particulars were determined: how a potential deal was considered, the strategy behind an effort to make it work, the pitfalls along the way, the reassessments and reformulating of the terms, the reading of the personalities on both sides of the table. These provide important life and business lessons even if you aren't sure of the difference between a unitholder and shareholder.

Just as each transaction is a journey, so too is Ken's life story—from navigating a rocky childhood, to working for a maverick Texan instead of Wall Street, to planting his flag in an industry where an investment model had to be invented, to reinventing the model after it stalled, to becoming the leader of an enterprise with traditional investors and wildcat partners, to creating a culture in which colleagues and staff were made to feel like family (constantly entertained and generously compensated), to embracing philanthropy, to, most recently, pursuing a second career in the not-for-profit sector, where his boss is a former U.S. president (and reinventing that model, too).

Finally, as in many a journey story, there is the unexpected, which happened during our writing process. In the age of COVID, a marriage falls apart, and there's a life-threatening, life-changing health scare. Still, the fellow on the journey learns and is energized.

So this collaborator has no regrets for going along on this journey and helping chronicle it. Indeed, I'm glad that I got into the foxhole and that the stranger with whom I agreed to collaborate is now a friend.

Steve Fiffer
February 2023

CHAPTER 1

RAISE YOUR HAND

STEVE FIFFER: *We have all heard the expression "There's no such thing as a free lunch." But you've said that if you hadn't taken advantage of a* free dinner, *your life might have taken a different path. Can you explain?*

KEN HERSH: Early in my senior year at Princeton, I saw an ad in the *Daily Princetonian* for a "shrimp dinner information session" hosted by the firm of Morgan Stanley. Because I didn't have a meal plan, I'd become pretty good at finding free food around town. At the time, I was thinking I would go to law school and then enter private practice. I thought Morgan Stanley was a law firm. That *and* the promise of a free meal just for listening to their pitch was good enough for me. A twofer!

When I got to the dinner, I was told Morgan Stanley was an investment bank, not a law firm. I had no idea what that was. "Bank?" I thought, "Like a checking account?" I had one of those. They said no, their clients didn't have checking accounts. I was confused, but the shrimp was good. So I listened. They talked about big corporate merger and financing transactions, showed slides of fancy buildings in the Manhattan skyline, and described their two-year financial analyst training program. For a politics major, it all seemed a bit foreign. Maybe the mystery of it added to the allure.

That session got me thinking about perhaps adding business school to my plans. Since I was already planning to go to law school—a three-year commitment—adding a fourth year to get an MBA would only amount to tacking on a single year to the plan. That didn't seem so bad. Heck, I was only twenty-one at the time. The problem was that to get the dual degree, I had to be accepted by both the business and law school admissions offices independently at each school.

So, in addition to my coursework and senior thesis, I spent the rest of the fall applying to business and law schools, ready to lock and load my resume for the rest of my life, while simultaneously requesting interviews with some of the top consulting and financial firms, just in case.

I was fortunate that Morgan Stanley invited me to an interview. I went. A few weeks later, they offered me a job, and I took it. Instead of going off to law school, I headed to Wall Street for a two-year internship. Then it was off to Stanford Business School and back home after that to help Richard Rainwater and three others start a new private equity fund, Natural Gas Partners.

STEVE: *Lucky for you that you were probably one of the few people at Princeton who didn't know what Morgan Stanley was.*

KEN: Luck certainly plays a role in life. But I think you put yourself in the position to have luck. That is the key. When I tell my story to people, I don't say I was a born leader or risk taker. It's more that I put myself in situations where the rewards outweighed the risks. What was the downside of going to Morgan Stanley? It was a brand-name firm. My resume was not going backward by doing it, and I was young. I could still go to business school or do something else if it didn't work out. I was excited about the unknown of going to New York City and trying something new. It did not really dawn on me that I could fall on my face. Maybe my naivete was a blessing.

I feel the same way about making investments: If you have your downside protected, you can really let the upside run. It is a way of managing risk, and your life, by putting yourself in places with opportunity.

STEVE: *When you gave the 2017 commencement address at St. Mark's, your old high school, you used the shrimp dinner story to illustrate a point.*

KEN: Yes. The title of the speech was "Be Uncomfortable." That's one of the lessons I've learned and now try to share with others. As a kid from a middle-class Jewish family from Dallas, I was definitely uncomfortable heading to a blue-blood firm like Morgan Stanley in New York City. I felt even more uncomfortable when they immediately placed me in their energy group. They figured that since I was from Texas, I must know energy. But my mother and stepfather were both economics professors. I didn't know the difference between natural gas and gasoline. So there I was, a Jewish liberal arts major in a finance job at a, shall we say, WASP-y firm, focused on an industry I knew nothing about. Completely uncomfortable. On my first day, a fellow analyst sat me down in front of a computer with a spreadsheet program and said, "Use this spreadsheet and create a debt-amortization table." Having missed the training pro-gram, I recall saying to him, "What is a spreadsheet?" and "What is a debt amortization table?" He must've thought I was a total idiot. I don't recall feeling like one. But I do recall realizing that I had better get caught up. And fast!

STEVE: *And the lesson?*

KEN: I really believe that if you aren't completely uncomfortable on your first day on the job, you're probably in the wrong job. It is important to experience the full learn-ing curve, from the disorienting start to the accelerated learning phase through to the satisfying feeling of mastery. I told the kids at St. Mark's, "Put yourself out, set a high hurdle, back up, run, and then clear it. Let the fog of the future excite you."

STEVE: *Before we look into the future, let's talk a bit about your past. You were born in Dallas in 1963, the year JFK was assassinated there. As you said, you grew up in a mid-dle-class Jewish family with two older sisters. Your parents separated when you were ten and divorced when you were twelve, and your mom remarried pretty soon after that, as did your father. Your mom and stepfather were economics professors, and your father was a podiatrist. So you do not exactly come from a long line of private equity investors or presidential center CEOs.*

KEN: Not even close. Investment success was not in my blood at all. In fact, in my family it may have been closer to a bloodletting. My father, who was an accomplished podiatrist, fancied himself an investor, as doctors often do, but virtually every one of his ventures failed miserably.

STEVE: *Such as?*

KEN: There was a restaurant, a collectibles store, and a hot tub store—which was all the rage in Dallas in the '70s. All failed. These were his losers I knew. There were prob-ably others. He was the kind of guy who saw a retail store and thought they must be making a lot of money because they had a lot of customers. Or he saw something on a cover of a business magazine and feared he was missing out. He was not an investor but rather someone who looked for the quick buck. He made just about every classic mistake that unsophisticated retail investors make. But because he was a doctor and a smooth talker, he had a steady stream of income to recover from his losses, and he always seemed to get banks to lend him money for his next big thing. He made and lost a fortune, it seemed, several times. I have to admit, however, that he never really shared his record with me. I just picked this information up from seeing him operate around town, both literally and figuratively.

I have to give him credit for being an eternal optimist, though. Given his track record and his history of filing bankruptcy, without a sense of optimism, I guess he would have curled up in a ball and quit long before he passed away.

STEVE: *And your mom?*

KEN: She met my dad in Philadelphia when he was in podiatry school, and she was getting a master's degree. I am not that sure how they met. In our household, given the persistent rage between them, talking about Mom and Dad's history wasn't really on the list of hot dinner-table topics. They moved back to Dallas in 1960, and my two older sisters, Paula and Susie, were born in '60 and '61. Then I came along in 1963. All this time, my mother was working on her PhD in economics at Southern Methodist University. I think she took six days off after having me and then was back at it. In 1966, she was the first woman in the history of SMU to earn a PhD in any field. After earning her degree, and with three kids under six, she commuted thirty-five miles each way to teach economics at Texas Woman's University in Denton, Texas. She did this for some forty years.

STEVE: *An armchair psychologist might say that you developed your work ethic from your mother and something about money from your father—maybe, what not to do?*

KEN: Well, my mom never missed the opportunity to remind my sisters and me how hard she worked, and my dad eventually went bankrupt and recovered more than once. In fact, early on he lost the money that my mother had set aside for us to go to college. It was not a *Leave It to Beaver* childhood.

STEVE: *The Hershes weren't the Cleavers?*

KEN: Hardly. While they were married, my parents were always yelling at each other, and after they got divorced, my father was pretty much absent. My mom always seemed angry. Given the distance of her round-trip commute on I-35 north of Dallas in its perpetual state of being under construction, it now seems totally understandable. She was always rushed and harried. She boiled over frequently, given the pressure she was under to raise the three of us on a state employee salary with intermittent child-support payments coming from my dad.

My mother quickly married my stepfather, Kendall Cochran, in 1975. He was a positive influence in that he was a calming influence. He was a sweet man who also taught economics in Denton at North Texas State University—what is now known as the University of North Texas. Thus, my mother had an instant carpool mate who helped ease the commute's pain. He acted as a buffer between us and our mother. He probably taught me more than I realize just by being around.

Meanwhile, my father remarried and divorced several times and was basically on to the next chapters of his life. We were not that close after he moved out. Our interactions were reduced to weekend brunches with his parents—my grandparents. We were basically "punching in" on the family-visit time clocks.

STEVE: *How did that affect you?*

KEN: In a few ways. Before the divorce, I usually just retreated to my bedroom and read or did something to keep myself away from the violent arguments between my parents. Once I was a teenager, I was grateful that my folks had put in a second phone line for the kids. I spent a lot of time in my room with my door closed, my school backpack, a two-liter bottle of Diet Dr. Pepper, my phone, the family cat, and my television blaring. Nightly I would do my homework while watching something or calling friends—usually girls. My habit of retreating to the peacefulness of my room was so well entrenched by the time my parents divorced that it did not change much after my mother remarried.

From my middle school years onward, I really found a connection with the girls from Hockaday, our sister all-girls school located about four miles away, and from my Jewish youth group where I got involved. I guess the other guys around me were in that awkward phase where they could not talk easily to the girls. Given that I had two sisters in roughly the same age group, I did not find it hard at all. There was such a positive feedback loop from these conversations. We had a lot of fun talking and sharing stories. I grew close to many. Some became my "steadies" in those middle school years when that was in vogue. I was popular. Looking back, I think I peaked in seventh grade—puka shell necklace, mood ring, and all!

My friendships at school and with the few girls I would talk with almost nightly really made a difference. To this day, that cadre of friends still exists. We may not see or speak to each other that often, but when we do, it's like finding long-lost siblings.

As I grew up, I tried to spend as little time at home as possible. That behavior was modeled for me. From the time we were very young, my sisters and I had jobs, and I participated in just about every extracurricular activity possible at school, just so I would not have to go home. So, if you want to play armchair psychologist, I will say it was the school activities and working those jobs that had the most impact on who I am today.

STEVE: *What kind of jobs and school activities? Before you answer that, we should say you went to St. Mark's, a private day school loosely affiliated with the Episcopal Church in Dallas, from first grade all the way through high school. Any discomfort with being Jewish at an Episcopal school?*

KEN: Not that I can recall. There were only a handful of Jewish kids in each class, but we were never treated differently or made to feel like impostors. Since I started there in first grade, my friends were my friends. At age six, nobody in the class seemed to care about each other's religion. I went to the mandatory chapel and sat with the whole class and listened. It was not an evangelical atmosphere, which I came to appreciate as I grew up. I do sport a mean rendition of the Lord's Prayer, however. And I thought it was kind of cool that I got to take off on the Jewish High Holidays *and* the traditional holidays that the school observed. My mother tells a cute story of my introducing her to the chaplain at the school by saying he was "the rabbi at St. Mark's."

STEVE: *And the jobs during those years?*

KEN: My oldest sister, Paula, led the way. At age fourteen, she taught a Hebrew school class after her own bat mitzvah, and I remember her driving illegally at that age so she could get to the synagogue and to another job she somehow landed at the Tremont retirement home. When she was fifteen, she also got her hardship driver's license and worked at Target by lying about her age. That seemed to be great behavior to model. I pretty much followed in her footsteps. From my vantage point, she had it all figured out.

I taught Hebrew school the year after my bar mitzvah a couple of days per week after school, although I rode my bike to the synagogue. Then in 1978, when I was fifteen, I got a hardship driver's license, so I would be able to drive to and from a job. I worked the grill and then the cash register at a local McDonald's. I was happy to work the graveyard shift from six in the evening until after the bar rush at two in the morning during the summer. That was great, because my mom would be asleep when I got home. During the day that summer, I worked in the warehouse of the Horchow Collection catalog company. I opened mail in the morning and helped offload trucks and open crates in the afternoon. My days were full—and out of the house!

In the interest of transparency, I should confess that I lied about my age to get the job at McDonald's. You had to be sixteen to work there, so I changed my birth year on the job application.

It gave me an incredible sense of freedom. According to the rules of my license, I was able to drive to and from school and to and from work. Another confession: I did not really adhere to those restrictions. I figured that with my McDonald's uniform in the back seat of the car, as omnipresent as those restaurants were, I could tell any cop who pulled me over that I was heading to work. After a year at the McDonald's, I made a lateral move—to Jack in the Box. I tell folks that I got head-hunted away in the first fast-food war for talent. In reality, I think it was fifty cents an hour better.

STEVE: *Is there a lesson there that you'd like to share?*

KEN: The first lesson was how clueless the government is. I found it funny that I had to show a birth certificate to get my hardship driver's license, so there was no question that the DMV knew I was fifteen. Then, when I filled in the job application at McDonald's, I had to fill in my Social Security number, so my age was easily verifiable. Given the state's child labor laws, I had to say that I was sixteen. I kept waiting for someone to call me on it, but the call never came. For a teenager, it seemed crazy that the state and federal agencies were not coordinating. Now, I think it is silly that I even expected that they would! Oh, and I guess I would say that it is not good to lie on an official application.

STEVE: *And your extracurriculars at St. Mark's?*

KEN: Between jobs, girlfriends, homework, after-school sports, and activities, that period is kind of a blur. Once I got into high school, I thought I had died and gone to heaven because there was so much you could do until 6 or 7 p.m. There was a mandatory speech and debate class at St Mark's in eighth grade, which I loved. So, when high school came around, I joined the debate team. I was good at it, and it had the added benefit of consuming my nights and weekends. When they said it met every afternoon and all day Saturday, I was in. Something else that could keep me away from home. Same thing with the school newspaper, which involved doing the paper's layout during marathon weekend sessions.

STEVE: *How did your folks react to this?*

KEN: My dad wasn't really involved. My mom was so achievement-oriented that she was fine. I'm sure she was happy that I was becoming independent and to see my college application resume credentials pile up. She kept a running log of all three kids' resumes in her head. We knew that if the grades were good and the accolades came, the conversations would be positive, or we would just be left alone. She had such a hair trigger when it came to anything negative involving her that we learned to tiptoe around her emotions and just keep talking about what we were doing.

STEVE: *There was a lot of achievement. By your senior year, you had been admitted to Princeton, ranked near the top of your high school class, were head of the debate team, editor of the student paper, and on the golf team.*

KEN: Well, remember, St. Mark's is not a very big school!

STEVE: *It was more than St. Mark's. A magazine in Dallas did a cover story on the area's top high school seniors, and you were featured.*

KEN: Yes. In August 1981, *D Magazine* did a cover story on "super kids." The reporter was trying to focus on how to raise them, what they have in common, and tips for parents everywhere. When I got a call, I was both flattered and afraid. A cadre of students from around the area all met at a local house. We were gathered around a living room, and the reporter conducted a group interview, roundtable style. She found about a dozen different ways to ask the same question: "What's the secret?" "Why did you all turn out the way you did?" "Where do you get your drive to succeed?"

I'd describe the scene as pretty Norman Rockwellian. It seemed like everyone was giving credit to their parents, saying how supportive they were and how great life was at home. I found this pretty unsettling, so I kept reasonably quiet. I didn't think I belonged in this group anyway. Heck, I wasn't at the top of my class.

When the session was breaking up, I approached the writer and asked to talk privately in the adjacent room. "Excuse me," I said. "I think you should just exclude me from the article. It is clear that everyone in this room had a very stable home life. My parents went through a messy divorce, and I feel like I did a lot of this on my own, with minimal direction, except from the school. So why don't you please leave me out? I don't really fit the narrative you describe here." As the editor-in-chief of the St. Mark's newspaper that year, I was pretty proud of myself that I could use words like "narrative." Plus, as an editor, I knew what the existence of contrary evidence could do to the thesis she was trying to put out. I thought I was doing her a favor.

Unfortunately, this confession caused the writer to put me *in* the feature, not take me out. The paragraph about me said:

> Kenneth Hersh could have become a troubled child after his parents went through
> a bitter divorce when he was 11. Instead of withdrawing, Kenny plunged into his
> 6th grade schoolwork and has been absorbed in school ever since.

When the magazine came out, I was mortified. There was nothing inflammatory or factually incorrect in what she wrote, but I knew it would evoke a reaction. I didn't say anything derogatory about my parents. But after my mother read it, you would have thought the entire issue was devoted to defaming her. "What are you talking about, 'bitter' divorce? I kept you kids out of the courtroom. Your father lost all your college money, and now he barely pays child support! If you want to have it nicer, why don't you go live with your father and see what he and his new young wife will do for you."

I was pretty confused. It *was* a bitter divorce. They were at each other's throats constantly. Yes, we were shielded from the courtroom for any sort of custody battle, but that was about it. I could not help but think that her son was just featured in a magazine cover story about "super kids," and her reaction was centered on how it reflected on her. She so desperately wanted to keep up appearances with her friends and acquaintances in the community that this one phrase was tantamount to a complete airing of the family's dirty laundry.

STEVE: *What else did you take away from that experience?*

KEN: Good press is not all that it is cracked up to be. And be careful about what you say to reporters—it may piss off your mom!

STEVE: *I imagine you were happy to leave home and go off to college.*

KEN: Absolutely. When I was walking across the graduation stage in 1981, I would have told you that if I ended up back in Dallas, raising a family about three miles from where I grew up and about four miles from my mom, you could simply shoot me, and I wouldn't object.

However, I want to make something clear. My mother did not have the easiest of lives. Her father abandoned the family when she was a young girl. She faced a lot of discrimination in graduate school and the workplace because she was a woman. My father left her pretty much on her own to raise three kids on a teacher's salary. Her unhappiness and anger were understandable. Outwardly, she was always proud of us and bragged on us constantly. And, while things may not have been that great at home, my sisters and I survived and found ways to be happy. For me, my energy was spent at St. Mark's. It was like a parallel universe compared to life at home.

That's how I regard St. Mark's to this day. Aside from my girlfriends, it was the single biggest influence on my life, and I am grateful that my parents thought to give me that opportunity. The stability of a twelve-year run there from age six to eighteen was a key constant for me.

Time did not change things, either. In the spring of 2015, I gave a speech at St. Mark's annual alumni dinner when I was being given the Distinguished Alumnus

Award. I noted that the campus was unrecognizable to most of the people in the room because the buildings kept changing, and new buildings were built since we had attended. The sports field and the library were the only places that had not changed. "So why does the place still feel so familiar?" I asked rhetorically. "Because this is *home*, and that is why we all come back and have good feelings about the school, even if it bears little resemblance to the campus we knew. This place is *home*."

My mother was in the audience. I gushed deserved praise for her from the stage and thanked her for creating the opportunity for me and for modeling the value of education. I went on to talk about my appreciation for the school. True to form, when we got in the car, rather than saying how proud she was of my being recognized, she said almost immediately, "So the school was '*home*,' huh? Not the house?" Again, seeing the world through her lens distorted the joy of the moment. I ignored the comment, stayed quiet while I drove, and dropped her off at her house. After she got out of the car, I reflected on the moment: Her journey sure was a sad one, and it made me sad at the same time—not quite the Norman Rockwell mother-son moment.

STEVE: *How did you end up at Princeton?*

KEN: I got in. There was no question that in our achievement-oriented household, all three Hersh kids were going to go to good colleges. Applying to the best was a given. So was going to the best school that admitted you.

Paula graduated from high school three months before her seventeenth birthday. She was so intent on getting out of Dodge that she moved from a local private school she had gone to for ninth and tenth grades to a public school so she could jump straight to her senior year. She wanted to go into broadcast journalism, so she chose a school with a great program, Syracuse. Given my sister's age and my mom's knowledge of what happens on college campuses, she said to Paula, "You are not going away to college when you're seventeen." So Paula took a gap year and went and lived on a kibbutz in Israel and did all the things she would have done as a freshman in college anyway. She then went to Syracuse and got that degree in broadcast journalism.

My sister Susie was also an overachiever, although she never went to private schools (I never got a good explanation as to why). She applied and was accepted to Princeton a couple of years ahead of me, so I was well aware of the school's stature. Having visited her once, I knew the school. The guidance counselors at St. Mark's were optimistic about my chances of getting in there, as well as some other top-tier universities.

I ended up applying to several schools, including applying early decision to Princeton. When I got the big fat envelope saying I'd been accepted there, I was excited. It was one of the country's top schools, and I got in. The only thing that could have derailed my decision was if I'd decided to decline the offer to go to the same school as my then-serious girlfriend. We had each applied to Princeton, Duke, and Texas. I got into all three. She was incredibly accomplished and was more qualified than I was to get into these fancy schools. But coming from a suburban public school must not have carried the same weight as a tony boy's school with a national reputation. She only got into the University of Texas. Had she been accepted into Duke, I would have gone there for sure. We were that serious about each other. But again, in our achievement-first household, turning down Princeton for the University of Texas to be with a girl was just a bridge too far.

STEVE: *From what I understand, getting to Princeton may have been a bigger challenge to you than getting into Princeton.*

KEN: That summer before I was to go off to college, my mom and stepdad were on sabbatical in Australia. I lived with my dad, his new wife, and their two-year-old. It was not pleasant because their marriage was in the process of breaking up. I had seen that movie before. But I had a girlfriend and a full-time job, and I was out of that house 95 percent of the time. I had already boxed up my clothes, stereo, records, and books.

When it was time to head east, I took everything to the UPS office and shipped it to myself at my future dorm room. I also got on the phone and booked and paid for my own plane ticket. I was going to arrive a week early to go on the Outdoor Action preterm camping trip. That seemed like a good chance to meet people before school started and yet another way to get out of town. The best airline deal was Piedmont Airlines' "hopscotch" fare. If you connected multiple times and did not insist on a direct flight, they'd discount it. Two planes. Three stops. Ninety-nine dollars. Dallas to Greensboro to Raleigh to Philadelphia International. Ba-da-bing, ba-da-boom!

After landing, I took a taxi to the Thirtieth Street train station, found the New Jersey transit train to Princeton Junction, and then transferred to the "Dinky"—the single-car rail spur from Princeton Junction to the Princeton campus. I remember pulling into Princeton at midnight. The normally beautiful campus was dark, empty, and wet. It was pouring rain. I arrived in my jeans and T-shirt, with a single suitcase and my acceptance envelope. The notice in the envelope said that people arriving after-hours should go to the security office to get their room key. So I traversed the campus in the rain, frequently checking the campus map in my envelope; knocked on the door of Stanhope Hall; and told the guard that I needed a key to get into my dorm room.

He found my name on the list, gave me the key, and asked if I knew where to go. The dorm I was assigned—Princeton Inn College—was one of the few buildings I knew. I had to backtrack because it was right next to the train station. The campus seemed eerie. Hardly the Gothic masterpiece that shows the grace of age for which Princeton is known. The gargoyles atop the Gothic buildings angrily spewed rainwater at me from the rooftops. I was drenched. I walked into my room. Immediately on the left as I entered this old hotel room was the bathroom. Just past the bathroom door, the room opened to reveal two beds with bare mattresses, a couple of desks, and empty dressers. Thankfully, I had packed a towel for the camping trip. I laid it on the mattress and used my jacket as a pillow.

The next morning, I found the campers and went off for what was an awesome trip backpacking in the Delaware River wilderness area of western New Jersey or eastern Pennsylvania. Having not spent much time in the Northeast, I had no idea where we were. But I didn't care. I was there. I met several great classmates and felt I had really taken the jitters away.

The bus full of dirty campers desperately in need of showers returned to campus on move-in day. Now, the sun was shining, and the campus was in full bloom. All over campus there were station wagons with moms and dads helping their kids unpack. There were dads assembling shelves in dorms; moms and siblings were shuttling boxes and trunks, helping their new Princetonians settle in. When I walked into my room, I was taken aback by seeing the rear end of a heavyset woman on her hands and knees scrubbing the tiny bathroom's floor, toilet, and bathtub. She was my roommate's mom. I remember thinking how silly it was to have someone's mom cleaning his college dorm room. I squeezed past the woman, walked into the room to the bedroom area, and introduced myself to my roommate, Jeffrey, from Cleveland. Luckily, I had left my small suitcase on the bed I had slept in the week before, marking my side of the room. He did not seem to mind as he and his family continued to move his property in.

STEVE: *And you were on your own.*

KEN: Yes. That was my "welcome to college" experience. When I tell that story now, people are aghast. "You poor thing," they often say. "I can't believe you didn't have someone take you to college." But I did not think anything of it. Frankly, I think parents need to back off and let their college-bound children do more on their own. I have to give my mother credit, since I was pretty adept at making my way around by the time I went to college. Those skills served me well. Helicopter parenting cheats kids out of critical learning on how the real world works.

STEVE: *Even though your parents didn't come out to Princeton with you, your father had agreed to pay for your education, right?*

KEN: Well, according to my mom, the divorce deal with my dad stipulated that he would pay for all education. Once everything broke down between him and my mom, we kids were the go-betweens. During those years before we went to college, my mom would tell us to remind him to pay the child support payments when we saw him. She was never shy in telling us how many months he was in arrears.

STEVE: *So, did he come through?*

KEN: He paid for my entire St. Mark's education and my freshman year and for Susie's first three years. And then things deteriorated.

STEVE: *What happened?*

KEN: During the summer after my first year, I had a summer job working for the public defender's office in Washington, D.C. When I came back for my sophomore year in the fall of 1982, I remember confidently going to the gym where we were to register for classes. When I got up to the registration table, I was handed a pink card that was stapled to the course-registration papers. It said that I could not register until I visited the registrar's office. I had no idea what it was about, but I went. When I got there, I saw my sister sitting on the couch in the waiting room. She had been given the same pink card and was in the dark as well. So we went in together. The school official told us that there was an outstanding balance on our bill, so we could not register for the semester.

STEVE: *What? How much?*

KEN: It was something near $6,000 for each of us for the semester, $12,000 in all. We knew that our father was supposed to have paid this. Like being in jail, the registrar allowed us to make one phone call, so we called dad's office. We reached him there and explained where we were. In stride and without raising his voice in protest, he simply said, "I don't have the money to pay." He went on to remind us that he did make it all the way through twelve years of St. Mark's and three years of Princeton for Susie and one for me. I guess in his mind, he had done enough.

I was nineteen. Susie was twenty-one. She looked at me and said, "What do we do?" We could have called mom, but she would have blown a gasket. I thought for a minute. Then, I took my checkbook out of my backpack and wrote Princeton a check for $12,000. My sister had a shocked look on her face, like she was watching some sort of supernatural act. "Where the hell did you get $12,000?" she asked.

"Don't worry about that now," I replied. "Let's get this done, and then we can sort it out later."

STEVE: *And how did a nineteen-year-old college sophomore-to-be come up with $12,000? That's a lot of money, especially in 1982 dollars.*

KEN: The money came from two places. First, I had saved quite a bit from all my jobs in high school. And second, I had earned quite a bit during my freshman year at Princeton through my work on a student publication called *Business Today* magazine, or *BT*.

STEVE: *You actually made money doing college journalism? How did you do that?*

KEN: During the first week of classes, student organizations recruit incoming freshmen. The editor-in-chief of the St. Mark's newspaper a year before me was now on the staff of the *Daily Princetonian* (or as students called it, the *Prince*) and tried to recruit me. However, I didn't want to work on a daily newspaper; it seemed pretty intense. Another Dallas friend who was then a Princeton junior was on the staff of *BT*. He put the hard sell on me to join that magazine. "It's more laid back than the *Prince*," he argued. "It only comes out three times a year, and we have a lot of fun." So I signed on. Frankly, it didn't even register that the magazine focused on a subject I knew nothing about—business.

Steve Forbes and a few other Princeton students started *Business Today* in 1968. It's a totally student-run national organization and is still around today. The magazine circulated to about two hundred thousand college students across the country and was part of the Foundation for Student Communication, a not-for-profit that also hosted the Business Tomorrow conference series. Every year the group hosts a big conference that draws top students and business leaders from around the United States. There have been some pretty impressive Princeton students who worked on this, including Wendy Kopp, who later founded Teach for America. Wendy was a freshman staffer when I led the whole organization, and she became president three years after me. If what the organization did under her watch was any indicator, Teach for America's success was guaranteed. She put my record at that organization to shame.

STEVE: *So how did you make the money that helped you pay your tuition?*

KEN: The foundation had a budget of about $1 million. A lot of that came from ads in the magazine and contributions from alumni and corporations. Even though I started as a writer for the magazine, I quickly asked what else I could be doing to help. Funding was always an issue, so they were eager to suggest that I try to sell ads on the side.

We were a good place for corporate recruiting ads that wanted to target undergraduates as well as corporate identity campaigns that wanted to reach that demographic. I looked at the various lists around the office and started dialing. I had a ball. Turns out, I was a pretty good salesman.

I was shocked to learn that we got very nice commissions for selling ads. It seems funny now that I did not even know there was compensation. I thought extracurricular activities were volunteer. Of course, I didn't complain. In fact, it spurred me to do more. My freshman year extracurricular life was focused on *Business Today*. I wrote articles, helped lay out the magazine, and sold ads along the way. Just like in high school, the person who raised his hand and asks, "What else can I do?" seemed to be given more to do. Go figure.

I actually made a lot more money on commissions the following two summers, when I partnered with another *BT* student staffer and traveled around the country to solicit contributions. We went to major cities across the country and met with any executive willing to see us. It was a real sales job—lots of "asks"—and success was measured by how much we raised against a quota set out by the leadership. We even used the summer trips to scout for new conference locations. We learned that hotels would put us up for free if we were touring them to consider hosting a future conference there. Funny, most of the major cities we went to were prospective hosts for future conferences!

I eventually became managing editor of the magazine—not necessarily because I was the most qualified but because when they asked, "Who's interested in becoming managing editor?," I raised my hand.

STEVE: *You've raised your hand a lot. Not everyone is so bold or confident.*

KEN: I tell students—people of all ages, actually—"Please, raise your hand." It's amazing what happens when you do that. Often, people are afraid or self-conscious. They don't want to stick their neck out or look bad—whatever the downside of raising your hand means in a particular scenario. But raising your hand to do something, while involving a little risk, can lead to some really interesting things, even if the hand raise is to take on something as basic as grunt work.

I'm going to jump ahead to my time at Morgan Stanley to give you an example. I remember I was at the office one Saturday, and this senior partner was messing with the copy machine. I could hear him struggling in the copy room around the corner from my bullpen. Since I was a junior analyst, I had a lot of experience with the copy machine and the presentation collator. He came around to my desk and asked where the toner was for the copier. (I guess the "needs toner" light was on.) I knew how to work the copier and knew where the toner was, so that made me the resident genius on the weekend. So I got up from my desk, went to the copy room, added the toner, and said, "Why don't I finish this up for you?" He had a few copies to make and a simple presentation that needed binding. It was nothing, and I was the junior guy. *Why wouldn't I help the senior guy?* I thought.

He said, "Great. Thank you." It took me five minutes. I carried the small stack of neatly bound presentations back to his office. You would have thought I had hung the moon. He was appreciative as he put the stack into his briefcase and packed up. I went back to my desk to continue working.

Apparently, I was now "in" with this partner, and he wasn't even in our specialty group at the firm. A few weeks later we were in a group meeting and this same partner came to our boss asking for help on a deal. It turned out that a larger client had some oil and gas assets held in a division of the company, so our group could help in the overall valuation assignment that his industry group was undertaking for that client. He called me out and said to our vice president as he gestured my way, "I want him." The other analysts looked at me and seemed stunned that this senior managing director even knew who I was. I was a mini-celebrity for the moment—all because I changed copy toner and bound a few pages of his presentation. So yes, raise your hand and volunteer. And yes, put yourself in the way of opportunity, even if that is in the copy room.

STEVE: *Back to paying tuition for you and Susie.*

KEN: Being able to write that check to Princeton was one of the most gratifying feelings ever. When push came to shove, I was able to do that. At the time, I was thinking, *I cannot believe I am wiping out my checking account because my father broke his promise.* But now I think, *What a cool thing to have been able to do that.* That was the satisfaction that came from self-reliance. I had earned money, saved it, and it came in handy in an emergency. I was able to help someone else in the process, too.

STEVE: *Did making a lot of money become important to you because of that experience?*

KEN: In fairness to my father, he did pay me back most of it over time, and my mom and stepfather were able to make up the difference and paid for my last two years there. But I learned I would never be able to count on him for support again. I also knew that my mom was on a schoolteacher's salary. It was clear that if I wanted to be secure, I had to earn it. It was not even a question. This was the moment when my youthful naivete evaporated.

But making a fortune was never part of my constitution. I just thought about making sure my future was secure.

STEVE: *Were there other times that reinforced this motivation?*

KEN: One story in particular describes the feeling.

STEVE: *Go on.*

KEN: After graduation, my college girlfriend, Jancy Hoeffel, who was from a hard-working family in Rochester, New York, and I planned to backpack around Europe for the summer. We got really excited, because there was a sale for a $99 round-trip airfare to London on People's Express—the popular no-frills discount airline at the time. After hearing the announcement of that promotional fare on the radio by chance, we raced to our respective rooms and started dialing the 800 number with the understanding that the first one to get through would order two tickets.

I got busy signals. She eventually got through. So, after graduation, we flew to London armed with our two $99 tickets; $2,000 in American Express traveler's checks; two Eurail passes, which allowed us to ride trains all over Europe for the price of the pass; and the *Let's Go: Europe* book as our bible. We were set.

We backpacked all over Europe. From London, we made our way to Greece and then headed back north through Italy and France. When we got to Paris toward the end of the trip, we were down to the end of our money. To ration our final dollars, we carefully calculated what we could spend on each meal. Before meals, we would walk the streets and look at menus in restaurant windows to see if we could afford to go in. Usually, we couldn't. Typically, this led us to grocery stores, where we would buy cheese, baguettes, and perhaps some luncheon meats.

Of course, at that age, this was totally fine. We were being resourceful, and it really felt like we were locals, shopping in stores and pinching our pennies. But I do remember distinctly one night being hungry and wandering down a nice avenue in Paris and realizing that the entire row of restaurants was out of our price range. Resolute, I said to myself, *Someday, I'll come back to Paris and eat wherever I want and not even look at prices.*

It wasn't about making a million dollars. My salary at Morgan Stanley was going to be $22,000—a lot for a twenty-two-year-old in 1985 but not a king's ransom, especially after you pay taxes and a New York rent. My motivation was more about wanting to work to make a good living to be comfortable. I didn't know what wealthy was. I just became very focused on self-reliance because of my circumstances growing up, even though I never felt underprivileged.

STEVE: *Prior to your epiphany about business, you were focused on becoming a lawyer.*

KEN: Yes. My whole life, people had told me I was going to be the next F. Lee Bailey great trial lawyer, or specifically a great criminal defense attorney. To tell you the truth, all I knew about being a lawyer was what I saw on television in the 1970s. I did not even know there was such a thing as a corporate lawyer. But since I was an effective high school debater, it was an easy thing for people to say to a teenager. I guess I liked persuading people, and winning competitions didn't hurt the argument either.

So, entering my freshman year, I considered myself prelaw, even though Princeton did not have a prelaw major. I wanted to spend the summer doing something law-related. I saw a flyer in the career office binder for the internship program at the Washington, D.C., public defender's office. Never one to shy away from a seemingly unnoticed advertisement, I applied for a job as an investigator. Based on a letter and resume, I scored a phone interview with the director and was offered the position. I didn't know at the time that the program was really for recent college graduates who were entering law school. I just found a flyer in a binder on the shelf at the career office.

As the youngest and likely the most naive, I was assigned to the office's legendary public defender, Sally Brown. She had a reputation for chewing up investigators. My guess is that the older interns somehow knew the ropes and arranged to avoid her, leaving me to be assigned to her as the odd man out. Once again, as I entered the program, I felt like the admissions mistake wandering up to campus on a dark, wet night with a suitcase. In the end, I thought she was great. She was the senior trial lawyer there, so I got assigned to complicated murder and rape cases. I found myself walking into maximum security prisons to interview inmates for statements. I was issuing subpoenas and taking witness statements, recreating crime scenes, and even got a chance to testify in court. It was a fantastic experience—so fantastic it convinced me I didn't want to be a defense attorney.

STEVE: *Why?*

KEN: I did not like the mercenary nature of the job. I understand and believe in the idea that everyone is entitled to a defense. And I know the criminal justice system isn't weighted fairly. But I couldn't deal with the ethical dilemma of what happens when you know your client is guilty and you still have to defend him or her. In fact, one of my junior papers that I wrote at Princeton was titled "The Dilemma of the Criminal Defense Lawyer" and explored this professional dilemma. It was painful for me to reconcile that every citizen was entitled to be defended in a court of law, yet every lawyer takes an oath to uphold the law in the search for truth. Obviously, many lawyers are able to put judgment aside and defend clients, regardless of their own personal feelings. All I can say is that it just wasn't for me.

I also did not like the fact that you're always around a dispute. Conflict was the business of trial law. Even as an intern, I saw how I was perceived. We were given the opportunity to ride along with police officers if we wanted. Not shying away from an interesting experience, one weekend I signed up and hitched a ride in a squad car on a Saturday night patrolling southeast Washington, D.C.

The Anacostia neighborhood on a summer Saturday night was hardly a garden assignment. However, it was a slow-ish night from the officer's perspective. The only real action he was involved with was a call for a man loitering at a nearby gas station. We drove by to check it out. I guess he had been annoying some of the customers, but the guy had not done anything bad that I could see. My officer called for another squad car, and in a minute, there were two officers approaching the man. They told him to put his hands on the hood of the car, and then they tried to handcuff him. The guy was enormous. He was not resisting but was not helping, either. Given the man's sheer size and lack of mobility, I'm not sure they could have put the handcuffs on even if the man helped. With a small crowd now gathering, they roughed him up and finally got handcuffs on and put him in the back of another squad car.

As we were driving to the police station, I said to the cop, "This guy didn't seem to do anything." And the officer calmly explained, "Listen, my job tonight is to clean up the streets. Your job tomorrow is to get this guy out. I'm not judge and jury. My job is the street. That guy was going to make a scene."

The next day, I asked Sally to help me find out if he got out. He did. He wasn't aggressive, he just seemed kind of lost. But the cop's job was to clean up streets that night, knowing that the public defender was going to get him released in the morning. No thought was given to the indelible police record that would now follow him or any trauma a night in jail might cause. It was eye-opening.

STEVE: *Despite all this, when you went to that free shrimp dinner your senior year, you were still planning on going to law school.*

KEN: Yes. I had heard of corporate law by that time!

STEVE: *So what happened?*

KEN: Life happened.

CHAPTER 2

THE FOG OF THE FUTURE
EXCITES ME

STEVE: *I would like to talk to you about your two years in the analyst program at Morgan Stanley and then your time at Stanford's business school.*

You got thrown into the fire pretty quickly at Morgan Stanley, following your graduation from Princeton in 1985, when you were put on the Texaco deal team. For those who don't know or remember, this was one of the highest-profile legal cases of the 1980s. In January of 1984, Pennzoil announced that it had entered into an agreement to acquire Getty Oil. Shortly after the announcement was made, Texaco learned that the final papers had not been signed and made a $10 billion offer for Getty, which the Getty board accepted. Pennzoil then sued Texaco for interfering in its deal. After a four-month trial, a Texas jury not only ruled for Pennzoil but also gave Pennzoil the greatest damages award in history—almost $12 billion. Texaco then appealed.

How did Morgan Stanley become involved in a huge legal matter?

KEN: As in most cases of this magnitude, the losing side immediately appeals the jury verdict to a higher court. Under Texas law, the side appealing the ruling must post a bond equal to the size of the judgment to be able to make the appeal. In this case, Texaco had to post a $12 billion bond. That's a lot of money today, and it was a lot more thirty-five years ago. Speaking for an amount like that back then was almost unheard of.

Texaco went into full crisis mode. It wanted to appeal, but it did not have the money for the bond. So Texaco's lawyers came up with a theory, which went like this:

We do not have $12 billion. Therefore, we would have to declare bankruptcy to proceed with the appeal. That is not fair. If you have to bankrupt yourself in order to appeal, it's tantamount to not being able to appeal at all. But, since the Constitution stipulates that every citizen has the right to appeal, this renders the Texas bonding requirement unconstitutional. Texaco then went to federal court in a friendlier jurisdiction—New York—to seek a temporary injunction preventing enforcement of the judgment.

STEVE: *Which is where Morgan Stanley comes in?*

KEN: Right. As with big financial deals and restructurings, companies looked to the big Wall Street firms to help them, along with their army of top-flight law firms. This was a huge financial burden that was just sprung on the company. It had not anticipated a loss in court, and it never would have imagined that a jury would award a $12 billion judgment against it. At the time, the largest corporate award in history was under $2 billion.

To make the argument that it was unable to appeal, the company had to prove it was unable to pay. So they hired us to run the numbers and make the case that such a payment was impossible. The firm's energy group was given the job. There were a lot of people on the team, and I was the low man on the org chart—a first-year financial analyst assigned to the team. If Texaco was going to win its argument, it would first have to show that it couldn't come up with $12 billion without bankrupting itself. The judge had granted Texaco a 105-day delay in posting the bond, apparently so the company didn't just rush to bankruptcy court and deny Pennzoil the award outright.

STEVE: *You, a first-year analyst only a few months on the job, ended up being the guy everyone looked to for the numbers.*

KEN: Again, luck presented an opportunity. The jury had delivered its verdict on November 19. Ten days later, I was at my girlfriend's home in a suburb of Rochester for the Thanksgiving holiday. I recall that I was in the shower at her house when her father knocked on the bathroom door. It was rather awkward in that I had no idea why he would feel compelled to interrupt my shower. Maybe I'd taken too long and depleted the house's hot water. I had a moment of panic before he told me that my office was on the phone. I told him that I'd call them back. "They said that it can't wait," he said. *Holy shit, what does this mean?* So I got out of the shower and got on the phone, and they said, "You need to get on the next plane to New York and get back here now."

Turned out John Berg, the group's second-year analyst who would normally have been running those numbers, was leaving for Sydney, Australia, in two weeks to work in Morgan Stanley's office there. He was going to have to pass the baton to me, and I had to get up to speed. Fast.

Morgan Stanley analysts were notorious in those days for wearing beepers—those paging devices that doctors used so their call services could get in touch with them anywhere. Wherever we went in New York, you could tell we were the Morgan Stanley analysts. We felt so important at the time. Truth be told, we rarely got beeped. But I guess it was reassuring for the directors of the firm to know that we could be reached if need be. Wouldn't it figure that the first time I got beeped, I actually didn't have my beeper on. In fact, about the only time I was out of earshot of my device was when I was in the shower. But, true to form, we had to provide backup phone numbers, just in case. Maybe this explains why I am so addicted to being responsive to my emails and texts to this day.

STEVE: *This time you hadn't even raised your hand. What was your role?*

KEN: I had to help build the analysis of every money-raising possibility for our team to present to the bankruptcy judge so Texaco could say, "Your Honor, we cannot raise $12 billion." I ran the analysis to answer questions like: How much common or preferred equity could Texaco issue? How much additional debt could the company's balance sheet stand, given their credit profile and the capacity of the credit markets? What if we broke the company apart and sold off pieces or took certain subsidiaries public?

Today, that would be about a weekend's work for a company's corporate finance team. But in a time before spreadsheets, we had to build the models by hand, crunching every number with a hand calculator. For about a month, I got in a car every day to go to Texaco's headquarters in White Plains, New York, where I worked with a treasurer from the company. I pulled all their numbers from their corporate mainframe system and ran them through our worksheets. It was really a crash course in corporate finance and company valuations. About the only thing that I didn't have to analyze was a merger.

STEVE: *And in the middle of this, something else happened.*

KEN: Someone on the team asked, "Wouldn't it be cheaper for Texaco to just buy Pennzoil?" The market value of Pennzoil had only increased a few billion dollars since the judgment was issued, so paying a premium for Pennzoil would be cheaper than paying the $12 billion judgment. As the junior person on the team, I had no idea whose brainstorm that was. But I thought it was ingenious. Amid all our work, Texaco delivered a bid for Pennzoil that was a big premium to the prevailing stock price at the time.

STEVE: *And?*

KEN: And then we waited. A Morgan Stanley banker was going to personally deliver the bid to the Pennzoil executives, I recall, in Nashville. Sort of a surprise bid to let them know how serious the overture was. Once the approach was made, the banker was to report on the approach. The call came in on a Saturday when the full banking, legal, and company teams were at the Texaco office in White Plains on their executive floor, working.

Someone said, "Come in the boardroom. We're going to get the report on the offer." The moment was full of nervous anticipation. I followed everyone else into the boardroom—a stereotypical boardroom for an old-line company, complete with dark wood paneling and a lineup of large portraits on the walls of all the company's past and present CEOs. In the center of the room stood the largest dark polished wood table I had ever seen. A couple of dozen high-backed dark leather chairs surrounded the table, all neatly spaced to precision, like a team of silent soldiers standing at attention. Around the outer edges of the room, smaller chairs were stationed, clearly for the subordinate lieutenants of the generals seated at the table. For a young capitalist, this was like going into some sort of temple. For a Saturday, when we were all casually dressed, going in there seemed like getting a tour of the White House while the president was away.

As the speakerphone situated in the middle of the table was ringing, we all quickly grabbed a seat at the table to listen, anxiously awaiting the report from the other end. I took the last seat after all the others had sat down. I recall being so far from the speakerphone that I had to stretch forward to hear as I took notes on my legal pad. Our teammate calling then reported that the offer was hand-delivered to the CEO of Pennzoil, who gruffly said they'd consider it but basically signaled that this wasn't going to go anywhere. The Texaco and Morgan Stanley senior executives around that table were deflated. I joined them in their disappointment, mostly because I was pretty tired of working twenty-hour days, and I was looking for a break.

While I can't remember the actual amount Texaco bid for Pennzoil, I will never forget the reaction that the Texaco CEO had coming out of his revered boardroom on that Saturday afternoon. As we all filed out, he pulled our senior-most managing director aside and cast a quick, casual glance in my direction as I trailed behind them. I was straining to overhear, to catch his feelings about the company's potential demise. Instead, he said, "Excuse me, but can you have your junior people not sit at the board table? That table is reserved for the board and senior executives. There are chairs around the perimeter of the room they can sit in."

I was aghast. Here we were on a Saturday afternoon. Everyone was working hard and participating in a pretty stressful exercise. I remember thinking, *This guy is about to lose his company, and he's worried that a junior member of the team dared to sit at this table after hours on a Saturday, when there were ample chairs available. No wonder this company was in the shape it was in.*

It was my first experience watching a leader crumble under pressure.

The legal and banking teams went back to the drawing board on building a case that would challenge the constitutionality of the Texas bond requirement while, at the same time, the company was feverishly preparing for an eventual bankruptcy filing. This all took place during the fifteen-week period from Thanksgiving through February. It was very exciting for a young guy. But it was also very instructive. I loved the fact that it was a super high-profile deal and that when everyone was talking about it, they were referencing *my* numbers. Heck, we were reading about conclusions based on my work in the next day's *Wall Street Journal*. I enjoyed being in the thick of it, but there was something artificial about it all.

STEVE: *You just realized then that Wall Street was artificial?*

KEN: You have to remember that that was 1985. I was twenty-two years old. My real-world lessons where just beginning.

STEVE: *Go on.*

KEN: As the hard part of my Texaco work wound down, one task I had remaining was to prepare the head of the Morgan Stanley natural resources group to testify in front of a judge as to Texaco's financial capabilities. He was going to be the expert testifying that there was no way Texaco could come up with the bond money. I had taken my models and summarized them all and assembled a briefing book organized by financing technique or money-raising strategy. Each tab concluded that the company would be shy of the $12 billion target.

Each day for a couple weeks, I would take a car service early in the morning to the managing director's house, wait for him, then hop into his car and accompany him wherever he was going. The goal was to quiz him on the briefing book and get him prepared. I found the whole exercise a perverse power play. I had the book organized, color coded, highlighted in key concluding parts, and easy to read and follow. It wasn't difficult. However, he insisted that I get to him before the crack of dawn and stay with him like a butler to walk him through the book page by page.

While it was great to get such senior exposure, I remember being perplexed that he wanted to be spoon-fed something from me. During the week, we were in the back of a chauffeured sedan heading back into the city, and he was listening to me with half an ear as he read the morning papers. On the weekend, he seemed to enjoy driving me around in his sports car. I had the book in my lap and was talking to him while he went driving. I didn't go to the courthouse the day he spoke, but it ended up being much ado about nothing. The legal briefs did most of the talking. At the time, $12 billion was so much money, a judge didn't need much convincing that that kind of dough wasn't just dropping into Texaco's lap any time soon.

Between my Texaco board table "scandal" and the great "Briefing Book Traveling Tutorial," I saw that the folks who were written about in the newspapers and who commanded respect wherever they went were just fallible people, complete with idiosyncrasies and peculiarities. No better or worse than anyone else. They just had fancy jobs and were paid a lot of money. I swore that I would not get that affected, no matter how successful I became.

I continued working my ass off on that deal, and ultimately the company had to declare Chapter 11 bankruptcy to stave off posting the Texas bond. The work did calm down and that exposure gained for me some profile in our group and the confidence of our senior managing director. Importantly, *I* gained confidence. Over the ensuing year, I had more responsibility given to me. How ironic that the junior analyst in the group, with the least amount of corporate finance training, was getting assigned to the most complex transactions. If they asked me to do something that I did not understand, I'd figure it out. And I'd stay late enough to get it done.

STEVE: *Stay until it's done. Another Hersh mantra?*

KEN: Yes. I arrived at Morgan Stanley a political theory junkie, not some corporate finance jet jockey. I hastily signed up for the one economics class offered at Princeton that covered corporate finance, but I was not an investment banking whiz kid. I had only a rudimentary idea of what they did when I walked into the building on my first day. So I got into the habit of arriving early, in time to read the day's *Wall Street Journal* and *New York Times* business section and whatever internal memos had circulated since the previous day. I felt like each day was the start of something new and I had to be more prepared than the others. Once I got into that rhythm, I enjoyed that feeling.

Similarly, when the chaos of the workday was done, I got into the habit of staying late. Usually, I was working to get a grip on what I had faked during the day. The extra quiet time was also perfect for checking to see if there were errors in the work I had done. I relished the nighttime when it was quiet, and I was also able to prepare for the next day. I got into the habit of not going to sleep until my inbox was empty and all of my deadlines for the next day had been met.

STEVE: *Since you are so detail-oriented, I guess that this pattern served you well?*

KEN: I thought I was a decent editor, but I learned the hard way that nobody is perfect.

STEVE: *Sounds like a juicy story is coming. What happened?*

KEN: As I moved up the learning curve and gained confidence, people came to trust my work. In fact, they rarely even checked my work prior to taking the numbers and the presentations to the client meeting itself. At times, I was incredulous that big companies were relying on the analysis of someone with so little formal training. But I was proud that I had a handle on what I was doing. I thought I was fairly meticulous in reading and checking the presentations before hitting the "publish" button, taking pride in my old editor-in-chief skills. I was humbled, however, when I sent out a presentation that discussed the merits of a company doing an "initial *pubic* offering."

STEVE: *Oh my God, did anyone notice?*

KEN: I handed out the fancy presentations and right there on the cover was the word "pubic" instead of "public." I also had thirty-five-millimeter slides for the presentation on the screen for everyone to see. The partner began talking. I was manning the button to advance the slide carousel, so as he spoke, I advanced the slides to the table of contents page, which was the page after my porno-title page. He said, "Ken, go back please. I am just doing the introduction." I pretended not to hear him. He quickly went into the meat of the presentation, and I was able to advance further. I have no idea who noticed it, but I was mortified.

That taught me how hard it is to proof your own work. I try to make sure more sets of eyes are on every document before it goes out. I also use that story to remind everyone that, once upon a time, I made quite an error!

These experiences really shaped me. I am still typically one of the first in the office and one of the last to leave. Luckily, electronics have replaced the need to be omnipresent in the office. However, I still find contentment in knowing that I have no unread emails in my inbox before I retire for the evening and that, no matter my rank, I don't want to miss deadlines. Some might call it OCD. I call it respect for the work, my colleagues, and the joy in taking ownership of my work product.

STEVE: *So, what is the takeaway from the "don't let junior sit at the table" incident? How does that differ from your leadership style and your team approach?*

KEN: That's simple. Keep your eye on the prize. People can easily get distracted by unimportant, emotional, or petty things at precisely the wrong time. Having seen that up close, I have always tried to take a breath, remain calm, and focus on the important next thing to do when pressure builds.

Also, I want to get my hands dirty along with my coworkers. My job is as a teammate, regardless of rank. I want to be in the trenches with my coworkers and not just someone telling everyone else what to do. I call it the foxhole. I want to be in the foxhole with my colleagues, producing while enjoying the camaraderie and satisfaction that comes from a solid group accomplishment. I want to feel that sense of teamwork and trust, not hierarchy. I am a social person, and I enjoy the social aspect of a work environment.

A positive culture is what makes it all worthwhile. I figure that if I work ten hours a day, a majority of my waking hours during the week are with my work colleagues. I had better like the work and the culture. What I learned at Morgan Stanley was that you don't have to be in charge to contribute to a positive culture. That can happen at all levels. In fact, some of the best culture-carriers are effective team members in the middle of the org chart. But if you're the leader, establishing a great culture not only is job number one but also is the fun part of leading.

STEVE: *To finish the Texaco story—Pennzoil rejected the bid. Then in April 1986, Texaco filed for bankruptcy protection. The matter moved slowly through the courts, and finally, Texaco agreed to a settlement that would pay Pennzoil $3 billion. By then you were working in Morgan Stanley's Chicago office.*

KEN: Yes. I went to Chicago in January 1987 and worked there until my program was over in August. During the summer of 1987, Texaco and Pennzoil started settlement talks and ultimately agreed in December 1987. So, true to form for the investment banking business, the bankers are usually out of the thick of things once a deal really concludes.

STEVE: *Why Chicago?*

KEN: At that time, the Morgan Stanley office in Chicago had no analyst. I went to the woman in charge of the analyst program and said, "Have you thought about putting an analyst in the Chicago office? Because if you would, I'd be willing to be the groundbreaker there." She called the lead partner in Chicago, and he said they would love to have an analyst. Again, I have always been one to raise my hand and say, "Hey, have you thought of this?" In this case, the worst thing that could have happened was that they'd reject the idea.

STEVE: *What were your responsibilities in Chicago?*

KEN: This was an interesting move, since it was everything *but* energy work. The Chicago office partners covered the companies in Chicago and the Midwest, regardless of industry. It was more of an office where the bankers' job was to maintain a strong relationship with prospective clients, and if any transaction assignment emerged, the staffing would be done out of New York, where the work would get done. The word-processing and presentation-preparation capabilities were in New York, as was the library and other resources. But during the time I was at Morgan Stanley, the personal computer was just becoming an office fixture. This, combined with the first versions of the Lotus 1-2-3 spreadsheet and a laser printer, was a game changer.

I took my computer and my software skills to Chicago. I was able to put analyses together for the partners in that office more quickly than they ever imagined. They quickly figured that out and asked me to work on transaction ideas throughout the office. So I was on another steep learning curve since I was working on deals across a range of industries. After a while, I was basically functioning as an associate, even though I was a second-year analyst. It was really fun showing those old-time bankers the power of a simple spreadsheet and the speed with which I could turn around a presentation after receiving their feedback.

Having an analyst really increased the Chicago office's productivity. When I left, they replaced me with two analysts. I like to joke that that made me a managing analyst.

STEVE: *The Morgan Stanley program was always going to be a two-year stint, so you knew you were going to be leaving the company and heading to school by the fall of 1987. What was the motivation to go to Chicago for such a short period—seven or eight months?*

KEN: Looking back on it, it was my first appreciation that every plant needs to be repotted. I was excited about the idea of a new city and learning something new. I had only been to Chicago a couple of times before and had some friends from Princeton who were from there. But other than that, it was completely foreign to me. At the time, it excited me. The thought of finding an apartment, setting it up, and finding my way in a new city was energizing, especially with a corporate relocation package! I was pretty up to speed on the energy thing in New York and, since Chicago had no financial analysts in the office, I saw it as a way to make my mark and learn something new at the same time.

It was a great experience. It is amazing how magnified this time of my life has become when I think about experiences that shaped me.

I really felt independent in Chicago. It was the first time I lived alone. In fact, I knew almost nobody in that town when I arrived. I searched for and found a nice place to live, furnished it, and made friends. To this day, I am close to the group of friends I made while living there.

STEVE: *So, in the fall of 1987, you head to Stanford.*

KEN: Well, I came back to Dallas first to do another thing that I had never done on my own—buy a car. Even that experience left an indelible mark on my path. In life, small things inform behaviors that can last a lifetime. When I bought my first car, an hourly auto mechanic influenced my business career, without even knowing it.

STEVE: *An auto mechanic? Let's hear it.*

KEN: Before I left for California to start business school in the fall of 1987, I went home to see my parents, and while there, I bought my first car—a new Acura Integra—from a dealership in Arlington, Texas. As I recall, the price was about $13,000. My mom gave me my $5,000 "starting-out money" (the same amount she said that she had given to my sisters when they graduated), and I decided to use that toward a down payment on a car. I had saved enough money for my tuition and living expenses at Stanford, but I needed help with the car.

In getting ready for my first major purchase at age twenty-four, I did my research. I read *Consumer Reports*, shopped around, and did some early negotiating on the phone with a couple of dealerships before deciding which dealer to visit. I didn't want to be a dumb consumer; I was ready to make my first big purchase.

At the dealership, I took my test-drive, all while staying as stoic as possible so as not to hurt my negotiating position. I did like the car I test-drove and was set to make a deal. I remember parking the car on the side of the dealership after the test-drive and then following the salesman inside to begin the negotiations game. I knew the dealer's cost from my *Consumer Reports* research, so I held firm to what I was willing to pay while letting the dealer have an acceptable margin on the sale. We went back and forth a couple of times, but I came up only a few hundred dollars in the end. I was pleased.

As we worked up the final drive-off-the-lot price, we calculated the monthly payment schedule using the dealer financing that was available for the balance. I was fine in having them finance the balance. Then we started talking about the other options. I knew that this was where the salesman was really trying to make his money, and I was *not* going to be a sucker. I had read all about this process. I knew the extended warranties were a bad deal, so I said no. I did not want special tire rims. I did not want tire coverage. I did not want windshield protection. I did not want tinted windows. I did not need the salt undercoat treatment. (I could not believe he was even pushing that. It rarely snows in Dallas, and I am not sure if the highway authority even knew to use salt.)

Then we came to the racing-stripe option for my white car. I was really proud of myself for not being seduced to buy crazy mispriced features I didn't need. But the racing stripe was only about $150 more, and it was kind of cool. He showed me a picture of a sleek blue stripe along the side of a new white car. I hemmed and hawed, reluctant to give this salesman a victory after I had stayed firm up to that point. Finally, he ran a number on his desk calculator. "If you go with the racing stripe, it will only add $1.50 per month to your monthly payments," he said. A buck-fifty! That was less than a cheeseburger a month, and I was a fancy investment banker heading to Stanford. What the heck! I went for it.

We shook hands on the new amount, and he left the room to process the title work and get the car ready for me to drive off the lot. While I was sitting in his office, I gazed out the window to the side lot where my new car was parked. I smiled, thinking about my first big purchase and what a great deal I had negotiated.

I started thinking about packing and cruising to California. Then I saw this guy come out from the service garage. He had a roll of skinny blue tape in his hand. He walked up to my car, started at the front, applied the sticky tape to a point near the side of the front headlight and unrolled it as he paced toward the back of the car. He carefully rubbed his finger along the tape line to ensure it was affixed to the car. When he got to the back, he pulled a small blade from his pocket, cut the tape, and pressed the loose end to the car. He then did the same thing on the other side of the car. Voilà! Instant racing stripe.

I felt like shit.

I had just paid $150 for a guy to spend thirty-five seconds with a $1.50 roll of tape. *I* could've done that! I felt *so* stupid. Then I realized what had happened: On a $13,000 purchase, the cost of the stripe was a rounding error. The salesman had made it even more insignificant by showing how little it affected my monthly payment when baked into my financing.

But in absolute terms and on its own, $150 was a meaningful amount of money, especially to a twenty-four-year-old kid. If I had someone approach me the day after I bought the car and ask if I would pay them $150 to run this strip of blue tape down the side of my car, I would have laughed. Perhaps $1.50 maybe. In the context of the larger trade, however, I had become numb to a real number and forgot to value that trade on its own merits. I was a victim of the bias that behavior economists have now documented well. At the time, I felt like I had been taken advantage of.

Similarly, I had negotiated a deal where the car dealer was only making about a $500 margin on the entire sale of the car, but then, with perhaps a full $150 margin on the racing stripe (assuming that roll of tape cost about nothing) the dealer was able to increase his margin by 30 percent to $650. From then on, every time I got into that car, I looked at that damn stripe and just shook my head. All I could think of was the mechanic with the roll of tape pulling $150 out of my pocket!

I learned from that experience. I let an emotion take over in the middle of a business deal and kind of lost my head.

STEVE: *So there's a negotiating lesson here?*

KEN: Absolutely. I tell my young guys, "When you are in a negotiation, you can usually get a racing stripe." They usually look at me funny until I tell them that story. I explain that you'll most likely get your way when you're negotiating a $50 million purchase and you say to the seller, "I'll do this deal, but I'd really need for you to add in that, say, $25,000 item." In the context of a large deal, a small rounding-error item has little significance. Even though, on its own, that item's value could be meaningful. "In every trade," I explain, "there may be something that is a 'rounding error' in the context of that trade but has value on a stand-alone basis. Don't be afraid to ask for it. The worst thing they can do is turn you down."

I think I learned as much from that damn racing stripe as I did in two years at Stanford—a real-world lesson taught by a salesman on commission, an hourly mechanic, and a buck-fifty roll of tape.

STEVE: *Racing stripe and all, you took off for Palo Alto and business school. What had happened to the idea of law school?*

KEN: Well, this was my first example of listening to the market after a good market-test. During my senior year at Princeton, I had decided to go get my JD and MBA degrees together. Despite my falling out of love with criminal defense law, I was still thinking that a law degree would be useful. Plus, I was intrigued by the business world, even though it was still kind of a mystery. Since I was still in my resume-building phase, I figured that if I didn't get training now, I never would. To make it work, however, I had to be accepted at both the law school and the business school of each university. There was not a joint application.

Then the market "spoke" to me: I was wait-listed or rejected at all of the top-tier law schools, but I had success in the business school process. I was accepted at Stanford. I got one of those "likely in two years" letters from Harvard. With the Stanford acceptance, I was given the option of attending the following year *or* electing to defer for two years. There was a simple return postcard with boxes to check: "I will attend in the fall" or "Defer." I checked the "Defer" box and put it in the mail. At the time, I had no idea how rare that was. It was only later that I learned that a handful of admits were accepted on that basis. Stanford Law School had put me on its wait list.

That changed my mindset on how I viewed a four-year JD/MBA degree. If I committed to two years to complete my MBA, getting a law degree on top would add two additional years—a full *doubling* of the time needed. If I was committed to three years of law school, then getting an MBA would only add a single year to the effort, from a third year to a fourth year of work. That was only a 33 percent increase in time. I think economists have studied this for years. The marginal cost for my law degree when I was starting with a two-year business school commitment was greater than the marginal cost of an MBA degree if I was committing to a three-year law school experience. Even though the four-year total is the same, the decision process is quite different.

I didn't really analyze it this way at the time. I just figured that the admissions officers knew what they were up to. I listened to the market and cooled on law school.

STEVE: *Listening to the market then served you well.*

KEN: Actually, that admission to Stanford really got me the job at Morgan Stanley.

STEVE: *How do you figure?*

KEN: Early in the fall of my senior year at Princeton, I put my name into the banking and consulting firm recruitment process, just to see what would happen. I was finding limited success. Although the recruiters came to campus to interview Princeton students, I was pretty ill-prepared. I had no real corporate finance background, and I didn't really work the New York network like some of my classmates. Heck, I'd never even heard of most of these firms. I guess a politics major with an affection for political theory writing a senior thesis on legal ethics wasn't in high demand. I only had one firm call me back.

So, after I had heard from Stanford, with little to lose, I thought I would try something completely different at my next interview. That interview was with Morgan Stanley, following their shrimp dinner information session.

The first-round interviews were held on campus. Typically, those interviews were done by second-year analysts who were eight or nine months away from finishing their program. I did not realize it at the time, but that fall, most were in the process of applying to business school themselves.

I put on my interview suit, trying to look like I knew something about finance, but hoping for a question about John Locke or John Stuart Mill. You could tell the interviewees because we were the only suits walking across a college campus. Little corporate cattle, awaiting the auction ring.

I went into the interview room with nervous anticipation. The chirpy second-year analyst started the interview by attempting to be super-friendly while still maintaining the "I have the job you so desperately want" attitude. He asked the stock "Why are you interested in Morgan Stanley" question to lead off. *Bingo*. I saw my opening to lead the witness. John Locke would have to wait. "You see," I said, "I am looking for a good two-year program and I heard you guys have one of the best."

I knew that was exactly the *wrong* answer according to the "how to ace an interview" book. So did my inquisitor. "Yes, that is true," he said smugly. "But *why?*" he followed.

Then, I dropped the bomb: "Well, I'm going to go to Stanford for business school in a couple of years, if, of course, I find a good program."

"You mean, *apply* to Stanford business school, don't you?" he asked, taking the bait.

"No." I explained, putting on my best pretend-innocent look. "You see, I applied to Stanford, and I got this reply card with my acceptance saying I could go next year or defer for a couple of years if I want, so I'm kind of looking around to see what's out there."

His silence was deafening. He tried his best to maintain his posture of superiority as he came back down to earth, realizing that I could be one of his Stanford classmates, *if he were lucky enough to get accepted*. He quickly became a salesman for the firm, explaining why it was the best on "the Street" and that I would have a great time there.

From that point on, I flew through Morgan Stanley's later interview rounds and was given an offer. I received a couple of other offers as well by applying the same interview tactic. It seems that the club really wanted people who were already members. Since Stanford had already sent me a membership card, the doors flew open.

STEVE: *You've said that when you arrived from Dallas, it was the first time you'd set foot on the Stanford campus. Have you ever bought a company sight unseen? Business school is a pretty big commitment. Why not check it out before signing on for two years that might determine your future?*

KEN: I guess it was a combination of resume-building and wanderlust. At the time, I was applying to all of the best law schools and business schools, and we didn't traipse around the country to inspect campuses like kids do today. Stanford was one of the best, if not the best, business school. I had visited California, so I could not complain about the weather. And I'd never had any real bias for or against that part of the country—other than the fact that I really hated the San Francisco 49ers!

Although it was sight-unseen, the product was well known, fully vetted, and well regarded—the MBA degree, that is. There was not a doubt that I would do the work and graduate. I figured that I was not getting *less* qualified by going to one of the top schools in the country.

Of course, at the time, I had no idea how life-changing the Stanford experience was going to be. It was there that I found lifelong friends, a wife, and an opening to write a letter to one of Stanford business school's 1968 graduates—Richard Rainwater.

STEVE: *Rainwater is central to your story. Before we get to him, let me ask if you entered Stanford knowing what you wanted to do after graduation.*

KEN: I was clueless. I had no set direction or plan. As I look at myself, I see that one thing baked into my DNA is that the fog of the future excites me. I seem to gravitate toward things that open up new doors, rarely needing a clear plan. We have all come across those gunners who seem to have their shit together and seem to know exactly what they want to do and where they want to go. I was never one of those people. I have never been deterred by uncertainty. Some would say that I am like a moth to the flame of the unknown. "Ready, shoot, aim," I liked to say.

STEVE: *What was Stanford like?*

KEN: For me, it was nirvana. It was like going back and doing my senior year in college all over again. I was on a vibrant campus, but two years older than I was during my last year of Princeton. While still close enough to college age to feel a part of the experience, I was now wiser, knowing that all the stresses of college would seem small once the real game of life started. I had worked in the hustle of New York and felt that I could take on the world.

There were many in my class coming out of Wall Street firms or the large management consulting companies. I was in my peer element and, having never taken formal courses in accounting, corporate finance, strategic management, taxes, organizational behavior, marketing, or negotiations, I was really looking forward to school. I didn't feel like the admissions mistake, but I definitely didn't feel like I was better than the curriculum. I was learning material for the first time and was challenged by it, but I did not feel like I was in the wrong place. There was a tremendous esprit de corps among the class. Virtually all of us had worked in the business world, and we were a few years older than most on campus. We knew how to approach school now. We took what we did seriously, but we took ourselves a lot less seriously. To say that we bonded would be a world-class understatement.

Going to Stanford was like going to school at a country club. The weather was so idyllic you couldn't help but be in a good mood. In and around classes, my life was full. We played some golf and even had a weekly bowling club. A local dive bar hosted a weekly business school night that served all the beer you could drink for those paying an annual fee. My buddies and I started a weekly low-stakes poker group. I was humor editor of the school newspaper and cowrote the class musical comedy show. Most important, I formed the friendships that continue to this day.

STEVE: *Was it competitive?*

KEN: Not really. Whether intentional or not, the school cultivated a unique culture. There were no formal grades, and there was an agreement among students that they would not talk about grades or class standing with recruiters. Amazingly, that agreement stuck. It was my first experience with a culture where people were encouraged to help each other and actually did. We acted cooperatively and cheered each other on. I think that is why our class has remained so close to this day.

I felt like I had found my people. I consider myself a person who wants to achieve but do so in the right way. Demanding does not have to be demeaning. Being competitive does not have to be ugly. I like to move forward in life, but not by stepping on those people around me.

STEVE: *As I understand it, Stanford had a core curriculum that everyone took for most of their first year, but after that it was totally free-form for folks to choose their electives from a big menu. Did you shape your curriculum to get you ready to be an investor?*

KEN: Looking back, you might say I was aimless. I took classes that interested me, but I did not weave any particular concentration together. Maybe it reflected the fact that I am attracted to so many different things. I enjoyed the "soft" classes like Organizational Behavior and Interpersonal Dynamics—affectionately called "Touchy-Feely"—as well as the "hard" classes like Statistics, and even Professor Myron Scholes's advanced tax strategies class.

STEVE: *Business school is also about finding a job. I imagine that the single summer you had between the two years of business school made that summer job an important one.*

KEN: We started school in late September, and before Thanksgiving people were already talking about summer jobs. I couldn't believe it. It seemed like we had just arrived on campus and the recruiters were already there. I interviewed with the usual suspects who came to campus—J. P. Morgan, McKinsey, BCG, Bain, and a few others. They all start to look alike after a while.

It was all so awkward. It was not like the undergraduate experience, where we were just bullshitting our way through an interview, pretending to know something about the firm we were interviewing with or repeating some well-rehearsed answers about our greatest strength or weakness. This was a much more real process. The good interviewers were simply seeing if you would be a good match. The bad interviews were from firms who sent some haughty young partner to sniff us up and down to see if we were worthy enough to grace their hallways. I had a few of each. Morgan Stanley sent out a partner to talk to me and a couple of other classmates who were in my analyst class. Now we were Morgan Stanley alumni and being courted away from the standard interview process. That sounded kind of cool. They wanted to give me an offer to return to the firm. I was flattered, but I said I wasn't really interested.

STEVE: *Why not?*

KEN: I had been lucky. While at the firm, I'd had good exposure to some of the firm's top people both in New York and Chicago, and I could really see who they were and how they worked. I also saw their quality of life. I have no idea why I did this when I was just twenty-three years old, but I recall asking myself if there was anybody there that I wanted to be like when I got to be their age. Of course, there were quality people there who were smart and very hard-working. But many of the men seemed a mess to me. Some were not married. Some were divorced. If they were married, it seemed like they never saw their families. They were always running—to or from the airport, to or from Manhattan, or to or from their weekend homes.

I am not being judgmental, but I looked around and there weren't many people about whom I thought: fifteen or twenty years from now, I want to be like *him*. Remember, this was the mid-1980s on Wall Street, the age of Michael Lewis's *Liar's Poker* and the beginnings of the junk-bond era. From a young man's perspective, it seemed like the mentality was "Work your tail off, make your number, hit forty, and figure out something else to do." I did not want to sacrifice ages twenty-five to forty to make a bunch of money yet become a wreck along the way.

Looking back, that was unfair. I have remained connected with some of the people I worked for back then, and they are quality people. We have had conversations about those days, and there is general agreement that the nature of the business is at fault, not the people. Remember that this is how it looked from the analyst cubicle.

STEVE: *That huge rush and feeling of satisfaction you got working on the Texaco deal wasn't enough to make you think you wanted to make a career of it?*

KEN: No, it really wasn't. Mostly because investment bankers were hired guns. I loved the fact that I was an essential part of a team at a very young age, that I was performing well, and that people were relying on me. But the Morgan Stanley people were basically getting a fee to tell the Texaco people what they could have figured out for themselves. I enjoyed this and other deals we worked on, but it seemed so odd to me that we were being paid transaction fees based on deal size, independent of whether the deal worked over the long term. The incentive structure just seemed off to me. Whether it was for acquisition advice or corporate finance underwriting, the fees were set as a percentage of the deal size and not on how much effort was expended. Moreover, the fees were due regardless of whether it was a quality deal. It was a pure transaction fee, with no regard to whether the ultimate outcome was good or bad for the client.

I know that in a normal market, if pricing is too high, then customers are always free to buy from a less expensive competitor, all other things being equal. That presupposes an efficient market with many competitors. But there seemed to be a general understanding that pricing for all firms was calculated this way, "because that is how we do it in the business." There were also only a few major firms, so it was a bit of an oligopoly. Charging someone a lot of money, just because they could pay it, felt icky to me.

That impression of this transaction business is what stuck with me. Bankers were only as good as their last deal or their last year's performance. Once their year-end bonuses were paid, they were back to zero. Bankers were making single hundred thousand-dollar salaries and then getting seven-figure bonuses. The lifestyle was supported by borrowing from a bank during the year and then paying it off when your bonus arrived. That dynamic forced an incessant insecurity, which resulted in this obsessive drive for everyone to make the year-end number. That pressure cooker *is* the investment banking business. I remember hearing one of the senior managing directors at the firm say that he really liked his bankers being "deeply in debt," because that meant they were hungry to hit their fee goals for the year.

STEVE: *You mentioned that you are still friends with some of your Stanford classmates. One of those classmates is Bill Browder. If that name sounds familiar, it's probably because he's the person responsible for Congress passing the Magnitsky Act, the 2012 law that allows the United States to sanction human rights offenders by freezing their assets and barring them from entering the country. The act was aimed at Russia*

and received a lot of attention during the investigation of Russian interference in the
2016 presidential election.

KEN: Right. Bill was one of the first to realize that the post–Cold War Russia offered real investment opportunities, and he eventually created a very successful investment fund to take advantage of those opportunities, Hermitage Capital Management. Long story short, he was banned from Russia in 2005 on a trumped-up charge that he was a threat to national security. When the stock market there crashed, as an investor, he spent a lot of time trying to get his money back and, in so doing, he exposed a lot of corruption in some of the largest companies there. I guess his discoveries got too close to some of the central authorities. They devised a scheme to accuse Bill and his firm of some really egregious activity.

Sergei Magnitsky was Bill's lawyer who helped defend him and actually uncover the real corruption. Instead of making him a hero, it made him a target in the thug state. Magnitsky was arrested, imprisoned, beaten, denied medical aid, and ultimately died in jail in 2009. Meanwhile, Bill was tried and convicted of tax fraud in absentia. To this day, the Russians would like nothing more than to get their hands on him. Their threats have not silenced him. He wrote a gripping account of all of this in his book *Red Notice* and its sequel, *Freezing Order*.

As you mentioned, he lobbied tirelessly for what became the Magnitsky Act, and he is still an outspoken critic of the regime and a champion for social justice against corrupt regimes worldwide.

STEVE: *How did you two become friends?*

KEN: I cannot remember exactly, but we connected early in our first term on campus. We have similar senses of humor. We're both pretty irreverent. We hung out a lot together, including starting our weekly poker game, which became a mainstay of my Stanford experience. We played every Thursday night for two years. I don't think we missed a single night of playing, even when things were the most hectic. It was like the perfect men's book club. No books!

Bill and I saw the world the same way. We took what we did seriously, but we took ourselves a lot less seriously. When we went through the interview process that first year, we had similar reactions to some of the more awkward interviews. When it was apparent that some firms were looking for a "type" to fit in, we both kind of rebelled. We made fun of the folks at J. P. Morgan who epitomized the blue-blooded, white-shoe New York banking scene. There was no way irreverent Jewish kids like us were ever going to get an offer. We joked that we needed old-line WASP names like

Chip and Winthrop to be given an offer. And we joked we should threaten to miss the interview because our sailboats at the Nantucket Yacht Club needed tending.

I am not sure anyone else thought it was funny, but we really cracked ourselves up. Coming to top-tier finance from "outsider" backgrounds was something we had in common. If ever there was handwriting on the wall that two guys weren't going to be spending the rest of their lives on Wall Street, this was it. We continued the "Chip and Winthrop" shtick throughout business school and still enjoy laughing about it to this day.

STEVE: *That brings up a good point about how you responded to your world. Did you ever feel that there were people on Wall Street who were uncomfortable about you being Jewish? Did you ever feel that you didn't belong?*

KEN: No. Never. I figured that with firms with Jewish heritage like Goldman Sachs, Lehman Brothers, and Salomon Brothers being so prominent, that was a thing of the past. If there was anti-Semitism there, I didn't notice it. Plus, I wasn't in New York long enough to even learn what the clubs were that I wasn't invited to join.

Looking back, it was ironic that I felt this way since I had succeeded at Morgan Stanley, probably the firm with the stuffiest WASP reputation. *And* they wanted me back after business school. On the surface, there was simply no reason for me to feel that I was an outsider. Regardless of the circumstance, I was determined to take my place wherever I wanted, and I didn't give much mindshare to thinking about whether I belonged. I saw no need to accept a rule book to which I had not subscribed.

Bill and I went so far as to do an independent study project in our second year to devise a more socially acceptable model for the investment banking business. We went through the analysis to prove that it was functioning as an oligopoly and demonstrating collusion in the pricing model and worked up an alternative for the industry. Professor Myron Scholes was our adviser on the project. We had grand visions of shaking up the Wall Street model.

How ironic that a decade later, Scholes was working at the hedge fund Long Term Capital Management, and his massive derivative positions were at the heart of the financial crisis of 1998. Somehow reality crashed into Professor Scholes's academic theories.

Good thing Bill and I didn't try to put our theory of breaking Wall Street into practice. We may have ended up the same way.

CHAPTER 3

DO YOU WANT THE QUOTE?

STEVE: *You never were going to go to Wall Street for that summer of 1988 between your first and second year at Stanford, were you?*

KEN: Not if I could help it. Since I was not interested in the transaction advisory business, I started reading to see what else was out there. I looked beyond the firms recruiting on campus and conducted an independent job search. At the time, there was an emerging activity called principal investing. Now, we call it private equity or high-net-worth family office investing. Back in 1988, the words "private equity" meant nothing.

I remembered reading about the Bass brothers in Fort Worth, Texas, who seemed to be managing their own money. As part of my research, I called around Morgan Stanley to ask for leads. I got through to Tom Hassen, the equity research analyst covering the oil and gas sector. When I was in the New York office, I always enjoyed helping him when I could, and he and I had pretty good chemistry together. It wasn't in my immediate job description, since he was in a different department, so I think he appreciated my going out of my way to help. The equity research department didn't have analysts like me and I guess the partners were expected to do their own processing. With his cherubic look, gracious smile, and easy manner, Tom always seemed out of place among the eat-your-young investment bankers. I would go out of my way to hang in his office for a few extra minutes to absorb some of his fascinating stories. I have no idea if his stories were true, but they sure were entertaining.

When I looked at my list of Morgan Stanley relationships, calling on Tom was a natural.

"Yeah, I know the Bass brothers, but . . . ," he paused.

"But—but what?" I stuttered, thinking he was about to pour cold water on any thoughts I had about this line of work.

He replied, "There's this guy in Fort Worth named Richard Rainwater who left the Bass brothers and went off on his own a few years ago. I've met him. He might need somebody. Forget the Bass brothers; I would get in touch with Richard."

That was the first time I had heard the name Richard Rainwater. So, knowing that I had little to lose, I figured out how to get in touch with him.

STEVE: *How?*

KEN: Duh! I called 411 information in Fort Worth, Texas, and asked for the phone number for Richard Rainwater's office. Then I called the number and politely told the receptionist who answered that I wanted to send Mr. Rainwater a letter but did not have the mailing address. She gave me the office address.

I drafted a cold letter to Richard that included my resume and explained that I had worked a bit with Tom Hassen at Morgan Stanley, who had suggested that I write. I said I was now thinking about the principal investment business as opposed to investment banking and was looking for a summer job.

I figured it would take a week or so for the letter to find its way to Rainwater's desk and that it was a total long shot for something there to materialize. In the meantime, I continued to put my name in for on-campus interviews. My two confidants regarding my job hunt were Bill Browder and John Berg. Recall that John was the one who high-tailed it to the Sydney, Australia, office for his second year at Morgan Stanley, leaving me as the lead number cruncher when the Texaco assignment came in. He was now a year ahead of me at Stanford, and I trusted his instinct on business and personal issues. Each of them encouraged me to write the letter to Rainwater, even if we all thought it had next to a zero chance of resulting in a job.

A few days after I mailed the letter, I was at home when the phone rang. A woman with a polite Southern drawl asked if I was Ken. "Yes, that's me," I said.

"Hold the line, please, for Mr. Rainwater," she said matter-of-factly. My mind raced. Since I had told Berg and Browder about the letter, my first thought was that one of them was screwing with me. But it really *was* Richard Rainwater.

STEVE: *What did he say?*

KEN: His first words to me were, "You want the quote?" Again, my mind raced. I knew there was a correct answer to this question, but I had no idea what it was. Remember, this was in early 1988. The stock market had crashed a few months earlier in October of 1987. That was a dark day. Given the time change, by the time we woke up in California and got to class on what was properly called "Black Monday," the market rout had already begun. So many of my classmates had money in the market—money they needed for tuition and expenses—that it caused a real panic. That memory left an indelible mark on our memory of our first year at business school.

I immediately thought there must have been another market crash and that this was going to be a quote about the market or some stock. But this was "quote" as in "quotation."

"Sure, give me the quote," I replied sheepishly.

Rainwater's voice chirped like a kid revealing a cool secret to a friend. "Morgan Stanley invented the Wall Street analyst program and has had more analysts than any other investment bank on the Street, and they say you are the best analyst they've ever had," he trumpeted.

I was speechless. He explained that he had called Tom Hassen, who had sung my praises. Apparently, Tom inflated my record at the firm. But, as a decent poker player would do, I kept quiet.

"Sounds like I need to meet you. When can you be here?" Richard asked.

"As soon as I can," I replied confidently. "I will figure it out and call you back and let your office know."

And that was that. My independent job search had just yielded its first interview.

Now, how could I get a ticket to Dallas? I didn't have a lot of spare cash lying around, so my wheels started turning. Then it dawned on me that I had a second on-campus interview with McKinsey in a few days. I knew from the first round that McKinsey was frustrated with Stanford students who, being the prima donnas they were, only wanted to work in the firm's San Francisco office. I figured that those willing to work in other offices had a better chance of making it further into the interview process.

When my interview took place that week, I joined the parade of well-dressed Stanford students making the procession to the Stanford Park Hotel on El Camino Avenue in Palo Alto, where McKinsey consultants took over a few guest rooms for the day. My second-round interviewer, Randy Kelley, was more relaxed than most of the interviewers I had met. A Stanford MBA himself, he was leading the recruiting process at his alma mater. As luck would have it, he was from McKinsey's Texas office, which is how the firm referred to their professionals in Dallas and Houston.

As the interview progressed, I worked in my bombshell. "I wouldn't mind working in your Texas office," I said, leading the witness.

"Really?" he said, seemingly stunned that I wasn't angling for a desk in San Francisco like the rest of the folks he was seeing that day.

"Sure," I replied. "I'm from Dallas, so it makes sense. But I would like to go see it first, just so I know what I would be getting into." I could tell by his body language that I was now in a club of one. That virtually guaranteed me a callback.

Lucky for me, neither Randy nor the guy who conducted the callback questioned why a kid from Dallas needed to go see an office in Dallas. They were happy to offer up the firm's money and agreed to fly me home a week or two later.

Voilà! I had my ticket.

I immediately called Rainwater's office and made an appointment to meet Richard. The date was March 10, 1988. I flew down on McKinsey's nickel and interviewed with them—legitimately, I might add. Among the partners I met was Jim Crownover, the head of McKinsey's Dallas office, who happened to be in the same Stanford business school class as one Richard Rainwater back in 1968.

After visiting McKinsey, I went to Fort Worth to meet Rainwater. Remember, all he had said to me was that he would like to meet me. I had no idea what to expect.

STEVE: *And?*

KEN: My first reaction was how stark everything was in his office. I remembered Morgan Stanley—not only the floors with the investment bankers but also the sea of screens, chairs, and phones that made up the sales and trading floor. This office was nothing like that. The plain glass double doors led from the elevator bank to a stark white reception desk, surrounded by white walls, with no name or logo.

Visitors were greeted by the receptionist, whom I came to know as Lois. She was a welcoming, warm, grandmotherly type with a throwback beehive hairdo that accentuated her bright red locks. She was the whole package: Her charming Southern drawl welcomed everyone to the office with a "Hello, hon," which spoke to another era. She made me feel at ease.

It wasn't long before Richard's longtime assistant, Nancy Pridemore, came to get me in the reception area. Like Lois, she had a friendly, maternal vibe.

Nancy escorted me from the reception area into the office. If I didn't know better, I would have thought I was in a semiconductor clean room or some sort of medical lab. Each office had a glass wall facing out to the core of the floor, but the three other walls were solid white, covered in a slick magnetic surface that turned every wall into a marker-board. Occupied offices had those walls filled with handwritten notes and numbers, giving off the feel that each room was its own deal lab. Stark white secretarial cubes filled the interior of the floor, all sitting atop the low-cut gray carpet.

Richard's office was large but nondescript. He sat behind a large white desk, and I took a seat in one of the two black guest chairs. His desk was bare except for two phones, a couple of photos of his family, a yellow legal pad, a black felt-tip marker, and a mysterious blue book.

As I would come to learn, his yellow legal pad guided his day as he took notes or scribbles during calls, meticulously coloring in the yellow pad as the calls went on. All work was done in a black felt-tip pen. By the end of every day, the pad was black. When he was ready to go home, he would tear off the top yellow page, now black (and sometimes the blank page behind it if the black ink had bled through), wad up that paper and throw it, and the used felt-tip pen, into the trash. One of Nancy's jobs was to have a new black felt-tip pen on his desk for the next morning, when he'd begin his day on a fresh, clean top page of the yellow legal pad.

STEVE: *How did that first conversation go?*

KEN: We exchanged some pleasantries, and then Richard just blurted out, "I don't have any summer jobs. It's just me, Nancy, and guys like Peter (Joost) and Tad (Kelly), who do their own thing. I work for myself. I don't have any real employees. But based on your resume and what Tom Hassen said, I just wanted to meet you."

Peter Joost had gone to Stanford for college and then on to Harvard Business School. Tad Kelly was a Yale undergrad, Harvard MBA. Others in the office then included John Goff, Richard Squires, Mort Meyerson, and now-Senator Rick Scott. At the time, the Rainwater office was a loose confederation of deal guys. Peter was really Richard's right-hand man, but he was not drawing a paycheck from him from what I could tell. Each person worked on deals and then when a deal got done, there would be some sort of board or monitoring fees that were negotiated as part of the closing. Those sources of income stacked up to cover overhead once someone did one or two deals.

Richard seemed to relish the fact that nobody reported to him, and that he didn't have a real payroll other than his assistants. I would later come to find out that a legacy investment fund that Richard oversaw when he was at the Bass organization continued to pay him an overhead fee after he went out on his own, so he didn't even really have to cover his office overhead.

The office was a collaborative deal "job shop" in which each deal professional worked on the deals that they brought in. There was a little collaboration. When capital was needed, the deal's leader would usually walk around the office and see who wanted to invest in it as well as solicit the participation of institutional partners. Richard used to say, "Go find partners, then walk the deal around the office, and I'll take whatever's left."

He later quipped, "I knew when guys were ready to leave and strike out on their own, because deals would only make it halfway around the floor or they wouldn't even get out of the guy's office before the entire equity check was spoken for." People soon developed their own capital base or group of coinvestors and could speak for deals without flashing Rainwater's name.

So there I was with this great investor who had so enthusiastically wanted to meet me, only to hear him dash my hopes of a job in the first five minutes.

STEVE: *That must have been deflating.*

KEN: It could have been, but there was a silver lining. Or a blue one. By chance, earlier that day, two McKinsey guys had presented a study to Richard. That was their trademark blue-covered presentation book shimmering on Richard's desk. It was an analysis of the U.S. natural gas industry prepared for numerous clients, including Richard. Incidentally, the two McKinsey presenters had been John Sawhill, a former deputy secretary of energy under Jimmy Carter, and a young associate from the firm's Houston office named Jeff Skilling. Yes, that Jeff Skilling, who would go on to become the CEO of Enron and, famously, would be found guilty in 2006 for misdeeds relating to the company's collapse.

McKinsey's study walked through the sequence of events occurring in the natural gas industry after the deregulation of 1986. As a result of sustained low prices, demand for the fuel was rising at the same time that the supply was starting to fall. Economics 101–type stuff. Since all oil and gas wells decline over time, the industry needed to keep drilling new wells to keep production up. If prices were too low, there would be insufficient cash flow for reinvestment drilling, and new capital would be deterred from coming into the business because returns were so low. The study concluded that demand would overtake supply in the winter of 1989 or the winter of 1990 at the latest. Natural gas prices would then go from a very low number to a very high number, as shortages would be inevitable.

In the silence hanging there after he dashed the hopes of this young capitalist, Richard noticed the blue McKinsey book, grabbed it, and pushed it over to me. "You were in the energy group, what do you think of this?" he asked as he turned the book around and slid it across his desk toward me. I took the book and began to page through it quickly. I remembered just enough to be dangerous, babbling about some of the trends that the McKinsey report explained. I was heading *way* out over my skis.

Then, *it hit me.* "Tell you what, Richard," I said as I closed the book. "Why don't I take the McKinsey view of the world and spend my summer coming up with some sort of an investment strategy around this?"

STEVE: *Where did that come from?*

KEN: Good question. Honestly, it seemed I was having some out-of-body experience watching my twenty-five-year-old self lay a "brilliant" idea on to one of the country's preeminent investors. But Richard had paid good money for McKinsey's report. I figured he might need some help in making sense of it all. Who better than a liberal arts guy who had spent one year crunching numbers for energy deals on Wall Street and a year taking the intro-to-everything courses of Stanford's first-year MBA curriculum? I was just what the doctor ordered!

Man, was I cocky, or what?

But Richard Rainwater bit. He told me to send him a proposal and he would look at it. I had no idea if he had asked just to be nice or if he was sincere, but I started writing it on the flight back to San Francisco. In the end, I suggested an analysis of who would win and who would lose, given the McKinsey view of the world and what type of investments would make sense. When I got back to California, I sat down at my Macintosh computer, complete with the companion dot-matrix printer to pretty it up.

As luck would have it, I did land the offer for a summer job at McKinsey's Dallas office, so I proposed something that I thought was a light lift for Richard. I said I would accept the McKinsey offer and complete the summer term there, which concluded in mid-August. But I proposed starting on the project from Palo Alto immediately so that I would have April, May, and then again from mid-August to mid-September, when classes resumed, to complete the work. This was a full three-month work plan.

I had no idea where this would go. I was just content to get something on my resume that would be interesting. It was setting up perfectly. I would be able to have a traditional summer experience with a top-tier management consulting firm while also doing something entrepreneurial on the side. I figured, *What the hell? I am not going backward at all.* My downside was covered, and I had a chance to make a good impression on one of the most enigmatic and revered investors of the 1980s.

Before sending the proposal, I had to make a pretty big decision, however.

STEVE: *Which was?*

KEN: I had to decide whether to charge him for my work. My two most trusted friends were of two minds. "Don't charge him. Just to get his name on your resume is huge. Make it easy for him to say okay," said John Berg.

Bill Browder disagreed: "Charge him! This is something of value, and if you give him something of value, he should pay you for it."

They were no help. I went back and forth for a while staring at the letter on my screen. Finally, I decided to go for it, adding a paragraph to my proposal, respectfully requesting a "stipend of $5,000 for this work." Then, upping the chutzpah quotient, I mentioned that my upcoming spring-break trip to Korea would preclude my getting back to him right away, as if to make me look like some international wheeler-dealer.

I faxed it to him and dropped a hard copy in the mail. Immediately, I had second thoughts. What if Berg was right? What would I say if he balked? *What was I thinking?* McKinsey was going to pay me well for the summer, and I was intending to live at my mom's house for free. With few expenses, I would come out just fine. I was all set. *Had I blown it?* I was ready to back off the demand for any money. I just hoped Rainwater wouldn't be so offended that he'd say, "Forget it."

I tossed and turned for two days wondering if I had blown it. Then, a couple days after sending off the proposal, to my surprise I received a FedEx delivery from Fort Worth. Inside the envelope was a check for $5,000. No note. Just the check.

I'd just landed my first client. Clearly, I need to include a copy of that proposal letter here, since it really has become a historical document of my life (see Exhibit 1).

STEVE: *You must have been floored.*

KEN: I thought, *Wow, 5K and I've only met the guy one time!* Then I had seller's remorse: *He was so quick to accept my offer; I wonder how much money I left on the table!*

No matter, it was March, and I was all set for my summer. I deposited the $5,000 in the bank and did what every enterprising grad student would do. I put an ad in the *Stanford Daily*: "Graduate student in need of research assistant." I said I wanted a senior who was an economics and finance major to help me on a project. I figured, if I offered $10 an hour for a hundred hours, that would set me back $1,000, and my researcher could do all the work for April and May while I was finishing up the year. I wouldn't have to lift a finger, and I'd be left with $4,000.

I was just a few years out of undergrad, and there I was at the Tressider Student Union interviewing Stanford seniors. I had interested students lined up around the corner.

I hired a guy—I wish I could remember his name—and took him to the Palo Alto public library and showed him how to find the *Oil and Gas Journal* 400—the top 400 companies in the industry. Remember that this was 1988. There was nothing online at the time, so I had to show him how to look up company directory information. I remembered doing that at *Business Today* while I was an undergrad, so I knew which books to look for. I asked him to call all the companies he could and request their annual reports, SEC filings, and investor packets and have them sent to my mom's house in Dallas. In all, he called about 300 of the 400 companies and was successful in getting the requested information.

March 18, 1988

Mr. Richard Rainwater
Investment Limited Partnership
First City Bank Tower
Suite 2000
201 Main Street
Ft. Worth, Texas   76102

Dear Mr. Rainwater:

I would like to thank you very much for meeting with me on March 10. I found our visit very informative and I am pleased to have the opportunity to undertake a project for you.

As promised, I have studied the McKinsey report and its implications. I have attached my preliminary analysis. In the report, I outline my initial thoughts concerning the implications of the McKinsey natural gas price scenario and I suggest an Action Plan to undertake in order to develop a rewarding investment strategy.

I would like to propose the following structure for my project:

- April 1 – June 1: Continued development of the strategy and basic research.

- August 22 – September 2: Work with you in Nantucket/Ft. Worth to fine tune the approach.

- September 6 – 16: Finalize the project.

I would plan to spend the first 10 weeks of the summer with McKinsey in Dallas working as a summer consultant.

I feel that this plan of action affords ample time to develop and plan an exciting investment strategy. This timetable would effectively allow me to spend close to 3 months on your assigment.

At this time, having thought about the time and resources needed to produce a comprehensive study, I would like to request a spring/summer stipend of $5,000 to cover the expenses and the time commitment to you.

I believe that, given the McKinsey scenario, very profitable investment opportunities exist and that a thoughtful "game plan" can produce exponential returns.

I will be traveling to Korea next week, but I will return on March 28. I will contact you at that time to discuss the next steps.

I look forward to speaking with you soon and I am excited about undertaking this project for you.

Sincerely,

Kenneth Hersh

Exhibit 1: Cover letter to Richard Rainwater outlining my original proposal to study the natural gas business, March 18, 1988

Some background: In 1985, the Federal Energy Regulatory Commission (FERC) had issued Order 436, effectively deregulating the natural gas industry. This was a huge event for the industry, and it had thrown the sector into chaos. Much of the McKinsey analysis stemmed from this chaos. So I taught my assistant how to use a microfiche reader to find old newspaper articles and asked him to research all he could find from credible sources about how the FERC order was reshaping the industry.

STEVE: *So, off he went to do his work. Sounds like you learned a lot about leveraging your time somewhere.*

KEN: He went to the library, and we met once a week. At each meeting, he gave me a set of articles he had copied, which I sent home. It worked out great. I didn't have to do much, and he had a nice side job for some senior year spending money. When I went home to Dallas in June, my bedroom was jammed with unopened envelopes from all of those companies. It was daunting, but I dissected them all with the help of my original Apple Macintosh, about a dozen floppy disks, and the 1.0 version of the Excel spreadsheet program.

I worked for McKinsey during the day, and I was bored out of my mind. Thankfully, my moonlighting project of putting the data set together for Rainwater kept me engaged. I worked on it every night. I probably only went out three evenings that entire summer.

Oddly, I did not hear from Richard between the time the FedEx envelope arrived and the end of the school term. I just took the money and started working. I figured I would check in with him toward the end of my time at McKinsey.

However, toward the end of June, I got a phone call out of the blue to my office at McKinsey. Rainwater was calling from his summer "office" at the Cliffside Beach Club on Nantucket. "How's my project coming?" he asked. This was my first conversation with him since I had left his office in March. I was thankful that he even remembered. Little did I know, he never forgot *anything*.

"It's coming along well," I said. "I'm working on it every night."

STEVE: *And that was that?*

KEN: That was about the extent of the call. One minute, tops. I think he just wanted to know that I was still out there.

STEVE: *Did McKinsey know you were doing this?*

KEN: When the summer was just beginning, I felt compelled to tell them I was moonlighting. I nervously went into Jim Crownover's office and said, "I know you know Mr. Rainwater. You should know that I'm doing a project for him on the oil and gas business as a sort of 'moonlighting' assignment. I just want to make sure you know about it, so you don't feel there's a conflict of interest if I get staffed here on an oil and gas client."

In fact, I suggested that it would be better if I got staffed on a client from another industry. No idea why I thought that Ken Hersh, lowly summer intern, was going to be so critical to major client work, but I felt like I should at least come clean, just in case.

STEVE: *I'm guessing that Crownover didn't have a lot of twentysomethings wandering into the managing partner's office alerting him to potential conflicts. What did he say?*

KEN: He thanked me for stepping forward and said he'd get me staffed on a non-energy assignment. I had no idea what he thought of me. I guess it was a good thing that he was friends with Rainwater. Otherwise, it may have been more awkward.

STEVE: *Seems like it may have been hard to juggle a job at McKinsey and a big project on the side.*

KEN: That summer was a slog. During the day, I was assigned to a team working on some cost study for a technology company there in town. For a summer intern, it was completely uninspiring work. However, the people in the office were nice and I got to see one of the most professionally managed organizations in the world. Their firm's culture was and continues to be outstanding. Even if I was uninspired by the work, I was very impressed by the firm.

But while my days were rather mundane, my evenings were stimulating. I assembled reams of data on growth metrics, cost structures, credit profiles, valuations, and oil and gas reserve quality for this entire group of companies and then went to work on sorting out who would win and who would lose in McKinsey's future scenario. It could be tedious, but it was fun and exciting at the same time. I was working on an independent project, and I could take the conclusions anywhere the data led me.

By August, my ten weeks at McKinsey were winding up, but my data analysis project for Rainwater was taking shape. I finally called him and said, "Richard, I am getting ready to present this. What do you want to do with it?" He invited me to come to the office to show him.

In advance of the meeting, I took my disks to print out at the local AlphaGraphics store and made three copies of my presentation. I put them in pretty binders with a pretty title page and made my way over to Rainwater's office in Fort Worth. I waited proudly in the conference room, ready to walk someone through the data.

After Richard came in, he summoned the entire group of deal guys working in the office that day. I would later learn that this was part of the fun of officing there. Everyone was able to meet people who came through and sit in whenever they were available. So, in walks a group of folks I had never met, including Peter Joost, Tad Kelly, Richard Squires, John Goff, and Rick Scott—yes, the Rick Scott who would go on to run Columbia/HCA and serve as governor of, and senator from, Florida. There may have been others in the room, but I was so overwhelmed that I don't recall. I just remember the room filling up, and I only had three copies of the notebook!

STEVE: *Uh-oh.*

KEN: Not to worry, I stretched them open, and we all leaned in, sharing books like schoolkids sharing some class project. It was clumsy, but we got through it. The discussion was lively. There was some good feedback and several good questions. Richard asked me to make some additional calculations. *Great! This meant I would get to come back.* We set a time for me to return with the requested information. He seemed content, but noncommittal about what he was going to do with this analysis.

It took me a couple of days to redo the study. My return to the Rainwater office was scheduled shortly after Labor Day, just before I needed to be back at Stanford. It worked out perfectly. Determined not to get caught with too few copies this time, I made twenty notebooks of the study!

STEVE: *This would be a good time to give a little background on Richard Rainwater. From what I've read, he was born in 1944 in Fort Worth. His father was a wholesale grocer. After a relatively normal childhood, he went to the University of Texas and then on to Stanford, where he graduated with an MBA in 1968. He worked for Goldman Sachs briefly after business school, but that changed when his lifelong friend Sid Bass summoned him back home in 1970 to help manage money that a relative had just left Sid and his brothers.*

As the story goes, from 1970 until he left to strike out on his own in 1986, Richard helped the Basses grow their net worth by more than $5 billion. Although he had some early fits and starts, the track record was pretty amazing. Fortune *magazine described his investment style as "analytically rigorous but opportunistic and Texas-sized in its audacity." Is that accurate?*

KEN: That's a good description. Richard had an electric personality and an amazing intellect. He was bold in his thinking, but cheap with his wallet. As an investor, that is a decent combination. It translated into the goal of trying to gain control of reasonably valued assets with as little money as possible. Borrowing from lenders is one source of capital. But that was too obvious. This approach required creativity more akin to an inventor. He was a master at finding unique ways to approach or structure a deal that made an investment idea compelling. It was a combination of intellect and sheer charisma. Being around the man was simply magical.

The Rainwater touch made partnering with him and the Basses attractive to many investors. Today, we would call these efforts private equity funds, but back then, they were just called partnerships. He really cultivated relationships that led to investing, not the other way around. It was impressive to see. At the time, remember, there was no private equity industry. So forming partnerships with institutional investors was one of the few ways to transact in bigger deals. In 1984, Richard and the Basses created one such partnership that ended up having particular relevance to me. The institutional partner was Equitable Life.

Big insurance companies like Equitable were always looking for higher-yielding investments for their portfolios to cover future claims. And so the $600 million Bass Investment Limited Partnership (BILP) was born. The Equitable put up $540 million as the sole limited partner, and a consortium assembled by Richard put up $60 million as the general partner of the partnership. Many notable investors from the heyday of the 1980s were included in that general partner category. But, as I have been told, Richard was the glue.

STEVE: *What happened to the fund when Richard left the Basses in 1986?*

KEN: Equitable insisted he retain some oversight. Even though he didn't manage it day-to-day—that was done out of the BILP headquarters in Connecticut—the new investments still needed his approval. When he left the Basses, they dropped the "Bass" in the partnership's name, so it just became known as Investment Limited Partnership, or ILP. By the summer of 1988, when I was moonlighting for Richard, that fund had participated in many leveraged buyout deals and had done phenomenally well. Equitable was very happy with the returns.

STEVE: *So how did this affect you, wandering into his world in 1988?*

KEN: Well, unbeknownst to me, during the summer that I was doing my analysis on oil and gas investment opportunities, Richard called Dick Jenrette, the chief investment officer at Equitable. Apparently, he reminded Dick that their $540 million investment had done well under his watch and that it was time to go again with a new investment thesis—natural gas. He stoked them up on McKinsey's conclusions to get them excited.

Then there was a follow-up call with his Equitable team, and Richard invited them to come to Fort Worth on the same day that he had scheduled me to come present my final report. I had no idea.

When I showed up in Richard's office with my big box of binders, the receptionist

Lois sent me directly to the big conference room in the back. It was empty when I walked in. I set myself up at the far end of this oversized conference table to be out of the way. I figured that as the junior schmo with all my notebooks, I belonged at the far end, leaving the center and head of the table open for the leaders of the meeting. I pulled my twenty books out of the box and set up two columns of notebooks, evenly divided. I took a seat behind them. Suddenly, Richard and these "suits" wandered in. I was floored. This was Equitable's senior investment team. Peter Joost was there, too, as was David Albin—a close friend of his who had traveled from Connecticut to be there.

STEVE: *Spoiler alert: David soon became your business partner for almost thirty years, so let's provide a little of his professional background.*

KEN: After getting his undergraduate degree from Stanford in 1981, David had gone to work at Goldman Sachs, where he was placed in the investment bank's energy group. When his two years were up, he had returned to Stanford for business school, graduating in 1985. Then, he'd gone to work in Connecticut for the BILP partnership. He had stayed on at the partnership after Richard left the Basses in 1986. When Peter asked him if he wanted to work on Richard's new energy fund idea, David had said, "Sure."

STEVE: *Okay, we're in the conference room now. Based on the original McKinsey multiclient analysis and the preliminary report that you had given him at your first meeting, it sounds like Richard had already made up his mind. What was this meeting about?*

KEN: That is how Richard worked. He was the proverbial "train that was leaving the station" and you had to decide if you wanted to be on or not. Richard had made up his mind that it was the right time to put some money together to buy natural gas assets low and then later to sell high. Equitable had come down to Texas to do its due diligence on the investment team.

Imagine this scene: Richard was standing at one end of the long black table in the stark conference room, surrounded by the same walls covered with floor-to-ceiling white grease-marker boards. I was on the other end behind this huge double tower of notebooks. Copies of the McKinsey study were in the center of the table. I was a twenty-five-year-old kid who looked like I was twelve. Richard took to the marker-board-covered wall and drew a line going down. "This is supply," he said. Then he drew another line going up. "This is demand." It was like an Econ 101 chart for dummies.

Richard continued: "The price is going to go up. The way to make money is to buy low and sell high. I've been so successful with my life because I've made moves like this at the right time. Where there is chaos, there is opportunity. There's chaos in the market, the deregulation has created chaos, and we've got a good team." He got more excited. "Let's do this. We'll do the same deal as before. (He was referring to the BILP partnership terms.) We'll put up 2.5 percent of the money; you put up 97.5 percent. We'll give you an 11 percent return, and after that, we'll take 20 percent. So you'll do really well, and if it doesn't work, we'll give you your money back." He extended his arm in a full arc toward my end of the table. "And we've done all this work, so we're ready to go."

Ten heads turned and looked at me. There I was peering out from between two columns of notebooks. I can't imagine how I looked. Richard said, "We can go through this whole study if you want."

I was petrified but ready to spring into action. Unbeknownst to me, however, Equitable had sent down the senior-most guys from New York, not the grunts, to go through the plan. They were not about to wade through three-inch binders full of analysis. My books could have been the Dallas phone book. Nobody opened them or looked at them. I don't remember if they even took them! Everyone just talked, and then it was over.

STEVE: *And that was it?*

KEN: Yep. I had no idea what was going to happen. I went back to the parking lot, changed from my suit into shorts, got into my car, and drove straight to California. I started my second year and soon began thinking about a job search, wondering what the future would hold for me.

STEVE: *Did you have any idea that there were further conversations taking place?*

KEN: Not at all. Remember, I was just a kid, and I didn't have a clue how this all worked. I didn't even really comprehend what was going on during that meeting. Putting an investment partnership together was foreign to me at the time, and they were talking a language I didn't understand.

Then, a bit of luck came my way. In October, Rainwater came back to the Stanford campus for his twentieth reunion celebration. This included a panel discussion with a couple of his classmates at the Memorial Auditorium. I'd seen some notices around campus that had the reunion schedules. Unashamed, I crashed the event. Why not? It was an hour of my life, and it was right there in the auditorium adjacent to the business school.

After a pretty interesting panel discussion, I lingered. Not sure what to expect, I went up to the stage to approach Richard. "Hi, Richard," I said, standing among the gaggle of people who had gathered around him. A couple of my classmates were in that cluster, having similar hopes of catching a word with the enigmatic investment celebrity who rarely left Fort Worth.

"Hey, Ken," he said, singling me out of the group of onlookers waiting to have a few words with him.

I perked up proudly as if being announced as an Oscar winner while my class-mates had that "Who the hell is he?" look on their faces. "Hi, Richard. What's up with that deal that I sat in on with those people from New York?" I asked, as if I was one of his full partners just asking to get caught up. Of course, at this point I had no idea what I was doing.

"Things are working great," he replied.

"Need any help?"

"You ought to call Peter," he said.

"Will do," I said as I retreated into the gaggle.

Bingo! Maybe Richard was just trying to get rid of me so he could talk with the others surrounding him, but this was all I needed!

I considered that a virtual first-round job interview. Full of confidence—whether justified or not—I immediately called Peter Joost. "I was just visiting with Richard when he was on campus, and he recommended I give you a call," I began the conversation.

Okay, so I exaggerated our fifteen-second exchange a bit!

After Peter confirmed things were moving forward with the partnership, I said, "I'd love to come work on it, if that is a possibility."

"Hmmm," he said. "We could work on that. Talk to David Albin." Again, he was probably passing me off to get rid of me, but I saw that as a virtual second-round interview.

I immediately called David, unashamed to describe the "momentum" of my inter-view process. "I was just visiting with Richard and Peter, and they said we should talk about my coming on full time if the partnership happens. You do need somebody, don't you?" I asked presumptuously.

When he said they did, I said, "Well, I'd love to do it." David seemed to concur and said that I should take a look at the partnership document.

I had shaken his hand a couple of months earlier and spent all of thirty seconds with the guy. In retrospect, I suspect that he thought I had already been vetted by Rich-ard and Peter. I think Peter thought David would do the vetting. I got the sense that I was falling through the cracks, but I knew I would do fine. Who was I to tell them that they needed to improve their interview processes?

You're going to ask me about the lesson. Again, I raised my hand. Richard Rainwa-ter was an emerging big damn deal in the deal business. I'd seen the work in his office; it seemed very exciting. What did I have to lose?

The next thing I knew, my name was added to the partnership agreement's distribution list. Almost daily, I started getting FedEx envelopes with the draft documents the lawyers were working. The fancy New York law firm circulated every draft to the entire distribution list, asking everyone to read it and offer comments. It was a limited partnership agreement. I didn't even know what I was reading, but at least I could track the deal a little.

In the original drafts, the partnership was tentatively called "[Gas Partners], herein after referred to as GAS." In drafting, placeholder words that will be altered later are generally put in brackets, so drafters know to come back to them before finalizing. I guess someone thought the reference to flatulating was kind of crass for a formal draft, so somewhere along the line it became "[Natural Gas Partners]" for subsequent drafts.

On November 16, 1988, the deal became official. In the final version, probably some legal associate took the brackets off, and—*poof*—our partnership had a name: Natural Gas Partners, or NGP, as it would be called. I came to appreciate later on that not a lot of thought went into naming things in the Rainwater world. Richard thought it was a waste of money to hire naming experts. The original investment partnership was called Bass Investment Limited Partnership. And the general partner of our partnership was named G. F. W. Energy, LP. Those letters stood for Greenwich Fort Worth—the names of the cities where the partnership's offices would be located.

I was anxious to get some specificity about my future. As soon as I saw the agreement was getting signed, I called David and said I'd like to confirm that I would be working on this with him. I knew he was based in Greenwich, Connecticut, and I had no desire to move there. I suggested that I work out of Rainwater's office in Fort Worth. "How can you have an energy fund and not have an office in Texas?" I asked, leading the witness.

"That could be fine with me, but you need to call Peter," David said.

STEVE: *And what did Peter say?*

KEN: I may have been a tad bit guilty of telling Peter that David said he was okay with it so long as I cleared it with Peter. Again, I think I wedged myself right between the cracks. But they had both seen my work during the summer, so I didn't feel that I was some unknown quantity. Peter said the arrangement sounded good, but that he wanted to talk to me one more time. Knowing I would be heading home for Christmas break a few weeks later, I arranged to meet him in the Fort Worth office. Once there, I told him I'd like to make NGP my full-time gig.

STEVE: *Ask and ye shall receive. Did he give you an answer on the spot?*

KEN: I don't recall exactly the words, but it sure did seem clear to me that he didn't have a problem with it. True to form, he bounced me back into David's lap, who seemed content with my just starting to work on it. The deal closed on November 16 and Equitable wired in $97.5 million to a new set of accounts. We had to get started on putting that money to work. With only a couple of people on board, they needed bodies. I was happy to start as soon as I got the green light.

Please note that I did not wait for an official offer letter. I didn't ask for some employment contract. I didn't inquire about the firm's health benefits or retirement plans.

Ready. Shoot. Aim.

That was that. Early in 1989, I went on the payroll of NGP even though I was still a student. David Albin was on board as the leader of the team based in Greenwich. Working there, too, was a former managing director at First Boston (now Credit Suisse) named R. Gamble Baldwin. Late in the summer, around the same time that the first Equitable meeting was coming together, Richard had called Gamble after reading an *Institutional Investor* magazine article that rated him the number-one analyst covering the natural gas industry. "How would you like to retire from the banking game, Gamble?" Richard had asked on a cold call to him. "I have these guys, and we may get this money, and I think they'll need an adult around them." I think Richard just liked the shock value in cold calling folks.

Gamble, who was in his mid-sixties in 1988, had never invested a dime in his life. But he had oil and gas industry street cred. After he signed on, also in early 1989, he enlisted John Foster, a young credit analyst who was working in the fixed income research department at First Boston to join them in the Greenwich office. And so, with me soon to be in Fort Worth, we were four. Plus, my Apple Macintosh computer.

This was really special. The four of us were partners from day one. David ran the Greenwich office with John and Gamble, who worked with us until he passed away in 2003. I "led" the Texas operation. As the only firm employee in Texas, I assumed the role with 100 percent support from the "team" there—me.

Richard Rainwater long preached: *Partner with great people. If you partner with great people, the documents don't matter. If you pick the wrong people, no document will protect you.* He was right. My partnership with David was the most special aspect of my professional life. We were partners running the firm for twenty-eight years, until we turned it over to the next generation in early 2016. We had plenty of knock-down, drag-out debates on matters, but in the end, there was never a nonunanimous vote. We never had a single sheet of paper between us outlining how we would share the money or govern the decision making of the firm. It was a true partnership based on trust and respect.

Richard was the catalyst who brought David, me, Gamble, and John together without any real interview process. Yet the four of us were honest, hard-working, optimistic people who stuck together. We grew our business, our families, and our life experiences together.

STEVE: *Do you remember your first salary?*

KEN: I think it was $75,000. Plus, I could put money into the fund. Unfortunately, I didn't have any at the time. In fact, I had a negative worth thanks to student debt. But Richard had Gamble cosign a credit line so I could borrow $75,000 to invest in the fund. I was my own leveraged buyout. Ultimately that became worth a couple of million dollars. It was my first taste of what ownership felt like.

It was also my first observation of the way in which Rainwater worked. He had an idea. He talked to experts. He waved his arms and cold-called people about the idea. Some of us bit and asked forward-leaning questions and he was willing to let it flow. Once it had some momentum, he rounded up partners and figured out a way to put in less money and to leverage the capital of others. The basic terms of the deal required his group to contribute only $2.5 million of the starting $100 million total.

Then, Richard apportioned out the $2.5 million general partner stake. True to form, the opportunity to invest got walked around the office, and everyone spoke for an amount. Richard was left with only $800,000 to invest. That was very small relative to his net worth at the time, but he acquiesced so that all of the deal team could take their fill. In my case, $75,000 was about all I could handle. Others in the office that day got a chance to invest as well. A fellow named George W. Bush, who was in the office that day with his Texas Rangers baseball hat on, got the chance to invest $50,000 as well. Others participating included Peter Joost, Tad Kelly, John Goff, Mort Meyerson, and then hospital investor and now Senator Rick Scott, to name a few.

It was the ultimate club deal.

STEVE: *Quite the understatement. All this was happening two months into your second year of business school. You were juggling this "pushy" job search along with classes and a social life all at once. How did that go?*

KEN: NGP wasn't the only partnership that was forming at the time. A Halloween party hosted by my classmates Ken Coleman and Steve O'Neill on October 31, 1988, changed my life as well. At the party, there was this cute girl who caught my eye. I worked up the nerve to ask her to dance. We danced and exchanged some niceties. I had never seen her around campus. Knowing that someone this cute would not have escaped my eye, I thought she must have been one of the new first-year MBA students crashing the second years' party. Turned out she was three years older than I and worked for a high-tech company, Octel Communications, near San Jose. One of my classmates, Paul Carberry, had worked in her group at that company for his summer job, and he had invited her and one of her female coworkers to the party.

I danced with her and thought she was great, so I asked Paul for her phone number. He wouldn't give it to me. As I protested, he said that he was protecting me because he thought she was way out of my league. In a brotherly tone, Paul told me, "She gets a lot of attention. Why on earth would she date a younger business student who doesn't even have a job at this point? Don't get your hopes up."

I knew that the longer the time between my call and that Halloween party, the greater the chance that she would forget who I was. Disregarding Paul's caution, I called 411 information in Milpitas, California, and got the number for Octel Communications. Heck, it worked for the Rainwater intro; why not for this cute gal?

I called several times over a two- or three-day span, trying at different times of the day, hoping to increase the odds of catching her at her desk. Each time, the receptionist transferred me to her line, but the voicemail recording answered. Knowing that we had just had a few dances together, I was too scared to leave a message, figuring that she would need some reminding who I was.

After several calls, I got quite familiar with her recorded message, which said she wasn't there but to press "0" in case of emergency. On about my fifth try, I relented. *What the hell. I need a date, badly. This is a borderline emergency.* I could justify pressing 0! So I did.

When the operator came on, I asked for Julie Kosnik. The operator was quite friendly and asked for my name. At the time, I did not know that this was the general operator for the whole company. Having been at a fancy Wall Street firm where busy signals rolled to a secretary seated outside the office, I had a vision that this call had rolled to her secretary, and her secretary simply peeked into her office to let her know that "a Ken Hersh is on the phone." But this was a technology start-up. Nobody had a secretary. The operator paged Julie over the loudspeaker, only telling her that she had a call holding.

When she picked up, I said, "Hi, this is Ken." Before I could elaborate that I was the guy at the Halloween party dressed as a Texas cowboy—okay, I'm not that creative—she jumped in: "Hi, how can I help you?"

She sounded so perky and familiar that I thought she remembered me from the week or so before. For a split second, I was quite proud of myself for making such a lasting impression on the dance floor.

"You can go out with me on Saturday night," I replied quickly and confidently, like some cocky high school senior asking a ninth-grade girl out.

STEVE: *Did that work?*

KEN: Nope. She had no clue who I was. She thought I was a pushy salesperson. She turned me down. Apparently, her dance card filled up quite a bit in advance. But in turning me down, she did say, "Maybe another time." I had no idea if this was her polite way of saying "forget it," or she really wanted me to call her another time. I chose to interpret it as the latter. So, a day later, I made up some excuse to call her and ask her out for the week after that. By then, I had jogged her memory that we had danced at the party. Ultimately, she said yes.

STEVE: *Man, you were quite the deal closer, even back then.*

KEN: In recounting this ninety-day period of my life, it seems that I was really poor at picking up on signals to get lost. Whether from Richard or Julie, I viewed every opening as a gaping opportunity. The uncertainty kind of excited me. Once on the phone or in the room, I guess I was just not afraid of what would happen. I had confidence that I would figure it out. In reality, these situations all had one thing in common: I had much to gain and little to lose. The worst thing that could happen was that they would say no.

After one date with Julie in early November 1988, I knew I would marry her. We quickly became steady companions. My hours at school were manageable, and she had fairly regular working hours. We had great chemistry, even though we were quite different people. There was only one problem: She had been through a failed engagement before and wasn't about to uproot her life in California without some certainty.

STEVE: *Uproot?*

KEN: Recall that prior to Thanksgiving, I had made my plan to go see Peter Joost in Fort Worth over the Christmas break, when I hoped to firm up a role at Natural Gas Partners. This coincided with the first three weeks of my relationship with Julie. We were in that honeymoon phase of dating, learning about each other. I was hooked on this gorgeous California career woman who was doing so well at her company, but I was not hooked on starting my career in gorgeous California.

I was in a predicament. On one of our marathon dates, the Christmas appointment with Peter came up. I knew I couldn't keep this topic off the table. *How can I broach the idea of moving to Texas with a woman I have been dating for all of three weeks? I'm not ready to propose. But it sure would be nice to know if she would move to Texas should things keep progressing.*

I had to figure this out before I left for the Christmas holiday. The way things were working with the Rainwater group, my gut told me that I would have to be ready to accept on the spot.

I was petrified. Standing in my rental house one evening before we went out, I summoned up the nerve. I crafted the most awkwardly circumspect sentence in my history: "Julie?" I stammered. "Do you think that maybe if things that sort of seem to be moving in the right direction between us continue possibly toward some future moment where it might look like this could maybe be something that one or both of us would think about doing forever, that, then, if I had an opportunity to work in Fort Worth, that moving there may be something that you might one day think about doing with me, maybe?"

She paused and looked up. I could hear her mind interpreting what I said as if English were my second language. I don't think she could have diagrammed that sentence if she tried. "Move to Fort Worth? Huh? Is that what you asked? Isn't it really flat there?"

"Dallas or Fort Worth," I responded, throwing in another city as if that would increase the odds of a favorable reply. "There are trees," I said, trying to resurrect the option as well as I could, desperately needing a Chamber of Commerce brochure.

There was a lengthy, awkward pause. "Well, yes, if you make it worth my while," she replied with a glimmer in her eye.

Bingo! I had my deal terms. Turns out, from September to December 1988, I was quite the twenty-five-year-old deal guy. Those ninety days would change my life forever. I proposed to her a week after graduation in June 1989. We married a year later.

STEVE: *You had an entrepreneurial opportunity on the horizon. You had the business partner of your dreams in David lined up. You had the girl of your dreams in Julie. The future was looking pretty bright.*

KEN: So it seemed. There was just one problem. Everything that was in the McKinsey study turned out to be dead wrong. The predicted imminent rise in natural gas prices never happened. In fact, prices went down steadily for seven straight years.

STEVE: *Ouch.*

CHAPTER 4

THROWING UP IN
THE SHOWER

STEVE: *As I understand it, the first couple of years of NGP were instructive but not very successful, given that the entire premise of your business plan was wrong.*

KEN: Right. It's important to talk about this period because it's almost a textbook study of how to reinvent yourself after your original model breaks. Or, in other words, what to do when it appears that the entire premise on which you based something is just dead wrong. I think psychiatrists refer to this as fight or flight—something to do with the amygdala in the brain, I think.

STEVE: *Let's start with that original model. You went on the payroll early in 1989 while you were still at Stanford, and the partnership had $100 million of equity capital to invest. Your partners had lined up a $100 million bank line to go with it. So, in all, you had $200 million to invest in the oil and gas business over time. What were those early days like?*

KEN: In hindsight, we were just making this up as we went along. We were guided by the goal of trying to make investments that would do well when natural gas prices rose as predicted. But that turned out to be more complicated than it sounded. As I mentioned, I was working from Palo Alto while David Albin and our two other partners, Gamble Baldwin and John Foster, were working full time in Greenwich—hardly the oil and gas capitals of the country. In those days, we were a relative unknown in the investment business. Gamble and John had decent Rolodexes of contacts in the industry from their work at First Boston. David had been a member of the investment team managing a generalist fund sponsored by Rainwater and the Bass brothers, so he had some investment experience, although it wasn't specifically in the energy industry.

Back in the late 1980s, other than the Bass-Equitable partnership, there were only a handful of groups in the entire country that had been formed to invest the way we think of it today. Sure, insurance companies, endowments, and pension funds existed, and all needed their capital managed, but it really wasn't until the emergence of Michael Milken's junk bond market and the related buyout business it spawned that deal shops emerged. There was no nomenclature at the time describing us as part of the private equity industry. Heck, we were so early, we didn't think what we were doing was part of an industry at all.

Since the three in Connecticut had worked at big Wall Street firms, they were making the rounds looking for investments. They talked to investment bankers in the oil and gas communities, accounting firms, and law firms and attended whatever industry conferences they could find. Initially, people looked at us sideways, wondering if we were smoking something funny. The oil and gas business was not terribly healthy in those days—remember, we were counting on it to rebound from historic lows—so when word got out that we had money to invest, people started calling us. Meetings were relatively easy to get since there was virtually no competition at the time. We learned relatively quickly that investing money in oil and gas was the easy part. It was getting it back with a positive return that was the problem. But we had this money burning a hole in our pockets, so we had to find places to put it to work.

STEVE: *What was your arrangement with Equitable?*

KEN: We got paid a 2 percent management fee, which paid our salaries and overhead. On the $100 million, that was $2 million a year. We had offices and several people to pay. We were comfortable, but not getting rich on our salaries. We didn't make any money above the management fee until we paid Equitable an 11 percent hurdle rate of return. If we cleared an 11 percent return, we started sharing 20 percent of the profit. In reality, we had to earn back the 2 percent management fee *and* the 11 percent return, so actually our hurdle to clear was more like 13 percent. That return was calculated annually, so we had to earn that *every* year. That wasn't easy.

It's important to note that the fund management business works quite differently today. Now, when we raise a fund, investors pledge capital to invest, but the money doesn't go in until the management team calls for it. The hurdle-rate meter doesn't start clicking until the capital is called. However, back in 1988, Equitable wired us all the money, and we had that 11 percent annual hurdle-rate meter clicking every day. Plus, we had to pay back our annual 2 percent management fees before earning any incentive compensation. By standing still, we were actually going backward in terms of getting closer to earning our percentage of the profits.

It's not easy to earn 13 percent compounded. In reality, we had to go make investments that would earn two or three times our money over five to seven years to cover that hurdle rate and make our profit share worthwhile.

We would meet with Equitable's representatives quarterly and show them our results and progress. We even talked about deals we had in the hopper. Our goal was to keep them apprised so they knew we were working toward that hurdle rate. Today, that kind of transparency is unheard of. But we only had one investor in the mix, so it seemed like the right thing to do. Sometimes, it felt more like we were working for them.

These quarterly meetings were a humble reminder that we were doing the job of managing someone else's money. This taught me a very simple lesson: Respect the investors because it is really *their* money. While people in the industry looked at us like we had a couple of hundred million dollars to invest, we were just custodians for it.

STEVE: *While David and the guys on the East Coast were making and taking the calls, what were you doing back in Palo Alto?*

KEN: Pretty rudimentary stuff. I still had a couple of classes to take at school during my final term before graduating. I began by helping out with research, number crunching, some valuation work, and lots of reading. It was similar to the deal analytics I had learned at Morgan Stanley. I was helping with the evaluations for the investment ideas that David and the others were coming up with. In early 1989, we were just trying to get smart on the industry and get our name out there. I didn't start diving in on new deals myself until I got to Texas after graduation. David was really the guy in charge because he had that experience working with Rainwater in the Bass organization. I followed along as well as I could and helped weigh in on the discussions. David made a huge effort to include me on things from three time zones away.

STEVE: *Rainwater had seen opportunities in oil and gas, and those were confirmed by the McKinsey report and your own research. But what was the state of the industry in 1988/1989? Were there other players like NGP who saw the opportunities and with whom you were competing?*

KEN: Historically, there were always folks who wanted to invest in oil and gas. I think it was the romance of the stories of Texas wildcatters getting rich. But in the early

1980s, it was apparent that the 1970s' predictions of a $100 per barrel oil price was not happening, so the exploration business in the United States was in free fall.

Only the tax code kept it propped up. You see, the tax code allowed people to write off 100 percent of drilling costs on their taxes, so even if an oil or gas well produced only enough to get someone their money back, on an after-tax basis, that was still a decent return. If a well really hit, it was a bigger return, and if the well was totally dry, Uncle Sam would pay 50 percent of the costs by giving investors a full write-off on their taxes. This made doctors and lawyers perfect targets for money raisers in the mid-1980s.

Tax code revisions in 1986 changed all that, reducing the tax deductibility of oil and gas drilling. At the same time, Saudi Arabia said that they were not going to support prices. Oil prices dropped from $20 per barrel to below $10 per barrel. Investors with money committed were in a world of hurt, and the commercial banks lending to oil and gas companies quickly retrenched. Bankruptcies and workouts were the norm.

So, when we showed up in 1988, there weren't many others around with capital to invest. There was one small group of investors working inside an investment bank named Dillon, Read who were interested in making equity investments in the industry. There were also some former commercial bankers who were assembling a practice in Texas to advise insurance companies on making higher-yielding loans to energy companies, since the banks had so dramatically reduced their lending.

STEVE: *Were there particular types of investments that you were looking for or that were looking for your money?*

KEN: As I said, we were kind of making it up as we went along. We had all this cash, and we needed to earn something on it since we had this 11 percent meter ticking every day. So we ran a public equities and fixed income portfolio to try to make some money while we looked for interesting private deals.

We structured early deals as a loan with an equity participation kicker so that we could earn our 11 percent and then have a share in the company's upside. Our mantra was this: Let's try to structure it right so that we can protect our downside and structure a deal so that we can benefit when prices go up.

At the same time, we were trying to put money to work in established companies trying to grow. It was a tough sell. If a company was credit-worthy, they could find cheaper capital. If they wanted our money, there must've been a reason. There was a real adverse selection problem here.

So we often settled on a structure that invested as subordinated debt in the capital structure and received some equity kickers for doing so. In the capital structure, we would be beneath the bank loan and still rank senior to the equity. For example, if a company had a $50 million deal they needed to finance, they could go to a bank and get, say, $30 million, secured by the assets, but then would need an additional $20 million to close the deal. They could sell equity, which would have been highly dilutive, or they could borrow the $20 million from us, and we would put it in a second lien or unsecured position with an 11 percent interest rate, with some agreement to share in the profits once our note was repaid.

For the right deal, this structure was ideal. It would be much cheaper for the company's owners than issuing dilutive equity, especially when the valuations of the sector were so depressed. From our perspective, our risk was reduced because we ranked senior to the equity holders in the downside, liquidation case. So we took this structure around to people who would listen and tried to sell them on how this was in their best interests if they needed growth capital.

STEVE: *You said that once you got to Texas you didn't know very many people in the industry. How did you get going?*

KEN: Well, that was pretty tricky. I quickly discovered that all my fancy schooling didn't do me much good in the oil patch. I wasn't part of the geology or petroleum engineering crowd that had graduated from Texas, Texas A&M, Texas Tech, Oklahoma, or Oklahoma State. Nor had I spent a summer as a roughneck on a drilling rig.

At first, I felt like I was going to a party where I didn't know a soul and everyone else seemed to know everyone. I felt like that Princeton freshman wandering up to campus in a driving rainstorm lugging my suitcase.

Undeterred, I started cold calling oil and gas companies. I picked up those same lists that I'd given my Stanford researcher just a year before. I would pick some dates out on the calendar and plan trips to Houston, Midland, Tulsa, Denver, and Calgary and smile and dial. The good news is that the oil and gas industry was pretty concentrated in about a half dozen cities. It was a club. All I had to do was break in.

Luckily, we had a unique entry ticket—money to invest. I quickly learned that that was virtually nonexistent. We became popular quickly. I thought it was going to be hard. In fact, the industry was so depressed and the capital so scarce that getting an audience wasn't hard at all. In that time frame, I might as well have been saying, "I'm handing out free lottery tickets. Want me to deliver one?" I targeted either the chief financial officer or someone on the finance team of the independent oil and gas companies when I called. Since I didn't have a technical background and, in the end, we were looking to invest money, I figured that the finance teams would be the most receptive. Sometimes, if they were small companies, I'd call on the CEO and drop Rainwater's name or Gamble Baldwin's name and try to get a meeting.

My pitch was, "I'm calling from Natural Gas Partners, and we are an investment partnership with capital available for oil and gas projects." But sometimes it sounded more like: "I'm Ken Hersh calling from Natural Gas Partners in Richard Rainwater's office, please don't hang up!"

Why *wouldn't* they want to see me? There were very few investors clamoring to put money into an industry that needed to outspend its annual cash flow every year to offset the natural decline rate in its production. In addition, commodity prices were terrible, operating costs seemed to escalate every year, and the banks and traditional capital sources were not that keen on increasing exposure to the sector. If you were an oil or gas company, particularly a smaller one, the only way to finance your growth was to find third-party capital—either debt or equity. Then I came along. Nine out of ten times, one way or another, I would persist until they'd say, "Sure."

My big problem was that when I showed up in 1989, I still looked twelve. These executives were often at least fifteen or twenty years older than I was. I knew that the only way I would be credible was to be prepared. I would read their annual report cover to cover. I would know who their shareholders were and everything about their major transactions and initiatives. If they were publicly traded, I read their shareholder letters. I prepped a valuation summary of their major assets. I knew how their stock traded against their peers. I read the *Oil and Gas Journal* voraciously. Unlike Rainwater's, my desk was a mess—piled high with stacks of research material ahead of these trips.

I had done my homework, so presenting myself as someone with company knowledge was fairly straightforward. From a style standpoint, I approached these meetings as if I were a student asking a professor about his or her area of expertise. I would go in loaded with questions. "When you sold your assets in that area last year and doubled down in that other region, what was your reasoning?" I would ask, making sure they knew that I had prepped for the meeting, but still wanting to get a meaningful answer. Or I'd inquire, "I read about your strategic plan and was hoping to learn *why?*" I quickly learned that people liked to teach a young kid how the industry worked. And they all appreciated that I had come to see them prepared with real questions.

I tried to keep them talking, usually letting them brag about their latest company opportunity, until the conversation came around to paying for their capital programs or expansion ideas. When I got the opening, I would gently let them know that we had money to invest and might be a capital partner if they needed it.

I was kind of jealous that they had a company with projects to do, so asking if they needed some capital was sincere. We each had what the other needed. I never thought, since we had a dedicated fund, that somehow we were better than they were. Today, a lot of people who have capital to invest feel that they're at the top of the food chain, deciding who does or doesn't get money. That attitude of arrogance really bothers me.

I treated these meetings as low-pressure affairs. My goal was to get networked into the industry and learn as much as possible along the way. I tried to make a lot of small talk, and I discovered that if you're not threatening and you ask people about themselves, they'll tell you things. I was an incredible sponge in those early years. I'd see these folks at industry conferences, follow up with a personal meeting, and be friendly. I always made sure to write personal thank-you notes for their time.

I also tried to offer something in return, which was important. After many meetings, I learned trends and even began to make some observations as to which strategies were compelling, and which were not. I offered up my views on what others were doing in the industry and how markets were reacting to various strategies. I tried to channel my best Richard Rainwater, having watched him in the office almost daily. He rarely did the deals that visitors to Fort Worth had come seeking, but he always offered them something in return—an alternative idea, a referral to someone else who they might try to solicit, or simply a quick analysis of their proposal. People left the office feeling grateful for his time, even though he usually rejected their idea. I tried to add value in every meeting just the same.

In time, I became familiar enough to be invited to meet folks at conferences or attend their next quail or dove hunt. Next thing I knew, I'd get a phone call from someone who'd say, "I remember you came to see me. I wanted to let you know that I heard about a company needing capital for a new deal. You should go see them." The deal flow started percolating.

STEVE: *Do you still conduct business that way?*

KEN: Absolutely. I like people, and I am genuinely interested in seeing what makes them tick. It is important to establish a personal rapport, regardless of the context. That is best done in live, face-to-face contact. It is the one thing I miss most in an email/texting world. I also see the courtesies in life losing significance these days. If someone is willing to share their precious time with you, then you should acknowledge that with a nice thank-you note. Simple, personal, and easy. I don't know why this is a lost art, but it is. To this day, I keep a stack of my personal note cards on the top of my desk, and I am quick to pen a personal note to thank a visitor or to congratulate someone on a job well done.

STEVE: *David was a Stanford undergrad and then Stanford business school. Gamble had gone to Princeton undergrad. You were a hybrid—Princeton undergrad, Stanford business school. John Foster had gone to Williams and NYU. Was there an old-boy or elite-type network that you guys were dealing in?*

KEN: You might think so, but nothing could have been further from the truth. When I started, David told me, "Ken, one of your biggest challenges will be realizing that the guys that run our portfolio companies are people you might never have thought of hiring." One of our best CEOs early on had graduated with an engineering degree from Oklahoma State, another CEO went to Ole Miss. That was a critical point on my personal learning curve. Growing up, what were my benchmarks? Twelve years at St. Mark's. Early admission to Princeton. Stanford business. Selectivity equals good, right? Not so in the oil patch. Nobody cared about my resume.

When I started making calls, I quickly saw how bright the engineers were. Just because they didn't go to fancy schools didn't mean they weren't smart or successful. As adults, they had the same drive as I had. Once I let go of my resume stereotyping, I began to connect with them. That was a key turning point in my maturation as an investor, and something that I see holding many people back today.

The independent oil and gas companies in the United States were, and still are, reflective of the Texas/Oklahoma culture—a little bit of a "screw you" attitude toward the Northeast. There are very few people with Ivy League pedigrees in the oil patch. I would talk about my Dallas upbringing more than about college. When people did ask where I went to school, I'd say, "I graduated from high school in Dallas and then went to college in New Jersey." That usually sufficed because they didn't really care once they realized I wasn't in their particular alumni association. I learned to "Hook 'em Horns," "Gig 'em Aggies," and put my "Guns Up." As a Texan, though, I drew the line and would never sing "Boomer Sooner."

STEVE: *Do you remember your first deal?*

KEN: Absolutely. I inherited it from David. He had started working on it, but I was happy to take over the lead on the evaluation and negotiation. It was in 1990. The company was called HS Resources, based out of San Francisco of all places. The "H" was from the last name of one of the founders, Mike Highum, and the "S" was from the last name of the other founder, Nick Sutton.

My kind of deal. No flashy name, and they were unafraid to run an oil and gas company from downtown San Francisco! They were not your typical oil and gas guys. They were lawyers who started in the business assembling drilling deals in the late 1970s, when the tax code provided favorable tax credits. They were adept at finding relatively low-risk drilling prospects. Between the tax credits and the resulting oil and gas production, their investments were able to generate great rates of return for their investors. Nick and Mike were good, both at raising money and finding oil and gas. Their tax-advantaged drilling fund capital had dried up with the tax code changes of

1986. But, more important, they were creative, hardworking people determined to do right by their partners and colleagues. Those personal characteristics were important to NGP when we decided to dive into a very complicated transaction.

STEVE: *What were the particulars of your involvement?*

KEN: I'll go into detail here because you always remember your first deal, and because this deal took a particularly novel turn at the very end.

STEVE: *Have at it.*

KEN: HS Resources was putting together a $30 million deal to acquire seventy thousand acres from Amoco for development in Weld County, Colorado, near Denver. As was typical of most deals, companies would line up someone to provide a senior loan covering as much of the deal as possible and then fill the rest of the cash needs with either subordinated debt or equity financing. In this case, the company needed a little over $100 million, $30 million to close the deal, about $60 million for future drilling needs, and $17 million to repay debt that existed in the company already. It was a big deal for a small company, one that had the potential to set HS on a long-term growth trajectory.

Its management team rounded up a good cadre of investors to close the deal. Chase Manhattan would provide senior debt to close the transaction and to provide a development loan to finance future drilling. So HS needed $40 million of equity to complete the rest of the deal. Goldman Sachs had agreed to provide $20 million of equity capital. We were approached to consider putting in a subordinated debt layer or preferred stock of $15 million after another debt provider, Westinghouse Credit, had dropped out. Trust Company of the West (TCW) was also considering making a $5 million preferred equity investment.

I first "met" Mike and Nick on the phone. At that time, we hired a consulting engineer to review their production estimates, and we prepared economic models to assist in our underwriting of the investment. We spent a lot of time with them and their consultants telephonically.

The fundraising process for a deal like this was difficult, but they were doing it. The deal was set with Chase, TCW, NGP, and Goldman Sachs to provide capital. It was not your typical deal because the purchase was for undeveloped acreage and all the cash flow was going to come after considerable dollars were spent on drilling. We all had to make engineering estimates as to the ultimate drilling results to get comfortable with the asset purchase. We did get comfortable and had a good agreement on the terms of our deal as we approached the closing deadline given to the company by Amoco. The respective deal teams agreed to meet in Denver to hammer out the final points of the deal. I volunteered to go, since I was running point on the transaction.

I remember that day vividly. After getting off the plane at the Denver airport, as was my habit, I stopped at the closest bank of pay phones and called in to our 800 number to check my voice mail. One message was urgent. It was from Nick Sutton. "Call the HS office immediately!"

I hung up and called Nick. "Ken," he said, "while you were on the airplane, we heard from Goldman Sachs. Their commitment committee rejected the Goldman deal team's recommendation to do the deal." He was really bummed out. "We're short $15 million and we have to close this thing in three days. We lost. It's over. There's nothing we can do. You might as well turn around and go home."

STEVE: *I'm going to go out on a limb and say you didn't turn around.*

KEN: No. We all had been working for months on this transaction. Their entire team from San Francisco had come out to Denver. Since this acreage was within an hour's drive of the city, they had started setting up an office there to operate the development program. Meanwhile, they were doing all the execution documentation work at the lawyer's office. I said, "Nick, we've never met in person. I'm this close. I can either get back on a plane to Dallas or I can get in a taxi and come to your office and meet you. Maybe we can go get a beer." Without thinking, I walked toward the airport exit and grabbed a cab.

In the cab, I checked in with our office in Fort Worth. Coincidentally, another Fort Worth oil and gas operator, John Snyder, had called his old friend Rainwater. Snyder and his business partner, Tom Edelman, had been keenly following our deal because they coveted the Amoco acreage as well. We later found out that they had been a close number-two bidder on the same acreage.

Snyder and Edelman were unaware of the recent decision by Goldman to pull out. Edelman got on the phone because we were approaching the closing date and wanted to fish around for some deal intelligence. "I hear through the grapevine that you are buying this acreage from Amoco. I know you don't need the money, but maybe we can partner with you somehow," Edelman told Rainwater.

I had briefed Richard and Peter Joost on the transaction as it progressed, so it was not a complete cold call to Richard.

On that call, I explained to Richard what I had just learned. With Goldman pulling out, the company didn't have enough money to close, and NGP was already at its maximum deal size for the transaction. Richard told me that since Snyder was interested in the deal, maybe we *could* do more. I could tell that Richard's competitive juices were bubbling.

I called Tom Edelman while I was in the cab on my way to the office. He reiterated what he had said to Richard: "We'd love to partner if you can't pull it together." I played it coy, never letting on that the deal was in danger.

Upon arriving, the lawyers' office felt like a morgue. I met Nick, Mike, their key lieutenant Ted Gazulis, their lawyers, Hovey Kemp and Jim Piccone, and several other executives of the company. They were dejected, watching this deal they had worked so hard on wither on the vine. There was a lot of frustration that a terrific opportunity for the company and its financial partners would fall apart because of an eleventh-hour surprise from Goldman Sachs.

I went on to offer my thought that HS was at a disadvantage by committing to a deal with Amoco before having all the money in hand. This allowed Goldman Sachs to push the company up against one deadline after another, resulting in a real negotiating handicap. Having talked with Richard and sensing that the likes of John Snyder wanted in, I felt this transaction had so much value that we couldn't allow it to fall apart because of Goldman Sachs. I felt that our downside would be covered, so moving forward would be a judicious risk to take.

I have to say, though, that Ted Gazulis remembers it differently. He recalled, "I saw black smoke coming out of your ears. You were hopping mad that Goldman was going to either steal or torpedo the deal!"

Maybe his recollection has some merit to it. Anyway, I told the team that NGP was prepared to cover the purchase price of the deal and then work out a refinancing without the deadline time pressure on all of us. I put on my best face and said, "Instead of putting up $15 million, how about NGP speaks for the full $30 million, so we can close it, and then we can work out a refinancing plan without the deadline pressure?"

Everyone perked up. This was 1990; I was twenty-seven years old. These guys were all at least fifteen years older than I was and had a lot more experience. Even though we had only done a couple of deals by that time, I *felt* like I knew what I was doing and started making shit up. I said, "If Chase will put in more money and go senior in the capital structure, NGP will do more in a subordinated position. Then TCW's equity will plug the hole. Let's tell Amoco that we can do it, but we need a bit more time. And then, once we have it tied up, we can figure out how to lay off some risk with the folks at Snyder."

They looked at me funny.

"*Snyder?*" Nick said, wondering where in the world that came from. The HS and Snyder teams knew each other professionally and had interests in some of each other's wells, but this was a whole new approach. I informed them of Edelman's call. I could see the "Who is this kid?" look on their faces. But here we were, crafting a term sheet on the fly. It detailed a deal with and without splitting the deal with Snyder. I remember sitting up that night with my yellow legal pad sketching out term sheets and talking them through with David. By morning, we had come up with a set of terms to present to the company.

We spent the next day working through the numbers and the various scenarios. It was a relatively complex situation, since HS also had to negotiate a senior debt facility with Chase and go back and forth with Snyder on their involvement. In the end, they agreed to split the deal in half. With the Chase, TCW, and NGP money, the company had enough to close on the smaller deal, if Snyder made good on its half. In the end, NGP only had to come up with about $17.5 million.

HS called Amoco to inform them of the development and, thankfully, Amoco gave us a short extension and was agreeable to work with two buyers if they closed on the same day. Amoco didn't want to be left with half of the acreage. They were exiting the field entirely.

As an aside, this is one of the aspects of the U.S. oil and gas industry that I really came to enjoy. It was a relatively small circle of people who were working to extract production from the fields. Even though they were in competition with others in the industry, there was a real collegiality among the participants. Companies that compete against each other in one region might be partners somewhere else. Most of the players went to a small circle of schools and were trained at a handful of larger companies.

With both the Snyder and the Amoco agreements in hand, we now needed a fast and fair way to split these seventy thousand acres north of Denver. I do not recall who came up with the idea, but the two companies devised a plan similar to a National Football League draft—with the teams selecting blocks of acreage instead of players.

A few days later, the Snyder people flew to Denver. The HS team set up two conference rooms on a Sunday afternoon at their lawyers' offices with maps of the acreage on the walls. One room was for HS, and the other for Snyder. Each team had two minutes to pick a section of the acreage. They alternated picks until all the acreage had been selected.

Once all the acreage was picked, we laid each company's completed maps next to each other. The HS people had concentrated their picks around the area that they knew best and supported their existing assets. The Snyder people had concentrated their picks around the opposite area. It was uncanny how each team had gravitated its picks toward different acreage. The division was relatively neat. But there were several stray picks that each team selected toward the end that crossed over into the other's core areas. When we looked at the map, there were some obvious swaps that each team could make to pull together the most contiguous acreage set as possible. The process was smooth, the conversations were friendly, and the outcome was fair. Miraculously, it was all done in one day.

As a first step in the financing, NGP bought $16 million of convertible subordinated notes and warrants, enough to close on the smaller Amoco deal and accommodating the split with Snyder. In subsequent weeks, Chase and TCW invested a combined $10 million for preferred stock and additional warrants, and Chase agreed to provide a $17 million Facility A Loan and a $30 million Facility B Loan with an agreement to syndicate another $45 million of the Facility B Loan should the company request it. NGP stayed in the capital structure with its subordinated loan.

With this financing package, the HS team was able to complete the deal shortly thereafter and then it was off to the races. At age twenty-seven, as a term of our investment, I joined the board of directors.

Not only was this my first transaction to lead, but it also led to one of the most rewarding relationships in my professional life. As the HS deal negotiations were heating up, we needed outside counsel to advise us. Rather than rely on the New York firms that were part of David Albin's professional circles, I persuaded my partners to try a Dallas-based firm that was less expensive and had a better understanding of the oil and gas industry. I leaned on some of my old contacts to suggest lawyers, intending to get a few firms to compete for the business.

Making calls late on a Friday afternoon, I was only able to reach one contact, Dick Covington, then a junior partner at the firm of Thompson & Knight. This contact had come through a hunting buddy of Gamble's who was the managing partner of that firm.

Dick listened, asked questions, and jumped at the chance to take on this assignment. We were a great pair. He was hardworking and able to explain to me the legal nuances exceedingly well. He helped throughout the negotiation of the final documents and was instrumental in getting the deal closed.

From that point forward, Dick became our trusted legal adviser and a dear friend. NGP would not have had anywhere near its success had Dick not been so involved. By the mid-1990s, he was so instrumental to the work at NGP that we were happy to bring him on board and make him a fellow managing director and general counsel at the firm. That was the best decision we ever made.

STEVE: *And the deal as a whole?*

KEN: HS Resources ended up being very successful. The company executed professionally on drilling the acreage it had acquired from Amoco and generated excellent rates of returns and cash flow. In subsequent years, it negotiated several more deals with Amoco and others, and actively worked with the Colorado Oil and Gas Conservation Commission to make land spacing more efficient and opening additional formations to production. By 2000, HS operated thousands of wells in the area and its oil production alone made it the second-largest oil producer in Colorado, behind only Chevron. By its calculations, it was producing the Btu equivalent of 25 percent of the natural gas consumed annually in Colorado.

NGP also did well with the investment. HS went public about three years later, and we ultimately sold our stock a few years after that. In the intervening years, we all stayed close as friends, and HS even found its way to acquire Tide West Oil Company—one of our early portfolio companies managed by Phil Smith and Doug Flint. I guess you could say we found ways to keep it all in the family.

In 2001, many years after I had left the board, HS was about to announce a sale of the entire company to Kerr McGee for about $2 billion. The night before the announcement, Nick called me at home to let me know and to thank me once again for playing a large part in the original formation of the company. In fact, the first well that the company drilled on the Amoco acreage was named the HSR-Hersh. When they told me that they were naming the well after me, I was petrified. I never was a fan of naming wells after people. Thankfully, the well was a decent producer.

Getting that call was a special moment. I had not spoken to Nick for a couple of years, and the company had done so much after our little deal that got it started. But Nick is a class act, and he remembered to thank the people who were with him at the beginning. That moment taught me a valuable lesson as well: Do not forget those who played a role in your life, no matter how long ago and no matter how seemingly small.

Of course, I didn't miss a chance to source a new deal. After he told me that the deal was going to be announced, I was thrilled to say, "Congratulations, and when your noncompete expires, let's do it again!" Which we did. In 2004, we formed Resolute Natural Resources with the nucleus of the HS Resources team after they fulfilled their obligations at Kerr McGee. Resolute, also, ultimately went public, and I enjoyed being on the board of it as well. Nick and the team became part of the fabric of my life as business partners, colleagues, and friends. Relationships like this that span three decades are the side benefit that comes from being immersed in a single industry.

I look back and can't help but think that without NGP's backing, financial and otherwise, the entire story would probably have been quite different. And, I might add, that HS's success contributed to the early success of NGP.

STEVE: *So, what should people learn from this?*

KEN: One big takeaway is that I didn't get back on the plane when it looked like the deal was dead. I made a couple of calls in that cab. It led to ideas. I improvised. We didn't give up. That was a seminal moment for me and gave me the confidence that I could do this job.

It also highlighted what I didn't like about the investment banking business. There's a big difference between getting a deal closed and investing in a profitable deal. In the investment banking business, the goal is to earn a fee upon a deal's closing, regardless of whether the client makes money on the deal. Success for the investment bank was independent of the client's success. There was complete misalignment. I recalled that feeling when the bankers were celebrating a deal's closing while, in my mind, there was no real reason to celebrate. We wouldn't know if the deal would be worth celebrating for many years.

For me, the real satisfaction came from watching these companies get built, while being a friend and adviser to the senior management along the way. I *enjoyed* being aligned with the management. I wanted to win only if they won. Being a partner in a company's growth is the great part of capitalism. We were sure to spread the equity ownership deep into each portfolio company, so that if the company became successful, many of the employees would share in the spoils.

Being able to see that repeatedly in the investment business was the most satisfying part of my job. Then, I saw the same thing at our own firm, NGP. As we raised and invested Funds 1, 2, and 3, we started to develop a reputation in the industry. I knew we had staying power when we raised our fourth fund in 1996. We were growing the firm with a loyal base of investors and now we had a loyal base of colleagues—all of whom owned equity in the funds and most of whom would come to own equity in the firm as time went on.

We implemented in our firm the same ownership mentality that we insisted on in our portfolio companies. We coined the phrase "owner-manager" to describe the senior executives of our portfolio companies. We wanted the decision makers to own equity and not just be hired guns working for salary. I wanted NGP to be run the same way. While this is commonplace now, it was unheard of at the time. Over the years, I concocted an ownership-sharing scheme that allowed every deal professional above the pre-MBA level to earn ownership. As the firm succeeded, we all succeeded—*together*. We never used a compensation or organizational consultant. I always loved sitting down with a clean sheet of paper and creating something. David saw this. He later said, "Ken, you dream shit up that no one else can dream up, and it works!" It was a skill that I developed over time and kept nurturing.

STEVE: *With HS Resources, you were twenty-seven, new to the business, and the others were clearly older. During that weekend, did you ever feel you were in over your head?*

KEN: I *was* in over my head from the day I started. I felt like I needed to go prove myself all the time. That's what kept me going. I fluctuated between this feeling that I didn't know what I was doing and the sheer excitement of making it up as I went along. Maybe I'm a confident impostor. The joy that I found in business was the room to be creative.

STEVE: *The HS Resources deal was a winner, but you've said that wasn't always the case with the investments in your early years.*

KEN: For sure. In 1992, I led a review of what we had done as a team up to that point. As I mentioned, we had managed a public securities portfolio that did okay, but not great. We had done a couple of transactions that worked well and a couple of others that went sideways. We had been obsessed with trying to structure deals to create a yield, since we were trying to clear the 11 percent hurdle rate while trying to find ways to get upside participation as well.

Natural gas prices kept dropping just about every year. We kept waiting for the McKinsey scenario to materialize. I remember sitting in a hotel room and looking through the few deals we had done and thinking through the common traits of the deals that had worked. You didn't have to be a rocket scientist or an oil and gas whiz kid to come up with what I concluded: We should try to do more deals that resembled the ones that worked and stay away from deals that had traits of our underperformers.

About the same time that we completed the HS deal, we made an investment in Atwood Resources, a small producer that specialized in drilling low-volume natural gas wells in Ohio. In that transaction, the executive team was competent, but they would not rank in any "executive of the year" competition. The assets were also relatively unexciting, and the development program on its face was set to earn a relatively low rate of return.

The company was debt-financed, and when we put that development plan through a big computer spreadsheet with an assumption that natural gas prices would rise, the returns on equity were great. Knowing that that was not guaranteed, we structured our investment as a subordinated note with an equity participation. Having a second lien on the assets would afford us some downside protection. This gave us the confidence to proceed with the deal.

Well, that didn't work very well. Natural gas prices didn't go up, and the leverage on the balance sheet came back to bite us. The management team was not strong enough to stay together during the downturn and to pivot their business plan to one that could succeed. In addition, they became somewhat adversarial with us when the going got tough. In the end, we were fortunate to get most of our money back, but the company did not succeed, and we made no real return. We tried to work with management to alter the business model in order to adapt, but they would have none of it.

STEVE: *I'm guessing you learn as much from the deals that go sideways as the deals that are winners. What did you learn from Atwood?*

KEN: This deal provided some interesting takeaways. Besides learning the route from Fort Worth to Dover, Ohio, we learned a real lesson in the value of alignment. The management team owned the equity, and since we were lenders, they didn't feel the need to treat us as partners. It was really uncomfortable. We were taking some risk in the deal, but since we did not have much ownership participation, once the returns started to slip, we shifted our thinking toward capital preservation instead of capital gains. Management, however, had nothing to lose by hanging on and continuing to find ways to not repay our debt. Since we weren't sharing in the upside alongside management, the team treated us like outsiders. Maybe that was why we always felt the need to travel there and check in on them.

In the end, we realized that if you're in business with mediocre managers, it doesn't matter how you structure it. If you're in business with really great managers, it also doesn't matter how you structure it. Winners will find a way to win. As an investor, I'd rather have more capital at risk alongside really good managers than need to rely on deal structures that protect my downside because management may not be that good. With mediocre people running the company, your downside may not always be as protected as you think. And with good people, you don't need to worry because they care about your money more than you do. Rainwater's lesson about needing documents to protect your investment rang loudly in my ear.

I remember Rainwater, who rarely traveled, asking me one time why I was on the road so much. He reminded me that if we really trusted our management teams, we shouldn't need to go check in on them—an amazingly simple yet important observation.

The winning deals had one thing in common. The management team treated us like partners, not just a financial source. We were all friends. We hung out with our wives together. We shared professional and social time together. We had grown to trust each other. This was critical. Given that the oil and gas business was so hard to succeed in, it was imperative that partners trust each other no matter what.

This trust works both ways. We wanted them to trust us, so it was important that we trusted them. I always wanted to be the person who could handle the call that came with bad news. Anyone can handle a call when good news is being delivered. But a true test of a partnership is when management has to deliver bad news to the owners. When we looked at the industry in this context, the successful path became rather straightforward to see. This was our light bulb moment. From that point forward, our mission was to find good, trustworthy people who knew how to make money even if prices went down. They knew the realities of the industry and that hope was not a business plan. Then, we set out to be the partner of choice in the industry.

Amidst the Atwood experience, I remember saying to David Albin, "Let's focus on finding more Nick Suttons out there and not bet on rising gas prices. Let's bet on the people instead."

It was so simple that it was almost embarrassing.

One more lesson. We learned that if you're in an out-of-the-way place and there's an interesting national monument or attraction nearby, don't just assume you'll stop there some day. Stop and smell the roses—or the pigskin! On our way to the Atwood headquarters, my partners and I must have driven past the Pro Football Hall of Fame in Canton, Ohio, at least a dozen times over a four-year period. We always said we would stop one day and check it out. We never did. Now, I try my best to stop and smell some of the roses along the way.

STEVE: *Was it really that basic? You mean even a writer like me could invest in oil and gas?*

KEN: You bet! We came to learn that investing in oil and gas is really *only* about making a bet on a management team. All oil and gas wells deplete over time. So, over the course of holding an investment for, say, seven years, the producing properties that are there on day one will become largely depleted. The assets that form the basis for the company's future sale will be assets that are acquired or developed over our holding period of the deal using the cash flow realized from those initial wells, plus our money. Looking at it this way, our initial valuation of the existing assets could be off by 20 percent, and if we picked a great management team that could create value, we could still win. If we picked a lousy management team that could not create value, then we would lose. It had less to do with the accuracy of the valuation going in. It had everything to do with how the team performed after our money had been invested.

Even transactions that seemed like they were based on a different thesis came down to people. One of the early transactions that NGP completed in 1989 was participating with the entire Fort Worth office in a distressed debt play to wind up taking control of one of the largest offshore drilling rig owners in the world, the Penrod Drilling Company. This deal was originated by Peter Joost and Richard Rainwater through their relationship with Carl Thorne. Carl ran Energy Service Company, or ENSCO, in which Richard and others in our office were large shareholders. This investment pre-dated the formation of NGP, so I had only heard about its origins a few years before. ENSCO owned a couple of offshore oil rigs.

Carl coveted the much larger fleet of Penrod and noticed that it was teetering on insolvency. Seeing the debt of Penrod trade at significant discounts got Peter's invest-ment juices flowing. In the end, the investors in Rainwater's office, NGP, Goldman Sachs, and Bankers Trust combined to accumulate a control position in the bank debt of the company, thereby allowing us to convert that debt into equity and take control of the company. This entire process took some five years to get done and was incredibly complicated, even tense some days between the various partners. However, we listened to Richard and Peter preach the gospel of staying aligned with Carl and his team, who were ultimately responsible for building a quality company. Each of the financial partners had an opinion, of course, as the drilling business went up and down violently during our hold period. But we remained committed to being aligned with Carl and held on to our position in the combined company for a decade. The deal ended up a winner.

Good people know how to make lemonade if the world gives them lemons. That was the epiphany of 1991. The oil and gas profit equation was rather simple. Revenue was simply price multiplied by the volume produced. Subtract costs to get operating profits. That means we had three variables: price, volume, and costs. As commodity prices were terrible and something we couldn't control, we decided to base our business plan on controlling what we could—volumes and costs. We stressed finding honest people who knew how to increase volumes and decrease costs. For a couple of MBAs, that seemed to be a much more manageable task.

STEVE: *Manageable, but a rather dramatic shift.*

KEN: Yes, but as simple as it was dramatic. It dawned on us: If analyzing assets brought to us to evaluate is really secondary to the judgment about the people, then why are we looking for deals where there are already existing assets in hand? Let's work to identify great people and forget about the assets. Let's get in business with them and go where they lead us. Give them a commitment to fund equity and let them go shopping with our money. If they commit some of their money to the deal also, they will be spending their money right alongside ours. So, if we think they are responsible shoppers with their own money, we don't have to worry. Perfect alignment.

Again, it was so simple, it was almost stupid. While it is common practice today, at that time, it was novel. While the few other investors in the industry focused on looking at assets in which to invest, we were simply focused on finding great people and aligning our interests.

Even our portfolio company management teams sometimes found our approach incredible. For example, after a somewhat lengthy negotiation in the fall of 1993, we had concluded a $6.2 million investment in a small company based in Baton Rouge, Louisiana, operated by two fantastic individuals, Bo Howard and Ben Jones. They had a small asset base at the time, but we were taken by Ben's understanding of the geology of southern Louisiana and his ideas on finding and developing more oil and gas. After we concluded the investment, David and I took Bo and Ben out to lunch to celebrate our new partnership.

We talked about all the transactions that were happening in the industry and some of the risky business plans that seemed to be getting funded back then. To express his incredulity at what seemingly crazy business plans were attracting capital, Ben exclaimed rhetorically, "Who would be crazy enough to invest in just people without any assets?"

Hmmm. David and I looked at each other; then we looked at Bo, who realized that Ben had just implicated what we were celebrating at that lunch. Then, we all looked at Ben, and I said, "We are!" Ben realized his faux pas, and we all had a good laugh.

As investors, those early deals taught us that we were really like absentee landlords. We were owners of the businesses *with* management. Rainwater would often say, "Whether you own 1 percent or 99 percent of the company, you work *for* the CEO and the management team. They are doing all the work, and you're just the money behind them. Your job is to be a great partner and find out what you can do to help them. Don't treat them like employees. They are the ones throwing up in the shower if they can't make payroll. For you, it's just one of your portfolio companies, but for each of them, it's their life."

David and I repeated that always. We were looking to find owner-managers who cared so much about making their company work that they would be throwing up in the shower at the panicked thought of their company's failing. *Employees* will cut and run. *Owners* care so much that they will see it through, no matter what.

I am not really sure how many of our management teams ever threw up in the shower. We had such a good record of finding winners that I don't know of many who would have felt that uncomfortable urge. However, by searching for people who cared deeply about being a good partner and making the company work, our business became much more fun. Once aligned, all we had to do was be a great copilot and get out of their way. We learned that on the job. When we made that our strategy, our business really took off.

STEVE: *What does "be a great copilot" really mean?*

KEN: In the investment business, money is a commodity. A dollar from us was no different than a dollar from someone else. We had to ensure that our business style was a point of differentiation. For us, it was all about relationships. Those relationships had to be built on open, honest communication.

As an absentee landlord—which is what all investors are—I would always say I didn't want the problem call at 2 a.m. If there were some major issues at the company, I wanted the call at 9 a.m. from the CEO saying, "I was up all night. Let me tell you what happened, and what I did to take care of it." And for that extra seven hours of sleep, I'd let that guy make his money. I knew I wouldn't be any help from afar, anyway. Plus, I am always grumpy if I don't get enough sleep.

STEVE: *Once you switched to the "partner with good people" model, how did you do?*

KEN: I can't say we were perfect at it, but it became a great guiding light that served us very well. To be sure, there were things we declined to invest in because the people were not quite right, but they went on to be wildly successful for other people. We tried not to let that bother us. Our goal was to earn a good rate of return for our investors, and it didn't matter if other people were earning good returns for theirs.

In the end, we wound up creating an investment model that has become the standard method by which capital is allocated to the oil and gas sector in this country. More than twenty firms today have funded over one thousand companies using the model we created. This has proven to be the engine propelling the unconventional shale revolution that has altered the industry, our economy, and our foreign policy forever.

I took our role seriously. We were entrusted with investors' money—Equitable's at first, and as time went on, university endowments, private foundations, major pension funds, and wealthy families. They were paying us a fee to look after their assets. In turn, we were giving those dollars to management teams that were essentially putting that money into the ground. *Holy crap!* There was a lot riding on our manager selection. The responsibility was real. I wanted to find people who understood and who took that responsibility as seriously as we did.

Our early successes also taught us a lot about people. Not only were Nick Sutton and Mike Highum great operators, but they were also quality people. We were lucky to spend a lot of time in Tulsa, Oklahoma, in our early days as well, because we found the people there to be down-to-earth, hardworking, and smart.

During those first three years of our partnership, in addition to the HS Resources investment, we also completed an investment in Mega Natural Gas and Draco Gas Partners—two companies affiliated with each other out of Tulsa. The senior management team of Mega and Draco was Jim Hays, Tim Jurek, Brad Karp, Jim Kincaid, and

Phil Smith. Just like the HS experience, good deals started with good people. Jim, Tim, Brad, Jim, and Phil were wonderful guys who treated us as partners and friends—never as adversaries. We watched them increase the value of their companies through careful acquisitions despite a lousy commodity price environment. Ultimately, we spawned several companies over the years with these folks. Backing winners over and over beats the hell out of trying to find new executives to back.

Phil Smith was more valuable to our franchise than he ever realized. He was in a league of his own. Phil is a Renaissance man disguised as a petroleum engineer. He is perhaps the most well-read person I have ever met. He combines an encyclopedic mind with an ability to explain the most complicated equation in terms every layman could understand. He is a walking contradiction. He can spend hours on end tearing apart oil well files, analyzing the volumetric charts to find the perfect technical remediation strategy to increase production or decrease costs. Then, he can break to discuss religious or political philosophy. Despite his gentle manner, he is a fierce competitor. From the beginning of my career, I was always able to ask him the most rudimentary question about petroleum engineering or geology and not feel stupid. He took the time to explain, and no matter how busy he was, he was always present when he was with me. I had his full attention.

That presence was felt in our portfolio as well. In all, Phil ran several companies for us over two decades and completed more than a dozen transactions with our capital. He helped us develop a corollary to our investment strategy: *If you have a relationship with a great manager, do as much business as you can with that manager.* Since picking managers was our biggest challenge, doing repeat business with someone we already knew and trusted took that risk away.

Not only did that practice guide us, but these owner-managers also became the standards against which we evaluated new people we met. We gravitated to the salt-of-the-earth types—not flashy promoters with fancy houses and private planes. While we did back some fabulously flamboyant executives with fancy houses and fancy planes, we wanted entrepreneurs who appreciated how hard it was to make a living and respected the challenges of the business. We could usually tell when people were giving us an honest answer as opposed to those who were trying to be slick and had a canned answer for everything. Even with these parameters, we still weren't perfect. So imagine how we would've done had we not had the discipline or the role models we did.

STEVE: *Did you have any tricks to make those determinations?*

KEN: Absolutely. I always wanted to get a sense of the culture created by the executives. Corporate culture is everything, in my opinion. It is the glue that holds people together, especially when business conditions become difficult. I think it is rather easy to see if people actually enjoy working at a company and if employees respect their executives. You could only see that on-site. I always liked to visit the company before we decided to invest with them.

I could tell by visiting with someone where his or her priorities were. Remember, we were in dialogue with companies that needed money. That was why they were talking to us in the first place. If they had to apologize for their office, saying something like, "Sorry that we're here, but a buddy of mine had three spare rooms, and this is saving us money while we put this deal together"—I loved that. Conversely, a person with big offices surrounded by fancy art and mahogany wood paneling didn't exactly exude parsimony. Maybe I was heeding that old lesson from the Texaco boardroom experience without knowing it. Sometimes, little signals mean a lot.

Anyone could produce a business presentation that ticked off all the boxes of our criteria. So the question was: How do we get beyond that? I think one of my strengths was being able to ask good questions, the right questions. I would often ask, "What are you passionate about? What do you spend your time on?" I would offer to take them to dinner. Then, you could see how they treated the waitstaff, treated the valet, or how they talked about other people. We wanted to be around decent human beings.

I gravitated toward these people because I wasn't an oil and gas guru. But I wasn't stupid, either. I was asking them to explain why they needed our money, what they were going do with it, and how the rewards vastly outweighed the risks. I listened. Did they have a contingency plan or were they going for broke? Could they explain to me what success looked like? Were they treating our money like their own?

People who really understood what they were doing stood out. Importantly, many of those people had already made a big financial commitment in their own company. They were capitalists looking for partners. They were excited by the chance to invest. They didn't view it as an obligation. While we gravitated toward these capitalists, we ran from the promoters who were happy for us to risk our money without taking any personal risk themselves.

STEVE: *Were there deals you walked away from that might have been profitable, but you just didn't want to get into business with the people?*

KEN: Dozens. We missed a lot of opportunities because we felt like we couldn't trust these people with our kids. That was our standard: *Would we trust our kids with them?* We'd do exhaustive background checks, and we walked away if the people were kind of iffy. Many times, these folks had good projects. But we usually stuck to our guns.

Inevitably, we did several deals that didn't work so well, but the people were sweethearts. Honestly, I'd rather have that type of dud in the portfolio if that was the cost of always doing business with honest, hardworking people we'd trust with our kids. The people all worked hard. We were never sued or stolen from. When companies started to underperform, it would have been easy for management teams to cut and run and for assets to be stripped from the company. As investors, our only protection against that was the character of the people involved and the level of trust we had established with them. Ben Jones turned out to be prescient in that we lost half the money we invested in his company, but we are close friends with Bo and Ben to this day.

I should add that David and I would speak on an open speakerphone just about every day, and the folks in the office would be able to hear us vet the deals and debate the merits and flaws openly. I would feel a sense of pride when I heard other people around the floor using some of our expressions in critiquing a deal. Even younger colleagues who had no kids were asking if they would trust their kids to this or that CEO. That was hilarious.

STEVE: *Any final thoughts on those early days?*

KEN: Being in Rainwater's office was a blessing. I tried to mimic his style. Everyone who made the trek to Fort Worth would get something from him. He was present, determined to make each visitor feel like they were the center of the universe. From the first time I set foot in his office as a wet-behind-the-ears, first-year MBA student looking for a summer job, I was amazed at how respectfully he treated everyone. He was able to turn people down and have *them* say, "Thank you." That was a real skill.

I always tried to make people appreciate coming in to see me as well. If they took the time to visit, I wanted to make sure I left them with something. I tried to push that mentality through NGP for as long as I could. We made a name for ourselves by being respectful and helpful. If we were jerks, we would have quickly been all alone. Instead, the word got around, and we were able to attract a lot of deal flow from all over the country. For a young professional with a fully drawn credit line funding his share of the investment, this was reassuring.

Julie and I were living in a house with lousy plumbing, and we already had to replace our shower pan once by then, so I doubt it could have withstood my throwing up in the shower if our portfolio ended up a loser.

CHAPTER 5

IF LIFE GIVES YOU LEMONS, MAKE LEMONADE

STEVE: *As we've discussed, the first NGP fund, seeded with $100 million from Equi-table, was started in 1988. As of today, NGP is up to Fund Number 12, which has over $4 billion from investors all over the world, bringing its total cumulative capital under management to about $20 billion. We'll look at the tremendous growth and success of NGP in future sections.*

For now, however, let's pause the story briefly to understand how your worldview evolved. Many in business keep their head down and maintain a focus that is rela-tively narrow to their field. However, your perspective seemed to get broader over time. I would like to talk to you about your thoughts on three big topics: government, energy, and wealth.

Let's start with your views about the role of government. When you were a senior at St. Mark's, you were among a group of Dallas-area high school student achievers receiv-ing the TACT (Teen Age Citizen Tribute) Award cosponsored by the Dallas Morning News *and the Zale Corporation. This was in April of 1981, shortly after Ronald Reagan became president. Here's part of what you wrote for the final presentation ceremony, under the heading "Credo":*

> The new conservatism which the nation demanded in the last election can lead
> to erosion (of the country's morality) in accordance with the current demand to
> justify governmental programs on the basis of cost-effectiveness. It may be nec-
> essary to eliminate the expenditures desperately needed for the poor, elderly, and

handicapped. Parentless children and medical research will also suffer. Legislative debate concentrates solely on monetary costs vs. the life-saving potential of the resolution. If lives cost too much to save, bills often fail.

However, I believe that monetary issues should not be more important than human issues. In essence, by comparing the two, bureaucracies are putting an arbitrary price tag on human life. As a result, the human element has been lost from governmental actions.

Overall, I believe that policies should be forced to fit the people, rather than people forced to fit the policies. The government is the servant of the people, according to Abraham Lincoln. I feel that it is time to re-evaluate our attitudes of conservatism. People should become more sensitive to human wants and needs, rather than to political dogmas. This would eliminate both the moral and legal crises that exist in the present system.

You now describe yourself as a compassionate conservative. And you've said, "If you want something to be inefficient, then government is the way to go. It's government's neat trick. If you want things to take three times as long, not work well, but cost ten times as much, give the job to the government." So how do these two square?

KEN: That is a great question. As an idealistic seventeen-year-old, I had high hopes about the human ideal and how government should serve. It's interesting to read that blurb today. It is apparent that I was searching for a way to do the most good and have government serve the people effectively.

I still maintain that view. However, now I believe that the best way to serve the human condition is through a narrower role of government. Governments should not create dependencies. I view the government's primary role as establishing the foundations on which human potential can be realized. Instead of dictating every solution, a government should serve its people by promoting equality of opportunity rather than equality of outcome. Then, it can focus its attention on providing a safety net for those structurally unable to participate in the opportunity equation and for providing public services needed to preserve the "commons"—like national defense and public infrastructure.

Creating conditions where people can achieve their potential is job number one for the public sector. This leads to compassionate outcomes that enhance human dignity. I still think outcomes measured in human terms are critical; I just now know that governments cannot be counted on to deliver the best results.

STEVE: *How did this evolve?*

KEN: I guess with age came cynicism. People are fallible. Government offices run by people are fallible. And bureaucracies only grow one way, inevitably crowding out the hardworking people they were once designed to serve. Working in the private sector, I spent three decades watching people navigate the labyrinth of backward government policy. I have watched the data accumulate to see what works and what does not. I would love for the public sector to function well, but the dysfunction is calcified.

And I've learned that the government doesn't *make* anything. Its revenue derives from taxes on the incomes and wealth of the citizens. It's a massive resource reallocation machine. Don't get me wrong, much of that is needed to address goals that we want as a society but cannot be provided by any single individual. Things like national defense, public safety, long-term research and development, and critical infrastructure. But when the government gets into the business of micromanaging sectors of the economy, it is way out over its skis.

The examples are endless. The health-care industry is in chaos, despite the fact that people from all over the world travel to the United States to receive its state-of-the-art, innovative treatments. Rather than take control of health care and stifle innovation, the government's role should be to provide proper incentives for the health-care industry to become more efficient, while preserving the forces of innovation and discovery. The federal government should become a partner in the push for efficiency, rather than the dictator of it.

The War on Poverty hasn't helped decrease poverty; we've spent trillions of dollars on poverty, and yet poverty rates aren't much better than they were in the 1960s. We spent almost $3 trillion on renewable energies, trying to pick winners, and yet fossil fuels have the same market share as they did twenty years ago, before almost any dollars were spent.

It's become apparent to me that an over-the-top solution decided on by 536 people in Washington and their staffs isn't always the best way to go.

While there are anecdotes that counter everything I just said, from a macro standpoint, the results are clear. The weight of the welfare state is a heavy burden to bear, and it is no substitute for the durability of creating *conditions* for people to lift themselves up. Remember, anything decided by legislation can be undone by a later group of legislators. As P. J. O'Rourke is famous for saying, "When buying and selling are controlled by legislation, the first things to be bought and sold are legislators."*

Look no further than New York State. You can't chase people away forever and then complain that they are leaving. I find it curious when a place makes it so difficult

---

* P. J. O'Rourke, *Parliament of Whores: A Lone Humorist Attempts to Explain the Entire U.S. Government* (New York: Grove Press, 1991), 210.

to do business that businesses flee, forcing it into a position of having to provide special incentives to entice new businesses to move in. Wouldn't it be cheaper and easier if the environment were hospitable to businesses in the first place?

How ironic is it that in 2018, the state threw $2.5 billion in incentives at Amazon to locate fifty thousand jobs for a second headquarters only to have the local community board in Long Island City create enough of a stink to have the company change its mind? At the same time, Apple announced it was locating fifteen thousand jobs in Texas, and they only got $100 million from Texas's opportunity fund. Fostering an environment where business can thrive is incentive enough. Then, public servants can really work on those things that are in their wheelhouse—like delivering the public goods of education, infrastructure, and public safety.

I chuckle because you can't have it both ways. You can't say, "We'll be hostile to everything you do," but then say, "We want you so badly to locate here that we're willing to pay you." Well-intentioned politicians have a hard time making the tough decisions that build a welcoming climate over the long term. I'm afraid that as a country, we're going to realize this one state at a time, with states like Connecticut, New Jersey, New York, Illinois, and California all living on the edge of financial meltdowns.

STEVE: *If this is so obvious, why do these places keep making the same mistake?*

KEN: Another great question. I believe we are drowning in good intentions. Good people in power positions see a problem and use their tools to fix it. Legislators make laws. That's their tool. Rarely are old laws repealed; we just keep piling on rule after rule to attack the issue at hand, unaware of the collateral damage they may cause. We have given a central planning authority this social obligation and it carries an incredibly blunt instrument. Consequently, the results are poor.

Compounding the issue are the politics of the situation, which favor putting out today's fires. Invariably, political considerations interfere. It becomes easier to enact a short-term fix that provides temporary help and delays tackling real issues that often involve real sacrifice. Politicians will pursue behavior that the system incentivizes. Kicking the can down the road is smart when viewed through that lens.

I would rather see the public sector recognize that good things happen when a person has a stable job, feels safe raising a family in the manner they choose, and lives in a community that offers good education and public infrastructure. When people thrive, communities thrive. The philanthropic DNA of Americans is then unleashed to allow community institutions to flourish.

I am not a libertarian here. I think the public sector has a vital job in ensuring the delivery of essential public goods—education, public safety, community infrastructure, long-range research and development, and a compassionate safety net for those unable to participate. And let's not forget the greatest of all obligations: the need for our public servants to establish clear rules and regulations that ensure level playing fields for market participants. This country's greatest asset is the sanctity of the rule of law. This allows our market-based economy to be the envy of the world. When our politicians try to pick winners and losers across the economy, the process gets corrupted, markets get altered, and unintended consequences become problems.

STEVE: *During your four years at Princeton, you went from someone interested in government and politics to someone destined for the business world. Can you explain that evolution?*

KEN: It started when I got involved in *Business Today* magazine at Princeton. I began reading the front page of the *Wall Street Journal* and its news digest daily. I flipped through *Fortune* and *Forbes* as often as I could. I spent two summers traveling around the country talking to business executives, asking them to sponsor the magazine and our national conference program. We had a zero budget every year, so if we wanted to put on a program and put out a publication, we had to sell. Once I became a leader of that organization, I realized that there would be no revenue if I didn't organize and motivate a national sales effort. Plus, I kind of liked getting on the phone and making calls myself.

We set a sales record in my senior year and were able to do things we hadn't been able to do before as an organization. We were able to see the results of our hard work quite quickly. I got addicted to the process of setting ambitious goals and then devising a plan to exceed them.

My year as president of the organization was 1984, the tenth anniversary of its national conference program. We devised the conference topic—remember, this was during Reagan's first term—as "An Analysis of Capitalism." Funny how history repeats itself. There was a debate as to the merits of government's role in the economy and whether markets were to be trusted. We held a debate between the president's economic adviser Martin Anderson and liberal economist Robert Reich, who would eventually become Bill Clinton's secretary of labor.

STEVE: *Who was more persuasive? The conservative Anderson or the liberal Reich?*

KEN: I don't remember much of the debate at all. My role was running the event and making sure the couple of hundred participants had a meaningful time. I remember looking around and trying to make sure that the food service was good and that everyone could hear the speakers. I wanted to put on a professional event, consistent with the tradition of the organization.

The success of the Foundation for Student Communication was built on top of its history, and I took that seriously. The organization was started, in part, by Steve Forbes when he was an undergrad at Princeton. Being a student and having such a connection to a New York scion was quite the eye-opener for me. Our success was directly proportional to the effort and professionalism we all put into it. But, as a student-led organization, the team turned over every couple of years. It was important that, as the leader at the time, I didn't mess it up. For some reason, my personal makeup thrived in that environment. I cared about the results and the manner in which they were delivered. I busted my ass to make sure it came off without a hitch. I have no real idea where that meticulousness came from. But I have come to accept that it is part of my DNA.

STEVE: *I get the sense that if you hadn't chosen the career path you did, you would have been a dynamic event planner! Seriously, though, were you politically active when you were younger?*

KEN: Meeting a young George W. Bush in the late 1980s when his father was president was as close as I got to professional politics during the early days of my career. But I was never really politically active. Of course, I always had opinions, but I expressed them through my votes and moved on. As I got older, I gave to a few candidates. I have settled in as a capitalist, not a politician. What I have learned, though, is that politicians have a way of finding the capitalists. So they became hard to avoid as I became more successful.

STEVE: *We'll get to your relationship with George W. Bush later, but this leads me to big topic number two: energy. We've already talked about how your initial exposure to the oil and gas industry as an analyst at Morgan Stanley was serendipitous. They mistakenly assumed that because you were from Texas you knew something about energy. You did some work outside the energy field for a few months before business school when you were in Chicago, but other than that your entire career was spent in that industry. Was there something particularly alluring about the energy field that kept you there? Or was it more the idea of investing that captivated you, and, in truth, you might have been just as happy and successful doing what you've done if the commodity was coffee or soybeans instead of oil and gas?*

KEN: For me, the energy industry had it all, even for a liberal arts guy with an MBA. I found it hard to follow the energy industry without also following economics, politics, and geopolitics. Moreover, it's impossible to understand the industry without some working knowledge of history. Intellectually, the industry was engrossing. I wish it was a bit easier to earn a good return, but from a professional standpoint, it kept me on my toes daily. It seemed like almost every headline mattered every day.

When we started NGP in 1988, it was only a few years after the deregulation of the natural gas business in the United States. So to understand the gas business was to learn the lesson of politicians messing up a market, impeding progress, and even creating harm. Allow me to give a little history. Even if oil and gas isn't your thing, I think you will find the process interesting.

Dating as far back as 1938, the federal government viewed the natural gas production business as an extension of the large, regulated interstate pipelines that transported that gas, thereby justifying the regulation of the wellhead gas price to protect consumers from monopoly power. That was solidified by a court case in the 1950s. Prices were federally controlled and set on a cost-plus basis. Producers were considered to be like small public utilities, and prices were set to protect the consumer, not to reflect the market prices needed to encourage exploration for new supply to replace the sold production. The artificially low prices caused demand to run up. Yet supply was inadvertently being discouraged because there wasn't a free market setting price.

However, the federal government was only able to control interstate commerce as opposed to intrastate commerce, according to our Constitution. So, within a state's borders, the price caps didn't apply. Natural gas that stayed within a state was able to fetch a market price. This obviously hurt the states that needed to bring production into their state. It wasn't uncommon in the 1960s and 1970s for Midwestern cities to suffer gas shortages in the middle of winter, while places like Texas had ample supply.

In the mid-1970s, about half the gas produced in this country remained within the state where it was produced. It was like an energy civil war brought to you by the federal government, whose job it was to protect and defend. Over the years, federal policy failed to rectify this situation. It wasn't until 1978 that natural gas shortages got so bad at the same time the country was experiencing an oil shock orchestrated by the emerging OPEC cartel that Congress acted. Even then, it made a mess of things.

The 1978 law enacted a seven-year phase-in of deregulation, freeing up prices for new production, thereby encouraging exploration. However, old gas wells that were already producing were left to receive the old, insufficient prices. This caused a real headache in the business, since old production was being sold at a loss and all the activity was artificially directed to new exploration. The number of drilling rigs searching for oil and gas shot up to four thousand. It has never been that high again. But that's emblematic of what happens when the government tries to "fix" a market. Supply ran up, and prices increased. However, as markets responded, demand fell, since natural gas prices were well above their historical norms. A supply glut ensued.

By 1985, when the full seven years was up and the prices were fully deregulated, supply exceeded demand. Prices fell and the drilling industry responded by dramatically cutting back. It was total chaos, with bankruptcies galore and consolidation of the industry needed. In 1986, the interstate pipeline business became deregulated as well, allowing the market to really get to work in the same way.

When I started at Morgan Stanley in 1985, you can see how I landed smack dab into an Economics 101 class mixed with a little political science on the side. I was hooked.

To make it even more interesting, in 1986, Saudi Arabia announced they were no longer going to lose market share by cutting their own production to keep prices stable (at around $20 per barrel) as other countries around the world increased production. They said they were going to keep producing, since they were the low-cost producer, and they would put the higher-cost producers out of business. Almost overnight, prices fell in half.

Between the readjustments of the natural gas business in 1985–1986 and the geopolitics of oil at that time, you can see why working in the energy group at a major Wall Street firm was so intoxicating. Companies were scrambling to get more efficient. Strong companies were looking to acquire. Weaker companies were looking to consolidate to stay afloat. Corporate raiders were looking at assets that were cheaper to acquire on Wall Street than to drill for.

Fast-forward to recent history. In the decade concluding in December 2019, we've had about 2 percent average GDP growth. If you exclude the domestic oil and gas industry, growth would have been half that. We have this incredible asset here in the United States and it was finally unleashed in the late 1990s and early 2000s. It's incredible what the combination of American ingenuity, its entrepreneurial spirit, private property rights, and functioning capital markets have enabled. There are countries with better geology than the United States, but they have no oil and gas industry since they have issues with rule of law, lack of protection for private property, and poorly functioning capital markets.

The energy industry has evolved so much since the late 1980s. Navigating that ever-changing environment has kept it exciting. I never got bored or felt the urge to go try something new. In fact, as I look back on it, sticking in a single industry has been one of the greatest lessons I learned along the way. Focus and perspective were rewarded.

Understanding that the industry is cyclical was critical. When times got bad, I didn't quit or lose faith in our business plan or investment process. We hung in there, adjusted to where we were in the cycle, and pressed on. Contemporaries who left the industry when it was down, only to return when times got good again, generally missed some of the best investment opportunities. Focus and determination have produced experience and discipline that I've needed to weather the volatility.

Maybe I'm stubborn. Maybe I'm just not a quitter. But, in the end, I made a commitment to our investors and my partners to see it through, so making some dramatic switch was never even a consideration. My goal was always to play the hand I was being dealt as well as possible, but never to fold.

STEVE: *So, as an energy investor, you never felt like you were being pigeonholed into some far-off corner of the economy?*

KEN: No. Energy is everywhere. If we sit down and start talking about energy, even if we don't understand geology or geophysics, we will have a lively and relevant conversation spanning economics, business, politics, and geopolitics. Today, the energy industry is at the epicenter of the climate debate as well. Having command of the facts around supply, demand, and the economics of oil, gas, and competing energy sources has allowed me to be both an effective investor and an advocate for the industry at large.

STEVE: *The third and final topic I'd like to address in this section is wealth. I'm assuming you didn't go to work with Richard Rainwater assuming that you'd make a fortune.*

KEN: No, not at all. I was broke when we got started. When Richard said I could invest $75,000 in the general partner of the first fund, I thought, *How do I get $75,000?* Unlike the young professionals today, I had no idea what the economics of a general partner in a private equity fund could be worth. Fortunately, Gamble cosigned a credit line so I could invest.

I didn't know what "2 and 20" meant. I learned that when I got to work. For the uninitiated, that is shorthand for the basic economics of an investment partnership. The investors pay to the general partner, or the GP, an annual 2 percent management fee, calculated as 2 percent of the investor's capital commitment. This was meant to cover the manager's overhead and administration costs. Then, the general partner would earn an additional 20 percent of the profits after some agreed-on minimum return threshold for the fund is exceeded. Today, it seems like the young executives are taught "2 and 20" in grade school.

At the start, we only had $100 million of equity to invest over a seven-year period. A 2 percent management fee amounted to only two million dollars per year. That amount had to support two offices, our entire staff, and all our annual out-of-pocket expenses.

We were just a group of colleagues trying to make a good return for our investors.

We didn't set out to create a large money management firm. It felt like a family business at the outset. I loved growing up with the private equity industry and playing a small part in that growth. I also enjoyed the challenge of turning a small partnership into a firm, complete with continuity and a lasting corporate culture. That was the evolution, and I discovered I had a knack for it.

STEVE: *Dating back how far? All the way to high school?*

KEN: Probably. As far as I can recall, I never got intimidated by a clean sheet of paper. I could always start with a clean sheet and make things happen. Some people are good with embellishing something that was already started. I guess I have always been comfortable making stuff up as I went along.

STEVE: *When did it become apparent that you were going to be wealthy? Was that important or was it just a measuring stick?*

KEN: At the beginning, we were comfortable, but not making over-the-top salaries. I really enjoyed what I was doing, and I remember being amazed at how I could make such a good living doing something that I didn't consider work. I felt that our real goal was to make our investors the returns we promised we'd strive for. When we sold an investment and got our cut, it just sort of showed up. Don't get me wrong, it felt good to earn a share of the profits that were so hard to come by, but watching this industry made me really humble. I knew that the volatility was real and that it was only a matter of time before any upswing would turn negative. The investment business is humbling that way. I guess Andy Grove, the former CEO of Intel, was right when he said, "Only the paranoid survive."*

My corollary to that quote was rather simple: You don't own oil and gas assets; you rent them.

Becoming wealthy was never part of my constitution. But from an early age, I did know that if I wanted to eat, I would need to earn it. I never forgot the lesson from that day in the Princeton registrar's office. That was the extent of it. I did not have some magical net worth total as my goal.

STEVE: *It sounds like you try to be the same person today that you were when you were trying to make ends meet.*

---

* Andrew S. Grove, *Only the Paranoid Survive: How to Exploit the Crisis Points That Challenge Every Company* (New York: Currency, 1999).

KEN: When I look in the mirror, that is the person I see today. Sure, I have more *things* than I had then, but I do not feel that different as a person. I guess knowing how transient the wealth can be keeps me grounded.

STEVE: *Grounded? Really?*

KEN: I've already told you the story of traveling through Europe with my girlfriend after college and not having enough money to eat in restaurants. Well, after my son Daniel's high school graduation in 2013, he and I went fly-fishing for a week in Slovenia. On our way there, our plane routing left us with a layover night in Paris.

I had never stayed at the George V, one of the fancy Paris hotels I had always heard about, so we splurged for a night. I wanted this trip, as a graduation present, to be special for him. When we arrived, there was an issue with our room, so the hotel offered to comp us a meal in the restaurant while we waited. We went to their lobby restaurant, and Daniel had a burger while I just drank a Diet Coke. We ate our lunch and watched the international glitterati parade through the elegant lobby. We were quite underdressed in our hiking and fishing clothes. I could see my nineteen-year-old son drinking it all in, not sure whether he was disgusted or enamored.

Once our room was ready, the bill came, and we looked at it together. Even though the meal was complimentary, I felt the need to tip the server. He caught a glimpse of the bill as I signed for it. It was eighty-five euros for the burger and a couple of soft drinks. Daniel was outraged. "A hundred and ten dollars for a burger and a couple of Cokes?" he protested, doing the quick exchange-rate math in his head. I was numb to things like that, but it was his first exposure to such excess. Later that night, even though we were tired and had an early flight, he insisted that we go out to find a cheaper place for dinner.

There is a nice symmetry to that story. In the one generation from me to my son, the Hershes went from wanting to eat at, but not being able to afford, the nice Paris places to being able to afford, but refusing to pay the price for, those same restaurants.

I think Daniel is going to do just fine. Thankfully for me, Rachel is even more thrifty!

CHAPTER 6

KEEP YOUR EYE
ON THE PRIZE

STEVE: *In this section and the next, I'd like to talk to you about two particular deals, one a success and one not so successful—in part because they were high profile but, more important, because you have stated that they each helped shape you.*

Let's start with the success. In the mid-1990s, you, Richard Rainwater, and his wife Darla Moore orchestrated the recapitalization of Mesa Petroleum, the prize jewel of legendary Texas oilman T. Boone Pickens.

KEN: Correct. When we entered the Mesa picture in 1995, it was heading either toward bankruptcy or a hostile takeover by David Batchelder, Boone's former lieutenant in the deal business. We recapitalized the balance sheet after infusing capital and arranged a comfortable amount of debt for the company and began what was a very nice turnaround for the stockholders.

STEVE: *Sounds good, but your relationship with Boone Pickens didn't survive the deal.*

KEN: That's also correct. While we did infuse equity into the company, it became apparent that the banking market and bond markets were not going to refinance the remaining debt if Boone was still in control of the company. So as part of the deal, Boone reluctantly agreed to work with us on an orderly transition to new management. I didn't think it would be such a stretch for him at the time. He was sixty-eight when the deal happened and had said publicly that he would retire by his seventieth birthday, so all I needed was that he reaffirm publicly what he had already said in many industry circles about his retirement date. Given the equity infusion that we were leading and the accompanying board seats that we earned with that investment, it was clear that our group would be in the driver's seat in determining the management's succession.

Although I tried really hard to work with him throughout the transaction, he seemed to resent me from the beginning and liked me even less when it was over.

STEVE: *How did it begin?*

KEN: Before the deal even heated up in 1995, Boone and his associates came over to Fort Worth to see Richard as early as 1992. Mesa stock was trading around $7 per share at the time, but they had just suspended the common distributions. Clearly their debt levels were beginning to bite. They wanted to see if Richard would make an equity investment in the company to provide funds to pay off some debt.

I pulled together my valuation of the company for the meeting, being the good number cruncher that I was. Unfortunately for Boone, my numbers valued the company at around $1.50 per share, well below the market price of the day. I had not intended to show Boone and his partners that analysis, preferring to give it just to Richard as briefing materials for his meeting.

Well, that didn't work out so well. Richard ended up referencing it, and I had to come clean with the paperwork. Boone was highly agitated. The meeting was essentially over at that point even though, in true Rainwater fashion, Richard invited the Mesa team to join us all for some cake and ice cream and loud country music in the office to celebrate a colleague's birthday. Richard entertained us all, but Boone was not amused. I later learned that on the ride home he had some choice words to say about me and my numbers.

At twenty-nine, I was so young to be in these types of conversations. I can imagine how brash I must have come across. With more experience, I learned how to soften the blow when delivering a tough message. Richard was always great at defusing situations and making people feel good, even if he had to turn them away. That is something that I both admired and tried to emulate as the years went on.

STEVE: *There's a passage in Pickens's autobiography I want to read to you: "Before I left, the company gave me a farewell dinner at Bob's Steak and Chop House. The Rainwaters and their short-boy Hersh did not receive invitations."* Short-boy?

---

* T. Boone Pickens, *The First Billion Is the Hardest: Reflections on a Life of Comebacks and America's Energy Future* (New York: Three Rivers Press, 2008), 56.

KEN: Well, I'm not the tallest guy in the world, but I didn't think that precluded me from eating at Bob's. In fact, I have had a bunch of great meals there over the years. Other than not being able to get on a few roller coasters when I was young, my height has never seemed to be an issue. I was as stunned as anyone to read that passage. I cannot imagine what it must have been like to be such a bitter person, but I saw that it made him a man who left a trail of broken relationships wherever he went.

While he did have a close-knit inner circle of friends and employees who he took great care of, there were many others who commiserated with me in the ensuing years about working either for or with him. Those he seemed to like were treated like kings and they stayed close to him forever. Those whom he came *not* to like were summarily tossed aside.

I guess the real takeaway is that Pickens was pissed about losing Mesa, and maybe a bit embarrassed about how it happened. He was one of the first executives I met who identified himself and his company as one and the same. If I had been such a high-profile magnate, I might have been pissed or embarrassed also. Who could think of Mesa without simultaneously thinking of Boone? As it turned out, most of Wall Street.

STEVE: *Explain.*

KEN: Mesa's financial situation and Boone's life were both a mess in 1995 when we re-engaged on a potential deal to save the company. Boone was about to lose Mesa to either bankruptcy or a hostile takeover by his former protégé while also personally facing a multimillion-dollar bill from the IRS for back taxes for which he had no cash to settle. It didn't help that he was also going through a high-profile divorce from his second wife, Bea. Looking back, I realize that his entire life was in turmoil, and that was a lot for anyone to deal with. So my opinion about the way Boone treated me at the time has mellowed a bit.

As NGP's lead for the transaction, and because I was also serving as Rainwater's chief investment officer at the time, I was the guy on the ground spearheading the deal. In a sense, I was the face for Boone's workout, and I represented a solution that he did not want to deal with. I sensed that he didn't like dealing with a young, Ivy League, prep school guy, who he thought of as some number cruncher who had no right to be in the oil business. He and I were quite opposite. I was the wet-behind-the-ears city-slicker and he was the geologist/oil man from Holdenville, Oklahoma. I think I knew his company's numbers as well, if not better, than he did. Thus, I earned a clever nickname from him—*wolverine*!

STEVE: *You're referring to the passage in his book that reads, "All too often there's a wolverine in the deal. Wolverines piss on everything they can't eat. Right or wrong, that's how I saw Darla Moore (Richard Rainwater's wife) and Ken Hersh."**

KEN: When I read that, it seemed weird. I think wolverines are kind of cute.

STEVE: *Let's take a closer look. As I understand it, Pickens started the company that would become Mesa in 1956. It went public in 1964. Then, in 1968, he put the company on the map—not with a big oil find but rather with the hostile takeover of Hugoton Production Company, a Kansas-based company with large holdings of natural gas. In the 1960s and early '70s, he coupled that with some exploration successes in the Gulf of Mexico and even in the North Sea. But those exploration successes faded when factored against the dry holes of the ensuing decades. By all accounts, however, the acquisition proved a winner for him, and by the early 1980s he was attempting hostile takeovers of biggies like Gulf Oil, Phillips Petroleum, Unocal, and Cities Service. While none of those were successful, it did build his profile on Wall Street and his stock gains were significant. David Batchelder was his associate at Mesa working on those hostile takeover attempts.*

KEN: Boone was a champion of shareholder rights and made the point at all those companies that the incumbent management teams were not working hard enough to increase shareholder value. Hence, his narrative went, he bid for the stock to reward the shareholders and get control. While the strategy didn't work in the end, in each case the stock prices increased from his purchase price, so he was able to sell out at a nice profit. This rewarded both Boone and the Mesa equity holders, of course.

STEVE: *He was ahead of his time, really. Buried inside this oil and gas company was, what we would call today, a hedge fund. He had a group of young guns working with him, just as Rainwater did. They were called "Boone's Boys," and one of them, David Batchelder, figured prominently in your story.*

KEN: Right. Batchelder left Mesa in 1988, having made a good amount of money. He started an advisory firm that would later become a hedge fund with the strategy of taking big positions in troubled companies to gain control. He accumulated a decent record at doing that.

---

* Pickens, *The First Billion Is the Hardest*, 50.

From the time Batchelder left Mesa through 1995, Boone ran up huge debts inside of Mesa as it acquired oil and gas assets around the country and continued to pay out generous distributions to its equity holders. But paying out hundreds of millions of dollars in distributions without the earnings to back it up, well, that money just left the company exposed to its creditors. He was confident in his strategy since most of the assets he acquired were natural gas reserves, bought in anticipation of an increase in natural gas prices. Sound familiar?

As natural gas prices declined, the company landed on Batchelder's radar as one with good assets, but a balance sheet with too much debt. He first advised industrialist Dennis Washington on the company, and Washington soon purchased a block of stock just under the 5 percent threshold. At the same time, another billionaire investor, Marvin Davis, did the same thing. In the parlance of the day, we would say that the company was "in play."

In early 1995, Batchelder paid Boone a visit and rattled his saber as representing a major shareholder in the company who was not happy with its stock performance. As a concession, Boone and the board agreed to nominate Batchelder and Dorn Parkinson (Washington's chief financial officer) to the board, and at the May 1995 annual meeting, they were elected.

There was a lot going on at the company as it tried to repair its balance sheet. They had been running a quiet auction of their Hugoton properties during the spring and in early June, but the board determined that none of the proposals they received were acceptable (Batchelder and Parkinson agreed). They were instructed by the board to continue to work with their adviser, Lehman Brothers, to broaden the scope and types of transactions that might stave off a potential bankruptcy when the debt matured in June of the following year.

Batchelder suggested that the process include the sale or merger of the company, but he was rebuffed. In late June, Batchelder filed a notice with the SEC announcing that Davis had joined Washington to create WDB Group, which, combined, owned 9.4 percent of the common shares. With that level of ownership clout, he formally asked that the board appoint an independent committee to run the strategic alternatives process and expand the scope to include "any and all options."

In early July, things got testy, and Boone dug in. The company filed suit against WDB Group, alleging securities law violations, and announced a process to be run under the direction of the entire board, not a special committee. The process would include consideration of any types of transactions. The board also approved a poison pill.

That same day, WDB announced that in a 13D filing that they would seek to replace the board via a proxy fight. (Schedule 13D is a form that must be filed with the SEC when a person or group acquires more than 5 percent of a company's common stock.)

In early August, WDB countersued and filed a preliminary proxy statement to replace the board at a time to be determined. After some furious behind-the-scenes "hand-wringing and teeth gnashing" (a clever term used by Garrett Smith, the number-two official in Mesa's finance department), the company made a temporary peace treaty with WDB Group in late September.

That agreement set up the timing for our deal by stipulating that a solution would need to be found by the end of February 1996. If the company did not find a transaction that met certain parameters by the end of February, then WDB Group could nominate a controlling slate of directors at their next annual meeting a couple of months later.

This was all being played out in the press and in SEC reports. It was quite juicy, especially given Boone's profile. It seemed that this group of shareholders was doing to him what he had been doing to other companies that he thought were poorly managed.

From my perspective, it seemed that the company was in a bad position to stay independent, with about a billion dollars of debt due in the middle of 1996 and very little cash flow to pay it off. It also didn't have enough unencumbered assets to secure new loans to refinance that debt. To use a legal term, the company was in a pickle.

For someone with such an imperial personality, this allowed Boone to play the victim card. From his perspective, nobody understood the value of this company and he was smarter than the marketplace. Anyone who was trying to take over was, in his eyes, simply trying to rip him off. Of course, we found out that it took a novel approach to turn the company around because his predicament was beyond his ability to repair it. At the time, the asset value simply was not sufficient to cover his debts.

STEVE: *How did Boone get the company into such a mess?*

KEN: To keep the flow of this narrative going, I suggest we put my answer to this question in this tome's appendix. It is a fascinating story to unravel, but I suggest you nerd out on this at the end. I think it's pretty juicy history, but you may not.

STEVE: *Fair enough. But I promise I'll happily turn to the appendix. What happened next?*

KEN: Boone hired Lehman Brothers to run an auction for the company, or for selected assets, or for investors to infuse equity in the company. They opened a data room with all the materials, and the industry came calling. More than 140 parties came through the data room, many of them multiple times. You see, the assets were pretty good. The issue was that the total debt of the company was more than the value of those assets.

Every proposal to sell assets would still leave the stockholders with some debt but no assets left to support that debt.

At the same time, no one offered to buy the equity of the company because the true equity value was negative. It made sense for Boone and the stockholders to hold out until the last possible moment.

STEVE: *Enter Ken Hersh, NGP, and Richard Rainwater.*

KEN: I'd never met Batchelder and didn't know the backstory of how or why the student was trying to take things over from the teacher. I just saw a puzzle that needed solving.

Just like the rest of the industry, we looked at the assets and tried to value them to find any way to structure something that would make sense for the Mesa equity holders and be palatable for Boone. In the summer of 1995, that was tough because the price was inflated because of all the takeover talk. Speculators would buy the stock simply on the hope that a bunch of competing offers would materialize and drive the share price up.

I remember throwing out the concept of a $100 million equity infusion to the Mesa CFO, Steve Gardner, during the summer of 1995. Not knowing that they needed a minimum of $250 million, according to the peace treaty standstill agreement with WDB Group and given that the valuation I threw out was well below where the stock was trading, my proposals fell on deaf ears. I did my best to explain the math, which he understood, but with time still left on the clock, there was no pressing need for Boone to accept a lowball offer.

Gardner and I had nice, open, and friendly conversations and I found his candor to be refreshing, especially in contrast to the folksy yet false hyperbole of his boss, Boone. He was a great CFO. I'm not sure Boone appreciated how lucky he was to have Steve stick with him as the company's finances deteriorated. He kept his eye on what the company needed but was realistic at every turn. That quality proved to be critical as our relationship progressed. In every transaction, there needs to be some level of trust established between the principals, or else it will fail.

STEVE: *What motivated you to stick with it, even after you were told no?*

KEN: I remained interested because we had this pool of money that was set up to get long natural gas assets. Our investors were paying us a management fee to do deals in the industry, so I wasn't dissuaded. Discouraged, yes; dissuaded, no.

STEVE: *Did Richard help?*

KEN: Absolutely. Each time David Albin and I ran the numbers, we talked ourselves out of even making another proposal. "They'd never do a deal to issue equity at a price *below* the trading value of the shares," we'd argue.

Richard was undeterred. "Think big, Ken!" he'd say. "Somebody's got to." He encouraged us to keep the dialogue with Gardner going just to stay in the mix.

As 1995 wore on, natural gas prices remained flat. No proposal emerged that made sense for Boone to accept. I recall succumbing to Richard's pressure and submitting a proposal in the fall of 1995, albeit at a lower price than we had offered a few months before. I sheepishly called Steve and floated it by him. He took it to Boone, but again the price was too low to interest the eternal optimist—especially with six months to go until the deadline.

Each time we had proposed to inject $100 million to $150 million of equity into the company, but at a lower share price than the trading value, *and* we wanted some control over the company. Boone basically said, "That's ridiculous. They want too much of *my* company." At one point in the fall, even Boone himself came to Fort Worth again to try to talk us up in price. I'm sure Boone felt that he could sweet-talk Richard and me into a price that he'd accept, as was his style. But the numbers didn't lie, no matter how sweet the talk was.

As 1996 began, the speculative premium was eroding from the share price as the market began anticipating a potential bankruptcy and the likely worthlessness of the stock in that case. The February 29 deadline was approaching, *and* the company had a very large amount of debt maturing on June 30. If no deal happened, bankruptcy was a real possibility.

STEVE: *Were you guys the only ones offering an equity infusion lifeline?*

KEN: We didn't know for sure, but the fact that Boone came over to see us personally to follow up a pretty egregious proposal a couple months before did seem to indicate to us that he didn't have many alternatives. It must have really irked Boone to come see us, hat in hand. It wasn't his nature to grovel.

STEVE: *Why didn't he have alternatives?*

KEN: By the mid-1990s, he had burned just about every bridge there was to burn. Folks just wanted to pluck gem assets from his burning building. He didn't seem to have a very strong negotiating position. For example, one of the other alternatives that they had to stay afloat was to sell one of their prize assets—the Satanta gas processing plant in the Kansas Hugoton field. This gas field was the core asset within the company, and the gas plant was essentially the channel that allowed that gas to get to market. Whoever controlled that plant controlled the marketing of the natural gas assets for any company using it, including Mesa. Think of it as the front door of a store, separating your inventory from your customers.

The cash offer they had on the table would have given the company a bit of a lifeline, even though it wouldn't have solved its long-term issues. Nevertheless, for a company playing for time, it would have given Mesa more time to work through its issues or for the natural gas markets to improve. However, in a prior convoluted debt transaction, the company had mortgaged its Hugoton assets against a series of bond issuances. The intricate structure made it a problem for the company to sell the gas plants. It would have violated those bonds' covenants. The company's lawyers tried desperately to find a way to interpret the bond covenants to allow them to sell the gas plant. I learned later that Boone was willing to take a less-than-legal interpretation of the bond indentures, but, in the end, Steve Gardner as CFO and Paul Cain as the COO acted independently and honorably enough to refuse to sign representations that would support that interpretation.

STEVE: *Given all this, you didn't mind being in business with Boone? Weren't you working on a proposal that would have kept his company alive?*

KEN: That's a complicated question. As part of each of our proposals, we stipulated that we would get control of the company. Our $250 million of equity would retire some debt, but we'd need to go to the bank and bond markets to refinance the rest of the debt and push out the maturities well into the future. I had had enough discussions with bankers and bond underwriters to know that they were fed up with Boone as well. There was no way they were going to lend any money to a company that he controlled. The lead banker on the high-yield bond refinancing project made that clear before we even got started. That emboldened me to stay firm in our demands.

STEVE: *So your strategy was simply to wait him out?*

KEN: I guess so. In hindsight it all looks so strategic. In reality, my partners in the fund and I had a fiduciary obligation to do smart deals, so we weren't going to chase it. Since our fund was taking the lead in the deal, with Richard saying he would put in some money and help us raise some from coinvestors, we knew that it had better be compelling to be successful.

Finally, in January 1996, I got the call from Steve Gardner asking us to dust off our proposal from a few months before. It was obvious to me that they were not getting another deal. The share price had declined even further, and the expiration of the standstill agreement or bankruptcy were real possibilities.

We started crafting a proposal. Although our proposals previously were for $250 million, we were asked to increase the number to $265 million so that the company would be able to comply with the terms of the WDB agreement. It started to look like a deal could actually happen. Now, we had to be certain that we could both close on the total refinancing deal and get invested on terms that we loved. Given the shakiness in the natural gas markets at the time, I felt that we could not buy common stock. We were going to have to structure our investment as a convertible preferred stock, because we needed to be higher up the capital structure to get some downside protection in case of liquidation.

The terms of preferred stock carry a liquidation preference that paid off the preferred holders at par before the common stockholders got anything. But at our option, we could make ours convertible into common stock so we could share in the upside if we so desired. Simply stated, at some point in the future, we could elect to either get our money back or convert our preferred stock into common stock and just ride the share price.

I crafted a term sheet with a bunch of blanks in it—which was typically what we did when we wanted to remain in conversation, yet not get pinned down to final terms. I relayed that to Steve but soon I learned that Boone didn't want to deal with me. I guess a thirty-three-year-old kid was beneath his pay grade. He asked to meet Richard. To do that, he would have to go to Tucson, Arizona. Richard wasn't about to alter his plans to see Boone.

At the time, Richard was spending the winter months at Canyon Ranch in Tucson. Canyon Ranch was a famous wellness and medical retreat for the stars that had caught Richard's attention. Richard was a fun hypochondriac, so it made sense that he fell in love with Canyon Ranch. He would live his life, playing golf, working out as well as he could, but maintaining a diet he called "fun"—burgers, fries, barbecue, and Snickers bars interspersed with salads and healthy eating. He was always in a great state of mind when there, happy to hold court in the dining room with whomever was there at the time.

After Steve called to alert me, I called Richard. "Boone is on his way to see you," I said.

Richard was one step ahead. "I know," he replied. "We tee off an hour after he lands." He was taking Boone to his eighteen-hole office.

"What do you want me to emphasize?" he asked. I ran through the key deal points that we needed to make it work. "Got it," he replied confidently. He didn't take a single note, but I knew he had digested the key points and registered them in his encyclopedic mental deal log. I'd been around him long enough to know that he would be just fine without my being there.

I said, "We need control of the board, we need our equity to be preferred, and we need the conversion price to be below today's trading price because the stock today is overvalued."

About two hours later, Richard called me from a tee box in the middle of the round on some course outside Tucson. Apparently, Boone was out of earshot. "I got control and preferred," he reported. "And we have a few more holes to play."

He seemed to be calling both to give me an update and to get an approving "attaboy" from me.

"Great," I said. "See if you can get it convertible, but don't forget that it has to be at a discount to the current share price."

"He'll never go for that," Richard said.

This was the first time I had to nudge to embolden *him*. "Come on, Richard. Think big!" I said. "The share price has run up recently, probably because word has leaked that we are interested in a deal, and the equity isn't worth the current price," I pleaded. "Tell him it has to be convertible at a discount, but we will do a rights offering to all his shareholders who want to participate. That way, if they think it is too sweet of a deal, we will let them participate in it."

I had winged it on the fly with the concept of a rights offering, but gave Richard his talking points on how that would make the deal more palatable. He went back to the tee box, and I waited anxiously.

He called back an hour or so later. "Got your convertible, *and* he agreed to make it redeemable." Richard had added *that* additional feature on his own. Giving the preferred stock an actual redemption date would serve to lower our risk even further.

In the scheme of things, that provision was not a huge give up for the company, but it did change our risk-reward ratio quite a bit. Without knowing it, Richard had secured the racing stripe for this deal!

I called Steve to report on the conversation, and we agreed to get together to hammer out the term sheet. I then called David Albin to get his help in thinking through the nuances of what just happened. "Holy shit, David," I gasped. "I think we just struck a deal to bail out Boone."

STEVE: *And had you?*

KEN: Not quite. We still had to negotiate the fine points of the agreement and then get it in a shape to present to their board. And we had to do it all by the end of February.

I called our legal team from Thompson & Knight. Dick Covington and Jeff Zlotky were the two people I came to rely on to get the details worked out. I recall a marathon negotiating session where we had the term sheet and worked to transform it into a preferred stock purchase agreement. The group hammering it out was small and cordial. From the Mesa side, Steve Gardner was put in charge along with Bobby Stillwell, Steve Massad, and Carlos Fierro from Baker Botts, the law firm representing Mesa.

During the meeting, we held our ground on the major terms, but found a way to get the Mesa team what they needed—an equity infusion of at least $265 million to satisfy the condition of the standstill agreement. I knew there were some key elements of the deal that needed to be included to clear the refinancing market. In addition to the dollars involved, I insisted that this class of preferred stockholders be able to elect a majority of the board.

STEVE: *Were you a tough negotiator?*

KEN: I knew that time was on our side, and we didn't *have* to do a deal. However, they did. So we were able to insist on things with the very credible threat of walking away.

The unique feature of this transaction was what was called a rights offering, to allow existing stockholders to have the "right" to participate on our exact same terms for up to just under half of the entire $265 million. This is an old structure that was used in the buyout business in the 1980s but had not been applied to the oil and gas industry. I had read about the deal structure but had never really seen it in action. This relative ignorance turned out to be an advantage, because I was able to concoct some aspects of the rights offering that were unusual, but I wasn't constrained by any "that's not the way these things work" complaint.

I made sure that the rights offering only allowed for existing stockholders to subscribe for $132 million of the $265 million offering so that we'd be able to control the entire class by holding over 50 percent of the preferred shares. This meant that with an investment of $133 million, we could vote the entire class of shares. And if the preferred stockholder class exercised control of the company, essentially that meant our $133 million investment would be able to control the entire multibillion-dollar enterprise.

The company had to be sure that $265 million would show up at closing to satisfy the terms of the standstill agreement and provide enough equity to support the debt refinancing. What if the shareholders didn't subscribe to the full amount of the rights?

The Mesa team needed assurances, and it was about to derail the progress we were making in the meeting.

I stuck out my chest and said that *we* would backstop the entire issue and take up any of the preferred units not taken up by the public. I remember Covington and Zlotky looking at me with that "What the hell are you doing?" look on their faces.

They knew the rub. Our NGP funds were too small to provide the backstop on the $132 million, and Richard was not keen on providing that backstop personally. Luckily, I was able to convince Richard that he should sign a credit line providing the financial backstop, but I had to assure him that it would not be called.

My chest was way out there now. For a little guy, I was pretty puffed up!

Now, I needed to be 100 percent certain that the stockholders would take up their portion.

STEVE: *That doesn't sound easy.*

KEN: It took some imagination. I dreamed up a concept that I called oversubscription privileges. We added a provision that allowed all the shareholders to get both the right to put up their share of the $132 million and their pro rata share of any piece of the $132 million *not* taken up by the other public shareholders. They had the chance to "oversubscribe" and have the option to take more of the deal than their share on day one.

STEVE: *I'm delighted to say that I am following you—and engrossed.*

KEN: I may be biased, but these transactions *are* interesting, even if you do sometimes need an appendix. Just nerd out with me for a minute and you may be surprised.

STEVE: *I'm a nerd. Go on.*

KEN: This oversubscription feature had a simple result. The sweeter the terms of the deal, the more desirable the "right" to participate in the financing would be, given that a single shareholder could get more than his or her pro rata share by exercising these oversubscription privileges. In short, the option to buy more stock had value. I understood the option value I was creating. This feature pretty much ensured that anyone buying the shares after the deal got announced was intent on exercising the option and taking any extra unexercised shares available, thereby eliminating the risk that we would be stuck having to fill the backstop.

STEVE: *What was Boone's reaction?*

KEN: Honestly, I'm not really sure. It was clear that there were no other proposals from which to choose, other than the problematic sale of the Satanta gas plant, and the Lehman Brothers team advising the company had to render an opinion that our deal would be good for the shareholders. There was a board meeting called once it was clear that we had a draft document in a form acceptable to both of us. I suspect Boone knew that the deadline to agree to something was imminent, but he still had time to accept our deal and try to break it up somehow later. With Boone, it was never over until it was over.

I remember the board meeting vividly. It was held February 27, 1996, two days before the standstill agreement expired. We had done everything we were supposed to do, other than show up for the meeting. But I didn't know where Richard was because at that time of year, he traveled back and forth between Canyon Ranch in Arizona and his house in Montecito, California. I called him to make the point that we should be at the meeting to present why our deal would be beneficial and suck up to Boone and the board a bit. I knew this was a tough pill to swallow and the Lehman team would be there to advise the company. He said I should go by myself, and he would call in.

I knew enough to never go into a meeting empty-handed, so almost as an afterthought, I made up two pages of bullet points on why the deal was worthwhile. I titled the deal "Project Halo." I wrote that our equity infusion and board control provision would give the public stockholders confidence in the future, based on our track record, and that we would be able to put the company in a position to play offense instead of being paralyzed by too much debt in its current form. I typed it up and made a bunch of copies, and off I went.

Exhibit 2 is that PowerPoint afterthought that hangs on my office wall today as a shrine to what can be done in five minutes.

PROJECT HALO

Financing Proposal
February 27, 1996

PROJECT HALO

THE PHILOSOPHY:
Value Creation in the Exploration and Production Business is the Result of:
- Transaction Capabilities
- Superior Re-investment Opportunities
- Maintenance of Credibility in the Financial Markets
- Maintenance of Financial Flexibility
- Low Operating and Administrative Costs

PROJECT HALO

THE FUTURE:

Ends

- Restore Transaction Mentality
- Restore Credibility in the Financial Markets
- Restore Financial Flexibility

Means

- Rainwater-led Financing
- Commitment to Rainwater "Transactionalist" Philosophy & Activities
- Additional Management Talent

Exhibit 2: Slides presented to the Mesa board of directors, February 27, 1996

Prior to my entering the room, the Lehman team took the board through the alternative of selling the gas plant, even though it was questionable from a legal compliance point of view. At the board meeting, Boone was impressive. He deferred to the team from Lehman Brothers, who then walked the board through the terms of our deal. They had big binders of books with the iconic green Lehman Brothers covers. The books detailed the entire process they had undertaken back to the opening of the data room some nine months prior. There were no other proposals, other than the problematic gas plant deal, that did anything other than wipe out the current stockholders. Ours was the only thing even remotely palatable.

The two WDB Group representatives sat there expressionless. They objected because they felt that the deal terms were too generous for our group. Boone coldly peered at Batchelder's colleague Joel Reed and Dorn Parkinson, Batchelder's men who were then on the board. Without missing a beat, he baited them with his deadpan monotone Oklahoma drawl: "We will now entertain a competing proposal from Joel Reed."

The room fell silent. Joel had no proposal. You could hear a pin drop. Boone then calmly called for a vote, and it passed with two dissents.

STEVE: *So, was that it?*

KEN: That was the green light we needed to move forward, but the story was far from over. It was clear that Boone only accepted our deal because he had to. We had to get busy. Working backward from the June 30 deadline when the company's debt would mature, we knew we had to do our own due diligence while simultaneously arranging a big bank facility and then hit the road to get a new public bond offering done. To make it more interesting, I knew that the whole thing would be of interest to the business press since Boone was such a controversial figure. The story line was irresistible: *Takeover tycoon needs to get bailed out himself.* The famed investment banker and former secretary of commerce Wilbur Ross even referred to it as a "bloodless palace coup."[*]

The next month was a whirlwind. Dick and Jeff worked on the legal due diligence and my associates Billy Quinn and Bruce Selkirk worked with me on the numbers. We had to learn everything we could about the company, knowing that the lenders would be willing to refinance the debt only if they felt that the company would be solvent and able to survive.

STEVE: *How did you come up with your numbers? In his autobiography, Boone makes it sound like you were the most obnoxious number cruncher, going so far as to tell them that the contracts for plants in the office were wasteful.*

KEN: Simply put, I wanted to position the company as the "New Mesa." That meant we needed to do some things better and also send signals to the public markets that the extravagant, imperial ways of the prior management would change. In dealing with the public markets, sometimes symbolic things mean a lot.

When we began our due diligence investigation, I really tried my best to honor Boone as the CEO of the company and work with his team to get the deal closed. At the outset, I honestly believed that he wanted to help save the company and do whatever it took to stave off liquidation. Our deal was the only hope at that moment. Steve Gardner and his team were terrific. They understood the big picture. The public markets had also responded well. Given the good reputation of Rainwater and NGP and with confidence that the company would no longer go bankrupt, the share price went up as soon as the deal was announced. It was only later that I learned how Boone was trying to undermine us from the very start.

We were cranking. Not only were we asking all the questions we could to understand the business, but we were also crafting the story of the New Mesa. I knew that we would have to make the case to the banks that our oversight was going to add fiscal discipline, so they would have confidence that the partnership would be creditworthy.

I reminded Boone that gas prices had fallen by half, and that the responsible thing to do was review all the company's expenses. We had to do something to show the bondholders and the banks that this was a new day. I pointed out that the company had three airplanes at a time in the commodity cycle when many in the energy industry

---

[*] Allen R. Myerson, "Pickens Plans to Step Down as Mesa Chief," *New York Times*, June 13, 1996, https://www.nytimes.com/1996/06/13/business/pickens-plans-to-step-down-as-mesa-chief.html.

were finally becoming cost-conscious and shedding the symbols of past arrogance—corporate jets in particular.

He was adamant that the planes were justified because company executives traveled to the obscure places where they operated oil and gas fields. I said, "Boone, you can charter a plane anytime you want for less money than it costs for you to keep the fleet. Let's sell them."

"Ken, you don't understand. Those planes pay for themselves," he emphasized, treating me as a schoolkid at the knee of a learned professor.

"I get that," I said, as the old high school debater came out in me. "But you have mechanics, pilots, hangars, insurance, operating costs, and depreciation. By selling the planes and chartering whenever you want, you can still fly privately, but you'll have $15 million from the planes we can use to repay some debt and send the right signals to the marketplace."

He would have none of it. He was living in la-la land. There were costs to cut all over the place that wouldn't affect operations one bit. The planes were obvious. I noticed other excesses as well and wasn't shy about pointing them out. We categorized them all. On the long list was the contract to pay some company $30,000 per year for care of the office plants. Somehow, he zeroed in on that one. All I was trying to do was reduce costs without laying people off and hurting operations. I was trying to create a path to get this sick company back to solvency. Part of that challenge was to arrange a new bank facility to anchor the new balance sheet. Bankers were keenly focused on their borrower's cost structure. Boone did not like that one bit.

Darla Moore, Richard's wife, proved to be a valuable ally in putting together the strategy for selecting our lead banker. She was a smart, ex-commercial banker, experienced in financing troubled companies. A South Carolinian turned New Yorker, Darla had a smooth, deep Southern accent that belied her steely resolve in dealing with companies who needed money, fast. Her words were piercingly precise and were known to send shivers through those across the negotiating table.

Our $265 million investment was going to be helpful, but it wouldn't be enough to get the company out of the woods. We needed a new large, syndicated bank facility, but we didn't know if *any* bank would lend us money. However, Darla and I understood that banks that had investment banking operations would be attracted to the junk bonds we were planning to issue as part of the deal. So, to get the bond underwriting business, we insisted that they make the senior loan to the deal.

The strategy worked. We had several banks competing for our business, offering us ever lower interest rates and easier covenants to win the junk bond underwriting business. We crafted good terms and selected Chase Bank as our lender and bond underwriter. We were off to the races.

Over the next two months, we completed our diligence, settled on a long-range corporate plan, and helped Chase syndicate the senior bank loan. We also drafted the SEC filings for the two public subordinated debt offerings that would be issued.

STEVE: *You had a lot of parties who had to sign on.*

KEN: For sure. This deal was complicated. We needed the stockholders to approve the issuance of the new preferred stock. We needed the SEC to approve the preferred stock offering terms since the public holders were getting the right to buy into it as well. We also needed the SEC to approve the bond prospectuses. And we had to get it all done in time for an investor road show to be completed so we could close prior to June 30.

Oh, and we had to line up the $133 million for our preferred stock investment and find a way to guarantee the other $132 million in case the public shareholders didn't exercise their rights. We were pretty sure that they'd be exercised, but the banks needed a hard guarantee in case the bottom fell out. This required us to find partners. The NGP fund had $30 million available to put in the deal, and Richard was nervous about doing more than $75 million. We were lucky that Richard had a few friends to call, but I needed to assure him that we were confident the $132 million would not have to be put up in any event.

There were some nervous moments as we assembled our equity group. Thankfully, with the help of legendary investor Ray Chambers, we closed the gap. We traveled to Richard and Darla's Montecito house to convene a final meeting of the group. I think holding an investor meeting in a gorgeous mansion overlooking the hills of Montecito made it a bit easier. Kind of hard to ask tough questions while sipping Pierre Lafond coffee.

Luckily, I took Phil Smith with us, and he was able to put his engineering degree to good use. He was a valued CEO and friend who, by that time, had led a couple of successful NGP ventures and had a lot of credibility. As a favor to me, I asked him to review the oil and gas reserve estimates of the company. I also enticed him to coinvest in the deal and be one of our board sitters after the fact. He explained the quality of the company's reserve report and where the risks were and how we should think about it. It was reassuring to be able to tap the network that NGP had established. It all came to bear on this transaction. In the end, we were selling confidence—confidence that we could manage the business effectively.

The meeting went well. Once again, I relied on a big, fat white notebook full of analysis. This time, though, I had enough to go around, and we reviewed almost every page. I was proud of the team and how well we knew the assets and operation of the company. It was not an obvious decision, but we crafted a good investment that managed the risk well. In the end, I didn't view our job as one of investing capital, but rather managing risk. If we protected our downside while positioning ourselves to participate in the upside, then everything would work out. We concentrated on the asset quality on which to build a new future for the company. Despite all the corporate shenanigans over the years, Boone had assembled quality assets and a decent team to operate them.

There was just one problem: Boone himself.

STEVE: *How so at this stage?*

KEN: Our terms included that we would control the board through our executive committee provisions, but Boone was still slated to be the company's CEO. As the filing deadline neared, we were stuck. Somehow, we needed Boone to agree to step down without taking the company down with him out of spite.

It was apparent from all our conversations with the bankers and bondholders alike that we needed to articulate an exit strategy for Boone if we wanted all the deals to get done.

In late May of 1996, amid the pressure to give birth to a new Mesa, I had to take a break to rush Julie to the hospital to give a different kind of birth. On May 24, our daughter Rachel was born, just two days after Boone's sixty-eighth birthday.

In the hospital, while basking in the joy of our second child's birth, I had what I thought was a brilliant idea: Since Boone had publicly stated that he was looking forward to retiring at the age of seventy, why not couch the new deal as the beginning of the "transition period" toward new management? We would make Boone a partner in the transition to which he had already committed publicly. The bankers agreed that this would fly.

I figured this would be an elegant solution. Boone could run the company, subject to the oversight of the executive committee, while he assisted us in finding a new CEO. I thought making him part of the transition while giving him a graceful exit would satisfy him.

The next week at the drafting session, we added a simple paragraph that our investor group, identified in the documents as the DNR group (conveniently standing for "Darla and Richard" as well as "Daniel and Rachel"),

> intends to implement an orderly transition and succession plan for Mesa's senior management. Such plans are being developed. In this regard, DNR has requested that Boone Pickens, the Chairman of the Board and the Chief Executive Officer of Mesa, assist DNR in identifying and retaining a new Chief

Executive Officer and then resign when such person is retained. Mr. Pickens, who will remain on the Board of Directors following the Recapitalization, has agreed to assist with this transition.

I thought it was pretty clever. The underwriters were happy. I didn't have to change Boone's previously announced retirement plan and we could begin to oversee the process. We submitted the text in an amendment to the SEC filings.

STEVE: *So Boone must've been happy. He got what he wanted and was able to stay true to what he had proposed as his timeline to retirement.*

KEN: You would've thought so. But no. His pride was apparently bruised by someone dictating the terms of his exit. Either that or he had no intention of following through with his public promise. Even though I was simply putting down on paper what he had said publicly, he balked when he saw the sentence.

STEVE: *Balked?*

KEN: Actually, he went batshit crazy. He called Steve Gardner and asked for an explanation. Steve held his ground and confirmed that the underwriters and bankers told us all that the deal would not clear the market unless Boone's exit was assured. In fact, the twenty-two months until his seventieth birthday was a negotiation in and of itself. I actually thought I had found an elegant way to help Boone. The Chase bankers were consistent and firm. They would have wanted him to leave sooner than that, but we were all trying to accommodate the ego of the man who had become synonymous with the company.

He would have none of it. Once again, he fired up the jet and called his lawyer Bobby Stillwell to accompany him to Montecito, where he would complain directly to Richard and Darla. Steve alerted me that Boone was on his way to go see Richard, intent on making his case.

I quickly called Darla and walked her through the latest development. She and Richard agreed with us and seemed somewhat annoyed that Boone needed to go see them personally to hear the same message again. But that was the state of play at the end of May 1996, some thirty days before the company was set to blow up.

Boone and Bobby showed up, and they pressed their case. Richard listened patiently to Boone's story of his adept management and how some wet-behind-the-ears young private equity guy wasn't going to push him out. Richard tried to be kind, reminding him that all we were saying was consistent with his stated retirement timeline. Finally,

Darla interjected in her direct Southern style, "Listen, Boone. You have to go. Hon, you're just not financeable. You cannot be anywhere near the road show."

That hit him hard, but he had no choice. In a huff, he reacted. He said that he was not going to have Ken Hersh run around and tell everyone that he was leaving. He wanted to tell his own story.

"Fine," Darla said. "We'll delay the road show a few days and let you go tell your story."

Boone and Bobby turned the jet around and flew back to Dallas, spending more of the money that the company didn't have. Along the way, Boone devised his swan song public relations strategy.

This worked out perfectly. Boone announced that he would begin his retirement plan with this transaction and invited all the local press for interviews. He recounted stories of the company's founding and relayed all the folksy lessons learned from his trials and tribulations along the way. The stories were nice retrospectives that were carefully curated by the local business reporters with whom he had a long relationship. He got what he wanted: to hold court with an adoring audience.

We got what we wanted. Upon this news of his retirement, the stock price shot up some more and our deal was even more in the money. We kicked off our road show the next week with the wind at our back. While I don't know what was going through his mind at the time, I think Boone believed that the announcement of his leaving the company would have made our deal impossible to sell, thereby killing it. In fact, the opposite was true. At just about every stop, the bond buyers we met started the meeting by thanking us for fixing the company and finding a way for the company to exist without Pickens. It was clear that the bankers' messages regarding his role in the company were not off-base.

Steve and I made a good team on the road show. We had developed a really good relationship and had become pretty good friends. He knew the company and the quality of its assets, while I represented the new capital and the control group that would be helping shape the future of the company. Plus, I had every intention of honoring Boone and taking our time after the closing to find a new CEO who would be agreeable to everyone.

Unfortunately, even though Boone publicly supported the transaction, he actively worked behind the scenes to undermine the deal all the way through the end of June. Had it not been for the honest efforts of Steve, Garrett Smith, and their Baker Botts lawyer, Carlos Fierro, who oversaw the documentation, I'm not sure the deal would have closed.

Boone was in blatant violation of the contract he had signed just a few months before. There was a clause in the signed agreements legally representing that the Mesa leadership was committed to the transaction and that they would stop shopping for a better deal. It didn't take much of an ear to the ground for me to learn that Boone and his advisers were actively making calls trying to scare up a better deal. Even once the bonds were priced, he tried to find a way to wriggle out by trying to scare up a competing proposal that would have him keep his job. But the die was cast. The bonds priced at the end of June. The bank credit agreement was signed, and our deal was inked.

STEVE: *That seems odd. Your deal was saving the company and if it had been unwound, the company would've just gone bankrupt, right?*

KEN: Exactly. I was amazed at his hubris. He had an obvious choice. On one hand, he could have watched the company fail and have everyone lose their jobs rather than let someone like us somehow wrestle the company from him. Or, in the alternative, he could admit that this deal was the best way for him to deliver the company to quality hands *and* preserve the jobs of the employees he had assembled while saving face. I couldn't understand his behavior once our deal was finally signed. This was not a hostile deal. He voted for our deal. In fact, our entire group was formed to stave off a hostile approach from his former partner. How ironic was that?

STEVE: *So how did you keep it on track?*

KEN: I have to admit, I almost let emotion get the better of me. Upon learning of Boone's efforts to subvert the deal while we were out selling the bonds for the new Mesa, I would have walked had Steve Gardner not talked me off the ledge.

Plus, every time I bitched to Richard about Boone's behavior, Richard would say, "You should thank Boone. If he were a good guy, we wouldn't have this opportunity. You need to thank him for being a jerk that nobody will touch."

That logic was so perverse that it was compelling.

"Keep your eye on the prize," he maintained.

That helped me stay focused on getting the deal done. Plus, there was a weird quirk to the deal that made it even more desirable as it got closer to the deadline.

STEVE: *What was that?*

KEN: Remember the "oversubscription privileges" concept? Well, what I had inserted as a way to ensure that we didn't have to put up all the money actually worked to seal the deal.

STEVE: *How?*

KEN: In the drafting sessions, the team worked out the plan that let those who wanted the option to take up the extra rights to buy them. It involved creating a three-week trading period after closing, when the rights separated from the common stock, and each right traded on the stock exchange separately from the common stock of the company. This gave people who wanted to exercise their rights the chance to buy all they wanted.

Then, after that trading period, holders would be allowed to exercise these rights to buy the convertible preferred stock and any amounts that weren't subscribed. It also allowed those who didn't want to put up more money to sell their right to those that did. The $132 million rights thus ended up in the hands of investors who were intent on exercising the option, thereby eliminating the need for us to fund under our backstop.

This aspect of the deal, combined with the fact that our fixed conversion price of $2.26 per share was now *below* the trading value of the shares, made the entire package incredibly valuable. Imagine having the chance to buy a stock at $2.26 that was trading at $4.00. It was profitable on day one to exercise the option at $2.26, buy the stock, and if someone wanted to, sell it immediately for $4.00 and net the $1.74 per share profit, or a gain of some 77 percent.

This feature created the dynamic where investors who bought the shares prior to the deal's closing would be intent on supporting the deal so they'd later get those valuable rights to exercise an "in the money" option. By the time we got to the shareholder meeting, the share price was about twice the value of our negotiated price. We had a double on our investment, and it hadn't even closed yet. None of these shareholders were going to vote against the deal. The structure made closing a fait accompli.

STEVE: *So how did it end?*

KEN: The only step remaining at that point in June 1996 was the stockholder meeting where the stockholders would need to affirmatively approve the entire transaction. Given the dynamic, there was no way the vote was going to fail.

For me, the meeting was kind of surreal. Normally, these shareholder meetings are pretty perfunctory matters. Votes are tallied by the brokers well in advance, and the script is laid out ahead of time. This one was no different, though the substance of the meeting was quite something.

We drove downtown to the Fairmont Hotel in Dallas on June 25, 1996, a few minutes before the stated time of the meeting. The hotel is a beautiful business hotel on the edge of downtown. The elegant lobby seemed more appropriate for a major fundraising gala than a mundane corporate shareholder meeting. But Texans build elegant buildings for just about any reason.

A decent crowd had gathered. There were probably a hundred people there, comprising a few shareholders, a good number of company employees, a lot of press, and then Richard and members from my team and the teams of lawyers, bankers, and accountants that had been working on this deal for the past six months. There was an anticipatory mood in the air, like standing at the end of an airport runway watching planes take off. This was Boone's official send-off. Everyone expected to watch a smooth outcome, but we all knew that with Boone involved, anything was possible.

I reflected for a minute as Richard and I entered the ballroom with our team. This was the place where the final curtain would come down on the corporate career of one of the original corporate raiders in America. His longtime shtick was being the good ol' boy from Amarillo who could waltz into fancy corporate boardrooms and tell those establishment moguls a thing or two about how to operate for the good of the shareholders.

Now, after an arduous ordeal, he was about to cede control of his company, which, prior to the deal, was on the precipice of collapse. This ending was being written in a windowless hotel ballroom in Dallas, Texas. Probably not the Broadway ending he would have written.

I knew it was going to be painful for him, so I just lay back and didn't interact with too many folks there. It was his show. The officers of the company and the lawyers knew the drill and how to conduct a meeting. Boone presided. He called the meeting to order and announced that the only piece of business that was properly entered into the agenda was the consideration of the recapitalization transaction and all the component parts.

He ran through the formalities and then called on the secretary of the meeting to call for the votes. Boone then made some forced, unenthusiastic remarks about the future of the company and how he was looking forward to working with Richard Rainwater and his group. He then opened the floor for questions or comments. People looked around.

One gentleman in the audience raised his hand. I later learned that this was some gadfly who had been put up to cause a bit of a stir at the meeting.

Boone calmly called on him, and the man stood up and began to critique the entire deal. He recounted that the conversion price on our preferred stock was too low. He cited the stock price that morning, which of course had already priced in the fact that the deal was going to close. He made the points that the dilution was too great for the shareholders and the company could have made a better deal.

Normally, a speech like this would have been given by Boone. Many of the criticisms sounded like they were lifted from Boone's prior speeches. But this time, they fell flat. The critique ended. Boone looked at him stoically. Then, he scanned the room and asked, "Anyone else got anything?" It was that same voice that had called on Joel Reed to offer some nonexistent competing proposal back in the late February board meeting.

There was silence. With a glance, he had closed the polls.

"The motions have carried. This meeting is adjourned," he muttered as he stepped off the podium.

Again, there was an eerie silence.

As the people got up from their chairs, the crowd began to assemble in smaller groups, some around Boone, most around Richard. I stood by Steve Gardner as we watched the luminaries absorb the attention. I caught Richard's eye as he was asked a question about the company. I usually stayed within earshot since I knew a lot more about the company than he did and didn't want him to get out over his skis in answering. He motioned for me to join the collection around him.

I had an immediate flashback to Stanford's Memorial Auditorium some eight years earlier, where he picked me out of a group of onlookers after the panel discussion at his business school reunion. What a stretch of time this had been. This time, he deflected the attention from himself on to me. He told the gaggle of folks that he had just followed my lead on the deal and let me decide how to do it. He said that he just played my cheerleader. Typical Richard.

There was some truth in his statement. He always cheered me and David on. He never told us what to do, but he had a way of making it safe for us to say, "What if?" This allowed us to think big and, sometimes in my case, just to make things up on the fly.

I migrated into Richard's circle and answered a few basic questions before the group dissipated. As we broke, I glanced over at Steve, who was finishing up with the few folks who had finally surrounded him after the meeting. Someone asked him, "Do you think Ken Hersh will be the next CEO of Mesa?" He glanced at me out of the corner of his eye with a wry grin, winked, and replied, "I don't think so. He's already got a job."

I glanced back with a smile. My associates and I prepared to head back to the office.

STEVE: *And that was that?*

KEN: Yep. Over the next three weeks, the rights detached from the units as planned. They traded independently into the hands of those who wanted them. Then, we funded our $133 million piece of the preferred stock, and the public holders exercised their rights and took up the full $132 million amount offered to them. All the bonds and credit facilities closed, and the company was no longer headed for bankruptcy. Our group had assumed control of the board. In that capacity, we had one more thing to do—plan our management transition away from Boone.

I knew we needed an industry veteran with a record of success. Richard had asked me who might be the best person to take over from Boone to run the company. I had one name on the list—Jon Brumley.

Jon, a longtime friend of Richard's, was a legendary Fort Worth independent oil and gas executive who'd had a phenomenal career in managing companies. I was not close to him, though I had met him casually before. As luck would have it, he had just turned over the CEO reins at his second company a few months prior to the conclusion of this transaction and had planned to set up shop with his son to start a new company. While I really wanted to approach him, I figured it would be nearly impossible to entice him to take on a turnaround situation this late in his career.

"Let's go get him," Richard said.

I agreed to make the contact, although with resignation that it would be a fruitless exercise.

We called on him together, and I started talking about the value of the company and how it was poised to go up. Then Richard put the hard sell on him: "You'll never get to sit on top of a gas asset like this again in your life, Jon. You've got to do it!" I guess the way to appeal to an oil and gas guy is to give him control over a mountain of oil and gas assets.

Jon said he would consider it if he could bring his son Jonny into the company as well and if we understood that he'd only take this post for a limited time to get the company stabilized. We said yes to both. We wanted to reach an agreement with him before the first post-closing board meeting in late August, so we agreed to meet prior to that board meeting.

On the morning before the August 23 board meeting, the three of us met for breakfast at the Four Seasons Hotel in Irving, about a mile away from Mesa's office. Jon had a list of requests that he would need to accept the job. He asked for a bump to the compensation and equity options package we had suggested on the phone and a different title for Jonny's position. He also requested that his wife, Becky, be allowed to accompany him on all business trips he took that required an overnight stay. He also wanted assurances that he could fly first-class. Richard and I glanced at each other at the breakfast table and quickly agreed to everything without hesitation.

Jon laughed, "Heck, I should've asked for more."

Probably so, I thought.

We had a deal. Jon shook Richard's hand. I think I hugged him. We immediately drove over to Mesa's office on the fourteenth floor of Williams Tower in Irving's Las Colinas development. The board meeting was just convening.

Richard and I entered the boardroom just ahead of Jon. We had not told anyone what we were about to do. When Jon entered, I caught a glimpse of Steve Gardner, who smiled with anticipation. Boone's lawyer and confidante Bobby Stillwell gave a curious wince. Boone forced a wry grimace. He knew.

We walked Jon around the room. He was truly a legend to most in attendance and a friend to many. As his reputation was beyond reproach, civility demanded he be welcomed.

"We would like to call a vote," Richard said.

The meeting began. Jon was installed as CEO and appointed as one of our group's designated board members. Boone was asked to remain on the board.

Within thirty minutes, Richard and Jon were three blocks away at a local studio doing a live CNBC breaking-news segment announcing our new CEO. I stayed behind with the rest of the board, and we made small talk until the segment appeared on the TV in the boardroom.

We watched it quietly. I can only imagine how it felt to Boone—kind of like watching his own funeral being broadcast while he was still alive. Beneath the shot of the jovial Richard and affable Jon was a running scroll of the Mesa stock price. After the announcement, it headed up immediately. The paper gains we had on our investment of just a month ago took another 30 percent leap. I'm not sure how I would've felt if my company's stock went up significantly the day I got the boot. But on this day, we were all stockholders, and the company was getting a fresh start. And let's not forget Boone's stock was now worth a whole lot more as well.

The board meeting concluded without fanfare, and we all went about our business. Thankfully, the senior officers at Mesa were good lieutenants and went back to work now knowing the new chain of command. Jon and Jonny quickly assumed their roles and took offices on the executive floor.

Some days later, Boone emerged with a document claiming that the company owed him a $6 million severance payment that was part of some deferred compensation scheme he had awarded himself years before. The document was valid, although it was totally an insider deal since he was both the controlling officer and the recipient. I was livid, given that the company was now counting every penny and this document had not been shown before. I quickly complained to Richard.

Richard remained calm; he just wanted this chapter to end. "I have an idea!" Richard exclaimed. "Let's give him the bigger of the airplanes. He was always saying it was worth $10 million or more."

"That's brilliant," I replied, since we had not yet sold the planes that he was so enamored with. "He will get *more* than the $6 million he is owed, and the company will get to divest of one of the planes. It's a win-win." I couldn't wait to deliver the news to Boone. I knew he loved his airplane, and he kept insisting it was worth a whole lot more than $6 million.

"Boone?" I called, reaching him after a few tries following the fateful board meeting. "I have a resolution for your severance deal." I put on my best Monty Hall *Let's Make a Deal* voice and said, "Why don't you take the $10 million Falcon plane in lieu of the cash? You will come out way ahead, and you will get your favorite plane to boot."

There was silence on the other end of the phone.

Then, he replied, "That's a bad deal for me, son. Don't you know how expensive those things are, with the pilots, hangars, mechanics, and all?"

"I thought you said that they paid for themselves," I retorted, returning to my high school debate roots, trying to show the judges that I caught my opponent in a cross-examination trap.

"That's cute," he said in that same monotone voice that targeted Joel Reed and the gadfly at the shareholder meeting. "I'll take the cash I'm owed." He hung up.

Upon hearing that exchange, Richard determined it would be better to pay him the cash and let him go on his way. I lost the battle but won the war.

STEVE: *And to think you could pull this off despite being a "short boy." Someone who, as Boone later wrote, was too short to be a CEO.*

KEN: How petty was that? Jon Brumley, by the way, was over six feet tall, thereby removing another pointless Boone objection. More importantly, Jon and his leadership of the company were just what the doctor ordered. He restored a healthy culture and got Mesa back to thinking about operating as a growing oil and gas enterprise. He got costs under control. He made some strategic acquisitions and divestitures. And he kept the team together. I knew I wasn't the seasoned operator that he was. I learned a lot from him during that time, and it was a real honor to sit on his board of directors.

Of course, I'm just being sarcastic. Height has nothing to do with anything. But calling it out sure does. I remain clueless about Boone's motivations. But I sure was clear on mine.

Less than a year later, I encouraged another height-challenged friend, Scott Sheffield, to merge with Mesa and move from Midland to the Dallas area and lead the combined company. Scott's company, Parker & Parsley, comprised virtually all crude oil reserves, while Mesa's assets were predominantly natural gas.

Together, the combined company would have one of the largest, most balanced portfolios of oil and gas properties amid the independent oil and gas sector in the nation. It would have a formidable reserve profile, balance sheet, and management team, led by Scott, a savvy leader with a phenomenal track record. I knew the company would be in great hands. This would also be a nice exit opportunity for the Brumleys.

The strategic combination made a lot of sense. In 1997, I helped negotiate that transaction which, when combined, created Pioneer Natural Resources, one of today's largest and most successful independent oil and gas companies.

STEVE: *A happy ending?*

KEN: Looking back on it, absolutely! And for everyone involved. Boone was reborn. It gave him the perfect time to resign from the board and finally sell his stock, which had rebounded dramatically from its near bankrupt position in 1996. The big gain enabled him to cover his IRS debt, to settle his second divorce, and to have enough left over to set up the commodities trading business he always wanted. He went on to experience some wild ups and downs in the trading business, but he landed on his feet. He ended up well, having made hundreds of millions of dollars that funded some impactful philanthropy in our region. He had a good twenty-five-year ride that was well documented prior to his passing in 2019.

Sadly, and despite my many overtures, we never spoke to or saw each other again after the final Mesa board meeting in 1997, when we announced the merger with Parker & Parsley. Through friends we had in common, including some that subsequently worked for him, I was frequently reminded that he considered my actions as tantamount to stealing his company rather than orchestrating its rescue while simultaneously arranging for his graceful exit. Over the years, I offered several times to go see him to bury any hatchet, but he chose bitterness instead.

STEVE: *Sounds like you got over it pretty well.*

KEN: For the most part, although it still gnaws at me. I didn't ruminate too much on Boone's history, but over the years I was amazed at how he seemed to manage his public reputation more than he cared about his private relationships. Honestly, however, when I read what he wrote about me so long after the fact, it hurt. I vented to those close to me, but I never engaged in that sort of pejorative talk while we were both pursuing our professional careers. Dallas is a small town in many respects, and I knew that the high road was the better road.

But to be honest, I would have preferred that we'd buried the hatchet. The relationships I have built over the years are my most prized asset. I'm proud of the fact that I've maintained positive friendships with almost everyone with whom I have done business—even those whose ventures failed. I tried my best to let time heal whatever was eating Boone, but to no avail. I can sleep at night knowing how my record of successful relationships compares to Boone's wake of failed relationships, be they personal, marital, or professional. Some people just live their lives that way and I had to let it go.

STEVE: *The deal seemed to put NGP further on the national map, both inside the energy industry and within the investment business altogether.*

KEN: I didn't think that much of it at the time. But in 1996, others began to take notice of our little eight-year-old firm. For example, a young professional we had hired at NGP relayed a story from his time working at Enron back at the time of the transaction. He reported that Jeff Skilling, who at that time was in charge of the Enron trading and finance businesses, gathered his entire team around a large conference table and laid out a stack of Mesa's bond offering prospectuses and the stockholder proxy documents, all of which outlined our transaction from top to bottom.

He was upset, since Enron had had several groups trying to dissect the Mesa assets for several years to concoct a way for Enron to gain control over the company's coveted natural gas assets. Those attempts failed.

"Ken Hersh just schooled us!" I was told he said as he tossed the stack of prospectuses across the table, so they unfurled like a deck of cards being spread by a blackjack dealer. "I want this deal dissected," he commanded to a roomful of lieutenants. "I want to know why we weren't able to come up with something like this."

Having met the now-legendary Skilling a decade earlier when I was a summer associate at McKinsey, I found this account especially gratifying. Not that the student had schooled the teacher in this case, but it was close. There was a strange symmetry about that moment, given the fact that Skilling's McKinsey study was part of the reason there was even a firm called Natural Gas Partners in the first place. Since the conclusions of his study never materialized, it made this moment all the more gratifying.

Finally, as the dust settled on the story, another indication of the importance of the deal crossed my desk. As the Mesa deal unfolded, Joel Reed, the dutiful colleague of David Batchelder, remained opposed to both Boone and our proposal. Their ultimate goal was to capture the company somehow as well.

After it was apparent that the company wouldn't fail and that he and his partners wouldn't end up with it, Joel sent a cordial letter to his old friend, Darla Moore, that read, "Although the Mesa deal found us on the opposite side of the table, I still recognize a masterfully structured and executed transaction when I see it. Congratulations to you and your group and best of luck in the future."

When she got it, Darla passed the letter on to me with a smile. "Well done, Ken," she said.

Joel's letter was a class act. It demonstrates what I love about business. Two sides may oppose each other, but that doesn't mean they are enemies. This great country was built on the constant tug-of-war of competition and cooperation embedded in our form of capitalism. This is what drives growth and innovation. When a deal is done, if all sides played fair and honest, life goes on. People go on. The relationships are what survive the most. Competitors on one day could become partners the next. In fact, Steve Gardner and I stayed close, even though we were on the opposite sides of the table on the Mesa deal. When I needed a trustworthy and hardworking CEO for NGP's mezzanine lending business some ten years later, I called on Steve and he accepted the challenge. We remain friends to this day.

STEVE: *From that point on, it seems from looking at your speaking schedule, NGP became part of the fabric of the United States' independent oil and gas business, and you became established as an emerging thought leader in the industry.*

KEN: By the end of 1998, I was sitting on the board of Pioneer, a large company that I helped create, attending to a growing portfolio, and raising a large new fund. I can see how it all just seemed to follow like it had been planned from the very beginning.

At thirty-five years old, I didn't think about it at all that way. I just went about my business, making stuff up as I went along.

CHAPTER 7

THE FOXHOLE

STEVE: *If Mesa was a success, the Sunoma deal, which was going on at about the same time, was, as you say in the energy business, a dry hole. How did that one turn out so badly?*

KEN: I could sugarcoat it and call it a learning experience. Unfortunately, it was much more than that. It was a disaster. At the time, we lost 20 percent of every dollar we had *ever* invested as a firm, and it made up 20 percent of our fifth fund. We lost all the momentum that the Mesa deal had given us just twenty-four months earlier. With time, I have gained some perspective, and there are some very important takeaways from that experience.

I want to describe it in detail because it's an undeniable part of NGP's history. Aside from the bath we took, it's an important case study because it uncovered a particular flaw in our model, tested us as young professionals, and simultaneously revalidated our business ethic. Most important, it gave me a healthy dose of humility as an investor that I have never forgotten.

STEVE: *The story starts with NGP falling in love with a guy named Rick McDermott.*

KEN: Right. If they ever made a movie of this, Rick would be played by a young Ben Affleck. He was your quintessential rural Canadian businessman. He was a big, athletic guy (at least to me), with a rugged, weatherworn look. Clearly, he'd been a hockey stud when he was younger.

When we met him in the mid-1990s, Rick was the kind of oil entrepreneur we loved. He didn't attend fancy schools. He came from the school of hard knocks, and he was an experienced oil and gas operator. He had grown up in a rural farming town in southeast Saskatchewan and worked in the local field for Imperial Oil, the Canadian affiliate of Exxon. Like a lot of executives with whom we did business, he hadn't liked working for a boss or for a big bureaucracy. So he struck out on his own. He began by purchasing small oil properties around the town where he grew up, several from Imperial Oil itself.

He would tell us nostalgic stories of strapping his young son to the back of a snowmobile as he visited his own oil wells to see to it that they remained flowing during ice-cold temperatures. This was the personal owner-manager behavior we loved. He was totally focused on his wells. He improved production and decreased operating costs. It was hard work but straightforward. The value of the wells in his field went up nicely. Ultimately, he sold the operations for millions more than he paid for them.

He became a household name and a bit of a celebrity in his small town after the sale. He recounted that everywhere he went, his story was all people wanted to talk about. This became so uncomfortable to a man who generally kept to himself that he decided to move to Calgary, a big oil town where he could become just a face in the crowd again. He fit the profile of the NGP executive we were seeking.

STEVE: *So?*

KEN: Rick was still hungry. So, in early 1996, while the Mesa deal was in the final stages of closing, we structured a deal with him to match his $3 million nest egg with our capital to create a war chest for acquisitions targeting small public companies. In Canada, companies could go public at sizes much smaller than those in the United States, so a strategy to pursue public companies was not necessarily a big-dollar game. David Albin used to joke that he could buy many of the publicly traded junior oil and gas companies in Canada by using his Visa card. We always thought he was joking, but we never really checked his Visa card limit.

First off, Rick bought a small company called Sunalta. The deal size was less than $30 million. We put up some equity from our NGP 2 and NGP 3 funds, borrowed a little bit, and voilà, it was done. At the time, we were just finishing up investing from our first NGP fund that started in 1988. As an aside, in 1993 and 1994, we added two funds from which we could invest, which we called NGP 2 and NGP 3, to serve as funds that coinvested alongside NGP 1 until the end of 1995, which was the end of Fund 1's contractual investment period. In 1995, Funds 2 and 3 were the ones open for us to draw from, and therefore, the original Sunalta investment was drawn from those two funds.

About six months later, Rick had his sights set on two other targets, a smaller company called Orbit and a bigger one called Paloma. They were several times larger than Sunalta, but since we had confidence in Rick, we listened. We did our due diligence and didn't really blink. Everything looked good. The Sunalta deal was on track early; we had our owner-manager invested, committed, and aligned. So we put in more equity (this time finishing out Funds 2 and 3 and utilizing Fund 4, which had been raised in the latter half of 1996), plus we borrowed additional capital to complete the deals. We didn't think we were in too deep. It followed our formula. We started small, letting the team establish its track record. Then, as the business plan was validated and the company's value was growing, we looked to feed our winners.

STEVE: *It does sound like this guy fit the NGP partner profile.*

KEN: He did. We're the financial backer, and our job is to align ourselves with moneymakers, right? In the oil and gas industry, that means finding people who love to acquire oil and gas properties and operate their wells efficiently. If you can get your production up and keep your costs down, you win. And what we found was that invariably the more the team works an area, the more likely that good opportunities will present themselves—either making further acquisitions in the same area or finding other undrilled locations in the fields they owned in order to increase production.

The Sunalta deal and the Paloma deal really fit well together and had all the ingredients we had grown to love. In fact, they fit so well together that even the name of the company was a natural evolution. I remember being in a bank meeting where Rick was talking about Sunalta acquiring Paloma. In talking about the combo of Sunalta and Paloma, he made a slip of the tongue and inadvertently called the company "Sunoma." Bingo! We had even renamed the combined company on the cheap, without any need for a fancy naming consultant.

STEVE: *You must have been quite confident in that deal to put money from so many funds in a concentrated bet. Were your investors okay with that?*

KEN: By that time, we had established a decent track record and assembled a great group of long-term investors. You might say we were pretty proud of ourselves. We had taken the lemons that the oil and gas industry had given us and turned them into some pretty sweet lemonade. We were riding high.

Our business had grown accordingly. The investor in NGP 1 was Equitable, a large insurance company. The largest investor in NGP 2 was Harvard's endowment. NGP 3's major investor was the American Airlines pension fund. When we were out of money from Funds 1, 2, and 3, we decided to open it up to more investors in creating NGP 4, our first multipartner fund. We were excited that each of our cornerstone investors from Funds 1, 2, and 3 all wanted in, so that made it relatively easy to attract some new investors. From 1988 through 1995, we invested $150 million in the aggregate. So it seemed to make sense to raise another $150 million. We figured it would hold us over for another five years or so. In late 1996, we easily completed the fundraise for NGP 4 at our $150 million target.

When it came to the Sunoma investment, our investors had given us a lot of leeway, and a 20 percent portfolio limit in any one company was a common fund term at that time.

STEVE: *Back to the story. Sunalta acquired Paloma, and then, as the renamed Sunoma, it bought Orbit Oil & Gas. Did it immediately go off the rails?*

KEN: Not at all. The acquisition was relatively straightforward and manageable. The size was well within the capabilities of our management team. Early returns were pretty good. And then, in late 1997, Rick got the idea to make a run at publicly traded Barrington Petroleum Ltd., a $500 million company headquartered in Calgary. This was a real gulp.

STEVE: *Seems like it. Twenty million dollars or so for Sunalta. One hundred for Paloma. Half a billion seems like a big leap to take.*

KEN: At the time, it didn't seem like a real stretch. We had a team that was building a good track record with acquisitions and our "feed the winners" mentality was being rewarded. I always say it's easier to take a company that has already doubled in value to double again than it is to take a company that has fallen in half and double it to get yourself back to even. Companies with momentum are a safer bet. And it is much more fun to be thinking about how to build your stack of chips higher than to try to win your money back. Our investors encouraged us as well.

In fact, we had invested much of the $150 million NGP 4 by late 1997, taking full advantage of the momentum we had as a firm and in what we thought was a market bottom caused by the unfolding Asian economic crisis. That came to a head in July 1997, when Thailand devalued its currency and the Asian financial crisis spread. Oil prices took a hit, and the public stock prices followed. It was a buying opportunity.

To that end, we began doing what we do when we have a fund start to run out of money—we launch a new fund. In this case, we began raising NGP 5 with a $300 million target. We circled around to all our investors, reminding them of our track record through 1997 and even giving them a healthy report on the Sunoma deal at that time. We quickly surpassed our target and closed NGP 5 at $320 million in April 1998.

From 1994 through 1998, we went from a single fund with a single partner to five funds with about $540 million more in capital. We were proud to back some great owner-managers like Theresa Kilgore, Randy Hill, Steve Gray, Dave Macfie, Ken Cairns, Bob Anderson, Kyle Travis, Mark Doering, Greg Wood, Dale Wood, and Tim Carey, who joined the family of our owner-manager partners from NGP 1. We had a stable of great partners, and we could brag on them to our investors. Our relationship with them was our secret sauce and the essence of NGP's investment franchise.

John Foster, one of our original four along with David, Gamble, and me, set our closing date for NGP 5 for April 15, 1998, since his wife, Doon, had an appointment to be induced for labor on the 18th. Once again, at NGP, family comes first! At least nobody could argue that that wasn't a good reason for the deadline.

With confidence that we would be closed on the fundraising of NGP 5, we encouraged Rick to keep going.

Barrington seemed like a good buy at the time. The stock price was at a historic low because of the market weakness. Given that it was publicly traded, we were able to review their public filings and get a description of its assets. On paper, the assets looked to be trading well below the value Rick and his team ascribed to them. The company was being advised by bankers who were used to doing deals with public companies, relying on the public numbers, which included audited financial statements and credible third-party consultants that valued its oil and gas reserves.

STEVE: *So, what was Rick's strategy?*

KEN: First, he approached the company. Not surprisingly, management didn't want to sell. Fortunately, Canadian takeover laws were such that it was hard for a company to resist an offer made at a big premium to the prevailing stock price. With that in mind, in the summer of 1998, we agreed that he would make a public tender for Barrington and take the offer straight to the company's shareholders.

We went to a bank we'd worked with before to line up the financing for our bid. They looked at the value of our current company, Sunoma, and the value of our target, Barrington, and came up with the number they would lend. Coming off the successful Mesa financing, they had a lot of confidence in us, so they agreed to lend us about 80 percent of the value of the deal. We committed to make up the difference from NGP 5 with a $64 million investment. After considerable thought and advice from our advisers, we announced our intention to buy all the company's stock. There were no competing bids, and the shareholders had a month to review the offer.

STEVE: *Sounds okay so far.*

KEN: It was going as planned. The shareholders had until early September to tender their shares. Once we had control of the majority of the shares of Barrington, we could then merge that company with our private company, Sunoma, and complete the take-private transaction. It was considered a two-step transaction.

I remember it well. As the tender offer period was set to expire near the first of September, we needed to fund the purchase of the shares that were tendered. We funded our investment and wired it to the stock transfer agent. The bank wired half the loan amount to make up the difference. We succeeded in buying 97 percent of the company.

Step one was complete. Now, all we had to do was draw the remainder of the money promised by the bank, and we could finish step two to merge Barrington with Sunoma and combine the two companies into one private enterprise. This would force the cashing out of the remaining 3 percent of the holders who did not tender.

STEVE: *Again, sounds very typical, and I'm not even a deal guy.*

KEN: Remember that our funding of this deal happened the first week of September 1998, and the bank *did* fund half of its loan commitment. I felt we were just executing as planned. But sometimes, things that happen half a world away can sting you.

STEVE: *Sounds ominous. Go on.*

KEN: In mid-August, after we launched our tender offer, a financial crisis had begun to grip Russia. The ruble had been devalued, and their dollar-denominated debt had defaulted. This roiled the oil markets as well. We were concerned and stayed in almost daily contact with our bankers. Since our tender offer to the Barrington shareholders was open for the month of August, this all transpired as we were asking them to vote to sell their shares.

At the time, it didn't seem to be affecting us, since the bank had said we were still on track and even funded the first chunk of money that first week of September. All the oil price action and the Russian troubles were known when they funded the first half of their commitment. From my perspective, it was game on. We bought the Barrington stock on a Tuesday. We planned to combine the companies that Friday, so we needed the bank's remaining commitment to pay off Barrington's debt to merge Barrington with Sunoma.

On that Thursday, the day before the funding was due, my contact at the bank called to inform us that they were not going to fund.

STEVE: *Come again? Why? And how much money are we talking about?*

KEN: We're talking about $100 million. I surmised that events unfolding at the bank led them to conclude they would rather renege on a firm commitment than send money out the door to us. We had paid them a couple of million dollars in commitment fees for the money a few weeks earlier, before the tender offer was launched. There was no "out" for them in the language of the commitment letter. They had a contractual obligation to fund. But here they were, ready to default. My contact said, "Oil prices have changed, and we need to complete some more due diligence."

Reminding him that oil prices had started to collapse in August, I said, "If oil prices are the reason, why did you fund the first part on Tuesday? You should have said no then." From my perspective, nothing new had happened between Tuesday and Thursday.

This bank had been our lead bank on another deal, and we had a great rapport with everyone there. There was a lot of trust and a healthy history of communication. I felt blindsided. Sure, there were events happening around the world, but those events preceded the conclusion of our tender offer.

My contact said, "We're going to come and restructure the loan somehow and figure out how to make it fit the current climate." He also reiterated that we were a great client, and he expected we could work something out.

STEVE: *But that didn't happen.*

KEN: No. He couldn't deliver. He flew to Calgary to work with us, but September and October 1998 were a bloodbath, with each week worse than the one before. The Russian default, combined with the Asian financial crisis, caused the New York hedge fund Long Term Capital Management to come perilously close to blowing up. That fund had over $120 billion in assets with derivative exposure, designed ironically by my Stanford professor Myron Scholes, that some estimated to be north of $1 trillion. There was a real fear that if it went under, there would be a global financial crisis. Given that we all went through a global financial crisis in 2008, we know now what they were afraid of. The oil markets do not like global financial crises.

NGP had already funded its share of the money for the company to purchase the tendered shares of Barrington, and now we were frozen. We were the proud owners of our portfolio company called Sunoma, which, in turn, owned 97 percent of the stock of a company called Barrington, whose other 3 percent of the shares were still traded publicly.

We had money from all our funds in that deal, and it was quickly going south.

Rick had to run two companies separately because we couldn't consolidate the two or build any efficiencies between them. We were basically stuck until we could get the money to merge them, but we were about $100 million undercapitalized—the amount that the bank decided not to fund.

One of the biggest challenges in creating value in an oil and gas company is the need to develop new reserves at a faster rate than your existing wells decline. Since all oil and gas wells decline with each passing day, it is critical that management not waste a minute. So you can see how things could deteriorate quickly. Both Barrington and Sunoma were short on money, so our anticipated consolidated capital expenditure program never happened; nor were we able to put in the oil price hedges we were planning to implement the day the deal closed. Their wells declined, and we didn't have the capital to put back in the ground. For a company with a fixed amount of debt, every dollar in lost value goes straight against the equity account.

STEVE: *What was happening to the rest of your portfolio at this time? Were you putting out fires everywhere?*

KEN: That is a good question and an important part of the NGP story at the time. In the summer of 1998, we had committed 20 percent of NGP 5 to the Sunoma-Barrington deal. But at the time, we also had a full investment team continuing to invest the rest of the fund. Our deal flow was strong, and we were investing capital with management teams who had sold earlier companies and wanted to go again. Plus, we had existing companies, like Sunoma, that needed more capital. Our investment business was rolling.

Managerially, it was important for me to keep the Sunoma troubles compartmentalized so that they would not distract from other work going on at the firm. The same conditions that were pinching Sunoma were creating some interesting buying opportunities elsewhere.

But we were quickly getting into a predicament. When we committed 20 percent of Fund 5 to Sunoma's tender offer for Barrington, it put us in a position that Fund 5 was getting closer to being fully committed. So, in the summer and fall of 1998, we began to raise a new fund—NGP 6.

We were still quite confident in the summer of 1998, because we had not yet closed the Barrington deal. Mesa and Parker & Parsley had merged in 1997 to create Pioneer Natural Resources and our position was still well in the money. When we began our road show, things were stable in our portfolio, and we spent time talking about our good track record and the anticipated returns of NGP 4 and 5.

Then, toward the fourth quarter of 1998, Sunoma's valuation started to crack.

STEVE: *Now, that doesn't sound okay.*

KEN: Over the next six months, we sent two people to Canada nearly full time to try to work things out. We kept working with the bank, although they were of little help. They didn't want the full loan exposure and were trying to find syndicate partners for the money they did lend, which also impeded the ability to raise the $100 million that they *didn't* lend. They kept promising to find us the rest of the money. Unfortunately, the financial crises and resulting collapse in oil prices had every bank in the energy business shut down.

At the same time, Rick was now CEO of both Sunoma and Barrington, so he was able to see the information behind Barrington's public filings. These revealed that the prior Barrington management and its accounting and engineering reports significantly overstated both the land position and the reserve estimates of the company. Ugh! Everything that could go against us did.

By early 1999, it was a lost cause. Once we did a thorough review of Barrington's assets and financials, it was clear that putting in more money would just be throwing good money after bad.

STEVE: *Looking back, whose fault was all this?*

KEN: A good portion of the problem stemmed from the underlying financial information we uncovered at Barrington, but the macro environment hurt also. Yet, had the bank funded as they had planned, we could have merged the two companies right away, consolidated overhead, and stopped the bleeding sooner.

Most important, we could have hedged our oil price exposure like we did in all our companies at the time. The bank would not allow us to implement a hedging program in the state we were in. Frankly, it's illogical for banks not to let their clients hedge, since they have a lien on the client's assets. After all, hedging against a commodity price collapse protects *their* collateral. But bankers are not always logical. When conditions get bad in the banking business, they tend to freeze up.

STEVE: *Was the discovery of the issues at Barrington something you guys should have found sooner?*

KEN: We could not have discovered it based on public financials. The biggest issue was in the audit done by the outside consulting reserve engineers. The company was only required to publish a summary of the report. We didn't see the assumptions behind the valuation estimates until we were on the inside. Most companies are honest and put out a report based on reasonable and truthful assumptions. We got a real-life lesson in broken trust, and it hurt badly.

Now, it was my turn to throw up in the shower.

STEVE: *After throwing up, what did you do?*

KEN: First, we needed to focus on the company and do the right thing there. Our portfolio companies were our engine room, if you will, and we needed to make sure we did everything we could to keep them afloat if they were in trouble. Our mantra was always to be helpful to management. We brought in another executive to help Rick. We came up with plan after plan to keep the companies going. I figured we were aligned with the bank, since they didn't want to foreclose on the assets, and it was their fault we were so undercapitalized.

We all tried to find ways to weather the storm. Ultimately, my counterpart at the bank was completely unsympathetic. He said, "You're in default, and the loan is going to the workout department to get as much of our money back as possible." We were cooked at that point. We worked to show them new business plans that would realize a greater recovery for them, and we were willing to do that for free.

Here is evidence that banks often do the wrong thing at the wrong time. When the loan becomes what they call "nonperforming," they send it to another department. That department does not care about the relationship; they don't have any pride of ownership over the original loan. Their job is to liquidate and take whatever comes back.

In Sunoma's case, it was a very surgical, dispassionate, detached approach. At a time when we needed businesspeople to listen and understand the situation the most, the bank put the loan in the hands of people who aren't supposed to listen. Their sole job was to get assets off their books.

This was a real lesson for a young capitalist: Do not count on rational people to behave rationally. Institutional norms of big institutions overwhelm personal judgments. This causes financial crises to deepen instead of softening, as we later saw in 2008 and 2009.

So that is what happened in Sunoma. The equity became worthless when the bank guys put it in their workout department. They liquidated the company, and they did not even get 100 cents on their bank debt back. They lost about 30 percent of their money. If they had held with us for one more year, they would have gotten all their money back, and the equity value would have been positive. It was very distressing.

STEVE: *Distressing is a good word to use. What was the impact of all of this on you? This seems like it was the biggest business failure of your life at that point. We have not talked much about your personal life. Was there an impact on home life?*

KEN: Funny you should ask. At this point in my life, we were rockin' and rollin'. Daniel was four, and Rachel was two. They were at great ages and a lot of fun. Even though Julie had been doing really well at Octel Communications working on their national sales team, she decided it made more sense for her to stay at home with the kids and be the anchor of our family life.

At this time, we were actively thinking about where our kids would go to school and the neighborhoods where we might want to live. We had looked for houses to buy and couldn't find one we liked. So we decided to build a house. In 1997, we purchased a lot and were in the process of building a rather large home while the Sunoma drama was unfolding.

When we planned for and budgeted the house project, we had just raised NGP 4 and NGP 5 in rapid succession. I had decent visibility of my near-term income, and the profits interest in the prior funds looked secure. That is, until the Sunoma write-down. At that point, things didn't look as sure.

It was a very stressful time, but in hindsight I wasn't paralyzed. I tried to keep the work challenges away from the family, although I didn't hide the fact that the business took a big step backward at that time. Julie picked up the slack at this point, and we were pretty sober about it all. If something happened and we couldn't move into the house, so be it.

STEVE: *So, what lessons should we take away from this case study?*

KEN: Good lessons did come from this whole experience. In a perverse way, it validated our entire business plan.

STEVE: *Wait a minute! You lost all your money in that deal, which represented about 20 percent of every dollar you had invested in your entire career and put a dent in four of the five funds you had ever raised, plus a full 20 percent of your largest and most recent fund at the time. How did that validate your business plan?*

KEN: Hang with me here, Steve. Central to our business plan is our insistence that our owner-managers put up a meaningful chunk of their net worth in the deal. If they are asking us to invest, nothing says more to me about how confident they are in their plan than their willingness to put skin in the game alongside us. Of course, we are generous with profit-sharing incentives, but we want the basic alignment with management that comes from their investing alongside of us in the beginning.

If all someone has is a profit incentive, there is a perverse incentive to swing for the fences and try to make a large return, independent of the associated risks, simply because they have no downside in the equation. However, if the decision maker has a large personal stake from the beginning, then they feel the downside in that their original investment is at risk. So swinging for the fences and missing has a real cost. Risks get factored into that equation for sure.

Rick had put $3 million of his own money into this deal. Not only did he want the company to succeed for his personal reputation, but he didn't want to lose his hard-earned money. Through it all, he never quit working hard. It was validation of our investment principle: To get alignment, you must have people put skin in the game. If he were only working for his stock options, then it would have been apparent right away that his stock options would have been worth zero, and he would have had no incentive to stick around.

Second, we want to back good people, who care about their partners—us. And partners do not leave other partners in the lurch. We didn't just write off the investment and quit on it. We kept working it even when it was apparent that the bank didn't care about resurrecting the business. In fact, we kept working on it even after we stopped charging our limited partners a management fee on the capital we had invested in the deal. We did that because it was the right thing to do. It was not the best economic decision, but we had made a commitment to our investors, and I wasn't about to quit on them.

Rick was cut from the same cloth. On our side, nobody stole; nobody cheated; nobody lied. What the Barrington directors and officers did was hidden from public view, so we couldn't really beat ourselves up that much. Barrington had reputable auditors and reserve engineers who made the choices they made. They were playing a different game, comfortable with crossing the foul line. That part of the deal was a real learning experience.

From our perspective, it was just a deal that did not work out. While it really stung, the loss was not related to backing bad people. We just swung and missed. That happens when you are in a risk-taking business. As much as we try to manage risk, there are still risks we assume. "People risk" we can control. As hard as the Sunoma experience was, it would have been that much harder if we had to wrestle with our CEO throughout.

After all the dust settled and Rick went on to do other things, I got a call eighteen months later from someone who was looking at a deal with Rick. Apparently, I was still on Rick's reference list. I paused after that call and reflected. It was gratifying that our greatest business failure did not result in a failed relationship. I was happy to be a reference for him, and we stayed in touch for a long time. I learned that it's okay to fail in this manner. It's not personal. We picked people we wanted to be in a foxhole with, had each other's back, and worked through tough issues together. That is better than the alternative.

We also did not make it personal with our bankers. We had some investors who thought we should sue the bank for not funding. We probably had a case to make, but our desire was to treat the bank like a partner as well. Had we become adversarial, all communication would have stopped, and we could reasonably predict that we would spend the next five years fighting, expensively. In that case, there would have been no winners.

We had lots of other business at that bank, and our other bank relationships were watching this unfold. Remember, the entire energy industry was reeling, so pain was everywhere in the industry. I knew we would be judged by how we carried ourselves during times of stress. We kept the holistic relationship with those banks in mind as well as what it meant to be a partner. So, from fall 1998 to summer 1999, we kept working diligently on the company like a stubborn emergency room doctor working on a dying patient, until it was finally apparent that the patient had no heartbeat.

STEVE: *During this time, were you bouncing ideas off anyone, or was this just you following your own instincts?*

KEN: David and I were in constant contact. We were also open and honest with the whole team. Remember, we had about twenty other portfolio companies at the time. Some of those companies were very new, and they were excited by the downturn and market chaos since it presented great buying opportunities. We had to be careful to keep everything in perspective.

We had a big portfolio in a volatile business. Our time was spent on some calls where we heard all the good news because the company had bought assets at the perfect time in the cycle, while other calls were tough to handle because we were dealing with issues like this. Understand that some win, some lose, and some go sideways. This was a big loser, and we had to do the right thing.

STEVE: *Which was?*

KEN: The right thing to do was to do the right thing. You'll recall that our partnership agreement allows us to charge a management fee of 2 percent on capital invested in a deal. But we didn't do that for Sunoma once the trouble started. It didn't seem like the right thing to do, even though we were still working on it and had manpower dedicated to it. We had invested real dollars, but if the dollars had evaporated, it made no sense to charge a fee to manage what might not be there.

I also realized at this point the value of having a great business partner. My relationship with David and our younger colleagues was tested here but came through with flying colors. Most firms would have split apart, and finger-pointing would have become the dominant firm sport. Somehow this experience actually drew us closer together. We never doubted our approach. In fact, we put the same discipline on ourselves that we put on our portfolio company executives. We invested heavily in all our funds. With this much skin in the game, our fight was more than a fight for our reputations. It was for our own net worth.

We did not make it personal, either. The deal was "ours." It didn't belong to any one of us. Assigning blame would have been futile. At the same time, working on solutions became a team effort. David and I kept each other level, focused, and positive. I'm not sure if the firm would have come out of this experience so well if we hadn't been each other's partner. John Foster continued to be a fantastic partner as well, working with our investors to keep them informed *and calm*. His steady demeanor was an important aspect of our success.

I would also add that, at the time, our younger associates, which included Bruce Selkirk, Billy Quinn, David Hayes, and others, really came of age. They worked hard trying to turn around the company as well as hold down the fort with the rest of the portfolio. I do not want to underestimate how important it is for the more senior partners to model the behaviors that they want the entire firm to exhibit. I think that much of our success through later cycles came from the ethic that was established during this downturn. Anyone can thrive when the market and returns are all up. Real investors are made during downturns.

STEVE: *This is consistent with your theme that success is a function of the people involved.*

KEN: Every relationship matters, and relationship-building doesn't happen by accident. It's critical to be intentional in investing in them. We spent so much time working on ensuring that we established the best relationship with new CEOs, it would have been easy to take our own internal relationships for granted. Luckily, David was a low-maintenance partner who was easy to talk to and work with. We always got along, even when we disagreed. There was so much mutual respect and inherent trust between us that splitting up was never an option.

This is where I began to develop my view of what the foxhole mentality was like in a corporate setting. I had his back and he had mine and we never played the blame game. We celebrated each other's successes and dug in together to work on problems. John, our other senior partner, was in the foxhole with us as well. I slept well at night knowing that we were all in it together and working through it as a team.

This allowed us to reach a pivotal conclusion: The same conditions that were causing Sunoma to fail were creating great opportunities for our other portfolio companies. The executives leading our other portfolio companies were watching us carefully. We were humbled, but we couldn't lose confidence in our business model. We could not forget to practice what we preached and do it consistently.

It was then I realized an important element of leadership. Even though we were investing in a volatile industry, our job was not to get too depressed when times were bad and not to get too excited when times were good. *Slow and steady would win the race.*

STEVE: *Sunoma turned this thirty-five-year-old racehorse named Ken Hersh into a tortoise.*

KEN: I realized the secret to my success was to be the fastest tortoise in the race. Our investors noticed, our owner-manager CEOs leading our companies noticed, and my partners inside of NGP noticed.

STEVE: *Did Sunoma's plight affect NGP's fundraising efforts in 1999? How were you able to keep a straight face when asking investors to commit to your next fund?*

KEN: Importantly, it turned out that being open about the lessons learned was appreciated by our investors. Apparently, they were so used to "masters of the universe" telling them how the world works that when they saw our refreshingly honest assessment of what we'd done well and what we hadn't over the first ten years of our firm's life, they responded positively. We did not realize it at the time, but we were building trust with them. They appreciated the story that we had forgone charging fees we were legally entitled to charge, and we took the high moral ground in continuing to work hard on an investment until the bitter end.

We also were quick to apply the lessons we had learned. First, we developed a new process internally by which we evaluated deals brought to us by our winners. When we had a successful portfolio company led by a great CEO, each subsequent commitment of capital became easier because the team had built up so much goodwill with us. We became pushovers for just about any approval being asked for by the management teams of our successful companies. I always believed that if you fed your winners and starved your losers, your portfolio would flourish. However, not everyone gets a hit at every at-bat. In this case, Rick was three for three on his first set of deals and everything was working.

So, when he asked for approvals to go ahead with the Barrington takeover, he had maximum credibility, and we probably looked at his analysis through rose-colored glasses.

This was a flaw embedded in our business model of backing our winners over and over again.

After this experience, we found ways to address this flaw. I adopted a policy of rotating internal teams that monitored each investment about every year and a half. This had the effect of putting fresh eyes on every deal halfway through our expected hold period of that deal. We made a conscious decision to not just be a rubber stamp for folks, even though they were on a successful run. That's the hardest thing in investing: When people have great track records, how do you know when they're about to swing and miss? We kept asking that question and tried not to be complacent.

STEVE: *Other big lessons?*

KEN: Besides humility?

STEVE: *Yes, besides humility.*

KEN: We became quite leery of anything we saw in the public filings of energy companies. We learned the hard way that securities regulators cannot legislate morality. All the accounting rules in the world cannot deter someone who has a mind to deceive. We no longer made any investment based on information we read in public filings.

We also learned that no matter how much conviction we had on an investment, we should be wary of taking on too much debt and be sure to never again get our portfolio overly concentrated in a single asset. The energy industry cycles are often violent. No matter how much we thought we understood about the energy markets, we needed to stay humble. Putting 20 percent of a fund into a single deal was not wise, no matter how confident we were.

That lesson about investment concentration served us well, *sort of*. More on that later when we talk about Energy Transfer.

The big takeaway for me was that we really had the makings of an investment franchise that was built to last. Despite Sunoma, we had all the ingredients we needed to not only survive but thrive. We'd been in business for a decade, experienced a couple of up and down cycles in the industry, and still put up good numbers despite the volatility *and* the Sunoma write-off. Internally, we were able to hold our team together with no turnover of staff along the way.

We never lost confidence in our people, or our business plan, and we kept fighting. In fact, the deals we did between the beginning of the Sunoma debacle and the summer of '99 turned out to be some of our better deals several years later. Investments made during this downturn supported great chief executives like Phil Smith in his third venture, Jon Brumley after he left Mesa, and new deals spawned by the likes of Bob Anderson, Kyle Travis, Eric Pitcher, Duane King, Bob Dunn, Charlie Stephenson, Mark Doering, Rich Talley, Randy Hill, Steve Gray, Flora Gillespie, and Theresa Kilgore. Without exception, these all produced winning returns for our investors. In addition, we found that relationships formed during incredible industry upheaval turned out to be the most durable. I guess we were in the foxhole with them when the world was bombing our entire industry.

For example, we accomplished an innovative carve-out of marginal, hard-to-sell assets from Pioneer, led by Phil Smith, in which we allowed Pioneer to retain a one-third ownership of a newly formed company called Prize Energy Corp. Prize took control of a hodgepodge set of assets that Pioneer couldn't sell for much money, and we put in about $45 million for two-thirds of the business. We also convinced a key Pioneer executive, Lon Kile, to join the Prize team. We were able to offer him an equity incentive structure that was typical for an entrepreneurial NGP company but hard for a big public company to match.

After three years of hard work rationalizing the asset base and making follow-on acquisitions, we were able to sell the company and make about $200 million on the investment, or over four times our cost. Once again, giving mediocre assets to a great management turned out to be the right call. Phil and Lon along with a stellar team of experienced executives worked their magic once again.

We even went on to make an investment in a new venture led by Jon and Jonny Brumley that kicked off during this time as well, thereby turning our Mesa/Pioneer investment into one that gave birth to two corporate offspring.

Internally, after all the volatility, we could have retreated and acted as if we were a distressed firm. But we did not. We did not lay off anyone. We did not treat it as a "sky is falling" moment. Without knowing it, the firm's foundation and our culture had just been solidified.

To top it off, we included our investors as an important voice in quantifying the meaning of Sunoma's collapse to our investment franchise.

STEVE: *How did you do that?*

KEN: We gave our investors the chance to vote on whether to shut us down.

STEVE: *That seems like a risky move. Did you know the answer to the question before asking it?*

KEN: I told you I didn't go to law school and become a litigator. If I did, I probably would've never asked a question I didn't already know the answer to.

STEVE: *So, what happened?*

KEN: Beginning in 1995, we began holding biennial summer retreats with our investors and portfolio company executives in Santa Fe, New Mexico. The third one was planned for July 1999. The idea for a portfolio company and investor retreat emanated from the first successful meeting we had in Fort Worth in late 1992. By that time, we had several companies in our portfolio. I thought it would be a good idea for us to convene a strategy session with our portfolio company's executives to share ideas and discuss broad strategies as a way of learning from each other. One thing we could offer was some perspective on the industry. Taken as a whole, our portfolio companies would be well served by sharing stories and winning strategies. If they all felt like they were part of the NGP family, I suspected that would be a net benefit.

In the summer of 1995, we decided to hold our second portfolio company/investor retreat and move it to Santa Fe, where David and I had decided to spend the summer, much in the same vein as Richard Rainwater did throughout his career when he moved his summer operation to the beaches of Nantucket. Richard's practice of moving his office for the summer ended in 1988, so I never got the chance to experience it. I only had heard the stories that became legendary. My hope was that our summers in Santa Fe would become for NGP what Rainwater's legendary summers in Nantucket had been for his network of friends and companies.

Ironically, our working patterns were so ingrained by then that even though we were in the same city together for the entire summer, we each worked most of the day from our respective homes and got on the phone to debrief at the end of the day, just as we did when we were 1,600 miles apart. John Foster, working diligently from the Greenwich office all summer, thought that was kind of humorous.

The 1995 retreat was the real legacy from that summer, and the biennial seminar became a tradition for the firm that continued for decades. Holding the event every other year allowed enough time to pass to make the reporting interesting and the strategy discussions meaningful. Not enough happens in one year, but over two years the industry and portfolio changed enough to make lively discussions easier to design. Plus, we had fun.

Our 1999 Santa Fe seminar was eventful. It was our third one there and our fourth one overall, counting the 1992 event. We were good at creating an agenda that mixed business strategy discussions and some fun after-hours diversions. We put a lot of time into designing the agenda to make it interesting and informative.

By the summer of 1999, our investor group had grown with the advent of NGP 4 in 1996, NGP 5 in 1998, and, at the time, those who had committed to our new NGP 6 fund that was in the market. Whereas the 1992, 1995, and 1997 summer seminars were dominated by our portfolio companies, the attendees in 1999 were about equally split between our portfolio company leaders and our investors. This posed a particularly delicate situation, since we now had some really bad news to discuss when going over the portfolio.

STEVE: *What did you do?*

KEN: We had decided to turn the first day of the session into an investor-only meeting that would serve as our annual limited partner meeting as required by our fund agreements. That way, we could discuss the portfolio and all the ins and outs the day before day two, when our portfolio company executives showed up. Investors could stay for the next two days of sessions that were geared more for our portfolio companies, or they could leave. Most stayed. Our NGP summer session really became something special in the energy investment community. Over the years, people planned their summers around it, and the sharing of ideas and experiences there became one of the defining elements of NGP's investment franchise.

We designed the agenda of the investor portion of the meeting to end with a detailed discussion of the Sunoma transaction—with a full forensic analysis going back to the first day of the investment. We described it all thoroughly and ended with a recap of our conclusion not to throw good money after bad in trying to resuscitate the company. We described how we applied the Sunoma lessons learned across the rest of our portfolio and would make up for the Sunoma loss by overachieving elsewhere.

We also did two very unconventional things at the same time. We announced that we would reopen NGP 6, which had either closed or was near closing on $450 million in commitments. This meant that investors who had already committed to the new fund could freely withdraw from it if they wanted to. In addition, after we went through the entire story, we decided to allow our investors to hold an executive session without us. We left the room and allowed them to discuss among themselves how they viewed their investment in NGP and their impressions of how we conducted ourselves.

STEVE: *Am I right that this was out of the ordinary?*

KEN: To say this was unconventional would be an understatement. General partners never allow their limited partners to hold private sessions together. In fact, most fund managers don't share the roster of investors among those investing. As mature as the private equity industry is today, it's rare that investors know the full complement of the other investors in the fund. Not only did we have them all in one room, but we also let them have free rein to tear into us if they wanted.

We didn't announce it ahead of time, and we didn't have the executive session on the printed agenda. After we outlined our lessons learned from Sunoma and indicated that we were reopening NGP 6, we just left the room.

STEVE: *Just like that?*

KEN: Yep. "See you all at dinner," I said, as we departed. People were floored. We gave them the opportunity to shut us down.

When telling that story to colleagues in the industry years later, they were amazed that we would have ever allowed such a session to occur. Yet in this case, it was clearly the right thing to do, so we did it.

STEVE: *What happened at the meeting?*

KEN: I have to admit, I did some reconnaissance at dinner to find out what happened. We did have a few investors who had become particular friends. And we left Phil Smith in the room to answer questions about us from his perspective as a CEO who had led more than one company for us over the decade.

I learned that two guys stood up and said they thought we cared more about our relationship with the bank than with our investors. They thought we should've sued the bank to hold them accountable for the loss. Then Mark Yusko spoke. He was then the head of the University of North Carolina's endowment, but he'd had a long history with us, since he had been the lead relationship manager at Notre Dame's endowment when that school committed to invest with us. Apparently, he stood up and said that he was going to stick with us. He boldly proclaimed, "These are good guys. They learned their lesson. I will go on the record to say that Fund 6 will be their best fund ever!"

I was told that his contribution stemmed the negative groupthink that was taking hold at the meeting. His contribution to the longevity of NGP's investment franchise cannot be overstated.

In the end, they had a good conversation, and people got complaints off their chests. Some investors did pull out of the fund, but a couple of them actually increased their allocation. A net of $80 million in commitments ended up being withdrawn from Fund 6, which reduced its size to $370 million in total. As I'm sure we'll discuss, Fund 6 made 7.5 times its investment, and the $80 million that was withdrawn would have been worth over $400 million to those investors who pulled out. It was the single best fund we ever had. Yusko, who has his own investment firm now, continues to remind me of his clairvoyance.

As time went on, even the final results of NGP 5 turned around nicely. Despite losing all our money on the fund's piece of Sunoma—20 percent of the fund—that fund still earned a good rate of return. We redoubled our efforts to enhance the value of the remaining companies in the fund and ultimately earned a 25 percent rate of return for our investors.

Ultimately, the efforts did not go unnoticed. In fact, when NGP 5 was finished and the returns were realized, I got the nicest letter from a *former* investor, the late Bill Dietrich, a retired Pittsburgh steel executive, written in his cordial but matter-of-fact style. He called it as he saw it, and his weathered skin and thinning gray hair were evidence that he saw a lot. After his retirement, he spent his time managing his own money, choosing to dive into the private equity industry head-first. He got to know a great cross section of investment managers and did his own due diligence. He showed up at all our annual meetings and Santa Fe seminars. I always enjoyed my meetings with him. They were no-bullshit, challenging sessions. I learned from him as well. We became friends.

After investing with us in NGP 5, he changed strategies and didn't come into our subsequent funds. Yet he still showed up at our investor meetings and was all ears when we spoke about the returns. Several years passed after that 1999 meeting, and we lost touch. But, as we wound down NGP 5 in November 2005, he graciously sent us a note of thanks. He wrote:

Dear David, John and Ken:

I just received my last distribution from NGP V. As I mentioned a couple of years ago, after the bad luck with Sunoma, this fund had the greatest comeback since Firpo knocked Dempsey out of the ring. As I told you, I made the decision after my NGP V commitment that I was confining my investing to venture and private equity funds. In retrospect, perhaps not the best decision, but I'll live with it. I do see the day when we will broaden our asset categories again, and I hope there might be a thin slice of a future NGP fund available for a broken-down steel guy from Pittsburgh.

Many thanks for a fabulous job on Fund V and also for taking on the University of Pittsburgh and Carnegie Mellon, both institutions with which I have been intimately associated.

Wishing all of you the best for the holiday season.

Bill

It was so nice to get that note. It's funny how few investors acknowledge the hard work and commitment put in by investment managers. Sure, we are well compensated, but that doesn't mean we don't like to be appreciated. To this day, I'm sure to send my thanks to people who are working hard to manage my family's money, regardless of how much we are paying them to do so.

Knowing that people like Bill Dietrich were out there watching was constant motivation to keep working hard.

STEVE: *Still, Sunoma sounds like an expensive way to learn these lessons.*

KEN: Well, we also got some nice Sunoma swag. But in the end, I think $83 million was a bit much to pay for a coffee mug, a shirt, and a sleeve of golf balls.

CHAPTER 8

THE FASTEST TORTOISE

STEVE: *Over the years, NGP had a lot more of successful Mesas than unsuccessful Sunomas. The story of your firm's growth was quite astounding, given the fact that there was no real model for what you were doing. Did you ever think you were going too fast? From my perspective, it seems like your team would have had a hard time keeping up.*

KEN: People would comment that it seemed like we were able to raise money rather quickly, especially as the firm reached its teenage years. As I described, for our first fund we had about $150 million to invest and it took us about seven years to invest it. We had no rule book, and the industry was so immature that we were working by trial and error. Since we were such neophytes in the energy investment business, though, we adopted the posture of being students of the industry, which was important. We were always learning from those who had been successful and trying to decipher why the industry failures happened.

David and I were both humbled by our early experiences, and I think our humility infected the firm. Now, don't get me wrong, people who know me well may not use the word "humble" to describe me. But while I have a lot of self-confidence in my abilities, I recognized at the time that I didn't know much. I've combined being a fast learner with the ability to pull the trigger.

Early on, I recognized that if we took a bunch of small steps first, we could always correct our course if something went awry. If things went well, we would have momentum to continue. This investment approach worked well in a volatile industry. If the winds of the industry somehow shifted and started blowing directly in our faces, we could recalibrate our investment assumptions to the new, tougher industry conditions and average down our purchase prices, for example.

If the winds were coming from behind, we'd have our sails wide open to enjoy the appreciation of our assets. In this manner, our slow, steady investment pace was our secret sauce. We had a lot of portfolio companies going at once, creating a diversified set of bets. I likened it to placing a chip on every space in a roulette wheel. But our payouts were not capped like in Vegas, *and* we got to add money to those companies that proved their worth and were on a roll. Imagine being able to place more money on a spot on a roulette wheel table as the wheel slows down, and you have a good sense of where the ball will land. That was the game we invented.

For the first ten years, we raised funds smaller than we could have so as not to put too much pressure on ourselves to leave our investment sweet spot. Smaller transactions tended to work better in the early years, before the massive capital expenditure supercycle that began around 2000 with the advent of the unconventional shale revolution.

STEVE: *We might explain here that the "shale revolution" refers to the industry unlocking vast amounts of oil and gas production through the combination of hydraulic fracturing and horizontal drilling technologies. Today, shale formations account for about half of U.S. total oil and gas production.*

KEN: Correct. With the explosion of the shale revolution came the need to place larger upfront bets, since it was impractical to start a drilling program until massive acreage positions were acquired. That meant the business plan migrated from smaller acquisitions that produce positive cash flow on day one to a point where companies had hundreds of millions tied up in raw acreage before they started drilling to produce cash returns.

We also applied that philosophy to our investor base. We took smaller amounts of money from investors than they may have otherwise wanted to give us. I wanted the most diffuse investor base possible. That way, no single investor would have undue influence on our operations. It may have been more labor-intensive to manage a larger investor base, but it was worth it. I let them build up their exposure to NGP gradually over several years by investing in multiple funds.

I described our goal as to be the fastest tortoise in the race. We wanted to build small companies into medium-sized ones and then sell them to larger companies up the food chain. We wanted to educate investors on the merits of adding the oil and gas acquisition-and-exploitation strategy to their portfolios because of its favorable risk-reward nature. I thought this was perfect for endowments, foundations, and pension funds.

They wanted to preserve capital at all costs, but also to have upside exposure when things went well.

In the 2000s, when we looked back at our returns since 1988, we were able to document with solid statistics that when things went well, we did really well, but when things went south, we still did okay. We had results that were *not* statistically correlated to the oil and gas sector or commodity prices. We had lower volatility than the market. Our slow and steady approach *was* winning the race. By our fifteenth anniversary, the investment community took notice.

STEVE: *While you were developing as an investor, how were you evolving as a leader? Today, you speak a lot about that, but was there a grand design when you were growing your business?*

KEN: I think being in a commodity industry where you can get whacked pretty hard by uncontrollable external events made me humble, if not perpetually scared. So I was in this weird place of leading an organization that was trying to navigate a lot of uncertainty, feeling insecure inside, but realizing that my colleagues around me needed me to be confident about pulling the trigger on the deals we wanted to do. Truth be told, I was nervous after every deal but couldn't really show it. Our team and our investors needed assurances that we knew what we were doing.

STEVE: *So, what did you do?*

KEN: When I reverse-engineer the leadership style that most matched what I was evolving into, it would have to be the servant-leader model. I felt that our job as investors was to help the management teams of our companies. "We work for them," I would always emphasize to our team, channeling my best Richard Rainwater, referring to our obligation to support the management teams of our portfolio companies. "Even if we own the majority of the stock," I would stress, "our job is to support them." This was always Richard's mantra.

In the same vein, I felt that my job was to help my colleagues have a great experience in working at NGP. I wanted everyone to enjoy coming to work, from the receptionist right up to my most senior colleagues. I wanted the working conditions to be great and to be accommodative of each colleague's life circumstances. Spouses and significant others were welcome at virtually all our social functions. I shared personal stories often and created a culture where that was not taboo.

Small things mattered a lot. For example, we had lunch brought into the conference room every day to serve the entire team. This was a holdover from Rainwater's office, where the lunch hour became a social hour, as well as a working hour. It was part of the serendipity of the office. By doing this, we ended up mixing as people, independent of our position in the company. As the leader, it would have been impossible for me to regularly take some of the administrative assistants to lunch without raising eyebrows. But sitting around the conference table with whomever happened to be going through the lunch line at the same time made sitting next to anyone perfectly acceptable.

We shared stories with each other. We laughed. We talked business, and whoever was there at the table became part of the conversation, regardless of title. It created a real camaraderie among the people at NGP. It made it fun.

As we grew, I felt obligated to work harder to ensure that all the NGP employees were able to enjoy work, develop professionally, and share in the profits. Once so many of my colleagues were invested in the funds, I felt like I was working for them. By the early 2000s, I had made enough money for me and my family to be comfortable. But what if the returns declined and the other colleagues who had just invested didn't do as well? I didn't want to let them down. I took that responsibility seriously.

And, when things did work out, I took so much pride in watching the folks at NGP send their kids to nice schools, move into nice houses, drive nice cars, and more important, build financial security. I loved it when my younger colleagues had children. We used to track the NGP kids as they grew.

STEVE: *Were you successful, do you think, in sticking to that philosophy? There had to be times where the pressure was pretty intense. Was it hard to always stay optimistic?*

KEN: Your question is spot-on. I can honestly say that there were pressure-packed stretches of time when I was a real jerk as a boss and as a partner. We were evolving as a firm through the first fifteen years, and I was evolving as a person. I was learning about volatility as well and how to handle that as a leader. We were all in it together, but it was not always easy. It's easy to look back on it now with a relatively dispassionate eye and analyze what was going on, but at the time, it was choppy.

Not only did we have to navigate the industry volatility during the 1990s, but we also had that near-death experience with Sunoma. We had all made commitments to our families, to our investors, and to each other. Plus, we had virtually all our individual net worth tied up in the funds. Keeping things moving during those times was hard. To say that I did it with a perpetually cheery disposition would be laughable to those who worked around me.

I kept trying to keep my eye on the prize, but life was crazy. As noted, Julie and I had two children during the first eight years of the firm. We started building a new house in 1997, which was completed in 1999, and it added a huge amount of stress to my time outside of the office. I was trying to be a good father, a good husband, a good boss, and a good provider. It was full, to say the least. But our core group of partners was going through the same personal growth.

David Albin and his then wife, Pam, had an equally full life during this period. In 1996, they moved across the country, from Greenwich to Santa Fe, where we opened an office around his being there. They had a son, Ben, who was born seven months after our daughter, Rachel, was born. Pam kept working for her family's real estate business based out of Boston, so they were living a bicoastal existence.

The other partner our age, John Foster, was expanding his family in Connecticut as well. We shared in the Fosters' joy when Doon delivered twins, Evan and Julia, after a lengthy fertility process. But fifteen months later, tragedy stuck when Evan died mysteriously in his crib. We were all devastated. Their daughter, Julia, needed to be raised, but at that same time, John and Doon grieved and mourned the loss of their son. It was a very tough period. David and I made sure to try to pick up whatever slack we could at the office to give John the time he needed.

Then, two years later, John and Doon welcomed a new child to the family when Lillie was born. Things were right again for our Connecticut office where John worked. He had been transitioning during the 1990s from deal work to that of investor relations. But he and our senior partner, Gamble Baldwin, were holding down the fort in the Northeast.

That all changed in November 2000 when, tragically, Lillie died suddenly one morning while on the couch watching television with Doon. She had an undetectable viral condition, myocarditis, and just expired in her mom's arms.

Burying two children inside a five-year span is more tragedy than most couples could bear. But John and Doon's strength was amazing. How they survived I have no idea. But they continue to inspire me to this day. Their outlook on life is positive, and they continue to move forward, surrounding themselves with family, friends, and a strong community to which they give fully.

The flip side to running the firm like a family is that we share in each other's family joys as well as our tragedies. I never shied away from spending time talking about personal matters. I believe that if you take the time to know your colleagues on a personal basis, you'll be better partners. Trust builds at times you'd never expect.

STEVE: *This sounds like everything boils down to trust—build a culture of trust, trust in your instinct, and trust in the decision to act.*

KEN: It was my goal to have a culture of trust all the way around—inside our firm and between our firm and our portfolio companies.

Within our firm, I think the best way to build trust was to think of it like savings. You needed to build it before it could be used. I tried to never forget that we were a bunch of real people who just happened to be working in the same office.

I wanted everyone to know they were valued. Having great compensation plans was one way, but having a caring culture was even more important. Trusting people to track their own time instead of micromanaging their hours showed trust. Giving people ample time to deal with personal matters was important, knowing that whatever work they missed would most likely get made up several times over.

Achievers achieve. We hired achievers. I didn't have to worry about their productivity. Ensuring that they had awesome benefits demonstrated that we cared about them and their families. When bad things happened, they came to appreciate that aspect of working at NGP. In short, like soldiers in a foxhole, we had each other's backs.

Rewarding that trust with real foxhole-type interaction mattered. This took the form of traveling together, socializing together, and helping each other through whatever life brought us. We were all going through young adult experiences together, independent of our rank at the firm. We all experienced the ups and downs of child-rearing and balancing work and family. I never felt that I could not show my human side to those in my foxhole.

STEVE: *These relationships were personal lifesavers for you, given what was about to transpire in your family.*

KEN: When Julie had a suicidal depressive episode and was hospitalized in May 2001, the first call I made was to David Albin. A couple months later, after Julie's return from a specialty-care residential program, I asked Dick Covington's wife, Mary, and Doon Foster to keep her on a twenty-four-hour watch without her knowing it during our 2001 Santa Fe investor and portfolio company strategy conference week. Talk about trusting people with your wife and kids. Mary and Doon went above and beyond. They jumped at the chance to be helpful for the family of a colleague in need. I will be forever grateful.

STEVE: *Sounds like you were as deliberative and selective with respect to your colleagues as you were with your portfolio companies.*

KEN: We were very particular about making sure we did things right. In the oil and gas business, people are always watching—regulators, activists, litigators, you name it. We needed confidence that our companies were doing things the right way. People are amazed to learn how few legal and environmental problems our companies have had.

I am not, because we made it a point to, as Richard Rainwater would say, "stay as far away from the foul line as possible."

I'm not sure if this was a tennis, baseball, or basketball analogy. He played them all. I never asked, since I knew exactly what he meant.

As for being selective: If people in New York State don't want oil and gas development, despite the fact that there are thousands of gas wells in that state and the reserves in the ground are massive, then we wouldn't go there. We stayed away from environmentally sensitive areas. We stayed away from difficult regulatory authorities for the most part. If we did venture into those areas, we would heavily discount the price so that we were sure to be compensated for taking on that added risk.

Living by the adage that "the best place to find oil and gas is in old oil and gas fields" had a corollary: "Only go where oil and gas development is wanted and appreciated." In addition, since our management team's money was being invested alongside ours, their risk aversion typically enforced both of those rules. We went where it was easier.

I'd rather be a strong follower than a groundbreaker. The groundbreaker struggles with what I call the double-double problem. They're fighting all the normal challenges of the industry, *and* they are doing it in a place where people would prefer that they fail. With all this headwind, things tend to take twice as long and cost twice as much. There's plenty of oil and gas in Texas, Oklahoma, and Louisiana. I don't need to go to Yellowstone to try to drill wells just because there may be oil and gas there.

I might have been able to make a lot more money if I had been a groundbreaker, but that was not my philosophy. In the oil and gas business, those groundbreakers were known as wildcat explorationists. There were legendary stories of the wildcatters who created great wealth by discovering new oil and gas fields.

We heard about such legends, but the business graveyard was full of people who tried and failed. The library has only a handful of books on the few dozen or so who made it. When I compared the number of those who were consistent winners to those who ultimately lost it all, the answer became obvious. Trying to have your name show up as one of the great explorationists was a bad bet, especially for a liberal arts guy with an MBA wandering around the oil patch. I wanted to find ways where the returns were good, and the risk was far lower. For me, this meant backing trustworthy people with boring business plans and being a great partner.

Richard Rainwater emphasized, "There are so many ways to make money, so don't make it harder on yourself than it has to be." He meant that, in business, there is a lot of gray area in between the black or white that separates right from wrong. Operate in the white areas. Don't get comfortable in the gray zones. That's when someone can get close to the foul line.

I wanted NGP to be a stabilizing force, whether the news was good or bad. Our job was to not get too excited when things went well and to not get too pissed off when things went awry. It was important to be a good partner and work through any problem issues together.

This became NGP's defining trait, and that reputation spread throughout the industry. We became the partner of choice for so many entrepreneurs in the oil patch. It also had the side benefit of solidifying our friendships with certain of our CEOs. Given that we had so many experiences with them through ups and downs, it was almost impossible not to get close. Many of them became lifelong friends as close to me as David, Dick, and John.

STEVE: *It's hard for me to imagine that the firm would have had so much success and so little turnover if you were the "jerk" you've alluded to in some of our conversations.*

KEN: My jerkiness, if that's a word, came when I had someone who was lagging in some way. I was shorter with them than I should have been. I took the attitude that the train was leaving the station, and you had better hop on, or you'll get left behind. We hired a bunch of highly educated professionals, paid them well, and included them in everything. So, if they were somehow underperforming, I had high expectations that they could take the critique, adjust, and move forward. In the office, I figured that I wasn't there to manage their feelings. I expected thick skin.

I think my management style really became defined during this period. I embraced having a double standard when it came to people around me—those who were in my foxhole and then those who were not. Of course, central to my foxhole philosophy is that there is unlimited room in my foxhole. I want everyone in there. I want everyone to have each other's back and to care deeply for each other's success. I relished having that team chemistry with high-performing type A people around who were motivated to do good work and pushed themselves. With those people, interactions were fun and rewarding. We challenged each other. We argued. We agreed. We disagreed. We laughed.

When people performed, the sky was the limit, and I was very hands-off, just checking in on the progress along the way. When someone underperformed, I tended to micromanage their work more. This often caused friction. Our business was pretty fast-paced, and we didn't have a ton of time to redo work or to undo a string of bad decisions. Whether it was a colleague at NGP or one of our management team executives, when I lost confidence, I bore down a little harder.

John Foster, who had a great vantage point to watch my style in dealing with colleagues, summed it up nicely one time. He quipped, "Ken only micromanages when you suck!"

As a lifelong Dallas Cowboys fan, I took a cue from the successful coach in their championship run of the early 1990s. Jimmy Johnson was accused of having a double standard because Michael Irvin broke team rules. When a less accomplished player pointed that out when Johnson was disciplining him for something that he had let slide with his All-Pro receiver, the coach responded, "You're damn right I have a double standard. Michael is a star! Now, get back in there and go back to work!"

At that time, I was probably more of a servant-leader with the top performers. The others may have called me an impatient micromanaging tyrant. But I meant well and always tried to make amends.

Much later, those few who incurred my immature wrath would say that I was more like that tough high school or college teacher who was a real hard-ass but who they respected and who, in the end, taught them a lot. Folks jokingly, *I think*, would remind me of my style by posting on the lunchroom bulletin board a few wayward envelopes that found their way to our office misspelling my name as "Ken Harsh."

The administrative staff was different, however. They were along for the ride and relied on us to make sure they had a future. They weren't so highly compensated that I could take the "get with the program" attitude. And, significantly, they were more of a risk-averse bunch who wanted a stable work environment and were not necessarily looking at the firm as a place where they would make millions. Hence, my double standard. I think I was much nicer to them.

STEVE: *Looking back, do you think you were inventing a new leadership mantra?*

KEN: I sure didn't feel like an inventor. I felt like a blind man feeling his way through a maze.

STEVE: *Or a tortoise on a circuitous road.*

Mona Hersh with her children, Susie, Ken, and Paula, circa 1966. (Hersh family photo archives)

Susie, Ken, and Paula, 1978. (Hersh family photo archives)

Ken as a sophomore at Princeton, fall 1982. (Hersh family photo archives)

Ken in his Morgan Stanley office in New York, 1985. (Hersh family photo archives)

Ken with Kendall Cochran and Mona Hersh-Cochran at Princeton graduation, June 1985.

(Hersh family photo archives)

Ken, with St. Mark's and Princeton classmates Richard Dzina and Gil Wolfe, Princeton graduation, June 1985.

(Hersh family photo archives)

Bill Browder and Ken, traveling to Europe, March 1989. (Hersh family photo archives)

Ken at Stanford Graduate School of Business graduation, June 1989. (Hersh family photo archives)

Julie and her brother, Tom Kosnik, Monterey Bay Aquarium, August 4, 1990. (Hersh family photo archives)

Ken, Julie, and Daniel, October 1994. (Hersh family photo archives)

Ken, Rachel, and Daniel, May 1999. (Hersh family photo archives)

Dr. Stanley Hersh (Ken's uncle) and Dr. Bernard Hersh (Ken's father), August 2010. (Hersh family photo archives)

Hersh family, Seattle, August 2002. (Hersh family photo archives)

Ken and Daniel doused with champagne in the clubhouse of Globe Life Park when the Rangers clinched the AL pennant versus the Yankees, October 22, 2010. (Photo by Scott Rosuck)

John Foster, David Albin, and Ken celebrating NGP's 25th anniversary, Santa Fe, New Mexico, July 2013. (Photo courtesy of NGP)

Ken speaking at the World Economic Forum alongside energy industry experts, including Fatih Birol (executive director of International Energy Agency), Davos, Switzerland, January 17, 2017. (Photo copyright by World Economic Forum/Jakob Polacsek)

Ken speaking at St. Mark's Distinguished Alumni Awards, Dallas, April 2015. (Photo courtesy of St. Mark's School of Texas)

Ken speaking at the Milken Institute Global Conference, Los Angeles, May 2017. (Getty Images)

Ken with President George W. Bush and Bono, Prairie Chapel Ranch, Crawford, Texas, May 2017. (Hersh family photo archives)

Jon Mosle (president, board of trustees), Ken, and David Dini (headmaster) prior to delivering commencement address at St. Mark's graduation, Dallas, May 2017. (Hersh family photo archives)

Ken interviewing Jeff Bezos at the Bush Center's Forum on Leadership, April 2018. (Grant Miller Photography/George W. Bush Presidential Center)

Ken golfing with President Bush when he recorded his first hole-in-one, Trinity Forest Golf Club, Dallas, March 2019. (Hersh family photo archives)

Rachel and Ken at Rachel's college graduation, Evanston, Illinois, June 2019. (Hersh family photo archives)

Ken accepting the ADL Henry Cohn Humanitarian Award, Dallas, November 2019.
(Photo by Jason Janik for ADL)

Rachel, Julie, Daniel, and Ken, November 2019. (Hersh family photo archives)

Ken with Jay Leno at the Bush
Center, March 2020. (Grant Miller
Photography/George W. Bush
Presidential Center)

Ken's happy place—on the Pecos River in New Mexico, September 2020. (Hersh family photo archives)

Ken at the Nantucket Yacht Club, July 2021. It took 58 years . . . (Hersh family photo archives)

Ken, Peter Joost, and David Albin at David's son Ben's wedding, November 2021. (Hersh family photo archives)

Regen Horchow and Ken, Mexico, December 2021. (Hersh family photo archives)

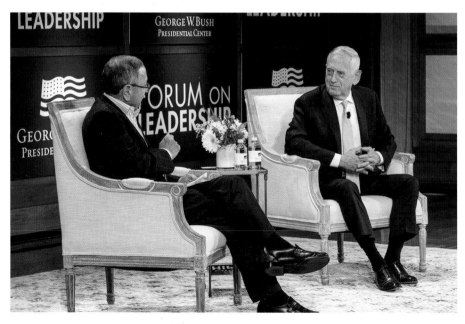

Ken interviewing former secretary of defense Jim Mattis at the Bush Center, April 2022. (Grant Miller Photography/George W. Bush Presidential Center)

CHAPTER 9

FEED THE WINNERS

STEVE: *Seriously, I think you were developing the makings for a new leadership school.*

KEN: I am not sure about a new leadership school, but in hindsight, what I was doing was feeding my winners internally, just like we did with our portfolio companies. In fact, you could boil down a lot of my philosophy around investing and management with this one phrase.

STEVE: *You used that phrase earlier. What exactly does that mean?*

KEN: Our investment style was built on this philosophy. We started a bunch of companies with no assets except for the people who we thought had some sort of an edge in a particular region. We would give them an equity commitment to serve as shopping money for them to go acquire assets in their target area. They would buy oil and gas wells and acreage and then try to add value to what they bought. If they were successful, we could go out and borrow some money against those original assets to buy more. If their success continued, we could add more money to our investment and let them shop some more. The more success they had, the more money we would keep adding to the enterprise. As they grew and continued to enhance the value of what they bought, the value of our equity investment would go up. Simple as that.

In the end, the more success the company had, the larger our investment would become. For those who were unsuccessful, we would, in essence, cut them off sooner. Thus, we fed our winners and starved our losers. Over the entire portfolio, then, the lion's share of the capital went to successful companies. Our profitable investments grew to be bigger ones, even though they didn't start out as large bets. Our losses were smaller. By doing a lot of little things right, our tortoise philosophy won the race and, as a whole, our funds performed in the top quartile of all funds in the country.

I guess I did the same thing with people. I think John Foster was right.

STEVE: *How did this leadership philosophy play in the hallways?*

KEN: What I learned was that if you have a "feed the winners" strategy with the people around you, the organization reacts.

First, it's fun to reward those high achievers with more responsibility, more reward, and more engagement, so long as there's no quota to the number of people in the winner's circle. I operated that way. I wanted everyone to achieve because I knew they could. When they did, we operated as a well-oiled machine.

That is how you would have described NGP during those years. David, John, and I, plus our junior colleagues were getting a lot done and having fun doing it. We challenged each other, but we never had a doubt that we wouldn't stick together.

We were real partners. As we added people, they fit the bill as well. Dick Covington, Billy Quinn, David Hayes, Brian Crumley, and Bruce Selkirk were all important early adds who became key parts of our growing franchise. On the administrative side, Don Shore, Laura Futrell Beagle, Lauren Garner Davila, Patty Davis, Judy Ingram, Nancy Buckland, and Helene Haston, among others, provided the firm support.

They worked hard, had thick skin, and excelled as part of the team. We had a good division of labor between deal sourcing, document execution, accounting, investor relations, and office management. Everyone on this team knew that my bark was worse than my bite because, in the end, any frustrations I had stemmed from the high expectations that I had for each. Today, I remain close to each and every one of these great people, and they know how valuable they were to the early success of NGP.

Everyone saw that the winners were being fed. Cash compensation, responsibility, and office attention were real. I wanted everyone to see and understand. When this happened, there was so much great give-and-take, and I welcomed it.

In the end, I found that having this "feed the winners" management philosophy resulted in three things over time. First, people who were not in this group but wanted to be had the behavior to model right there in front of them. They worked at it, improved, and made the cut.

Second, others looked at the work required to be in that winner's circle of favorites and opted to remain outside that circle but were quite happy to ride along. This group was indispensable to the firm. They provided a ton of support for all of us and enjoyed the growth of the firm and being a part of it.

The third group, which thankfully was small, was made up of those that somehow couldn't advance or were resentful. They ultimately left the firm, which was an acceptable outcome altogether. During the first twenty years or so of the firm, that group comprised only a few administrative workers who came and went. We were really fortunate with our hiring.

Now, I have a PowerPoint presentation I use for speeches titled "Leadership and Organizational Impact," and I always close with "Ken's Axioms," hoping that some tale from my set of experiences will be a nice nugget that someone can apply to their own situation and benefit.

STEVE: *It's a great presentation that I think would be very instructive to anyone reading this. You begin by describing three types of leadership styles. There's the servant-leader—which you say you were—the autocrat, and the smartest person in the room. How do these differ?*

KEN: The servant-leader is the person who asks their team, "How can I help you succeed?" This leader believes the progress and development of others are more important than the leader's. This leader understands the goals are of the collective and that power and the spoils of success should be shared. This type of leader thanks more than scolds and is secure enough to hire great people—and actually listen to them.

A good servant-leader can be demanding without being demeaning. I worked on that all the time, even though I didn't always get it right. I can only ask for forgiveness to those who stumbled onto Ken "Harsh."

STEVE: *As opposed to the autocrat, who asks, "How can you serve me?"*

KEN: An autocracy may work when the autocrat is inspirational, but a successful autocracy is almost impossible to sustain. They don't have to be mean and ugly. In fact, the successful ones often are wonderfully driven, inspirational leaders. But the autocrat had better be a benevolent dictator, or the talent will leave. When the autocrat adopts a "What have you done for me lately?" attitude, that's a recipe for instability and perhaps a mass exodus. Selfish people rarely have a loyal following for too long. They are then forced to govern by fear. Clearly, this is not the building block for a sustainable franchise.

STEVE: *What about the "smartest guy in the room" model? I'd think that people would love to follow a leader in whom they had confidence.*

KEN: You'd think so, but this model isn't sustainable either. The smartest person in the room, who proclaims, "I know better; here is what we are going to do," presents a thorny issue. Quite frankly, many successful companies emerge because of the brilliant and charismatic leader who either founded the enterprise or was at the helm in the formative stages. That person may *actually be* the smartest, and this approach may work when an organization is young, but rest assured, there will always be smarter people who come along.

STEVE: *Then what?*

KEN: That's when a company enters the danger zone. The leader can either become an autocrat who shuts out the smarter generation or transition to a servant-leader who recognizes that the up-and-comers are smarter and should be put in positions to lead. Ultimately, that requires remarkable self-awareness, since this is the beginning of the passing of the torch. Many leaders whose identities are tied up with their business find out that this is nearly impossible for them to do.

Moreover, it is a challenge for that emerging group, since a charismatic leader can be a very tough act to follow. That is where many organizations that are led by the smartest guy in the room falter in the long term. Examples are everywhere. GE after Jack Welch's reign. Apple after Steve Jobs's first run at the helm, and IBM after Lou Gerstner. Each of those companies stumbled before regaining their footing when a new leader was appointed to succeed the charismatic smartest guy in the room.

STEVE: *You have a section in your presentation called "The Problem."*

KEN: Yes. Great leadership that gets celebrated often augurs its own demise.

STEVE: *That sounds hard to believe. Can you explain?*

KEN: We often celebrate strong individual leaders without noting what they're doing to the organizations they lead, sowing the seeds of future problems. We applaud these leaders, their financial success, and corporate size. *Forbes* and *Fortune* built their respective publications' franchises around lists of the world's richest people and the world's largest companies, equating those two measures with success overall. They are good indicators of financial success for sure, but not necessarily staying power.

Cultures adopt the norms perpetuated by these leaders, and those norms can become entrenched in corporate lore. There are vast numbers of failures out there that never get dissected. But think about some of the nation's most successful companies that have romanticized stories around the quirky personalities of their leaders when the companies were young—Sam Walton, Herb Kelleher, Ross Perot, and others like them. They were all unique personalities who led organizations and became legendary. Taken out of context, many of their behaviors would be reprehensible. However, when associated with a corporate success, they become positive parts of the corporate culture. Their companies reflected their styles.

Now, think about what happened when those leaders left their businesses. It's very hard for a new leadership style to take root without a wholesale makeover. An autocratic-style leader could find it impossible to live up to his or her predecessor. If a servant-leader comes in to lead the company to the next level, a workforce that is accustomed to dogma and charisma may not be capable of responding well. How can the corporate culture shift from a command-and-control style to one of collaboration and consensus? If a muscle is not developed, it is hard to flex. The same can be said of a corporate culture.

This problem is compounded if the charismatic leader was the enterprise's founder. Here you might think of Travis Kalanick at Uber. His drive and inspiration were needed to start the company, but different skills were needed to manage the company's growth once it became established. His successor has found that the job of managing a company in an ever-changing industry is hard, but it is made even more difficult if he has to engineer a wholesale cultural change while also fighting off tough competition.

STEVE: *It sounds like you have personally seen each of these three dynamics in action.*

KEN: I can safely say that I've *been* each of these three types over the years, occasionally to the chagrin of those around me.

Over the decades I probably wasn't the model of consistency. I can speak from experience now. I only hope that the folks who were around me during these years will forgive me for learning on the job.

STEVE: *With so little turnover in those first twenty-five years of the firm, my bet is that they have.*

KEN: Hope so.

STEVE: *I'm guessing you had a pretty good data set of leadership lessons going on in and around your firm.*

KEN: I saw each of these three leadership styles in practice at our various portfolio companies over the years. With over 250 companies spread around the NGP portfolios, I witnessed just about every senior management style that could exist in corporate America. We backed some very seasoned executives like Jon Brumley, from whom I learned a ton. We also backed a lot of very young management teams who, like us, were figuring it out as they went along.

Our role in helping these executives execute their business plans often turned to helping them manage their senior managers or junior partners. We became the de facto human resources department for our portfolio companies, since most were too small to actually have an HR manager. This afforded us a lot of opportunity to see what was working and what wasn't in the field.

One thing became apparent to me over time: Small personnel issues portend bigger problems later on. The tendency in management is to try to "coach up" workers who are showing signs of trouble. Whether these are performance or personality issues, the default behavior often is to try to work through them. Performance reviews, professional coaches, and training programs are all part of the remediation effort.

Managers obviously had hired all the employees, so throwing in the towel on someone was really a sign that the hiring decision itself was a mistake. Nobody likes to admit a mistake, especially when they can try to fix it. That's what often happens. Time and time again, performance issues are addressed, with all good intentions.

In my experience, with the more senior colleagues, personality or performance issues never seemed to go away. Maybe they went into hiding for a while and fooled those around the company. But invariably the behavior appeared again, became more disruptive, and ultimately led to a difficult personnel issue.

It never ceased to amaze me how coaching and counseling failed to produce new behavior. If the issue was a skills gap, then it was relatively easy to rectify through teaching and experience. However, when the issues related to personality or character traits, those small signs were often perfect indicators of larger issues—issues that would inevitably grow over time.

What I realized was that yellow lights don't turn green. By this I mean that when we had to make a personnel decision at our various companies, we almost always had plenty of small "yellow lights" warning us that concerning behavioral patterns were emerging. Invariably, we ended up making changes, but realized that it would have been a heck of a lot easier if we had just owned up to the issue and made the change sooner.

I'm generally an optimist who wants everyone to succeed, so I was always reluctant to throw in the towel at the first sign of trouble. But, almost always, once we made the change, we kicked ourselves—saying we should have done that months or years earlier.

The same thing could be said of company performance. It is also telling how few times companies that performed weakly in the very early stages of operations were able to turn it around. Again, in many cases, we were more forgiving of weak early performance since the team was just starting out and the stakes were much smaller. But, many times, the mistakes that were being made on one or two assets were just magnified when the company had hundreds. From a portfolio company standpoint, we definitely learned that yellow lights don't turn green. We got this message early enough and used it to keep our losses smaller.

In the end, we were lucky that we had a lot of "green lights" around on which to build relationships that lasted—relationships with each other, relationships with our management teams, and relationships with investors in the industry. It took time to build those, but we took the time, and it worked out well.

We were pretty happy tortoises.

STEVE: *Speaking of time, how did you—as a leader of an enterprise on which so many depended and on which so much money was riding—balance the time between work and family? You had two young kids during those early years, and as you noted, Julie was battling serious depression. I don't want to play armchair psychologist, but you had grown up in a dysfunctional household. I'm assuming that you didn't want to repeat what you considered the sins of the past. It's one thing to be a CEO. It's another to be CEO and husband and father.*

KEN: That was the tough part. Life was really full, but in a good way, from the start of NGP in 1988 until 2001. Growing our business while navigating the uncertainty of the industry was a challenge. But doing it with partners who were all going through it together made it more fun.

As a private firm with a family feel, we were fortunate that we were able to make time for family. Of course, as we grew, my work and travel schedule made it impossible to make all the family dinners or events. That was the sacrifice I had to make.

Julie also made a sacrifice. She had a flourishing career at a telecommunications technology company in California and was able to transfer to its Dallas office and take on a sales role. She was very successful in that capacity. However, once Daniel was born, it became obvious that she could be a 100 percent performer at her company or a 100 percent great mom but not both. Having tried for about a year to burn the candle at both ends, she realized the difficulties. It hit her hard one day when Daniel, then a toddler, ran into the outstretched arms of our nanny instead of her. She quit working right then.

She sacrificed her career so she could devote the time to our family and be the rock that I needed in order to go out and do battle every day. She bore the lion's share of child-rearing from 1995 until 2001, managing the household, moving into a new house, and keeping tabs on two rambunctious toddlers.

This worked until that rock cracked. In 2001, shortly after Rachel began going to school full time, Julie began to question her identity. With both kids now in school for a full day and less reliant on her, she hit a wall. Because of some unknown combination of environment, chemistry, and electricity, her brain tripped into a depressive break. She became suicidal and quite despondent.

Reality hit me right between the eyes. Our cozy world was shaken; time seemed to stop. I throttled back my work life for a while and ensured that the kids were taken care of and that Julie was able to get the best care possible. I relied heavily on our friends who were in our family's foxhole. Nothing would have been possible without the love and support of so many around us. It was amazing how people came out of the wood-work to help. I knew we had built a strong community in Dallas, but I didn't know how strong it was until I saw people drop what they were doing to help. Julie saw it too. I will forever be grateful to our Friday night supper club, affectionately known as our Shabbat Group, who seemed to drop everything to be at our side.

With the help of many, both inside and outside of the office, I juggled, and we got through it. I wasn't about to give up on the challenge of dealing with her condition. Reading and talking to experts on mental illness helped. It is a disease like many others, and it was important that we realized that. Julie was not somehow defective. We finally found a treatment that worked and are blessed that Julie did not end up as a suicide statistic. The often maligned but quite effective use of electroconvulsive therapy (ECT) worked wonders for her. We were fortunate that the doctors at the University of Texas Southwestern Medical School facility in Dallas were fans of this treatment for medica-tion-resistant depression.

She recovered in 2001. Although she relapsed several more times over the years, the ECT treatments always seemed to do the trick. She has demonstrated courage not only by being open about her struggles with depression but also in her willingness to help those in need. She wrote a popular book, *Struck by Living*, about her own path in overcoming depression, and she has dedicated her philanthropy, in part, to the search for effective measures to prevent and treat depression.

In addition, part of her recovery has been to recognize the tendencies she has had toward depression throughout her life and to take steps to stay well. More on this later, but recognizing that she needed to take steps to stay well led her to make the difficult choice to end our thirty-year marriage.

Personally, I can't help but think that I had something to do with her depressive episodes, although she is quick to point out that it's a chronic medical condition that afflicts millions. If she had diabetes, she argues, I wouldn't run around saying I caused it. However, the life of a professional woman who makes sacrifices for a husband and family is complicated for sure. While she has not realized the cash compensation that I've earned, I haven't realized the clutching hug of a child around its mother's neck or the feeling that fills a mother's heart when her child beams and giggles with her. That connection is compensation that I will never receive. It was hers and hers alone.

Not standing by her was never an option when she was sick. We were a family. Like any chronic disease, her depression didn't go away. It became an added element of our life together—one that we would have to tend to like a member of the family. A serious illness is life's not-so-little way of reminding us that we are not superhuman but rather mortals who need to appreciate that imperfection and weaknesses are part of our existence.

This master of the universe got a real-life lesson in the spring of 2001 that life is precious, and nobody is immune. That lesson would continue for some twenty years. And, just like other serious chronic illnesses, mental illness can wreak havoc on any family and, ultimately, contribute to permanent change.

CHAPTER 10

FEED THE DUCKS WHILE THEY'RE QUACKING

STEVE: *No less an authority on the oil and gas business than the singer Kenny Rogers is famous for advising on when to hold and when to fold. I don't know if "The Gambler" is on your musical playlist, but you seem to have taken his advice to heart with great success.*

In this section, I'd like to talk about a high-profile, high-stakes instance when, under your leadership, NGP made the decision to cash in some chips. This was your involvement with a partnership called Energy Transfer Equity (ETE).

KEN: Other than the name Kenny, I don't think I have much in common with Kenny Rogers, at least as far as that song is concerned. I'm not much of a gambler. I credit that to an early trip to Atlantic City during my sophomore year at Princeton.

STEVE: *Explain, please. I feel another racing-stripe story coming on.*

KEN: There were promotional lines that ran a bus to Atlantic City from Princeton just about every day. The cost of the bus ride was $35 round trip and when you got there, the casino gave you a $25 roll of quarters and a coupon for a free all-you-can-eat dinner buffet. It was a no-brainer way to spend a long day. Put an extra $60 in my pocket, leave Princeton around four in the afternoon, and be home by midnight. I figured I'd spend $60 on a fun night out, so spending this would be just like that.

That all worked fine as far as the dinner and trip was concerned, but I remember losing the extra $60 I had in my pocket at the tables on that first trip. It felt like crap. I usually didn't feel that way after a night out.

I didn't have that much extra cash lying around—my lucrative summer job had yet to occur, and I had to clean out my savings to pay tuition for myself and my sister. Since it was a self-inflicted loss, I couldn't help but feel stupid for freely losing money that meant something to me at the time.

I'll never forget that feeling of watching a dealer scrape away my chips. It wasn't fun at all.

As to the song itself, I have come to appreciate that in cyclical businesses, it is best to know when to hold and when to fold, or as I like to say, feed the ducks while they're quacking. There are times when everyone is saying that the only way things can go is up. These are the times to sell. Cycles tend to repeat themselves. So good times often set up the bad times and vice versa.

When you're selling a business, it's best to sell when buyers are interested. That tends to be a time when people are clamoring for assets, like ducks vying for loose bread-crumbs. I know it sounds intuitive, but I'm always amazed when people think about selling an asset on their timetable, instead of the buyer's. In fact, I don't think you actually ever *sell* anything. I think that you have an asset available when a buyer comes along. A grocer doesn't sell an apple. A grocer has a pile of apples available should shoppers for apples wander down the aisle. That's how I tried to manage the business.

STEVE: *So tell me about the Energy Transfer investment. How did the opportunity present itself, and how did you decide whether to make the investment?*

KEN: This investment started much like all our others. It was a bet on people. At an annual industry social retreat put on by three friends in the oil patch, aptly named Tres Compadres, I had shared a golf cart with Ray Davis, a very successful operator who I had known just casually up to that point. I must admit that I kind of wormed my way into his golf cart by begging to be his partner at one of the prior Tres Compadres outings. It was the spring of 2002. The Lake Whitney setting outside Hillsboro, Texas, was comfortable. The two of us were partners in a tournament format for the day. We weren't that compet-itive in the matches, but we had a good time getting to know each other.

Over the course of the day, we talked about getting positioned to buy assets that might be divested as part of the unwinding of the Enron debacle at that time. Amid the internet boom of the late 1990s, Enron and other gas transmission companies attempted to transform themselves from stodgy utility mentalities to that of merchant growth, defined by savvy trading operations and repositioning their fixed assets into growth opportunities.

That worked for a while. But the tech wreck of 2001 and the California power crisis of 2000 and 2001 brought the game to a screeching halt. Their trading operations came under scrutiny and their strategies were called into question. No longer did their stocks trade at high levels. With access to new capital severely limited, their excessive debt loads began to weigh on them. Plus, regulators began to focus on the concentration of natural gas assets held by the few large trading companies. Whenever the government turns its sights on an industry, chaos usually erupts. And, wherever there is chaos, there seems to be opportunity. It seemed inevitable that companies in the gas transmission and marketing sector would have to divest assets to survive.

Ray talked about the emerging company that he and his partner, Kelcy Warren, had created. That company, Energy Transfer (ET), was based in Dallas and was in the business of acquiring natural gas assets inside the state of Texas. I had known Kelcy since the early 1990s, when NGP had looked at making an investment in the company he ran before starting Energy Transfer.

This time around, NGP was more seasoned, and my instinct around people was more developed as well. Ray and Kelcy made a great team. Kelcy, who understood the gas business like nobody else, was able to sniff out a deal and was not afraid to pull the trigger on big assets. Ray was a great operator with a calm demeanor who could ensure that the i's were dotted and the t's were crossed. They had assembled a nice nucleus of people around them and had a good start on assembling a portfolio of assets. In many ways, Energy Transfer was a lot like NGP.

Although our backgrounds were different, I think I found my deal-making kindred spirit in Kelcy. He grew up in East Texas and went to the University of Texas. He spent time as a natural gas pipeline operator and gas trader and had a keen sense of how the molecules moved around the system. He loves the Texas hillside, country music, boots, and a good story. Except for taste in music and boots, we were alike. We each had what some might view as an unreasonably positive outlook—an outlook that, I'd argue, is exactly what was needed to survive the wild swings of the natural gas business.

Not only does the gas business cycle about every three to five years like most other industries, but it also cycles *during* the year. The demand for natural gas varies so wildly throughout the year that prices swing wildly too. Given that about half the annual natural gas demand in the United States occurs in the winter months, an unexpectedly warm or unseasonably cold winter can cause wild volatility. The weather can be as impactful to results as drilling a successful well. This is the perfect industry for someone who can sense where the market is heading, assemble assets in strategic locations, and then keep a cool head throughout the year. Kelcy was that guy.

I also liked managing in an arena of uncertainty. It required a simple understanding: Never get too excited when times are great, and never get too pissed off when times are bad. *Think clearly and act accordingly*, I would think, trying to calm myself during times of extreme volatility. *What should I do that, five years from now, will have everyone saying, "Man, that guy was so smart for doing that five years ago"?*

Just as I had David Albin, Dick Covington, and John Foster around me to help execute, Kelcy had Ray Davis. And, just as I respected and relied on David, Dick, and John to help wrestle my wild ideas to the ground, discarding the foolish and helping refine the workable ones, Kelcy respected his partnership with Ray.

Soon after my day of golf with Ray, NGP committed to investing in Energy Transfer to get positioned to pounce on distressed assets that we thought would hit the market soon. To consummate the deal, we had to value ET's existing business, so we could come to an agreement as to how much of the company we would own for our investment. We also had to structure an incentive package for Ray and Kelcy to earn more return after we had achieved certain return thresholds.

I went out on a limb with my partners on this one. The hodgepodge of assets that existed in Kelcy and Ray's company at the time was okay but not great. They had decent cash flow, but their internal projections were wildly inflated. Of course, they wanted us to value their business off those projections, while we would have liked to base ours on the lower actual numbers.

In my mind, it didn't matter that much. The lion's share of the future value of the company would be based on what they did with our money, plus new money that we would ultimately have to go raise. If we made a bunch of smart investments and raised future money at higher and higher values, then any mistake I was making by overvaluing these original assets would be small in the ultimate scheme of things. If they blew the money we were putting in, then the value of the whole thing would go away, and it wouldn't matter then anyway. Zero is still zero.

More important, I didn't want to have a knock-down, drag-out fight with my new partners. Ray and Kelcy were seasoned executives, and we had big aspirations. I didn't want to start the relationship with a bitter negotiation. I acquiesced to the value that they suggested. Some of NGP's young number crunchers who had worked on the valuation materials thought I was nuts. But David and the other partners trusted me.

I kept my eye on the prize. The prize was building trust with my new partners and focusing on capturing a set of assets that would position the company for a big valuation jump someday.

STEVE: *How did you get started?*

KEN: Energy Transfer's first deal with us in the mix was the $265 million acquisition of the South Texas gathering and transmission assets from Aquila, a Kansas

City–based utility. That utility had no business owning these assets and was now in the process of divesting.

Kelcy and Ray found the assets to buy and negotiated the price. They came to me to confirm that we were in agreement with the bid and would help them get the capital they would need to close the deal. This was right up our alley. In this instance, we were able to arrange a decent bank line but had to come up with about $100 million of equity capital. As usual, we stuck our chest out and committed to the deal, confident that we could raise the money. We spoke for $37 million, since that was 10 percent of our $370 million fund. This amount was enough to get us started, and we offered the balance to a series of coinvestors—some of whom were investors in our fund and some who were friends of NGP, Ray, or Kelcy. That deal closed in the fall of 2002. Believe it or not, that was the last equity we would put into the company.

STEVE: *Fast-forward about five years, and through a combination with Heritage Propane Partners, several major acquisitions, and numerous organic growth projects, Ray Davis and Kelcy Warren grew Energy Transfer from a small private company into the third-largest publicly traded midstream master limited partnership. How were you involved in that evolution?*

KEN: As with any good partnership, it's hard to tell where our influence ended, theirs began, and vice versa. It was really the model for how I wanted NGP deals to work.

That dawned on me during a conversation at a Young Presidents' Organization (YPO) social function with a friend who ran a competing investment fund. "We looked at that [Energy Transfer] deal too," he said with a competitive undertone that I think was secretly wishing for us to lose money. "But we just couldn't figure out how to control Ray and Kelcy."

I blurted out a response. "That was our analysis too. But we came to the conclusion that *we didn't want* to control them. We were happy being their partners and seeing what we could do together."

That was the secret to our success. If we lacked so much trust in a management team that we *needed* to control them, then odds were that we were picking the wrong management team in the first place. As I've told you, Rainwater used to say to us, "Regardless of whether you own 99 percent of the company or 1 percent of the company, you work for the management teams. They are doing the heavy lifting, and they know way more than you do about what is going on." We never forgot that.

With that philosophy in hand, we helped Kelcy and Ray navigate a series of acquisitions that assembled a set of gas-gathering and processing-plant assets around Texas and Oklahoma, as well as one of the long-haul pipelines that transports gas across

Texas. We were helpful in ensuring that they were always financeable and did our part to find creative structures to access cheaper capital. If the bond market was open, we issued bonds. If the public equity markets were open, we looked at going public.

In the end, we were able to merge our company in 2003 with Heritage Propane Partners in what many thought was a crazy idea. Heritage Propane was a publicly traded, low-growth, tired, master limited partnership valued on the basis of its steady cash flow distributed to its unit holders. Energy Transfer was more of a growth company that needed as much cash as possible to fund future growth. Most thought that it made no sense to merge the two companies.

However, we saw it as a way to use the Heritage units as a currency with which to do future transactions. Plus, we felt our assets were good enough cash generators not only to be able to sustain a decent dividend but also to reposition us as a growth company that would trade at a higher cash flow multiple.

When the teams identified the Heritage merger opportunity, Dick Covington sprang into action to work with Energy Transfer's finance and legal teams. Dick knew the ins and outs of partnership agreements better than anyone in the country. He knew our transaction documents with Energy Transfer and also knew how to work with the Heritage partnership agreement to make the merger happen.

Along the way, a light bulb went on. To control the Heritage public company, it was more critical to control the general partner entity of Heritage Propane Partners. This was very familiar territory for me and my partners at NGP.

STEVE: *How so?*

KEN: First, this was the structure of our own partnership. We raised money under the name Natural Gas Partners, but each fund was actually an individual partnership with a distinct general partner entity that controlled it. Our investors purchased limited partnership units in the partnership, but we owned 100 percent of the general partner and, thus, retained full control over the operations of the whole partnership. At the time, we were operating our sixth fund, so we knew firsthand the earning power of this structure for the general partner who was entitled to earn 20 percent of the profits.

Second, having been through the entire Mesa transaction, we were well aware of how these vehicles traded publicly. We knew when they traded well and when the public market punished them. Growth vehicles of this structure can work, but it's challenging, since the public unitholders expect a strong sustainable cash dividend. Growth companies typically don't pay out good dividends, if at all, since they need to retain their cash to fund growth.

However, if you have a growth vehicle that can grow *and* pay out a good dividend, then there is a big market for the units and the prices should rise. If the unit prices are rising, then the partnership can issue more units to fund its growth. The key is the partnership needs to have compelling investment opportunities for the unitholders to appreciate. The assets that Kelcy and Ray were assembling had such a profile at a time when interest rates were declining and, hence, the public was receptive to securities that paid a decent yield.

As a no-growth propane partnership that paid out all its free cash flow, the general partner of Heritage really wasn't worth much. Its cash flow was barely covering the administrative costs of running the public partnership. In addition, the ownership structure made it difficult to think it would do anything differently in the future. It was equally owned by four different utility companies. It was what we called a stepchild asset because it meant very little to these utilities. The gas utilities had merged their disparate propane companies in early 2000 as a way to begin the exit process. So this deal was a natural evolution. It didn't take much convincing for them to sell it to us. We only needed to agree on price. For them, we were the quacking duck, and they fed it to us.

The four owner utilities wanted to sell it to us for $30 million. This was an insane asking price, given the entity's meager cash flow. Kelcy complained that he was never going to pay that price for the general partner. Dick, who's as good a negotiator as they come, agreed that this price was crazy. But we needed to buy the Heritage general partner to make the merger go. This was the entity that controlled the limited partnership.

"Pay it!" I said impetuously.

I argued that the vehicle was worth way more to us than to them and that we probably couldn't take Energy Transfer public on our own without tremendous delay and costs. Also important: The Heritage general partner agreement allowed the general partner to collect 20 percent of the profits above a certain rate of return. These were known as the incentive distribution rights. As a propane company, the general partner wasn't receiving much, if any, profits distribution. Arguing about the value would have wasted time—time that was critical to us. The few million dollars between their offer and what we'd pay would not matter much in the end. I knew the power of that profits interests provision in the agreement. The general partner of Heritage wasn't in a position to profit from that provision, but I knew we could. So we proceeded.

In mid-2003, with an agreement in hand to purchase the general partner, we were able to structure a transaction that passed muster with the investors and orchestrated a reverse merger of Energy Transfer's assets into Heritage Propane Partners, changing the name to Energy Transfer Partners, LP (ETP). Just like our structure motivated us to work hard to generate investment profits for NGP, this structure would motivate all of us to work hard to increase the equity value of the new Energy Transfer Partners.

Separately, our Energy Transfer Company paid the $30 million to buy the general partner of Heritage and renamed it Energy Transfer Equity, LP (ETE). Then, the operating assets that we had purchased up to that point were swapped for limited partnership units of the new Energy Transfer Partners, LP.

As a result, ETE—the entity that was owned by Kelcy, Ray, NGP, and those coinvestors who helped fund that first Aquila purchase—now owned about 30 percent of the limited partnership units in the publicly traded ETP, plus ETE's general partnership interest of ETP, which entitled it to earn up to 50 percent of ETP's cash flow once the dividends exceeded specified levels.

The Heritage unitholders voted for the deal under an agreement that was struck in November 2003. I knew this vote would not be difficult to win because we were replacing a stodgy business plan with one that was built on growth. In addition to Heritage's old propane assets, the new Energy Transfer Partners would have some gas-gathering and processing assets in South Texas, one of the largest gas pipelines that traverses the state of Texas and connected the state's major gas marketing hubs, plus some odds-and-ends assets in Texas and Oklahoma. From the limited partner perspective, it was straightforward. Plus, we retained the chief executive of the propane business and added him to our board, so there was already an insider who had agreed to vote for the deal. The deal closed in early 2004 and the company never looked back.

Over the next phase of the company's growth, Kelcy and his wonderful team completed further acquisitions inside of ETP—each time using both the credit markets and the equity markets to finance the growth. Each deal led to the ability to increase the distribution to ETP's unitholders. Remember from the original deal: Energy Transfer Equity, the vehicle into which we all made our investment, held one-third of the ETP common units and 100 percent of its general partner. When ETP paid out its distributions, one-third went to ETE. Plus, after a while, ETP started paying its general partner more of the cash flow, since it had exceeded its original hurdles. Now, the general partner was positioned to be a cash machine. With every deal that ETP did from that point forward, ETE got one-third of the distributions paid to the common unitholders plus a share of the cash flow exceeding certain levels laid out in the partnership agreement.

With that in place, the ducks started quacking. Understanding the option value of an entity that gets up to 50 percent of the cash flow from the deals done by the multibillion-dollar partnership it controlled, we approached several investment banks to assess the public market's receptivity to such a vehicle. The train wrecks of the early 2000s were now cleaned up and the unconventional shale revolution was just getting under way. That meant large volumes of new natural gas production were being discovered across the United States, and that natural gas needed pipelines and processing plants to get it to market. Energy Transfer was well positioned in the Southwest with an existing network of pipelines and processing plants to add on to. Given the growth of the natural gas business, the growth trajectory for ETP was an easy sell, as was an interest in the general partner that got up to 50 percent of the cash flow.

The only problem was we had yet to earn much of that incentive payout. We knew that if we kept going, we would generate a lot of cash, but we hadn't up to that point because we were just getting going.

I pushed the idea of taking public our general partner entity, ETE. I pitched it hard to Ray and Kelcy and a few investment bankers. Enter again Dick Covington. He was masterful in working with the team at Energy Transfer to do what nobody was doing at the time—attempting to monetize the option value inherent in a structure that receives a disproportionate share of the cash flow of another related party. We were undeterred by the novelty. Ultimately, we got a group of investment bankers on board with the idea.

In late 2005, we filed to take ETE public with that profile. We showed the bankers the cash flow growth that could take place from future deals done by ETP. Those bankers were generally in agreement that the incentive distribution rights (IDRs) were valuable options, but they weren't generating as much cash flow as the batch of ETP limited partnership units held by ETE. So they were reluctant to place that high a value on them.

"Then let's just offer them 50 percent of the IDRs," I said. "Let's call their bluff."

If they felt the IDRs didn't add much value, then our keeping half of them outside the deal shouldn't diminish the value very much. If they were just trying to negotiate a better price for their clients who would be buying the units in the IPO, then that would tip their hand.

Kelcy and Ray loved the idea. They delivered the message to the underwriters, who said that our keeping half the IDRs on the outside would not change the value much at all. So we proceeded accordingly.

My message here was simple: If someone doesn't value an asset, don't give it to them.

In the IPO completed in early 2006, we raised about $350 million by selling a minority stake in ETE, thereby raising capital. But we still retained control of ETE and, hence, ETP, since ETE owned 100 percent of ETP's general partner. This deal valued our original $37 million investment at over $600 million. Kelcy and Ray's stake was valued at about the same level. In fact, since we had given Kelcy and Ray a profits interest in our investment, their pieces were growing disproportionately against ours. I couldn't have been more proud. Everyone was aligned and the incentive structures we put in place from day one were working beautifully.

And we were not done. Our original investment had then been translated into public units of ETE, yet the original investment group still collectively owned the other half of the IDRs separately, which would have a higher value someday. That day came soon. As the cash flows of ETP increased, the IDRs generated cash flow. So much cash flow that the public markets began trading ETE units at a higher multiple in anticipation of ever-increasing distributions. Along the way, we finally exchanged the other half of the IDRs for more ETE units and netted the original founding group of Energy Transfer investors an extra several hundred million dollars. My retort to the bankers a year earlier really paid off.

Over the course of the next year, the unit prices of ETP and ETE appreciated nicely. Our $37 million had appreciated to a paper value exceeding $1.3 billion. The markets, of course, have a strange way of validating one person's idea. About the same time that ETE was persuading bankers to take it public, several other natural gas midstream companies took their general partner entities public and monetized their IDRs similarly. Imitation is the sincerest form of flattery.

One such company was Enterprise Products Partners, LP, which was run by Dan Duncan, a Houston-based entrepreneur similar to Kelcy. A few months before ETE completed its IPO, Duncan had completed the IPO of Enterprise's general partner. Enterprise was equally acquisitive around Texas, and the two companies seemed to be bumping into each other frequently as they competed on deals.

Seeing the frequent clashes and understanding that their capital needs would keep growing as demanded by the emerging unconventional shale gas revolution, both Enterprise and Energy Transfer knew that size mattered. It was inevitable that the two principals, Kelcy and Dan Duncan, would explore a combination. However, a combination inevitably meant that one party would have to be the survivor and the other would have to be the acquired. Enterprise was based in Houston, Energy Transfer in Dallas. Kelcy and Dan were both headstrong. No merger was possible.

Dan, however, knew that Energy Transfer had a major shareholder, NGP, and that we were not a long-term holder because of the nature of our partnerships. We had to sell at some point, according to the terms of our partnership agreement. We had telegraphed that behavior to the industry since the early 1990s, and the fact that private equity funds had a finite life was well known. Kelcy knew we were getting an itchy trigger finger to get some money off the table. He suggested that Dan purchase some or all the NGP position as a way of getting involved with the company but not taking control. He seemed intrigued.

At the same time, Ray Davis wanted to sell down some of his holdings. We all understood that when two big holders of a company want to sell, it is almost impossible to sell it in an orderly manner without tanking the trading value of the units. So, in essence, we needed to find a creative way to sell our stakes.

Enter Dan Duncan.

Ray and I decided that together we would negotiate so as to offer him a nearly $1.5 billion stake in ETE. Half would come from NGP and half from Ray. Kelcy was not interested in selling any of his shares.

Our shares together represented about a third of the partnership. Normally, bankers would help trade such a block of stock, but the market would command a pretty big discount to the prevailing price to move it all at once. Neither Ray nor I wanted to mark down our investment. We also believed that the value of the shares would go up in the future. This presented a dilemma. How could we ask for a *premium* price when the industry norm was to sell large blocks at a *discount* to the last trade?

I invited Ray, Dan, and his Enterprise team to NGP's offices in Irving. We figured that if NGP led the negotiations, then Ray could avoid having to take some sort of adversarial position against Dan—a hedge against the realization that if no deal transpired, we would have to return to being friendly competitors coexisting in the same industry. As a financial partner, we were not involved in anything day-to-day at the company, so it was a bit easier for us to lead the negotiations. If no deal was reached, I was okay with being the bad guy.

On the day of the meeting, Dan entered our large conference room first. I had never met him but had read up on the bold corporate moves he had made in assembling Enterprise. His story read like many Texas oil and gas success stories, full of swagger. When I laid eyes on him, I was taken aback. He was unlike what I had imagined. He was short—about my height—and rarely showed anything but a pleasant smile. He spoke with a sweet, gentle, almost melodic Texas twang. His soft voice was barely audible, as if he was reading a nighttime lullaby to his grandkids. He reminded me of my grandfather, only replace the Polish parts with Texan.

Dan was followed by two of his associates. They took their seats across the conference table from me, Ray, and Dick Covington. We exchanged niceties and gave each other short, rosy updates about each of our companies.

Then, Dan, in his understated way, cut to the chase. "We are interested in buying into Energy Transfer," he said. "But my bankers have told me that a block this size would cost something like a 20 percent discount to today's price." He slid two pieces of paper across the table. One was a stock price chart of Energy Transfer, and the other was a list of some discounts paid for comparable large blocks of energy companies that traded in the recent past. They were easy to understand.

He continued, "At today's price of $36 per unit, I think the right price would be in the high 20s or low 30s for us to buy the block we have been talking about."

Ray glanced at me. He knew I couldn't stay silent. My team had prepared some projections for the company and boiled them down to a couple of pages as well. We handed out those pages.

As Dan started to look at them, I chimed in to walk him through the analysis. "Dan," I explained, "this is pretty simple. Energy Transfer Partners is in the middle of a growth phase, so we have shown here how the dividend of Energy Transfer Partners will increase pretty quickly. This will cause ETE's share of the cash flows to really take off, given the disproportionate sharing of cash flows between ETE and ETP."

I showed him a table projecting the value of the units in five, seven, and ten years using the same multiples that today's market was placing on our cash flows. "The analysis returns a present value of $40 to $50 per unit," I said.

He couldn't argue with the math, since *his* GP entity was also trading at a huge multiple, and he'd been selling his unitholders on the same type of growth. I had heard his investor presentations in the past and used the same logic that he and his team had used to justify their value. It's always critical to be prepared when entering a negotiation.

"We won't do anything for less than $42 per unit," I concluded. Ray glared at me as if to ask if I knew what I was doing.

Dan tried to make the points again about how big blocks needed discounts to transact and that $42 was a *premium* to today's price. "That never happens. Minority positions don't go for premiums. I don't think we have much more to talk about," he tried to explain to me in a fatherly tone. We each swapped our same logic again, but in different words, trying in vain to persuade the other of our position. Clearly, neither of us was going to budge at that moment.

"Then, we don't need to do anything," I replied calmly. There was an awkward silence that engulfed the room.

But then I had a wild thought. "Tell you what, Dan," I said. "We will leave you three alone in the room here to chat about it. You know where we stand. We will go down to the corner conference room at the end of the hall and just wait there. You guys think about it a little bit and come get us when you are through." I said that we had made dinner reservations across the street. No matter what, we would be happy to just enjoy a casual, friendly dinner, even if we couldn't agree on a deal.

Dick, Ray, and I got up from the table, walked out of the conference room, and shut the door behind us. We walked the fifty feet to the opposite corner conference room on our floor, where we would wait. That was a long walk. Ray looked at me and said, "I hope you know what you are doing, Ken. I didn't think $30 per unit was such a bad price. I expected him to offer a discount."

"Let's just be patient, Ray," I said, hoping to God I was right about this one. Sticking at $42 per unit when we both would have been okay with something around $30 was a gamble. That was a $400 million walk down the hall!

Dick, Ray, and I sat in the conference room nervously making small talk. The minutes passed like hours. Finally—after what was really only ten minutes—there was a gentle knock on the door. I opened the door. Dan stood alone in the doorway. He extended his hand. "Forty-two dollars. I will do it."

I let Ray go first, making way for him to shake hands with Dan. I put on as flat a smile as I could and then shook his hand as well. I needed to keep my face saying that I was a reluctant seller of an undervalued stock, even though inside I saw the same little boy jumping up and down on the bed celebrating the 1972 Cowboys victory over the Dolphins in Super Bowl VI.

"Thanks for coming over, Dan," I said. "Would you all like to join us for dinner?" I had made reservations across the street at the local Italian restaurant in case the negotiation got protracted and carried on into the evening.

"No thanks," he replied. "I should get back to Houston, but my colleagues can stay."

Ray and I walked over to the restaurant with Dick Covington as the rest of the Enterprise team made their way over there on their own. As we strolled on the sidewalk on the bridge over Las Colinas's faux canal, Ray looked at me, smiled, and said, "From now on, I want you with me whenever I negotiate anything."

These are the moments imprinted in my memory and that make our business approach so gratifying. We enjoy that relationship to this day.

Over the next couple of days, the lawyers worked furiously with the bankers and brokers to cross an enormous block of units at a premium to the last trading price on May 7, 2007. Something like that is rarely seen by the market makers in the stock, but, on that day, they saw it. It was a good day.

STEVE: *So there you were in May 2007, selling approximately 55 percent of your ownership stake in Energy Transfer Equity, LP, for about $740 million, reflecting a per-unit price of $42.*

Given that you had invested only $37 million in the deal, this represented about twenty times your money and you still retained 45 percent of your position. In other words, you knew when to fold 'em.

KEN: We weren't folding. That implies somehow that we were bluffing. ETE was a strong company with a lot of momentum. But the song implies that there is a time to walk away from the table with your winnings. This encounter allowed us the best of both worlds: We were able to cash in some chips and still retain 45 percent of our position in the company for the future. The company continued to do well, although the market volatility did hit the entire industry when all commodities got crushed in the global financial crisis of 2008 and 2009. Energy Transfer stock went down substantially, although it did keep up its strong distributions to unitholders. We were able to distribute the remainder of our units to the limited partners of NGP, although at a price much lower than $42 per unit. Still, the total return was fantastic.

In the end, the $37 million we invested in 2002 turned into over $1.3 billion by the time we distributed the final units in 2008. Plus, the management team of the company, not just Kelcy and Ray, all did phenomenally well, and the philosophy of aligning our investment with the management team performed wonderfully. There was an incredible amount of financial security created for hundreds of people as a result of this investment, not counting the many endowments, foundations, and pension funds that were investors in NGP. Our coinvestors and the public unitholders also did really well.

This was a great testament to how innovative management and entrepreneurship combine with an ownership mentality to produce strong financial returns. Today, Energy Transfer is a company with an enterprise value in excess of $30 billion. It is amazing to think that our involvement with it all started on a golf cart outside Hillsboro, Texas, back in 2001.

STEVE: *To wrap this up, what is the takeaway from Energy Transfer?*

KEN: This is a hard one to answer in a sound bite. In many respects, the Energy Transfer story is a validation of the investment model that we pioneered and our approach to remaining aligned with great management. Kelcy and Ray are great American entrepreneurs who were open to NGP's support and the financial creativity and acumen for which we had become known. We could not operate a gas field or a gas plant, but we did know our way around a balance sheet and the capital markets.

We paraphrased the words of philosopher R. Buckminster Fuller atop our firmwide promotional literature: "Do not oppose forces, use them."* When the market windows open opportunities, you take them. When buyers come along, you talk to them. You raise money when you don't need it. And, most of all, don't ever let anyone tell you that something is unworkable simply because it has never been done before.

During the time we helped that company grow, there were lots of ducks that were quacking. We fed them.

---

* Fuller's words are "Don't fight forces, use them." R. Buckminster Fuller, *Your Private Sky: The Art of Design Science*, ed. Joachim Krausse and Claude Lichtenstein (Zurich, Switzerland: Lars Müller, 1999), 174.

STEVE: *Quite well, it seems.*

KEN: Yes, but to finish the Energy Transfer windfall, I should return to our discussion of the fallout from Sunoma. When initially contemplating the investment in Energy Transfer, we determined that we should commit an amount equal to 15 percent of NGP 6, but when it came time to close, I was gun-shy. We recalled the lessons from Sunoma and I decided to pull back our investment and put only 10 percent of the fund in that deal. Knowing the perils of concentrating too much of a fund in any single deal, I felt comfortable with this lesson learned.

Yes, the ETE transaction turned out to be the single best deal ever done in the energy private equity industry up to that point. Yes, our $37 million turned into in excess of $1 billion in a few short years. But had we stayed at the 15 percent level and invested the extra $18 million, we would have earned an extra $600 million. That, my friend, would have fed a lot more ducks. This really was the ultimate cost of the Sunoma transaction. The investment business can be mighty humbling. But that sense of humility would continue to serve me well, even though it cost me dearly in this case.

CHAPTER 11

READY, SHOOT, AIM!

STEVE: *Well, deal number two made up for some of that opportunity cost. This was your sale of a 40 percent stake in NGP to Barclay's Capital, the investment banking division of Barclay's Bank. When this was announced in October 2006, you said the following to explain the decision:*

> Over the past two decades, we have established NGP as the premier provider of capital for energy companies in North America. However, in such a global industry as energy, we felt the need to align ourselves with an investor who would position us for whatever the future holds. The energy industry is becoming more complicated each day and is influenced by economic and political events worldwide. An investment by Barclays Capital now gives us access to all of the world's leading economies. Each of our investment initiatives is impacted by events around the world.[*]

A shorter, but equally telling, explanation can be found in your list of "isms" or maxims that we explore in depth in a later section. The pertinent maxim here is: Get the money when you don't need it. *Was it as simple as that?*

KEN: If you step back and look at the picture of Natural Gas Partners from, say, 2000 through 2004, we were on a roll at a time when the unconventional shale revolution was just beginning to emerge in the United States.

---

* "NGP Energy Capital Management Announces Investment by Barclays Capital," *Chron*, October 25, 2006, https://www.chron.com/news/article/BW-NGP-Energy-Capital-Management-Announces-1900661.php.

Since the inception of NGP in 1988, U.S. oil and gas production was declining every year. The large multinational companies viewed their U.S. holdings as no-growth assets—sources of cash that those companies could reinvest abroad in the emerging oil and gas plays of West Africa, South America, and the former Soviet Union. Those were the areas where large oil and gas finds were thought possible. The only area in the United States that was getting attention shortly before the turn of the century was the deepwater Gulf of Mexico, where new drilling technologies were introduced that allowed the industry to explore for larger reserves in water several miles deep.

Other than that, there was little attention paid to trying to get more out of the ground in the lower forty-eight, except by the industrious independent oil and gas producers, many of whom NGP had financed. These entrepreneurs combined the elements of hydraulic fracturing that the industry had been using for fifty years with the new horizontal drilling techniques. This combination produced something astounding—the ability for the U.S. oil and gas basins to actually *increase* production. Yet again proving my maxim—*the best place to find oil and gas is in old oil and gas fields.*

Think about it. When a traditional vertical well drilled through a twelve-inch-diameter pipe intersects the producing zone, it only intersects it for that twelve-inch diameter times the height of the producing geologic zone underground. Picture a vertically shaped cylinder and you get the idea. But with horizontal drilling, the producer can turn the drill bit *into* the producing geologic zone and take it as far as it mechanically can go. Now, if you think about the amount of producing zone you have, your cylinder is lying sideways. It is the same twelve-inch diameter, but the height of the cylinder is the entire length of the horizontal leg of the well. Today, those horizontal legs are up to three miles! By comparing the simple geometry of the two cylinders, you can see how exponentially the volumes recovered have increased. I know my geologist friends will kill me for this oversimplification, but they'll get over it. Exhibit 3 presents a clear illustration.

Anyway, starting around 2000 and continuing through the next few years, these techniques were being tried and perfected all over the United States and even into Canada. The industry was recording growth for the first time in decades. The growth was driven by entrepreneurial independent oil and gas operators. For the better part of a decade, the major oil and gas companies maintained that this was all a fraud.

At the same time, China, India, and the emerging markets were in the midst of a demand growth boom as their economies were expanding at impressive clips. Demand growth in the developed economies like the United States and the European Union was fairly steady, so when the Asian economies expanded, there was a marked increase for commodities of all types. Demand went up and prices went up, thereby

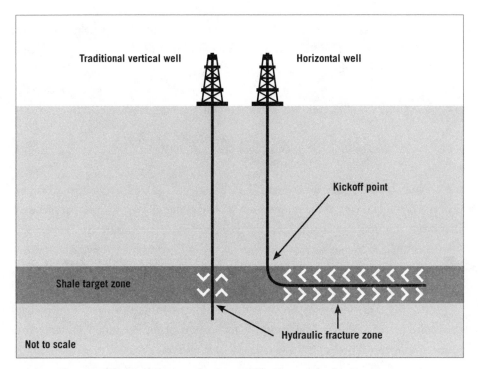

Exhibit 3: Illustration of how much more reservoir is intersected by a horizontal well

incentivizing companies in places like the United States to try new things to reverse the production declines. And it worked.

Against this exciting backdrop of the turnaround in the way people thought about the North American oil and gas industry, NGP grew.

Our signature deals of Pioneer and Energy Transfer were well known, and the dozens of smaller companies we had invested in had done well also. We had taken a number of companies public and had realized strong returns on others that stayed private. Our fifteen-year investment record was near the top of every list. With this momentum, I saw increasing interest among our investors to expand their energy allocations. I was repeatedly asked by our long list of investors to offer them free advice on how they should build out a broader energy portfolio so that they could get exposure to this commodity supercycle, as it was called.

It was gratifying that people were looking at me and NGP as thought leaders in the industry. I was never shy about telling the NGP story or offering my opinions as to what I saw as the future of the oil and gas industry. I enjoyed speaking at conferences, and I put a lot of time and energy into making sure my conclusions were well researched and well reasoned.

I guess my old high school debate background came in handy. It was always amazing to me how many people pontificated about the oil and gas industry. Since stories of the

Middle East were in the paper on a daily basis, everyone fashioned themselves as experts on the region and therefore had an opinion about oil prices. Yet so few people actually could tell you some of the most rudimentary facts about the industry. I prided myself on knowing the facts and tried to play myth buster to people who drew large conclusions about one of the world's largest industries based on the most recent anecdote.

STEVE: *Did you see things happening that others didn't?*

KEN: Well, I don't think I was particularly prescient. I was just trying to grow our firm and take advantage of the momentum we had going. It was obvious that the asset allocation community was searching for more ways to get exposure to good energy investment managers. Seeing that we were just about the best energy investment manager going, I thought we should grow our firm by increasing the amount of capital that each investor could place with us.

It's always easier for a company to get more revenue from existing customers than to acquire new customers. That is one of the axioms of the restaurant industry and many consumer businesses that spend a heck of a lot of money to attract new customers. If they can offer more to existing customers, then growth is a whole lot easier.

I convinced my partners that we could utilize our investment record to both increase the size of our main NGP funds and, at the same time, increase the types of funds we could offer to our limited partners. We set out on a serious growth binge beginning in 2002, when we planned our seventh fund. Our NGP 6 fund, which was closed in 2000, was $370 million in size. That fund was fortunate to have made the investment in Energy Transfer. In 2003, after that fund had been fully invested, we closed on an oversubscribed NGP 7 at $600 million and began investing it. That fund hit the maximum target we had set for it relatively quickly. Rather than increase the size of the fund, we cut back certain partners and chose not to accept some investors. Being oversubscribed put us in an enviable position. Talk about momentum!

As a good first step, we decided to expand our investment products beyond equity investments in energy companies. Our deal flow was expanding to the point where we had the chance to see so much more than just the narrow type of investment we liked for our main fund's capital. There were numerous investment opportunities where a loan structure would work better and be less dilutive to the business owners than a straight-up equity investment.

We extended our aperture in 2004 to launch NGP Capital Resources Corporation. It was what was known as a business development company, a form of a publicly traded lender. It was an interesting structure in that it did not pay taxes if it was able to pay out virtually all its cash flow as a dividend. The concept was created by the federal government as part of the Small Business Administration and its desire to find ways to encourage private capital to flow to smaller enterprises. The structure seemed ideally suited to the energy business, since we were able to make loans that had positive yields on day one.

We put out feelers for managers with a credit background and found some quality lenders who had bounced around the street, but always in the energy-lending arena. With a capable team in tow, Dick Covington again worked his magic to ensure we'd be able to manage the company within our existing operating company framework, and I took our show on the road with the two energy lenders to meet investors.

We succeeded in raising $240 million as the opening kitty from which to lend. On top of that, we arranged a bank loan syndicate that we could draw on once our equity capital was loaned out. Leverage would enhance our returns. We created an investment committee, and I served as chairman of the company, putting my name and reputation on the line. Given the success we were enjoying in the investment arena, that was an easy sell. If that business could scale, the economics to the NGP management company would be a nice piece of business for us.

To give the feel that we were more than just Natural Gas Partners (the name of our successive main private equity funds), we transitioned to the name NGP Energy Capital Management to refer to the operating entity that served as the ultimate controlling vehicle for the Natural Gas Partners funds as well as the new NGP Capital Resources Corporation.

STEVE: *To quote a wise man, you were off to the races. I feel like that was a major transformative step for you personally as well as for the firm. While you were one of four original teammates for the original Natural Gas Partners partnerships, David and you were the cofounders, and you were the acting CEO of NGP Energy Capital Management—a much broader asset management franchise.*

KEN: Yes. And in 2005, we followed that up with the creation of NGP Energy Technology Partners. That fund was formed to appeal to investors clamoring for renewable energy technology deals because of the emerging fears about climate change and the coming realization that this global boom in energy demand might not be met by fossil fuels, or if it was, it wouldn't be cheap. To make the fund a reality, I followed the same formula. I wanted to find a capable partner to lead the fund's day-to-day operation, and I would serve as chair of the investment committee and lend my name and reputation to the enterprise to get it launched.

Then an old acquaintance gave me a call that would change both our lives. Phil Deutch had been a first-year analyst at Morgan Stanley back in 1986 when I was a second-year. He had gone to Stanford Law School after his time at Morgan Stanley and then returned to Washington, D.C., to practice law.

Since Phil was an entrepreneur at heart, he chose to leave the practice of law (which he was good at), to become a principal investor. He joined Frank Pearl, a private investor based in Washington, D.C., who had assembled a pool of capital in the 1990s to invest in just about anything that struck his fancy. Phil became the in-house expert on energy technology, in part, because he raised his hand when his firm needed someone to focus on it. When he called me, some twenty years after our Morgan Stanley days, he had amassed a decent track record in the energy technology sphere.

Phil and I were kindred spirits. We were both sure we weren't qualified to be admitted into any place that ever admitted us, and we knew we always needed to work harder than anyone else to stay even. He wasn't trained in energy technology, just like I had no technical training in oil and gas. But we were humble enough to ask a lot of questions of people who were way smarter than we were. Besides, Phil is someone who I would trust with my kids.

Just as I had immersed myself in the oil and gas industry to learn it, Phil had done the same in the energy technology sector. He had a nice network of experts from places like Harvard and MIT's engineering schools and had befriended some of the leaders in the industry. Also, we were equally skeptical of just about everything we heard, which made us good partners. We didn't get seduced by every new idea destined to save the world.

We struck a deal to form a fund that would be co-owned by him and NGP Energy Capital Management to invest in growth companies within the energy technology industry. We knew enough about the sector to stay away from pure pre-revenue venture capital–style investing and, instead, focused on identifying companies already making and selling a product.

Our story got some traction. He and I went on the road to pitch the idea to investors, and after a few months of meetings, we succeeded in launching the fund with $148 million of capital. Again, my name and reputation combined with his sector experience carried the day. Phil hired a few colleagues to help run the fund, and we opened an office in Washington, D.C., where Phil lived.

STEVE: *And you did this all while simultaneously managing the main NGP funds?*

KEN: That's where a great team comes in. Our team was continuing to execute on our business plan. Of course, when we ran out of capital for NGP's main oil and gas fund, it came time to reload. Given that the energy technology fund did not cannibalize capital that would otherwise get invested in our main fund, we didn't miss a beat.

That same year, we hit the road again to reload our Natural Gas Partners franchise. We announced the opening of NGP 8 in mid-2005 and we closed it prior to year-end. Again, there was good demand, and we exceeded our stated goal to allow some new investors to join us, completing the fund at $1.3 billion in total. We had little trouble raising that fund since the full results of NGP 6 were apparent. NGP 6 settled with an approximately 90 percent rate of return, with investors realizing about six times their initial investment.

Taking that track record for a spin didn't end there. As projections for North America's oil and gas production growth from the emerging unconventional shale revolution took hold, there were insane estimates of the amount of capital that would be needed to add the infrastructure required to move all these hydrocarbons around.

STEVE: *How so?*

KEN: Natural gas wells don't just magically send gas to stovetops. Every well drilled needs to be connected to a gas-gathering system, a spider web of small-diameter pipelines that crisscross the oil patch. Those small pipes connect to larger-diameter pipelines that usually connect to central gas processing plants, which sift and sort the gas into various products and then send them down the line in more pipelines or trucks. In between, a mountain of compressors, valves, and gauges are needed to account for and move the product along. As fields develop, this infrastructure needs to keep up.

There's an entire industry that sits between the upstream oil and gas production companies, with their producing wells, and the downstream users of the oil and gas. These midstream companies were all the rage at the time, and we had credibility because Energy Transfer was one of the midstream company darlings of the industry. With that experience, it was an easy extension for us to raise a dedicated fund to focus on the midstream sector. In addition to the Energy Transfer story, a couple of the early Natural Gas Partners funds had invested in midstream deals, and they all were working at the time. So, with no blemish on our midstream track record, we set out to extend our brand further.

STEVE: *How did you do that?*

KEN: Colin Raymond, one of our deal professionals, suggested that we speak to his brother John, who had done a couple of transactions as part of a larger company in the energy midstream space. Together, we could start a dedicated fund specializing in the energy midstream industry. In mid-2006, I went on the road with John and another partner he recruited (an energy and minerals investment banker) to find investors for a large new fund. In the end, my reputation, combined with John's knowledge of the industry, carried the day. We closed on $1.4 billion of investment capital—NGP Midstream and Resources, LP—in early 2007. At the time, it was one of the largest first-time funds in the history of the industry. The two of them striking out on their own together never would have been able to raise such a first-time fund, but with my participation and the sponsorship of the entire NGP brand, it was possible.

It was a fun time. We were increasing our reach in the energy industry by establishing a broader footprint across the entire natural resources arena. We were absorbing increased investor demand with new investment vehicles. We were adding partners. We were a real firm, not just a bunch of deal guys investing a fund into deals. I could feel the change happening. We had a cogent mission and a clear set of practices, policies, and operating norms. We had evolved into a real franchise.

STEVE: *Can you describe some of those practices and policies?*

KEN: I deliberately created some internal practices that helped solidify the firm mentality in an industry notorious for having specific individuals take credit and blame, as the case may be. Not only did I broaden the investment committees of the funds to include a lot more people, but I also created systems to avoid being able to attribute success or failure to any single person. We were "all for one and one for all." In fact, I resisted keeping any accounting for what our investors called attribution analysis, a practice of assigning specific wins or losses to specific individuals. Investors always liked to see that so they could decipher who were the real moneymakers at the firm and determine if the firm was going to last. Clearly, if the chief moneymaker departed, then, as the logic went, the firm could be in trouble.

I did no such accounting. I intentionally rotated the teams that worked on each deal. The person who found the deal was not necessarily the person who worked on the analysis and closed the deal. The person who helped close the transaction would not necessarily be the one monitoring the investment and helping it grow over time. Finally, I would try to have others help with the exit of the deal when the time was right.

By the end of an investment's life, I wanted as many fingerprints on it as possible. Every deal was "our" deal, not "his or her" deal. We all took credit for the winners, and we shared the blame for the losers. I always maintained that when investors asked for attribution analysis, they were actually planting the seeds for the firm's destruction without even knowing it.

STEVE: *I'm assuming your partners bought into this.*

KEN: Not just the partners but up and down the chain. In 2006, we'd been around for sixteen years and, but for one employee going on to be the CFO of one of our portfolio companies, we had had zero employee turnover at the professional level. That continuity was recognized in the industry and by our investors, who took great comfort in the fact that everyone in the firm owned a piece of every deal, and we practiced what we preached.

As we aged, one of my principal goals was to knit us all together to transform us from a group of people managing funds into an asset management franchise. We already had the key ingredient—a positive corporate culture, evidenced by the low turnover, high morale, and positive working conditions. What we needed was a way to connect it all so that we'd all grow personally, professionally, *and* financially. If I was able to accomplish that, then I felt we had a chance to do what few had done in the private equity investment business—create a real branded franchise that would last beyond the professional lifetime of the founders.

STEVE: *So, in 2006, business was booming. The NGP funds are seemingly doubling in size every couple of years. Your two brand extensions, NGP Capital Resources and NGP Energy Technology Partners, have been successfully launched. The NGP Midstream and Resources fund is coming along. It's clear NGP Energy Capital Management was really taking shape. As George H. W. Bush might have said, you had the "big mo."*

KEN: Yes. Now the challenge was capitalizing on our momentum and finding a way to make this thing last. I thought about the investment industry and the lasting firms. Marcus Goldman and Samuel Sachs stopped working at Goldman Sachs a long time ago, but that firm had a strong culture that survived cycles and employee turnover. There were other great service firms that had established strong corporate brands that stood the test of time, such as McKinsey & Company.

STEVE: *And making it last meant finding a capital partner?*

KEN: To tell you the truth, I hadn't thought about selling the firm or even a piece of it for a long time. We'd been approached years before by General Electric when GE was expanding its energy finance business. A broker called us to see if we'd be interested in becoming a part of GE's energy group. That wasn't really a capital-partner-type deal; we were much smaller then, and they were simply looking for employees.

They saw buying our book of business as a finite purchase to get us as employees. They had no interest in thinking about our business as a franchise with real future value over and above the portfolio of assets we had at the time. This was reflected in the purchase price range they threw around. Even though we didn't think we had an investment franchise back then, I felt that if they wanted our book of business and our future earnings, they'd have to make us an offer we couldn't refuse. While the conversations did not advance very far, talking to them was an interesting exercise, since it got me thinking about what I'd need in the future to legitimately call NGP an investment franchise.

By 2006, we had accomplished that.

We had brand goodwill. We had name recognition and value in our name. We had a track record of applying investment practices that were tested. Think of it like the Campbell's Soup logo. That brand has goodwill in that a concoction of ingredients put in a can with that label will get instant consumer acceptance versus the same concoction being put in a can with an unfamiliar label. When a company establishes that kind of positive value, it has a real chance to succeed over the long term.

We had people who wanted to work at NGP, and they may not have even known who I was. We had developed a real brand in the industry, such that positioning ourselves as a durable firm, not reliant on any single individual, was credible.

Recall that we formed our firm without regard to coming up with a catchy name. That simple historical accident probably enabled us to accomplish something that nobody had accomplished up to that point. Had we named the firm after ourselves, it would have been nearly impossible to make the case that we were an investment *firm* and not just a collection of individuals led by a key person or two.

STEVE: *So how did Barclays come into the picture?*

KEN: I set out to find a capital partner so we could establish some permanent capital in the firm, which could invest across all our investment platforms. We already had it set up whereby each deal professional was able to invest in the particular fund on which he or she was working. But I needed to find a way to have people share in the returns of the affiliated funds so they would all feel connected financially. I also needed to find a way for people who didn't necessarily have capital to invest to earn an interest in all our investment funds. This was intended for all our fantastic support employees who were so essential to everything we were doing. Accountants, administrative support, office managers, investor relations, and even the receptionists were a key part of the firm and its culture. I wanted everyone to have a piece of the action.

When I looked around the industry, it was the ownership structure that caused firms to fall apart over time. New employees didn't share in prior fund successes, and when different funds performed differently, it became inevitable that the financial returns were shared unevenly. Without a strong culture, this contributed to the destruction of many investment firms. That, plus keeping close track of attribution analysis made it easy to see how someone could get resentful if they felt they were either being dragged down by an underperforming colleague or otherwise having to carry the load for others. Mix this dynamic with the type A personalities that populated the private equity investment business, and most firms were powder kegs waiting to explode.

I didn't want NGP to meet that fate. This was my life's work, and I didn't want it to disintegrate. Besides, it is no fun to work in a toxic environment.

Remember, this was shortly before the 2008 and 2009 financial crisis. The asset management industry was transforming itself from a series of portfolio managers into a real asset management business, and we'd done a good job of converting our business into that as well. Looking back, had we waited, the financial crisis would have killed any chance to do what we did. That's probably the best example of lucky timing in my career.

It also goes toward my predilection to move—to do something, as opposed to doing nothing. As I already told you, "Ready, shoot, aim!" If you feel like you have instinct about something and the conditions are right, don't overthink it. Trust your instinct to take a shot and then, if it doesn't work exactly as planned, have the confidence to be able to correct your course.

STEVE: *Can we pause here to explain what an asset management business is? I actually looked up the definition. An asset management company is a firm that invests pooled funds from clients, putting that capital to work through different investments including equity, both private and public, as well as bonds, real estate, venture capital, and more.*

KEN: Sounds good.

STEVE: *Sorry for the interruption. You were saying?*

KEN: Looking at the risk-reward equation, it wasn't like we'd go out of business if we didn't find a capital partner. But the opportunities that could come from finding the right one could be quite large. This made it a perfect situation for me: limited downside and lots of upside. Plus, I knew we had a pretty special thing going on at the firm. Surely, someone would take note of that. We also didn't *need* to do anything. This put us in a good negotiating position as we went looking for capital.

I knew this would be somewhat controversial because it had not ever been done in the private equity business at the time. This effort was before the advent of initial public offerings for private equity firms that were transforming into asset management companies. Blackstone didn't go public until 2007. KKR didn't go public until 2009. Carlyle didn't go public until 2012. In helping our portfolio companies, we always stressed to get the money when they didn't need it, because when you need it, it may or may not be there. This was true for us as a firm as well. I saw no downside in testing the market. Some of my partners thought I was Don Quixote tilting at windmills, but they knew me well enough to leave me alone while I tried.

STEVE: *What was your first step?*

KEN: I knew we needed help in the process. I made a phone call to Ray Chambers, a dear friend of Richard Rainwater whom we had included in the Mesa investment a decade before. I had stayed close with Ray and his associates over the ensuing decade. I asked him to connect me to Eric Gleacher, who had been in charge of the mergers and acquisitions group at Morgan Stanley in 1985 when I was an analyst.

STEVE: *Why Eric?*

KEN: When he left Morgan Stanley in 1990, he created a boutique investment bank that bore his name, Gleacher Partners. Six years later he sold it for $135 million to a large European bank, but it didn't go well, so in 1999 he bought it back for far less. I knew he had done the hardest thing possible in the service industry—monetize a firm that bore the founder's name. Plus, I have to be honest and admit that there was a certain gratification for the former junior-most analyst to get to "interview" the former head of the whole department some twenty years later.

I called Eric and introduced myself. He didn't remember me at all, but with Ray's introduction, he was receptive to my inquiry. "I've been thinking about selling an interest in my firm, and I might be interested in hiring your firm to advise us," I said.

This seemed to catch him a bit off guard. Private equity firms were not designed to pursue this sort of path. I persisted and explained to him our investment footprint in the energy industry and how I thought we had evolved into an asset management firm with a strong franchise. I also impressed on him the fact that the one brand extension remaining for us was to expand into international energy investments. He got it very quickly and agreed to take us on as a client.

STEVE: *Then what?*

KEN: Eric was based in New York, but he also had a London office. After we signed the engagement letter, we made our list of possible capital partners. The list was pretty long and disparate; plus, there were a few eccentric names on it. We set out to contact each of them. There were few takers. We had a few good meetings, but clearly the idea of monetizing the operating entity of an asset management company had yet to take hold. Once again, I seemed to have been early.

As the process prolonged, Eric floated the idea of talking to Barclays Bank. He said the folks at Barclays were looking to expand their presence globally and in particular wanted more energy exposure. It seemed like an odd match for an old-line stodgy British bank. But Barclays' job as a money-center bank was to get in the middle of capital flows. In 2006, the natural resource industry was in the middle of a supercycle of capital expenditures, as both the developed and developing economies were experiencing rapid commodity supply and demand growth.

The estimate at the time was that something like $2 trillion of investment needed to flow into the global energy industry to satisfy the world's appetite. The United States was going to attract a big part of that capital need. Based as it was in London, Barclays didn't have any real footprint in the U.S. asset management business. We fit the bill.

An aggressive American named Bob Diamond was their CEO at the time. He was working to transform Barclays from a stodgy commercial bank into a full-fledged global financial institution. The bank had expanded into wealth management and investment banking. It was establishing itself in the commodities and derivative trading areas, but its asset management business was nascent. Eric floated the idea of buying a stake in NGP to Bob, who responded that Barclays did indeed want to broaden its footprint.

"You *need* to just meet these guys," Eric pleaded with me when he heard the incredulous tone in my voice as he offered up the Barclays idea. Barclays was not a bank I knew well, but my mind was open. We quickly hit it off with the deal team running their principal investment business. That group, led by Roger Jenkins with an assist from Mark Brown, was akin to an internal NGP using the bank's capital for deals. They'd been working on transactions, but with limited success. However, they were real deal guys, not corporate bankers. After learning how we did business, they saw it as the perfect chance to get a foothold into the U.S. energy investment business and learn our secrets so they could apply our methodology outside the United States.

The negotiation was pretty straightforward. There were things I cared about and things they cared about. First and foremost, I wanted the value that they'd pay to be reflective of the real franchise value of NGP. We had created a reasonable cash flow projection that was quite achievable. It was a stretch, but not an unreasonable set of future projections. In addition, I knew we would have to retain absolute control over our operations. We had a good thing going, and I wouldn't agree to be absorbed by a large bank. Plus, I knew our compensation and ownership plans were not comparable to those of the London bankers. If they assumed control, it would have been only a matter of time until they made our pay plans similar to theirs, and that would be the end of NGP as we knew it.

We settled on discussing a sale of 40 percent of the revenue stream and profits interest that the firm was earning on its managed funds. That number was large enough for the bank to take it seriously and, importantly, smaller than 50 percent—meaning control was never going to be an issue. Now, all we had to do was agree on value.

After some back and forth, we concluded that they were willing to purchase the 40 percent stake for $680 million, with 60 percent of the amount paid up front and the remainder due once we hit some performance targets. It was a big step for us to take.

STEVE: *Your partners must have been excited.*

KEN: On the surface, for sure. I wasn't about to make this decision on my own, so it was important to me that my partners all agreed. If I was selling Barclays on the fact that we were "all for one and one for all," it would've been hypocritical for me to make a unilateral decision, especially one of this magnitude. I had been updating the team all along as the negotiations progressed, and Dick Covington was, once again, masterful in crafting a set of agreements that protected our interests while finding a way to make both sides comfortable.

It was also critical for me to make sure the proceeds went to the right places to achieve our objectives. I didn't want my partners to take the money and run, either.

The trickiest part of the deal wasn't dealing with Barclays but rather dealing with *my* partners. If, all of a sudden, 40 percent of our revenue was going to go to Barclays, but we were still on the hook for 100 percent of the expenses, it looked like our bottom line was going to be cut pretty heavily. Of course, the up-front cash paid by Barclays was the trade for that, so we all had to agree that we could withstand this change in our bottom line and feel that the trade was good enough for us.

I convened my partners in the cabana of my house one evening after the deal was struck, but before it was signed. I laid out the plan where we would all be able to get liquidity from the deal. Of the proceeds, about 50 percent went to people *other* than David, John, or me. Everyone in the firm got a payday. In addition, I intended to set aside about 10 percent of the proceeds to invest in our future funds to create a profits interest pool earned by those funds.

The plan was for that profits pool not to go to any of us, since we were all sharing nicely in the up-front proceeds. Rather, the money in the pool would be essentially free shares of the profits of all our funds going forward. We called that capital pool Incentive Program Partners (taking a page, the only page, from the Rainwater enterprise naming handbook), and it would be available for every non-equity employee (present and future) of the firm. A share would also be available for the management teams of NGP's affiliated funds as long as the folks worked at the firm.

Voilà! I had created a financial tool that allowed profits to be shared across the entire platform using someone else's money. In addition, we were able to monetize a portion of our investment franchise's goodwill, establish a solid, third-party valuation for the enterprise, and retain full control over our operations. What was not to like?

After a healthy discussion, everyone agreed to the transaction, and we proceeded to execute the deal. It was a special day. We all knew what we were doing and knew the pros and cons of taking in an outside capital partner, but in the end, we believed the valuation was a good one and it was the smart business decision to solidify our franchise.

Make no mistake, my senior partners and I took a whole lot of money out of our own pockets to ensure that everyone would participate. We all recognized it, and it felt really good to tell the rank and file how much they'd benefit. Tears flowed when I had the honor of telling some of our longtime accounting and administrative people how much money they would be getting. There is no better feeling in the world than sharing.

STEVE: *You obviously felt some moral or ethical obligation to those people below the partnership ranks, even though there wasn't a legal or contractual one. Can we take a detour here for you to explain the very deliberate way in which you had created a firm culture and identity—one that appears to have been so strong that a particular type of person wanted to work for NGP, and one where, apparently, few people ever left. It obviously went beyond the fact that they were just making a good living.*

KEN: This is something I often ask myself and wonder why I cared so much. Nobody ever told me to go out and create an investment franchise. Nobody ever taught me how to create a great corporate culture, and nobody in the deal business I saw was doing it.

Looking back, part of my motivation was for survival. Simply put, we were a firm investing in a single industry. If NGP had a bad culture and experienced a lot of employee turnover, then I would, in essence, be training future competitors. Eliminating turnover was a key ingredient for continued success.

If I were fearful that people would quit and go out and compete against us, then it would have behooved me to never let them near our investors or our portfolio company management teams. Doing so could jump-start their business and let them hurt mine. I saw this exact behavior in many firms inside the industry, and I would hear horror stories about the working conditions at other firms. I always took great comfort in knowing that we did things differently. And my colleagues responded. If folks never wanted to leave, I could leverage my time better and provide my partners and junior associates the professional development opportunities they wanted. I was obsessed with ensuring that our younger professionals had a phenomenal experience.

David Albin, Dick Covington, and John Foster were the best business partners anyone could have. We had so much trust among us. The rest of the team could see and feel the bonds between us. The camaraderie was infectious. It was modeled by the other, junior members of the firm. We had an "NGP way" of doing things. And it was fun.

I made it a point to have fun holiday parties that, by today's standards, would shock most human resource departments. All in good fun, we had a hypnotist come and make fools of a few of us. We had legendary talk show host Bob Eubanks come to a party and host a mock *Newlywed Game*; we had a reenactment of the *Family Feud* game show, complete with full set and a professional actor emcee.

We were also incredibly generous with gifts of time and money to ensure that people enjoyed working hard and felt aptly rewarded for their effort. They also saw the leadership team go all-in. Generally, I was one of the first in the office and one of the last to leave. I traveled at the drop of a hat and had a to-do list as long as anyone in the office. Everyone pulled their weight.

We also splurged on nice places to go for our firm-wide retreats, and we tried to make them special. Our biennial retreats in Santa Fe were meaningful gatherings where we came to know each other and our families. We also came to know the families of our investors and portfolio company executives. We shared stories and ideas. We learned from setbacks and celebrated successes.

At each Santa Fe enclave beginning in 2005, we also established two awards to recognize and celebrate our portfolio companies. We awarded the Gamble Baldwin award to one of our companies that demonstrated remarkable corporate citizenship, in honor of our late partner Gamble, who passed away in late 2003. In 2013, we changed the name of the biggest award to the Brian Jennings Award to recognize innovative corporate performance in honor of Brian Jennings, who served as the CFO of Energy Transfer and tragically died in 2012 at the age of fifty-one. These practices celebrated the history of the firm and established traditions that bound us together. Corporate traditions are such an important part of a firm's culture. I was always looking for ways to solidify our franchise.

STEVE: *For the first two decades of its existence, NGP had no employee turnover in its deal team. This is a shocking statistic that I would think is almost unheard of in a business like yours.*

KEN: Obviously, we were doing something right to achieve that stability. I think it was much more than fun parties and fancy retreats. We operated the firm with open doors and a flat hierarchy. We were inclusive to a fault. And I really felt responsible for the people around me. I appreciated the fact that they could work at other places, and I also knew they had a lot riding on the decisions we were making at the firm.

I wanted the work conditions to be great, including the benefits packages. I stressed the need to have gold-plated health benefits long before the time people needed them— just like a company raising money when it doesn't need it. Once upon a time, when I was first starting out, I tried to get long-term disability insurance but was denied because of my psoriatic arthritis. From then on, I counseled my young employees to get all the health insurance they could when they were young and healthy, knowing they could become uninsurable later.

That counsel was appreciated by most everyone, especially when an emergency occurred. One year, one of our young associates was out with friends celebrating his twenty-fifth birthday when the car they were in crashed and he was critically injured. Our gold-plated health insurance plan, which I made sure always had no lifetime expense maximum caps, covered his lengthy stay in the ICU, followed by the hospital, followed by the rehabilitation center. Years of recovery were made possible that would not have been available under traditional corporate health plans at the time. Our benefits programs were tapped for other experiences with illnesses, cancers, childhood psychological traumas, and all the other life events that happen in a large workforce. I knew that if colleagues were worried about their health or that of their children, then they would be no good in the office or anywhere else for that matter. This attitude made sense both as an employer and as a friend.

I was amazed when I saw other companies take a different approach.

My reasoning was this: If we hired the kind of people who had that "family" gene in their professional DNA and appreciated all NGP had to offer, my job was to just keep it going. The rest would take care of itself.

Which it did.

It wasn't until 2015, when I really started to telegraph succession planning, that sharper elbows came out. I guess it was apparent that if I was no longer going to be the glue, some folks had no choice but to look out for themselves. Fortunately, Chris Carter, one of my young professional hires who matured into a key part of our succession plans, has a strong sense of that "family" gene. He is now a key player in the firm's future and understands that if you lose your cohesive corporate culture, you might as well close up shop.

STEVE: *We'll talk about Chris later, but back to the Barclays deal now. Did the plan work out the way you had envisioned it?*

KEN: It did, because there was good agreement on the deal itself, and the senior leadership was on board. We distributed the cash proceeds broadly, so the younger partners got a good slug of the proceeds from the sale, and some of them had only been at the firm for a short time. We laid out the "free" equity participation in Incentive Program Partners to the rank and file. Who doesn't like free stuff?

The senior group, led by David and me, agreed to reinvest a huge amount of the proceeds back into our next fund. All the ingredients were in place so that people were incentivized to stick around and, if things worked well, everyone would get rewarded.

STEVE: *That meant that Ken Hersh was leaving a lot of money on the table—money many might say you were fully entitled to. Why?*

KEN: Our success was a function of everyone's efforts, not just mine. It was in my DNA to share and to do what I could to keep the firm together. I also was motivated to make sure that Barclays wasn't disappointed in its purchase.

I was doing fine financially, so I reduced my cash compensation. Henceforth, any financial reward would come primarily to me in my role as an investor in our funds, rather than through salary and bonus. Since we now had only 60 percent of the revenue coming to us, against which we had to pay all the expenses, the rest of the firm appreciated this. Now, my goal was to rejuvenate that 60 percent and get it back to where the 100 percent had been just a few years before.

STEVE: *And?*

KEN: It worked. At the time, our biggest NGP fund had been $1.3 billion. The Barclays deal closed in the fall of 2006, about five months before the final closing of the $1.4 billion NGP Midstream and Resources fund. Then it was time to raise NGP 9. Our track record was still intact, so we set an aggressive goal of raising $4 billion. We hit the goal, although it was a bit tougher this time, because we had to explain the logic of the Barclays transaction to an investor base that was accustomed to having their capital invested by a group of partners who owned 100 percent of their firm.

In the end, we achieved the goal. You can imagine a 1.5 percent management fee on $4 billion—that's $60 million of revenue. We were able to grow the assets under management and get our 60 percent share to be greater than the 100 percent was before the Barclays deal.

STEVE: *That was in a relatively short time?*

KEN: It only took a year and a half. I was focused on doing what no one had really done before: to create a firm whose identity was larger than the principals that founded it, to find a way to monetize its value, and to hold the team together. To me, that was the intellectual challenge of it all.

STEVE: *After the Barclays deal, did anyone say, "I'm retiring!"*

KEN: Nope.

STEVE: *Why? If people get a big payday, it stands to reason that they may become less motivated. Was it simply because everyone enjoyed what they were doing?*

KEN: Yes. And *where* they were doing it. We still made it fun, and we were still building. Besides, our partners made commitments to people in the firm and to our investors. The people at NGP were honorable and believed in upholding their promises. Plus, David Albin and I had a ton of money invested across all our funds. Talk about skin in the game! This alone told the investors, "We're going to stick with it."

Often, investors challenged us as to why we were working so hard and why we were so committed to the firm. I think many of them felt unsatisfied in *their* jobs, so they couldn't understand why we stuck around our jobs long after we were financially secure. I think they were projecting their circumstances on to us.

I made it personal because it was. I walked them through the economics of our old NGP 6 fund, the one with Energy Transfer in it. By 2007, the results of that fund were well documented, and it was easy to calculate that our 20 percent profits interests returned about 100 times our initial investment. I almost took it as a personal affront when people said, "Are you really going to stick with it?" So I would tell people, "If we were going to quit once we made enough to retire, that would've already happened. I still love what I do and am committed."

I would conclude simply by assuring them that I wouldn't let them down.

At some point, I'd encourage folks to ask about what motivated me. Clearly, it had stopped being about the money. With the passage of time, I have come to appreciate that I have what I think of as this unique American drive to keep moving forward. What drives Bill Gates or Warren Buffett? If your goal is to get to a dollar figure and then go to the beach, the beach would be packed with people who stop working. Instead, builders build. Inventors invent. Leaders lead.

From 2002 through 2007, NGP was wildly successful and grew ambitiously. At each step, we could have stopped and said, "That's fine. We've done enough." But we didn't. So it reveals what really drove us, what we were really made of. I guess I'm just a builder who likes to build. In my life, there is only forward. I was born without a neutral or reverse gear.

David used to say that my hobby was erecting a high hurdle for myself just so I could try to clear it. I guess he would know. Subsequent to my tenure at NGP, I dove into my work at the Bush Center, often the first car in the parking lot in the morning and the last one to leave in the evening. And it's a nonprofit! Clearly, money is not my driving force.

I'm hardly unique. That motivation exists across America in so many people and places. Whether it's part of our immigrant past, insecurity that it might all disappear one day, or our neurotic drive for immortality, I don't know. I just know there's an incredible sense of satisfaction that I derive from building something with lasting value and finding ways for that to enhance the lives of the people who make it possible. Along the way, I enjoy giving back to the community to enhance the quality of life for as many as possible. Seeing what others who have gone before me have done inspires and motivates me to go further. Working hard just feels right. As long as I don't forget to have fun. I always take what I do very seriously, even if I take myself a whole lot less seriously. As a leader, I believe that's important.

I believed it, and I modeled that behavior for everyone else in our firm. David Albin was cut from the same cloth, as were Dick Covington, John Foster, and our other partners at the time.

STEVE: *And it helps to have good timing.*

KEN: You can say that again! This growth phase and the Barclays transaction was complete by the end of 2007. We know what ensued during 2008 and 2009—the worst economic downturn since the Great Depression. The price of oil and natural gas collapsed. The capital markets crashed. The financial institutions around the world were rocked, including Barclays. And our portfolio was hit pretty hard.

Needless to say, the ducks stopped quacking, and conditions really tested the character of the firm we'd built and the promises we'd made.

CHAPTER 12

OUR KIDS THOUGHT WE WERE BROKE

STEVE: *You've already noted the importance of moving out of one's comfort zone. In 2008, you and your family took that one step further and moved not just out of your comfort zone but far out of your time zone as well.*

KEN: Just weeks before the 2008 global financial crisis hit, Julie, the kids, and I moved to London.

STEVE: *How did that come about? You had done the deal with Barclays in 2006, and from what I understand, business was good. You seemed to have a great life in Dallas. Why rock the boat?*

KEN: The short answer is that all the reasons you just cited for staying put convinced us there would never be a better time to get out of our comfort zone.

Let me expand on that. I had been a keen watcher of the global energy business and felt there was some selective opportunity to leverage what we had done in the United States on the international level. We had a good name and an investor following. Why not try to add some international deals and see if our model translated globally?

So, not too long after Barclays bought its 40 percent share in NGP, we opened a small office in the Mayfair section of London to help expand our footprint and see if we could get traction in the global energy investment markets.

STEVE: *Why London?*

KEN: Being closer to the Barclays team made that move logical. Also, London is where the international oil and gas companies are based or, at least, where those companies come to meet. I guess meeting in London beats places like Lagos, Nigeria. If you were looking at a deal in the North Sea, Gabon, or Russia, the meetings and the network of lawyers, bankers, and deal brokers seemed to be in London—although at the time, Singapore and Dubai were also picking up steam as business centers.

David Albin and his wife, Pam, volunteered to go for the first six months to get the office established. Julie, the kids, and I followed in the summer of 2008, with the intention of remaining there for a year.

My true motivation was to help our family. I thought time abroad would be good for all of us.

STEVE: *How so?*

KEN: To get away. When we moved into our new house in 1999, our profile began to change. Living in a big house in a nice neighborhood brought some of that on. While Julie and I tried to be the same down-to-earth couple that we were when we were living in our termite-infested, foundation-crumbling starter home in Irving, those around us often acted differently.

Dallas social circles converged on Julie as a fresh new face with philanthropic dollars to dole out. She often felt targeted. Similarly, our young children were getting old enough to begin to ask questions about money.

After the closing of the Barclays deal, Julie and I decided to make large gifts to our children's schools and allow the gifts to be written up in the local newspaper. We wanted to reinforce the messages to our children that we weren't necessarily going to leave everything to them and that it was important to be charitable.

We always emphasized to our kids that we would be sure to give them at least what our parents each gave us to start out—five thousand dollars. Coincidentally, both Julie and I were spotted the same amounts by our folks, some five years apart back in the 1980s.

It wasn't long after we made one of the school gifts that we were driving in the car and one of the kids asked from the back seat, "Dad, how much did our house cost?" I froze, not wanting to let the kids know the full price of our house but not wanting to lie to them either. Then, it hit me: "This house cost a lot of years in school and a lot of hours working hard." I was proud of the dad-comment I had just made up on the spot.

Clearly, they were now in tune with what was going on with us financially, so we knew right then that it was time to redouble our efforts to stay humble.

I didn't look back to see the reaction from the rear seats. No follow-up question came. Thank God.

In 2008, Daniel was fourteen and Rachel was twelve. It was their eighth- and sixth-grade years, respectively. The timing was perfect to take a year away from Dallas. We were between Daniel's bar mitzvah and Rachel's bat mitzvah. They were not yet in high school and knee deep in activities. We felt it was important for the kids to expand their horizons. They had lived a cushy life in suburban Dallas. I'd joke that if you had them draw a picture of the solar system, they would put the intersection of Preston Road and Royal Lane as the sun. That's near where our house was, and almost everything they needed or desired was at hand. Even school was right around the corner. London would definitely broaden their perspectives.

I thought it would be good for Julie, as well. Her depressive break in 2001 was a wake-up call for all of us. With the move into a new house comfortably behind us and the kids settling into full-day school schedules, I felt we were out of the woods. But her relapse in 2005 indicated that her depression was not just situational. As she described it, it was a crude mixture of chemistry and electricity combined with whatever was going on around her.

Her ECT treatments had worked like a charm, and our life was back to normal. She had become active as a spokesperson for ECT and recovering from a mental health break. She wanted to write a book and was actively working on it—which she could do very well overseas.

Also, on the personal side, I could feel the world's encroachment on Julie and me. Everywhere we went, people wanted something. Many wanted money. We had to say no a lot, and that made us feel like we were letting people down. We wanted to get away, a sort of metaphorical retreat to the mountains. During a year in London, I could establish an NGP office, Julie could finish her book, and the kids could experience a different school environment. Our world back in Dallas could go on pause until we returned.

STEVE: *The timing turned out to be interesting. The financial crisis hit right around then.*

KEN: We made the decision during the summer of 2007, about a year before the markets collapsed. This allowed us the chance to apply to the American School in London for our kids and find housing for the fall of 2008. Lehman Brothers crashed about six weeks after our arrival and so, too, did the regard for those who worked in the world of finance. It reached the point where bankers in London began to wear jeans to work, fearful that if they wore suits they'd be accosted on the Tube.

One more thing about the timing: Even as the financial crisis unfolded, the unconventional shale revolution was accelerating in 2008 and 2009. Oil and gas prices fell precipitously during the financial crisis, but behind the scenes, the price declines spurred another round of innovation within an industry trying to figure out how to stay afloat or make money at lower commodity prices. This meant entrepreneurs were working to dramatically lower drilling costs and find ways to extract more volumes from each well. With each passing quarter, it became more and more apparent that there were more exciting oil and gas opportunities two hundred miles from my house than there were half a world away.

STEVE: *But you didn't go back to Texas.*

KEN: Not yet. The intention was to try something new—to repot the plant. And that's what we did. We had committed to a full year in London, so we gutted it out. I liked learning a new city, a new neighborhood, and exploring new restaurants. It was fun crossing the famous Beatles Abbey Road crosswalk every day on my way to the Tube. We had no car, opting instead for the Tube, buses, and taxis. We had a small city house near the American School in London where our kids went. It was extremely nice by London standards, but small relative to our Dallas home. Despite the rent that exceeded the mortgage on our 11,000-square-foot home back in Dallas, the kids thought we were broke.

For probably the first time, Daniel and Rachel watched us operate outside our comfort zone. Our attitude was "let's figure it out, kids." We all made the trek on the bus to the grocery store, since we needed extra hands carrying bags home. At the house, not everything worked right. Living in Dallas, we knew who to call for what and we had people at the ready to help. That was the kids' normal, so this new life was really eye-opening. As much as they fought us about going, I think they look back and see it as a gift. My daughter cried when we got there and cried when we had to leave.

STEVE: *And Julie?*

KEN: She thrived there. She basked in the freshness of new people, many of whom were expats, and forming new relationships. She joined a neighborhood running group, and she explored London on her morning jogs. She even trained for and completed the London Marathon. She bonded with a great group of women. She worked hard and finished her book. From my vantage point, she was really switched on.

STEVE: *And how was your work?*

KEN: I was working hard, trying to network and learn the European business. The time change made it easier, since the London morning was still the middle of the night back in Texas. I was able to book a pretty solid morning and early afternoon around town trying to get plugged into the industry players. But because of the financial turmoil of the crisis, I could never really disengage from the office in Dallas. I found myself working a full London day and then, with a six-hour time differential, at 3 p.m. my Texas day would begin. Seems like I was working through dinner most nights. It was hard. But I saw how great Julie was doing, so I soldiered on.

From an industry standpoint, I learned quickly that the international oil and gas scene is quite different. We looked at deals in Africa, the Middle East, Eastern Europe, and the North Sea. Everything was cross-border and complicated from a tax, regulatory, and operating point of view. Nothing was easy. I came to realize how spoiled we were by doing business in the United States.

However, being in London was scratching an itch. Despite the financial crisis of '08–'09, the firm was solid and had a great base with our main NGP funds performing, our new expansion funds launched, the Barclays money in the bank, the cash distributed, and the long-term incentive pools established. But we were still perceived as a niche investment manager in North America. We were well known in the energy patch, but I felt it was critical to expand our profile to institutionalize the NGP brand. We had our London office, so the next move was to be more global in our exposure and expand our investor base around the world.

The seeds for that move had been well planted. As we matured as a firm, I wasn't shy. I always enjoyed speaking at industry conferences, and I took those invitations seriously. I intentionally worked to lift my profile to project NGP's position as the industry leader it was.

Not only did I enjoy doing this, but also it was important for me to do. I had become a real expert on the energy and climate topics at a time when everyone in the world seemingly fashioned themselves an energy expert, despite their shallow knowledge of the facts. I made those presentations fun to listen to and a chance to offer a substantive opinion about how we saw the industry trends.

While in London in 2009, I was nominated to join the World Economic Forum and, in 2010, I started attending its annual enclave in Davos, Switzerland. The following year, I began speaking there on one or more of its various panels that involved energy or climate topics. I had also been a relatively frequent contributor on the U.S. financial shows produced by CNBC, and I appeared on the CNBC Europe equivalent morning shows when I lived in London. My profile as a thought leader in the sector helped give NGP a certain panache in the marketplace. None of our competitors bothered with such a public profile. Building and maintaining a global network and profile was tiring work, but I loved it.

STEVE: *Did your philosophy about investing in people continue in your deals there? Or did you have to adopt a new business model to get something done overseas?*

KEN: I learned that the American entrepreneurial DNA is unique. Entrepreneurship means something different in other cultures. The willingness to take a risk and potentially fail is perceived quite differently around the world. In the United States, there is a sort of badge of honor that comes from trying to do something on your own, taking a risk, failing, learning from mistakes, and reinventing yourself. That risk-taking mentality is lacking elsewhere. People may have read the books and articles, know the vernacular, speak about it, but few really understood what it was all about. When pressed, it was obvious they weren't true entrepreneurs.

Internationally, business is done more by larger corporations rather than by young entrepreneurial enterprises. Perhaps it was cultural differences. Perhaps it was because every deal was so complex that only larger corporations could stomach it. Either way, it was quite difficult to find good partners who responded well to our investment philosophy. I guess we could have changed our philosophy, but we did not.

Also, arriving in London in August of 2008 and eager to hit the ground running, I learned about summer vacation in Europe. Let's just say the work ethic in August in Europe is not quite what it is in the United States.

STEVE: *How did you go about finding potential partners to add to your portfolio?*

KEN: It reminded me of the early days of NGP. I had a list of a few people to whom I had a close referral—mostly bankers and lawyers. They are great places to start, since their firms have important U.S. offices and our relationships there were deep. Barclays also was a good point of contact, as was joining the local YPO chapter and my alumni associations. The only thing I had to do was make calls and make the time.

After a few months of heavy networking, I became pretty plugged in to the oil and gas investment community there. They were very welcoming. Of course, having a multibillion-dollar fund and a relationship with Barclays didn't hurt.

STEVE: *Sounds like it was the perfect hunting ground for deals.*

KEN: It was for about two months. Then the financial crisis hit. The fall of 2008 was pretty ugly in the investment world.

STEVE: *How did the financial crisis affect you?*

KEN: When oil and gas prices collapse by more than 75 percent, it's hard not to be affected. Our portfolio companies were all reassessing their balance sheets and investment assumptions. Our investors were reeling as the markets collapsed. Barclays nearly went under, as did several other large London banks. The commodities investment team inside Barclays was distracted, to say the least.

But we'd seen huge swings before, and we tried our best to remain optimistic. We had a newly raised fund, and we had seen turmoil before. This is where NGP's DNA shined. Our team approach was evident. We didn't panic and we didn't quit. We patiently invested our new fund, pursuing an investment pace much slower than was our practice. We focused on the existing portfolio, *a lot*. We overcommunicated to our investors.

I was proud of the firm during this time, but that wasn't easy, either. We had been through a growth phase and had a cadre of young, ambitious deal professionals who had never been through such a dramatic industry downturn. Of course, the NGP leadership team had. But this downturn was different because it was global and affected just about every industry. My role, as always, was to not get too excited when times were good, and not get too dour when times were bad. I tried my best to reassure our team. I even went so far as to circulate a white paper memo to our team that attempted to put the global financial crisis into perspective and to offer some reassurances as to our approach. That memo is included in Exhibit 4.

Memorandum

To: Natural Gas Partners Employees
From: Ken
Re: Current Investment Climate
Date: October 6, 2008

As I write this, I am reminded of the scene in the movie *Jerry Maguire* where he is writing a "white paper" that describes the sad state of affairs of his business and then seeks to reaffirm a set of governing principles that will guide him out of the abysmal slime of the sports agent business. While not a perfect analogy, the current abysmal conditions in the finance industry are certainly causing many to reaffirm the importance of the prudent credit underwriting principles that were so carelessly cast aside in recent years.

continued

The turmoil in the capital markets reminds us that volatility and change are the norm, not the other way around. It is at times like these that experience is rewarded. As investors in the energy sector, we have been forced to follow global economic conditions, global capital markets, and geopolitical forces in order to understand all the factors that impact energy supply, demand, and pricing. That perspective has served us well.

I want to communicate to the whole firm that this economic condition is not unprecedented and, if we play our cards right, will sow the seeds of enormous returns down the line.

First and foremost, we are investors. As investors, we have developed a set of principles on which we base our decisions. When markets start to move, people who bet right are rewarded. In those times, it is impossible to discern between results of the lucky and results of the smart. In bull markets, we all look brilliant. However, as the markets progress through their inevitable cycles, the difference between the brilliantly lucky and the brilliantly smart becomes painfully clear.

Fortunately, NGP has not deviated from our core governing investment principles and, thus, has been unharmed by the current environment. Once again, our disciplined investment approach has been rewarded.

WHERE WE ARE NOW (IN CONTEXT)

In our 20th anniversary year (November 16, 2008, marks our 20th anniversary as a firm), it is important to review some of the cycles that have tested us or to which we were witnesses:

1987	October stock market collapse
	Oil and gas prices were low
1989–1991	Collapse of the banking system in Texas
	High-yield bond market collapse
	S&L crisis, collapse of real estate values
	Recession begins
	Oil and gas prices were still low
1994–1995	Mexico currency crisis
1998	Collapse of long-term capital management, Asian Tiger country currency crises
	Russia defaults on its debt; Russian stock market crash
	Oil prices went from bad to worse—$20 to $10 per barrel
2001	Tech bubble bursts, NASDAQ collapse, World Trade Center attack
	Mild recession
2002	California power crisis, Enron collapse, merchant power companies default
	Banks reeling
	At least oil and gas prices were beginning to recover from post-9/11 collapse
2008	Credit crisis, housing crisis, liquidity crisis, market collapse, emerging markets collapse, oil and gas prices peaking

We have seen this movie before. In each of these time periods, there was turmoil, and there were reactions. It is important to understand a few key common observations:

1. In all cases, the sun did come up tomorrow, although the next day did look different depending on the industry you were in.
2. There was generally market intervention (politicians just cannot help themselves), and the regulatory landscape changed accordingly.
3. Attractive opportunities did emerge, but they only looked "obvious" many years later.
4. The market averages did rebound in all cases. However, "tulip" values were rarely seen again in the sectors where the "bubbles" were.
5. Level heads did prevail, and conservative investment principles were rewarded. The weak went away.
6. The "Old Economy" did not die.

So, before we get specific as to NGP, it is important to emphasize that we will get through this current turmoil. The government will continue to be in our affairs (they already were), and there will be reactions and overreactions that will create a "new normal." It is also important to understand that there will be unintended consequences of every behavioral change that will only be realized once that behavior changes. While some we can anticipate, others we cannot. This will create extreme volatility and, most likely, sow the seeds for the next "crisis." For example, the housing bubble was a direct result of the decisions by the Federal Reserve to preserve liquidity in the system following the market plunges of 2001. To head off a recession in 2001, the Fed reduced interest rates dramatically and quickly injected massive amounts of liquidity into the system. That liquidity had to go somewhere, and the nation's mortgage brokers were happy to oblige. We are now unwinding the excesses caused by that phenomenon.

WHERE IS NGP NOW?

At NGP, we learned to invest against a backdrop of bad industry conditions and changing market conditions. Richard Rainwater was fond of saying to us as we toiled through the late '80s and early '90s, "If you guys can make a dollar in energy, you'll be able to make a hundred dollars anywhere else." He was trying to convince us to leave the energy industry. But we stuck to our knitting and built our franchise. We avoided the fads of the day, and we were always preparing for the sky to fall. That paranoia led us to act cautiously and to continue to refine our investment discipline. At times, we wondered why we were doing what we were doing when the silliness around us was seemingly producing returns without discipline.

While we are not flawless investors by any stretch, we have developed a cogent set of guiding principles that we follow, and we always maintain a healthy respect for the markets. They can turn against any sector, and when they do, the washout is indiscriminate. We have all seen this before. It is important to understand that the oil and gas business has always been about risk management. Since there is always a risk that any well drilled will be a dry hole, operators in the industry manage exposure to the wellbore. Since there is always a risk that elevated prices will retreat, financiers in the industry manage exposure to price swings. Since there is always a risk that banks will fail, borrowers manage their exposure to single lenders. And on and on . . .

continued

In short, we have adhered to our governing principles. We back prudent management teams who have a proven track record, share our conservative values, have an "edge" over the competition, and follow a defined business plan with extreme focus. We only back management teams willing to invest a significant amount of their own money in the deal. We do not get carried away when commodity prices go up because they have always retreated. While not always putting NGP into the "sexy" plays of the day, adherence to this set of principles has kept us out of trouble.

The same is true for our use of the capital markets. We have a tremendous amount of institutional knowledge of the capital markets. We have seen the "hot" structures of the day turn "cold." We have seen what happens when structures need to unwind quickly. As a result, we are very conservative in our interactions with the capital markets. Again, while not putting us into some of the "hot" structures of the day, adherence to this philosophy has kept us out of trouble.

Unlike hedge funds and leveraged real estate investment funds, Natural Gas Partners does not use any leverage or enter into futures contracts at the fund level. As such, at the fund level, we are not impacted by the current credit crisis.

At the portfolio company level, our investments are structured as equity investments in operating energy companies. As these companies grow, they typically utilize our equity dollars to build a base of capital and operations and then grow from there on the debt capacity of the assets that were built with the committed equity. The younger and smaller the company, the less leveraged it tends to be. Further, the lenders to our companies are diversified among a broad cross section of middle-market banks that specialize in lending against producing oil and gas properties. Since the arrival in 2003 of Tony Weber (Managing Director and Director of Corporate Finance), we have had a dedicated partner focused on the financing function. As a former commercial banker, Tony is aware of the issues involved in bank concentration. The first report he prepared for us was a comprehensive bank concentration report showing where we may or may not have been exposed to any single financial institution. Today, we are extremely well diversified with our banking business. Virtually all of our banks are still lending to oil and gas companies. The middle-market, regional banks are picking up the slack provided by the loss of the large, national money center banks' appetite to make small energy loans.

In addition, the lenders and hedging counterparties for our portfolio companies do *not* include Lehman Brothers, Bear Stearns, or Morgan Stanley and only have minor exposure to AIG through some insurance policies. Our companies have only a nominal amount of commodity hedge exposure to Goldman Sachs. Our standard practice is to use the same banks that are our senior lenders to provide the hedging services to our portfolio companies. This minimizes the complications that can arise if different financial institutions are competing for collateral coverage when commodity prices are extremely volatile.

Furthermore, when looking at the portfolio companies in each active fund, taken as a whole, they are on very modest leverage and are fairly well hedged against a dramatic fall in commodity prices. On an asset-weighted average, NGP 7's portfolio companies are over 70% hedged for 2009 and 2010 and 35% hedged for 2011. Debt/EBITDA is only 1.8x for the companies on a weighted average basis. NGP 8's portfolio companies are 65% hedged for 2009, 35% hedged for 2010, and 20% hedged for 2011 and their debt/EBITDA stands at 1.7x. NGP 9 is a very young portfolio with only $530MM funded of its $4.0 billion. The portfolio companies in that fund are about 20% hedged for 2009 and have debt/EBITDA of only 0.3x.

As a whole, all of our funds are prepared for the storm—not only to weather the storm but also to exploit the opportunities that the storm provides them.

WHERE DO WE GO FROM HERE?

Once the dust settles, the world will look similar to the previous "post crisis" periods. The pendulum will swing too far in the other direction. It always does.

In this case, it is obvious that there will be fewer lending institutions, more conservative lenders running them, and more conservative investors buying their paper. As a result, we will enter a period of reduced liquidity in the leverage markets. This should be a fantastic opportunity for a private equity investor.

The government will try its hand as both a regulator and as an owner of financial and real assets. It will mess it up further. Therein lies the opportunity for the people with the patience to work through the morass.

Taken together, it seems improbable that this will lead to anything more than sluggish growth at best, or a recession at worst. Increased government borrowing will crowd out private sector borrowing and restrict growth. Interest rates will go up as will inflation. Increased government regulation will restrict growth. The U.S. consumer will take time to recover. Geopolitical forces will become more, rather than less intense.

For commodity prices, this means weakness (absent a geopolitical flare-up in the wrong neighborhood). Slowing demand growth caused by economic weakness will lead to slack capacity in the producers' systems. This has always led to price declines, absent a tremendous amount of coordination inside OPEC. That coordination has only been possible when prices were at extreme lows, not just levels off their all-time high. As we said at our annual meeting in July, there are those who believe that the industry is cyclical, and there are those who believe we have entered a new paradigm. We are believers in the cycle. High prices cure high prices, the same way that low prices cure low prices. The high and low levels may change, but the volatile gyrations between highs and lows will persist.

It is a good time to be a buyer that is well hedged, under leveraged, and has equity dollars at the ready.

In the last month, we have initiated one of the largest calling efforts of our firm's career. We will initiate close to 100 meetings with different independent oil and gas companies in the U.S. and in Canada between now and year end. At a time when the public debt, public equity, and bank markets are constrained, private equity is the only game in town. As the leader in the industry with the longest track record of support for the independent oil and gas space, NGP is well positioned and well prepared.

We intend to redouble our efforts to enhance our management teams at every level and have less tolerance for mediocre behaviors. As we work through the deal flow, we hold the opportunity against the highest standard of care so that we can make sure to avoid common pitfalls. In times like these, our experience will serve us well.

We are blessed to have a dedicated and talented set of professionals at NGP. Every member of the firm serves a vital function, and I thank you for your dedication and commitment.

I am excited by the current environment and look forward to 2009.

Exhibit 4: Letter to the firm as the global financial crisis unfolded. (Lehman Brothers filed for bankruptcy on September 15, 2008.)

Looking back, I wish we had invested more during the crisis, but deals were hard to come by. In moments of extreme downturns, there's a real adverse selection problem. The quality companies are built to weather the storm and don't raise capital at super-low valuations. The companies that need capital are those you don't particularly want to invest in. It is a fallacy to say that it's easy to buy low and sell high. When times are bad, the deals that are usually available are the ones you don't want to do.

But there were real buying opportunities and I failed to pull the trigger on a couple of notable transactions. Even given all my perspective and experience at the time, I must admit I didn't always practice what I preached. It was a very difficult time, and a global economic panic was not the same as a commodity cycle swing. I was learning on the job again, except this time I was sitting in London watching the world nearly implode. I must say that I played better defense than offense.

STEVE: *From a portfolio perspective, you weathered the storm. Was the financial crisis just a fleeting event for NGP?*

KEN: The world did recover, and we were able to hold our portfolio together for the most part. On the surface, however, as time went by, it was apparent that the crisis had a lasting impact on my fundamental building blocks of the firm's future. I can actually trace the instability of the firm some eight years later to the financial crisis itself.

STEVE: *That's a pretty interesting realization. Explain.*

KEN: With the 2006 Barclays transaction, the growth in our assets under management, and the expansion through our affiliated funds, unbeknownst to me, I was making a bet on the future of the firm. We had doled out a lot of cash to people at the firm, both from the Barclays proceeds and the firm's profits, and reinvested a chunk as well. Pieces were in place for my colleagues at the firm to reap future benefits. The future payouts from the Barclays deal plus the expected appreciation from the IPP fund would combine with the returns from their ownership in NGP 7, NGP 8, and the newly raised $4 billion NGP 9. Taken as a whole, the design would keep people incentivized far into the future. If we performed, everyone would earn *a lot*.

Looking back now, unfortunately, it's clear that the global financial crisis set in motion forces that would undo my grand design. Commodity prices crashed. Capital markets crashed. And the ensuing response to the crisis would change the nature of the private equity business forever.

STEVE: *In what way?*

KEN: Simply put, the profits didn't materialize as well or as fast as projected. Unknowingly, I was counting on people having more patience than they actually did.

After the world's economic powers coordinated to save the global economies from a major depression and Barack Obama's administration was firmly in place, the markets entered a slow healing phase. Once the recovery was under way, I viewed 2008–2009 as another industry downturn like we'd seen at other times in our history and treated it as another chance to lock arms as partners, hunker down, and get to work. Our task was to focus on our portfolio and help our companies navigate through the crisis and survive until such time as they could regroup and return to growth. Most of the companies in that portfolio survived, although the returns from the affected funds were somewhat below our initial expectations.

Again, our investment style paid off, and we were able to adjust on the fly so that even our most affected funds were able to recover nicely and still earn a double-digit return, well ahead of most private equity funds of that vintage. Most funds raised in 2005 and invested prior to the crisis of 2008–2009 got wiped out. Contrary to that, our $1.3 billion fund, NGP 8, was able to recover and earn 1.6 times its invested capital, yet, given the length of time it required, it equated to only a 13 percent rate of return. I was really proud of the team. But with only a 13 percent return, the profits interest portion was relatively modest, and surely it wasn't what our team was expecting.

In addition, our affiliated funds did not fare as well. The energy technology industry faltered badly. Even though our risk-averse investment approach didn't get caught up in the hype, it was still affected. Our fund did manage to get the investors their money back, but it was years later than anticipated and the profits interest was not worth anything.

In addition, the energy lending business was affected as loans made to energy companies before the crash had trouble being repaid in full. Plus, the business development company model couldn't raise capital once losses happened, so the business ended up shrinking. Since our financial returns were linked to increasing the amount of assets under management, the income we would earn remained relatively low.

Finally, the NGP Midstream and Resources team didn't remain as part of the NGP organization. After I helped originate the idea and sponsor that team in the investor market, the management team there never seemed to integrate with us. From my vantage point, it was a lesson in understanding the importance of organizational culture. While they acted otherwise at inception, it appeared to me that team had difficulty buying into our family style of operating the business. Ultimately, despite the successful returns of that fund, they changed their name and raised subsequent funds on their own.

Despite all this, however, David, Dick, John, and I felt good about where we stood coming out of the financial crisis. Sure, the financial model we had developed for all the employees had to be revised, pushing out the gain further into the future, but given the crush of the markets, we were thrilled with the health of our firm relative to the bloodbath the industry had taken. This was the benefit that historical perspective provided.

STEVE: *Sounds like you were dealing with the aftermath of the crisis pretty well, and it wasn't the near-death experience Sunoma was. Am I missing something?*

KEN: As I said, on the surface, we were in great shape. However, beneath the surface, there was instability. Two camps began developing inside NGP, though they didn't really reveal themselves for quite some time. The old-guard team—me, David, John, Dick, and a few other partners who had seen the volatility before—redoubled our efforts. While we all had been financially rewarded by the returns from prior funds and received the Barclays deal proceeds, we had reinvested much of that into the firm. But more important, we had made personal commitments to each other and to our investors. We had never quit before, and we weren't about to quit now. We had confidence that our business model would yield great returns. We just needed to be patient.

As for my new-guard colleagues, I expected them to follow the behavior we were modeling and work hard as a team. And they did. The web of financial incentives and capital they'd invested was well structured and in place. They were looking at the money they would be leaving on the table if they left, so they stuck around and worked hard. We continued to have fun. We continued to work on all the cultural aspects that made NGP a special place. On the surface, everything was fine as our returns recovered.

STEVE: *And below the surface?*

KEN: Green lights were about to turn yellow.

CHAPTER 13

YELLOW LIGHTS
DON'T TURN GREEN

STEVE: *You left us hanging. That ominous theme from* Jaws *ran through my head. Sounds like something lay beneath the seemingly peaceful NGP waters after the global financial collapse.*

KEN: Not immediately. As I said, we survived that collapse better than most. But there were a lot of factors outside and inside NGP that made our success—you might even say survival—problematic.

President Obama's chief of staff Rahm Emanuel nailed it when he said, "Never allow a good crisis go to waste."* But before that, in 2010, Congress took that concept to heart and passed the Dodd-Frank Wall Street Reform and Consumer Protection Act—a conglomeration of edicts that put much of the financial industry in the regulatory sights of the federal government. Even though the private equity industry had nothing to do with the mortgage or banking crisis, the legislators saw us as a place where money and power had accumulated without much government oversight.

Dodd-Frank's 848 pages, which soon led to nearly 28,000 new regulatory restrictions on the financial industry, changed all that. Private equity firms now needed to register with and make periodic filings to the Securities and Exchange Commission

---

* Rahm Emanuel, "Let's Make Sure This Crisis Doesn't Go to Waste," *Washington Post*, March 25, 2020, https://www.washingtonpost.com/opinions/2020/03/25/lets-make-sure-this-crisis-doesnt-go-waste.

to report on their business. From that point forward, firms, NGP included, needed to have a significant and costly compliance department.

When NGP's revenue pie was growing, and we were sharing that pie across the firm, everyone was happy, but our newer colleagues had never seen a downturn until 2008. The old guard had seen several, and we remembered vividly when much of our take-home cash was reinvested into the business. We saw the chance to own equity as a gift. That was a clear holdover from the Richard Rainwater days. Getting to invest in the equity account of a deal was a plum opportunity for which we were grateful.

Now, after the Barclays deal, we retained 60 percent of the revenue of the firm, yet we had to cover all our costs. In addition, the costs of the London office and the new compliance functions were high. Even though the $4 billion NGP 9 fund was the largest we had ever raised, it was easy to calculate what it would be without Barclays taking its 40 percent. Under the surface, there was a "what have you done for me lately" attitude developing. This developed even though our 60 percent of the top-line revenue was greater than the 100 percent amount from before the Barclays transaction.

The storm brewing was masked by the professionalism of the people we had hired. They were quality people, and they were very appreciative of how we shared the economics of the firm with them, knowing that we didn't have to. However, as people, they just had different perspectives. The original core partners had all grown up in the industry and we knew how lucky we were. The younger set had come to just expect the growth in income to continue. I even had young partners compare their net worth to my net worth when I was their age. Of course, that was some twenty years prior, and we took on a heck of a lot more risk in building the mature enterprise that they were fortunate to be hired into. We suffered through some lean times that my younger colleagues had only read about.

STEVE: *Despite all this happening in 2010, you tried to expand your footprint even further into the agribusiness and climate adaptation arena. Why? It sounds like a stretch.*

KEN: As I said, the cracks were well below the surface. Our team was working hard, and we were blessed to have held together as a team. Other firms in our industry had come apart by 2010.

Yet our returns had recovered nicely, and the Barclays deal was far enough in our rearview mirror that I felt confident in spreading our wings once again. Given how close I was to the energy industry and the climate change debate, I saw an opening to do something innovative.

It was apparent to me that, despite massive efforts to increase the use of renewable energy, the world was still going to be hooked on hydrocarbons far into the future. The world's economic growth during the past century was enabled by the supply of reliable and relatively cheap energy. Fossil fuels would be hard to displace. It took a hundred years to build out the extensive energy supply chains that exist in the world, and the replacement cost will measure into the tens of trillions of dollars.

Hydrocarbons will be displaced someday, but not in the time needed to avoid the temperature change scientists have been warning about. The world's population will increase from seven to nine billion in the next twenty years, and up to two billion people will develop into middle-class consumers with the commensurate increase in demand for things like beef and plastics of all sorts. At the same time, the world will see massive urbanization, much of which is clustered along the globe's coastlines. This research is everywhere. These facts are not in dispute.

In my mind, there was no way the race to install uneconomic renewable energy would be won. The world needed to begin *adapting* to the inevitability of climate change, while it worked on developing and implementing the technologies that would ultimately reduce our reliance on fossil fuels. The numbers didn't lie. Since the early 2000s, the world had spent over $2 trillion on renewable and alternative energy, but hydrocarbons' share of global energy supply had not budged. It remained at 82 percent. Regardless of what people wish to believe, fossil fuels will be dominant in the energy supply chain for decades.

I tried to be forward-thinking and raise capital to get ahead of the trend. I assembled a team with experience in the agribusiness, water, and coastal infrastructure protection industries and off we went to make the rounds to see our investors. NGP Global Adaptation Partners would be seen as a trendsetter when it became inevitable that mankind would fall short of its greenhouse emissions goals and the necessity of adapting to a changing planet would become obvious. When that moment occurred, I argued, it would not be the time to *start* thinking about investing; it would be the time to have your portfolio ready to go. Rainwater used to say it was important to have your sail fully out when the wind changes direction and starts blowing from behind.

We saw that in the oil and gas industry. Since we were always investing in the sector, we saw firsthand the dramatic returns we generated when the markets turned bullish. Those returns were achieved by investments made many years before. The deals done when the wind was at our back were typically done at higher prices and in an environment when competition was everywhere—not a recipe for investment success.

STEVE: *In 2010, you also founded a nonprofit think tank. Where does that fit in to this narrative?*

KEN: To accomplish something more socially responsible at the same time we were doing our deals, we concurrently launched the Global Adaptation Institute. The goal was to stress the need for the world to incorporate adaptation into its thinking about dealing with climate change. This institute was to receive a share of our profits from the NGP Global Adaptation Partners fund. I thought that by adding a philanthropic by-product, many investors would rally more to the cause. At the time, investors had started clamoring for more socially responsible investment vehicles.

While today that fund would fly off the shelves, in 2010, not many investors were willing to do something new. I find it puzzling that I was lauded for having great insight and, sometimes at least, for being able to see around corners, but when push came to shove, investors in the endowment, foundation, and pension fund world had less ability to analyze trends and allocate capital in that direction, even when advocated by experts they trust.

Most investors agreed with the premise I was espousing, but they were incapable of pulling the trigger and getting ahead of the curve. The way to make outsize returns, I argued, was, to use a hockey analogy, to skate where the puck is going. You don't wait to see where it lands and then skate toward it.

Unfortunately, institutional investors are not in the business of being forward thinking. I was really disappointed that my investor base didn't want to back the team we had assembled, with my oversight, in a new endeavor. It was the first time I was unsuccessful in taking my track record for a spin. I was humbled. We closed on a small agribusiness fund to complete some of the deals we had in the pipeline, but the water and coastal protection team had to be disbanded.

At the same time, the returns in our main NGP funds had recovered nicely and we were excited about launching a new oil and gas fund. We launched the fundraising for NGP 10 in 2011, again with a $4 billion target. This fundraise was considerably harder. The senior team all participated in fundraising, aware that we needed to cast a very wide net for investors.

Here is where the aftermath of the Madoff scandal, combined with the financial crisis, hit us. Despite the fact that, on a relative basis, our performance was strong against the competition, the endowment, foundation, and pension fund community was dialing back its exposure to private investments. However, we persisted.

Given the continuity in the team and our stature within the industry, we were given the benefit of the doubt by many. I made trips to virtually all our investors to look them in the eye and give them my word that we would work hard and not let them down. We took in several large international investors and some sovereign wealth funds that were now emerging on the private equity investment scene. In the end, the complexity of our fund management increased, but we were successful in raising $3.6 billion for NGP 10, which closed in 2012. It was one of the larger funds raised that year, and we folded our agribusiness team into the overall firm and got investor clearance to allocate some of that fund to agribusiness deals.

We were back in good shape.

STEVE: *But you didn't live happily ever after.*

KEN: I'm afraid not. At a time when I felt NGP was as strong as ever, the complexion of the firm was changing. With growth and complexity came more people. We hired really strong people, and I worked a lot on culture at every turn. But sheer size made it more difficult to maintain that personal family feeling. Each group had a different cadence to its work. We were not always in sync.

The accounting team had a clear pace that worked toward reporting deadlines. The legal and compliance team needed their work to be completed on time and with great care throughout the year. The investor relations team was on the road frequently, and the ebb and flow of investor communications demands dictated its work. The deal team was growing with the addition of some remarkable young people and the maturation of the junior folks whom we had brought on over the years.

My goal was to institutionalize the NGP brand, and I did a lot to make sure it happened. Our institutionalization was solidified by the Barclays transaction in 2006 and the resulting incentive plans that were implemented. However, it was clear that a group of younger partners who had smaller participations in the funds were beginning to realize that the spoils of the future would need to be shared among more people. We were transitioning to a place that traded the opportunity for a massive payday for one that ensured financial stability and more modest wealth for everyone. Of course, there was always a chance for another Energy Transfer–type deal to occur, but the law of large numbers became evident—it was a heck of a lot easier to make seven times your money on a $370 million fund, rather than on a $4 billion one.

I missed what was happening. I was an open book about my goals for the firm and did not hide the ultimate plan. I figured that, with a much bigger pie and the huge amount of stability we had built, people would all be happy. The paydays were still enormous by any standard, other than what NGP had become accustomed to.

That was tested and confirmed again in the second half of 2012, when Barclays decided it wanted to divest its 40 percent stake in the firm.

STEVE: *Why were they looking to sell?*

KEN: Barclays was humbled by the global financial crisis. Their pedigree was as a stodgy UK bank and they had had this stretch where they transformed into a bulge-bracket commercial, merchant, and investment bank. Bob Diamond, the aggressive American CEO, aspired for Barclays to be both a money center bank and a full-service investment bank, complete with corporate finance, sales and trading, capital markets, derivative, and merchant banking capabilities.

The financial crisis brought this all to a screeching halt. Barclays nearly went under. Emergency capital was raised, and we all know how central banks made it possible for the global capital markets to remain functioning. The money center banks became shadows of their former selves. In Barclays's case, new management was brought in, and the bank sought to return to its roots and shed businesses that were not central to the operations. In addition, the Volcker Rule, enacted as part of the Dodd-Frank legislation after the financial crisis, said that commercial banks and asset management businesses should not be housed under the same corporate umbrella.

Some institutions acted and others took a wait-and-see posture while the Volcker Rule itself was being fully written and litigated. Barclays decided to act early and looked for a buyer for its 40 percent interest in NGP. Ironically, those that never acted were better off. The Volcker Rule ultimately was deemed too unworkable to implement cleanly, and it was watered down before it was essentially abandoned by the federal government. Being a foreign bank on U.S. soil, Barclays was keen to comply before the dust settled.

STEVE: *Were there a lot of buyers out there?*

KEN: I'm not sure. We had an agreement that they needed my approval to sell their interest, so I knew I would hear about it once a negotiation became serious. I didn't see my role as one of playing broker for them. The people I dealt with at the bank, led by Mark Brown, were solid. We had become friends and they were good partners.

As fate would have it, along came the Carlyle Group, one of the world's largest and most successful asset management businesses. It had investment funds all over the place and counted just about every major institution in the world as an investor in one product line or another.

On a much bigger scale, Carlyle was running the same play I was, but from a different playbook. While I had grown our firm into a more diversified asset management business, NGP was still defined as an investor in the energy and natural resources industries. Carlyle, on the other hand, was an investment supermarket. It was managing funds in the global private equity and dedicated investment pools focusing on real estate, power, emerging markets, Asia, Europe, South America, and Africa. It also had a large fixed-income management segment.

The strong leadership of its founders, David Rubenstein, Bill Conway, and Dan D'Aniello, was able to drive consistency of process across the platform. Their model was built on gauging investor appetite for a strategy and then starting a fund from scratch, by hiring an investment team, putting the Carlyle wrapper around it, and raising funds to target that specific strategy. Each fund had its own unique investment thesis.

In 2001, Carlyle deviated from its traditional methodology and formed a joint venture with Riverstone Holdings, an investment team focused on the energy industry. Although the joint venture was a fundraising success over the ensuing decade-plus, the returns faltered, and the firms parted ways after 2010.

That relationship failure left Carlyle without a vehicle to invest in natural resources. Given the explosive growth in global energy demand plus the unconventional shale revolution that was just becoming apparent in the United States, Carlyle remained motivated to find a way to manage capital in the sector. They considered starting a new fund from scratch as well as looking around for other firms to either partner with or acquire. In their process, they learned of Barclays's interest in divesting its holdings in NGP. I was contacted by my counterpart at Barclays and asked if it would be something I would consider agreeing to.

STEVE: How did you respond?

KEN: At first, I was confused. I knew of the Carlyle-Riverstone joint venture, and it seemed to me I'd be talking to a competitor. They had raised a couple of large funds in rapid succession and were making a lot of noise in the industry. I thought, *Why would I let the fox in the henhouse?* I was not keen to share our information with them and let Barclays entertain selling their piece to a competitor.

Then, David Rubenstein contacted me and explained the split between Carlyle and Riverstone and how we could actually be a strategic fit for them. Of course, I'd heard of David Rubenstein, the ever-present face of Carlyle, but we had never met. On more than one occasion, I had been in the audience listening to his speeches. His dry sense of humor and his humility belie his keen eye for macro trends. I always felt I would like him. For a private equity guy like me, getting a call from David Rubenstein was tantamount to someone in the stock-picking business getting a call from Warren Buffett. I had no idea how vast Carlyle's reach was, however, so it was fascinating to learn why he felt the fit was such a good one.

I was intrigued enough to encourage discussions and, after going over the possibilities with my partners, we moved the dialogue along. I traveled to Carlyle's Washington, D.C., office to meet its senior partners, and then we hosted an entourage from the firm in our Irving offices.

Immediately, there was great chemistry. The three founders of Carlyle were a team not unlike David Albin, John Foster, and me. They complemented each other well, and they had a very similar approach toward investing—find great people who can run good businesses and try to be the best financial partner possible. Their firm had grown steadily over the years from a private equity fund business into a full-fledged asset management business. They had multiple product lines, if you will, with separately managed funds all over the world. But each fund had a linkage back to the firm. NGP was a mini-Carlyle.

Carlyle was also in the midst of a transition, not unlike what we were telegraphing at NGP. Carlyle had gone public in May 2012, and as a public company, it was becoming important that the firm operate more like an established institution, not just a group of funds managed by three people with a supporting cast. This was exactly the challenge I'd embarked on going back to the Barclays deal and the launch of our affiliated funds. I had worked through the nuances of how to institutionalize the NGP brand from a culture and compensation perspective and was now thinking about the long gradual succession process.

It was apparent from our conversations that the three Carlyle founders were thinking through the exact same dynamics, although on a much bigger scale. And they were doing it in the public's eye. Helping them navigate this entire dynamic was Glenn Youngkin, a longtime Carlyle partner, although not one of the original founders. A former collegiate basketball player, he was a commanding yet pleasant presence in the room. His McKinsey background was apparent in his calm demeanor, yet his two decades at Carlyle had transformed him from a consultant into a real investor. After a long career at Carlyle, he transformed into a savvy politician, running for, and winning, the race for governor of Virginia in 2021.

Glenn had strong investor instincts and the ability to simplify a complex situation into clear insights. In many respects, that had become my role as well. Our business had long since outgrown my ability to manage, and increasingly I found my role to be deciphering the real investment bet that a new deal would be making, or to help synthesize for the group whatever issues were percolating in the portfolio. For the investor community, I was able to explain in plain English the nuanced investment process and the way to assess the risk and rewards of placing bets in the oil patch.

As the discussions around the business marriage between NGP and Carlyle evolved, Glenn and I worked well together. Clearly, we had to have a meeting of the minds on valuation, not only between ourselves but also with the folks at Barclays. More important, we needed to have a clear sense of how the two organizations would work together after the fact. Both Carlyle and NGP were mature investment franchises. Our cultures were unique *and different.*

STEVE: *In what ways?*

KEN: When working on transactions, too often the bulk of the time is spent on valuation, with each side trying hard to have the deal land on a price that is acceptable. Questions around cultural fit are often left to the end.

In our case, preserving NGP's culture was front and center on my mind. Buying into NGP would be a different path for Carlyle. We were already up and running, not some nascent team looking for a home. Our money was already raised, and we had our own deep relationships with investors and did not need Carlyle's sponsorship in the investor community. I had spent decades arguing that sector-focused investment efforts were superior in that we were able to really become a part of the fabric of an industry. Carlyle was the ultimate generalist firm trying to diversify into sector-focused efforts.

David Albin and I had grown up with many of the leaders of our industry. Corporate chiefs of 2012 were underlings in the 1990s. We made it our business to get well networked in the industry, and my goal was to always play the long game. As Richard had modeled, I always took a meeting. I always followed up. I always tried to be helpful. I always stayed in touch. After twenty years, these relationships were indeed special. My professional and personal lives were hard to separate. Our friendships ran deep. All of that became the goodwill of NGP's brand. There was no way I was going to let that be consumed by Carlyle.

STEVE: *Was that difficult?*

KEN: Thankfully, no. Carlyle was paying for that goodwill, so it had no reason to risk damaging it. We simply had to craft a set of governing principles that would allow the firms to work together and preserve the value of NGP's independent brand, while allowing NGP to have access to the resources of a global firm with much broader reach. Crafting that approach was fun. Glenn and I were both committed to making it work. Again, good people who are aligned in their motivations can make just about anything happen.

Of course, the team at Barclays had to agree on the value for Carlyle's purchase of its interest, and we had to determine how and who would sell a bit more, so the negotiation was intense. After nearly getting derailed at a couple of points in time, Youngkin, Albin, and I reached a framework for everything to happen by Thanksgiving of 2012.

Once again, I used the transaction as a tool to share the economics across the firm. The economic trade was fairly straightforward, and I had kept all my partners abreast of the discussions, so this was not difficult to digest. However, given that Carlyle was in the private equity business and its goal was to increase alignment over time, I wanted the entire senior team at NGP to be included in the decision. There was some risk to our franchise and our independence over the long term, even though the transaction was well structured to preserve it.

Knowing the importance of the decision, I called a special meeting of the senior NGP team. We holed up in the unfinished dining room of a condo that Julie and I had purchased to hash out the pros and cons of the deal. Dick Covington and I went over the entirety of the structure and valuations that were settled, and we discussed the deal in depth.

I'd had general agreement in the office hallways as to the deal itself, but I wanted to be sure everyone was in favor of moving forward. The discussion was robust, but the debate was minimal. Everyone saw the merits of the deal and appreciated the independence that we retained. However, with the Carlyle affiliation, we would have access to a larger set of potential investors and, crucially, we would have a built-in coinvestor for deals too large for our funds. The rationale made sense to the team, and the vote was unanimous.

From my perspective, it was most important that this deal set in motion the successful transition of the firm's management from David and me to the rest of the team. We sold an incremental 15 percent piece of the firm for $212 million. As was our style, David and I only allocated about 35 percent to ourselves, with the remainder spread to the other employees. We also made the point to the rest of the team that we would *gift* the remaining 45 percent of the ownership in the firm to them at a later date. I was proud to be providing liquidity for everyone plus a path for the next generation to be gifted the remaining half of the firm for free. Essentially, we used Barclays and Carlyle money to buy us out so we wouldn't have to have the touchy negotiation later when it became time for the next generation of partners to buy us out of our piece of the firm.

STEVE: *Seems generous of you and a great deal for that next generation.*

KEN: We thought so. But while the senior partners were all in favor of this deal, the next layer of junior partners was less convinced. I knew they were the most skeptical of the deal's merits, so I went to great lengths to make sure they were getting an economic windfall that they would not otherwise have received and reassured them that the firm would be in their hands in the not-too-distant future. These were professionals we had hired at a young age and who had matured to be in line to take over the firm.

STEVE: *And they were persuaded?*

KEN: Yes. Everyone was on board and excited. The deal closed prior to year-end 2012. NGP became further institutionalized as a branded investment franchise deeply woven into the fabric of the natural resources industry and had an identity fully separate from that of its founders. We had a strong institutional partner in Carlyle. Everyone was being taken care of. Our management succession was now indeed possible, even if key individuals were to leave the firm.

There were a few criticisms expressed by the junior partners about the deal. We listened to their points and adjusted. We made sure that the final deal spread more money their way and telegraphed succession planning clearly. They all expressed their pleasure and were happy to receive the proceeds. In hindsight, these criticisms were not criticisms of the deal, per se; they were expressions of the DNA of those individuals' character—their perspectives and priorities. I should have seen this as a yellow light that would later turn red.

STEVE: *Clarify what you mean by "yellow light" in this particular instance.*

KEN: Whenever I look back on a difficult period or tough personnel decision, I've been able to see there were early warning signs all over the place. As I've gained experience, I have learned that the best thing to do is to be intellectually honest about these early warning signs, because they rarely go away. Those same conditions tend to worsen over time, ultimately leading to the need to make a tough decision. If I had acted when I first saw the warning signs, life would have been easier. In investment parlance, it means cut your losses early, before they become bigger problems.

With regard to people, my tendency in my career was to try to coach the recalcitrant people and work to bring them into the fold. I was loath to admit either defeat or that I had made the wrong decision in bringing them into the firm. I was optimistic that people were coachable and that certain behaviors could be groomed. As I've already explained, I've learned that, just like a stoplight, yellow lights don't turn green.

It's important to see those yellow lights and act. Just like an investment that begins to sour, it is quite hard to turn things around if the problems relate to some fundamental core characteristic of a company or a person. While the issues may get swept under the rug for a period of time, it seems inevitable they will become problems again in the future—and usually at inopportune times and with larger ramifications. Whenever I have delayed, hoping for change, I have come to regret it. In fact, the yellow lights usually turned red, forcing me to make a tougher decision that could have been managed with fewer ramifications had I acted earlier.

STEVE: *We'll come back to that. But as for the firm, you were trying to do something unique in the private equity industry. Right?*

KEN: Yes. While the large investment banks and financial services firms like Goldman Sachs had all been able to reach this level of institutional maturity, almost nobody in our business had been able to accomplish this strategic maneuver. The industry is seen as one driven by single individuals or key partners. But I knew we had a great franchise and had developed a set of business practices and principles that could stand the test of time and weren't reliant on David and me anymore. I knew that ultimately the old guard would have to leave, and that employee turnover was inevitable, but I didn't want my professional life's work to vanish the way many partnerships unravel or wind up when the founders pack it in.

Now, all we had to do was keep our heads down and execute, and that we did. A flurry of calls and meetings with investors followed, assuring them that the Carlyle relationship would be positive, while not detracting from our ability or desire to work hard. Again, I had to make the points to investors that the added liquidity for us was not going to hurt our work ethic. In fact, I felt the need to work harder to keep my promise to them. And it was sincere. As crass as it seems to admit, money in the bank ceases to be a motivator after the bank account reaches a certain level. This was "look yourself in the mirror" time to determine what really motivates you.

STEVE: *And what did you discover?*

KEN: I'm a pleaser at heart. I really wanted to create a lasting business and make everyone happy. Proving it to investors who doubted my sincerity became a challenge in and of itself. Many felt that since we had pulled so much money out of the business, we'd be less motivated to work hard. Once again, we made the point that we could have quit after Fund 6 if money was our only motivator. I could only surmise that so many people who didn't enjoy their work would happily quit if they got a great payday. With that mindset, they couldn't understand why we wouldn't do the same once we got ours. But, man, I was having a ball. And I was doing it with people who had become my dearest friends.

More important, as a business builder, I had found a way to establish such a broad foundation of business practices and scale that we essentially de-risked our business model. Recall that the large Sunoma write-off earlier in our careers created an existential threat to the entire firm and our livelihoods. Now, in the 2010s, we were so successful in broadening our base and diversifying our risk that even a larger write-off was not a threat to our existence or our investment franchise.

STEVE: *Sounds like you are referring to another mess?*

KEN: Yes, you could call it that. In late 2011, we had the chance to participate along-side the big buyout firm Kohlberg Kravis Roberts, more commonly known as KKR. They approached us to partner on a $7 billion leveraged buyout of Samson Resources, one of the old-line private family oil and gas companies based in Tulsa, Oklahoma. This company was built by acquiring and drilling properties in the midcontinent region, a region with which we were intimately familiar.

However, the company was a private family operation, and it was run in a very unsophisticated, you might say sloppy, manner. We later learned that the internal controls and finances were not in good order. The team at KKR engaged an army of consultants from the top accounting firms to perform due diligence and examine the books. This is something that we never farmed out to consultants. We always did our own work, so this was a practice with which we were not familiar. While we tried to work our way into the due diligence process, KKR was firm in their lead position on the deal and stuck to their business practices. Shame on us for not dropping out of the deal. The two brand-name accounting firms charged the buyer group several million dollars and produced voluminous presentations with fancy charts full of numbers, yet they missed a $500 million expenditure that was caught at the first board meeting.

Needless to say, we deviated from our investment discipline to participate as a minority partner with a brand-name firm who turned out to be amateurs when it came to deal evaluation and understanding what makes an effective portfolio company executive team. Plus, it didn't help that natural gas prices took a nosedive soon after we closed the deal.

We were behind the eight ball for the entire time we held that investment.

In the end, despite four years of work by KKR trying to restructure the operations and enhance the value of the assets, the debt levels were too great to overcome. By 2015, we ended up writing off the entire $350 million investment, or about 9 percent of the capital in NGP 9. In fact, we had to start marking down the value of that invest-ment as soon as 2012, the year after we made it. But, given our scale, that fund still ended up realizing over 1.8 times our investors' capital. While this loss stung, it was not the end of the world. Looking back, surviving such a loss proved how resilient and strong our franchise had become.

But, sitting there in 2012, all the lights were green—firm, investors, and perfor-mance. The next year, 2013, was intentionally uneventful as we continued to manage the portfolios through market swings and prepared to launch our next fund. In 2014, we launched NGP 11 with a target of $5 billion, which we exceeded, closing the fund at $5.325 billion. The firm's growth of the prior ten years actually set up this successful fundraise, but for reasons exactly the opposite of what you'd expect.

STEVE: *How so?*

KEN: When we raised Fund 10 starting in 2011 and finishing it in 2012, we had a lot of explaining to do. Over the preceding few years, we'd asked our investor base to digest a lot of concepts that were out of the ordinary. We did the Barclays deal. We added the expansion-affiliated funds. We attempted to diversify away from energy into agriculture and water, but to no avail. Yet we kept moving forward and stuck with our plan.

By 2014, the expansion funds were not going as planned. Despite being in the upper echelon of energy technology funds of the time, the energy technology fund's returns were lackluster and not what we were accustomed to at NGP. Our timing was off. While we had raised a second fund in 2009, there was no plan at the time to raise a third fund. Also, by that time, the Midstream and Resources fund team had decided to go off on their own and raise future funds without the NGP affiliation—another yellow light that I should have seen coming back in 2006. Our lending business was also limping along on its way to being sold. It was humbling.

Having eaten that humble pie, we saw it was time to get back to our core competency. So 2014 became our back-to-basics year. We launched NGP 11 with a large target and our message was simple: The affiliated funds' distractions were gone, and we were singularly focused on the oil and gas investment platform. With that message, the Carlyle transaction became easier to digest, and we were much more credible to the investor market. It was a simpler pitch to make than the ones I'd been making for the past handful of years.

STEVE: *That must have been a relief.*

KEN: Yes, but it was a lot less fun. I enjoyed innovating and expanding and, frankly, I was kind of bored by the same story we had been telling for so many years. For years, when I described our perfect buy-and-build oil and gas company, I said our portfolio company's goal was to be the fastest tortoise in the race. We wanted them to build assets slowly and carefully while letting the power of compounding work in their favor. "Slow and steady" was our mantra. Boring was good.

Here's the great irony: We built a fabulous firm by investing slowly and steadily. Yet, at the firm level, I went fast. I took the firm out of its slow lane, shifted lanes, and grew us into a more diversified asset management business to institutionalize the brand

and to monetize part of the firm at a superb valuation. We never could have realized the firm value we did had we stayed in our original lane, but that original lane was where we thrived best.

Once we returned to our tried-and-true message, we completed our largest fundraise ever, closing NGP 11 at over $5.3 billion. That fund drove more profitability for the firm than all the expansion funds combined. We turned back into the tortoise and won the race, even if running that race was less fun for me personally.

STEVE: *Does having less fun mean restless, ready to look for a new challenge outside NGP?*

KEN: The fundraising effort for NGP 11 allowed me to be forthright with investors as to my long-term intentions. At age fifty-one, I didn't want to commit to leading the fund for the twelve years it would exist. The thought of doing this at this pace until my sixty-third birthday in 2026 did not sit well.

At the same time, I wasn't going to do what many in the industry did and hide that fact from investors. I saw several firms announce the departure of senior partners *after* a fund had closed, surprising the investors who had just committed capital. That type of behavior is reprehensible. So, in our actual offering documents for this fund, we were up-front with our investors about the future of the firm. We explicitly said that I would start out as CEO of this fund, then, during the fund's life, I would move to chairman and would not be in that capacity for Fund 12, whenever that would be raised.

We expanded the investment committee to include more of our partners, and the entire senior team took part in the fundraising efforts. We divided into teams and fanned out, so the investor community could see the depth of our team.

This felt good to me. We had successfully navigated the firm through quite a period of uncertainty. We had lived through the bullish price run-up caused by the synchronized economic growth in the United States and China before 2008, then the near-depression of the 2009 global financial crisis and the recovery through 2014. Through it all, we stayed flexible in our strategy and weren't afraid to try new things. We grew as a firm. We learned from our mistakes, and we were locked and loaded with a new fund, our largest in history.

STEVE: *So you were humming along?*

KEN: Well, in the energy business, it's only a matter of time until you get hit right between the eyes. We were humming along until Saudi Arabia decided to do battle with the U.S. oil and gas entrepreneurs.

STEVE: *In what way?*

KEN: Armed with data from some of the highest-priced consultants in the world, Saudi Arabia believed that the $90 per barrel oil prices supported by Saudi production restraints in late 2014 were enabling the U.S. oil producers to drill the unconventional shales. As a result, U.S. oil production had increased from 5.7 million barrels per day in 2011 to 8.8 million barrels per day in 2014. To accommodate that growth on the world stage and not have prices collapse, Saudi Arabia sequentially restricted its production growth, so it stayed essentially flat during that time period. With no end in sight to the growth in U.S. production, the Kingdom, as it's called, had to do *something*. It couldn't stomach their production going backward with each passing year.

Conventional thinking at the time was that unconventional shales were uneconomic when oil prices dipped below $70 per barrel. This made Saudi's calculus rather simple: Dial up production enough to cause prices to drop below $70 per barrel, and the U.S. producers would stop drilling because new production would be unprofitable.

Their expensive consulting reports turned out to be *very* expensive indeed, because they were so wrong. The Saudis decided to declare war against the ingenuity and creativity of the independent producers in the United States who were armed with entrepreneurial spirit and new technology. With necessity as the mother of invention, the independent operators slashed their costs and reduced the floor price at which their reserves were able to be sustained.

Beginning in late 2014, the Kingdom continued to dial up production, and prices, having averaged over $90 per barrel in 2014, began to fall. Ultimately, oil prices dropped to about $30 per barrel. At that price, Saudi Arabia was inflicting real pain in the oil patch. Companies that could not service their debt went bankrupt. The year 2015 was terrible for the industry. New drilling was reduced dramatically. The growth in oil production not only stopped but actually dropped. Another dramatic industry cycle was upon us.

Thankfully, in early 2015, we had a big new fund, and our prior funds were holding up okay. I rallied the troops to send a clear message: Hang tough; we have seen this movie before, and we know how it ends. The best cure for low prices is low prices. Demand goes up and supply drops. In fact, I emphasized, this will create unprecedented opportunities for our new and largest fund ever.

Then, on February 3, 2015, one of my yellow lights turned red.

STEVE: *What happened?*

KEN: Early in 2015, David Albin and I were asked by the CEO of one of our Tulsa-based companies to schedule a private meeting to discuss an issue. He agreed to fly in to see us, so we arranged a conference room for February 3 at one of the private hangars at Dallas Love Field.

That afternoon, David and I walked into the conference room, where we found not only the CEO but four others from NGP—one of our junior partners, a young associate, one of our internal attorneys, and our controller. They proceeded to tell us that they were leaving NGP to form a competing investment firm with the help of the CEO of our portfolio company, who had agreed to be a senior adviser to them. They suggested that this would be a good development for NGP, in that they could craft a deal whereby we could share deals, given the difference in size between NGP 11 and the much-smaller fund they set out to raise. It was a stretch of an argument, but they kept at it.

We listened, somewhat in shock, especially since the NGP colleagues had been so well taken care of by the Barclays and Carlyle monies and were important members of the firm. Uncertain what to do, particularly given the bombshell nature of the way they sprang the news on us, David and I offered very little reaction. We agreed to discuss their idea with our other partners and get back to them quickly. We asked them not to return to the office, as they had already essentially moved out.

This announcement hit me hard. I had been going to great lengths to include that junior partner not just in compensation and ownership incentives but in all the long-term strategy work of the firm. Had I suspected this junior partner was itching to go do his own thing, I would have tried to help. He never let on that he was motivated to go elsewhere.

I always tried to have an open communication with my colleagues about their individual long-term goals so that I could ensure that they were tracking in their professional development as we grew. I held frequent one-on-one meetings with each person to talk about where they wanted to be five and ten years out. These frank and open discussions were an important part of the culture of the firm.

For example, one of these discussions with one of our partners, John Weinzierl, revealed his long-term desire to operate a company and not just have a career as a financier of them. Thanks to that conversation, when I was looking for a CEO to lead an IPO, I asked John if he would take the helm. It was exactly what he was looking to do in his career. In 2011, I had a crazy idea to create Memorial Production Partners, which was an amalgamation of pieces of five portfolio companies held by our funds, and we needed a safe pair of hands to lead them into the public market. John did a fantastic job, and he was always appreciative of the way we worked to help him achieve his personal goal.

But this time, I was not rewarded for the openness. During my one-on-one with this individual who was now announcing his intent to form a competitor, he said his long-term goal was actually to be on the senior leadership team at NGP. We discovered, however, that his plan to create a competing firm had been in the works for quite some time. All the time I had spent with him during the Carlyle transaction discussing his professional development, my future succession plans, and making sure he approved of the compensation plans and monies that would be paid to him was misguided.

He was one of the young professionals who always worried how much ownership would come his way. At his prodding, we outlined to him the money we had set aside for him and how we intended to transfer ownership to him and his partners *for free* as the succession plan unfolded, and he seemed satisfied. This was a seven-figure payday arranged for him. During that time, he bought a house in Colorado and bragged to us that he named his vacation home, a picture of which was placed prominently in his office, after David's and my initials. He thanked us profusely.

I was so intent to keep the team together and continue to model the foxhole mentality, I missed some obvious yellow lights that hadn't turned green. His original gripes with the deal should have been all I needed to hear. I thought I had turned that yellow light green. I assumed he was still in my foxhole. Wrong!

I had been burned by not listening to my own axiom. Shame on me.

STEVE: *So then what?*

KEN: From that point forward, David and I redoubled our efforts to hang tight as a team. I had one other yellow light that I had to revisit. A second junior partner who had expressed concern after the Barclays deal, and again after the Carlyle transaction, was running our Houston office. He had all the responsibilities he could handle, and I made sure to let him know he was appreciated. We arranged similar compensation packages for him, and I assured him that he would be part of the long-term ownership and succession plans of the firm. He also seemed content. And rich.

Quickly, I took it on myself to lay out fully the succession plan and how we intended to implement it. I communicated it to the entire group of young partners so they would be content that their day to inherit the firm and our outstanding history was assured. I also pulled together a full economic analysis showing that the value of the non-Carlyle piece of the firm that the next generation would inherit would be worth, dare I say, hundreds of millions of dollars.

David and I made it clear they would be assuming that ownership for free. As I've said, David and I were compensated by the Barclays and Carlyle monies. Enough was enough. If we pushed too hard to get paid for the other half, people would leave en masse, choosing instead to take their chances striking out on their own.

But there was another side of our business equation to consider—our investors. To minimize the disruption to them, we created a plan whereby we would add a junior partner to the executive committee in 2015 and again in 2016. Subsequently, I would become chairman, and David would transition to an advisory role. This would result in a full transition over a smooth period of time as NGP 11 was being deployed. I described it as a hockey team doing a shift change on the fly. Players get added, and then previous players leave the ice. Everyone seemed on board, and they said as much.

With that consensus in hand, we took the first step and elevated Chris Carter to the managing partner title and added him to the firm's executive committee. I selected Chris because of his character. He exhibited no yellow-light characteristics, and so we began to implement the staged succession plan. We assured the next tier of partners that they would be added to the senior ranks in relatively short order.

Despite these assurances, I was quickly hit with another surprise: Tomas Ackerman, the outstanding junior partner who was then leading our Houston office and who was next in line for promotion, promptly announced his intention to leave and take one of our younger colleagues with him.

He was the other yellow light I thought I had turned green. Because of his concerns dating back to the original Barclays deal and then the Carlyle transition, we had increased his compensation and his equity sharing to keep him in the boat. We layered on more professional responsibilities, making him a managing director, and putting him in charge of our Houston office at a very young age. He was developing so well. I couldn't have been more proud.

Taken together, these departures hurt, but for different reasons. The surprise exit of the first junior partner stung more because I felt betrayed. In the second instance, Tomas Ackerman, the young partner who I had trained since he was a college intern, was always in my plans to comanage the firm someday. He felt he was ready before I did. I was committed to giving him every opportunity to grow and he was well on his way, but ultimately, his entrepreneurial streak made him less patient.

STEVE: *What's the lesson here?*

KEN: Team players are born, not made. And free agents play for pay. In the end, free agents do not make a sustainable team. They eventually become disruptive. And entrepreneurs need to scratch an itch that is hard to do in a larger enterprise.

After the Barclays deal and then again after the Carlyle transaction, each of these young professionals remained skeptical. With only half the firm's ownership left, they could always run the math and figure out that their ultimate piece would be diluted. Even if there were fewer mouths to feed, they couldn't look past that fact. Even if the size of the fund was significantly larger than they could do on their own, they couldn't look past that fact. Even as I continued to stress that my intention was to award them ownership of the other half of the firm without having to pay us a dime, they looked to leave.

I came from the school of making the pie bigger instead of complaining that there were fewer slices for me. I really enjoyed being a part of something larger than myself and building something that could include so many more and provide enriching opportunities for each. I was spoiled because that philosophy worked for such a long time.

Remarkably, we operated the firm from 1988 through 2014 with turnover of only four investment professionals, and one of those I don't really count because he went on to become the chief financial officer of one of our portfolio companies. None of these departures were people who sat on the investment committee. In the investment business, twenty-six years with such low turnover was unprecedented. Our continuity became one of the trademarks of NGP. When I discuss that fact today, people can't believe their ears. From my perspective, it was the norm that made NGP special.

However, some people are simply cut from a different cloth. Instead of appreciating what they have, they focused on what they *could* have had. Instead of focusing on the collective, they focused on the self. Chris Carter focused on the collective. That made him the logical first promotion. His maturity was remarkable. That behavior needed to be recognized. That winner needed to be fed. Unfortunately, that promotion caused my other yellow light to turn from green to red.

I was disappointed that the group we had recruited, hired, and trained did not hang together. I spent so much time with them over the years and expected that I would be for them what Richard Rainwater had been for me. I wanted to be a role model whose values would be adopted by the next generation of the firm's leaders. I worked hard at that over the years by spreading the economics of ownership deeply into the ranks of the firm and running the firm with a consensus-driven decision structure. David and I shared at every step. We celebrated loyalty. We enjoyed the foxhole and welcomed them into it.

Part of that mentality was a commitment to assist partners in achieving their goals. Typically, those goals were aligned with the goals of NGP. But not always. During this same period, Billy Quinn was itching to go in a different direction. Billy had grown in importance to the day-to-day operations of the firm and was a critical leader of our efforts. However, increasing complexity of the business and the scope of the firm did not appeal to him for the long term. At the same time, his elite gymnast daughter was deeply engrossed in her quest to be on the U.S. Olympic team and that took her parents, Billy and Stacey, all over the world.

As was my pattern, open and honest communication led to putting our heads together to create a win-win outcome. This was not unlike my experience with John Weinzierl. In the end, Billy started his own firm, Pearl Energy Investments, which would be a smaller version of NGP. NGP struck a deal to own a piece of Billy's firm and agree to share in deals that were too large for Pearl to do on its own. This put us in a position to help sponsor and endorse his new venture rather than treat it like new competition.

In the end, for a combination of reasons, my efforts were not enough to hold everyone together. However, with the passage of time, I have come to appreciate the role I played in their careers. Today, there are three successful investment firms, employing dozens of people each, who are following the playbook that we wrote. Just as Richard Rainwater influenced so many investment professionals who have spent a career trying to replicate his success, we had spawned a new generation of energy investors as well. I take special pride in the success of Billy Quinn's Pearl Energy Investments, Tomas Ackerman's Carnelian Energy Capital, and, of course, the continued success of NGP.

David and I continued to move forward, choosing to focus on the possibilities instead of looking back. That page had turned, and it made no sense to read it any other way. Tony Weber, the other senior partner who had taken on more responsibility, joined with Chris Carter to demonstrate the maturity and foxhole mentality that made NGP special. Tony and Chris were the firm's managing partners while I retained the role as CEO.

Over the course of 2015, Tony and Chris continued to take on more responsibilities. As time evolved, I began to encourage the team to think through how they'd like the firm to be managed if I wasn't in the room. Ultimately, when it came time to fully transition in 2016, rather than dictate the future to them, I decided to let them come up with their own "constitution." They did, and it included a consensus-driven approach, inclusive of the other senior partners at the firm.

With the benefit of hindsight, this was the correct decision. The firm has thrived since my departure and successfully transitioned both leadership and ownership to the next generation of investment professionals. This is a feat that few investment firms have been able to accomplish. Under Chris's leadership, the firm has gone on to raise over $4 billion more for NGP 12 while also revisiting my expansion strategy. The firm has relaunched the NGP Energy Technology Partners vehicle to take advantage of the energy transition momentum as well as expand into management of mineral and royalty funds. I reflect on the firm now with the confidence that my vision there remains.

STEVE: *Was it hard to just watch them figure it out on their own? You were demon-strating a lot of trust in letting them come up with their own governance model.*

KEN: Well, I had a choice to make. I could see who wanted to work under my con-struct of the future and stick around for as long as it took to rebuild the team around that vision, or I could let them set their own path. The former, while entirely doable, would mean that I would get sucked back into the day-to-day management of the firm and all its complexity for quite some time. The latter would mean my exit plan could remain intact.

I chose the latter. I wanted the next generation of leadership to define its own fox-hole and how it would work. For the firm to survive, the culture would need to reflect the style of its new leadership. As painful as it was for me to watch, I knew that when organizations cling to the styles of absent leaders, they generally stagnate.

NGP deserved a road with only green lights visible.

STEVE: *From the description, it appears that, in addition to Billy Quinn and Tomas Ackerman, Chris Carter has become part of your legacy, not just as the leader of NGP but as part of your personal legacy—not unlike how you are a part of Richard Rainwater's legacy. Am I making too much of that?*

KEN: When you put it that way, I guess so. Chris Carter is a special individual. I am honored to have played a role from just about the beginning of his professional life.

STEVE: *Can you start from that beginning, please?*

KEN: We started off with a quirky interview. In February each year, NGP participated in the North American Prospect Expo—an enormous industry trade show held in Houston. This annual gathering attracted about 25,000 people from all over the oil and gas industry of North America. We traditionally hosted a large booth, primarily so we would have a place to sit down in the cavernous George Brown Convention Center in downtown Houston. It was also a chance to socialize with friends in the sector, meet new industry players, and learn.

I always enjoyed walking around to learn what was happening in regions across North America. Companies selling prospects were all too ready to teach me about the latest geologic play, what industry competitors were doing in that particular area, the prices that deals were fetching, and so on. I was never sure why people talked so much about the information that formed the strategic basis for their investment judgments, but I was glad they did.

As our stature in the industry grew, it became harder for me to be anonymous as I walked around the hall. I seemed to spend more and more time just socializing with my industry relationships—so much so that I hardly got the chance to walk the halls.

At the 2004 expo, I was due to interview Chris, who at the time was a young analyst from Deutsche Bank's Houston office. He was interested in leaving his position at the bank and making the jump into private equity. Given my schedule, it made sense to carve out some time at the expo for a meeting. He found me in the NGP booth, and I tried to channel my best Richard Rainwater.

"Let's go walk around. See what we learn," I said. I wanted to see how this young man handled himself in conversations with people twice his age. We stopped at a couple of booths and traded industry gossip with the exhibitors. We met a couple of friends of mine and spent a few minutes talking about their impressions of the day. Chris held his own in the conversation just fine. He was respectful and a bit quiet, but engaged, nonetheless. Very mature.

"Let's grab something to eat," I said, as we walked toward the long counter where sandwiches were being handed out. We grabbed sandwiches and went in search of a place to sit down. Unfortunately, our timing was off, and we were a bit late for the lunch rush. Every seat in the dining areas of the hall was taken. We walked quite a bit. "What the heck," I chuckled. "Let's just sit on the floor."

Chris looked aghast that someone of my stature in the industry would just go sit on the floor with a twenty-something junior analyst, cross his legs, eat a sandwich, and conduct an interview. But that's exactly what happened. I felt comfortable around him and wanted to send the message to him that at NGP, we take what we do very seriously, but we take ourselves a lot less seriously. No job was beneath me, and I was not some sort of imperious CEO who commanded subjects. I was in there working with my colleagues every day and on any detail that needed my attention, and if that meant sitting on the floor for lunch, so be it.

He nailed the interview. I was impressed with his maturity and willingness to learn the industry and do whatever it took. He saw every deal as an opportunity to learn, and he exuded confidence without being cocky. Needless to say, we hired him. He worked hard and didn't disappoint any of us. He was diligent in his effort and always looked for opportunities to take on more responsibility. Most important, he was curious and intellectually honest. When we had a tough situation that needed a sharp mind, I often sought his help on the issue. While I was teaching him the business, I learned from him as well.

As the firm grew, his responsibilities grew. Ultimately, it was apparent that he would be in the small group that would assume the responsibility to manage the firm after David and I retired. He was the kind of builder I was. He cared about the team culture and the stability of the firm. He cared about the kind of professionalism that a service business should always display. In short, he cared about the NGP franchise we had built and was excited to build on that foundation. He was a winner, and I was happy to feed him.

The young guns who are attracted to the private equity business are bright, motivated, aggressive, and smart. Most are driven to build personal net worth and live the American dream of participating in the ownership society. To be an investor means to put capital at risk and work hard to realize a return on that capital years into the future. Gratification is virtually always delayed. But when those payoffs come, the adrenaline rush is real.

Often, the personality that thrives in this environment is *not* one of a servant-leader. Somewhere along the line, I realized that it was important to me as a leader to build something that would last. To do that, I needed people who cared about the franchise and about their colleagues. David, John, Dick, and I cared about each other deeply as partners. That care was NGP's cornerstone value. Chris distinguished himself among every professional in the firm, regardless of tenure or age. I could tell he cared. I could tell he was in it for the long haul. He was able to increase responsibility at work, even as he was a good father to four children and a loving husband and friend.

In short, Chris was a leader. He would get the first chance to rise through the ranks.

Fast-forward to 2015 when the succession decisions were being made. It was clear that Chris, then age thirty-seven, had earned his spot as a managing partner of the firm, and the future of the firm would depend on how he was able to bridge the relationship between the next tier of senior colleagues beneath David and me and the young guns whom we had hired along the way.

He has filled that role brilliantly, and it has been a joy to watch him develop the younger talent in the firm and lead the senior group. He believes in NGP's culture of consensus but doesn't shy away from difficult decisions. I trust him with the franchise. I don't have to pester him with input, because I trust that if he had a situation for which he needed my input, he would call. I feel proud to have been one of his mentors and to play a part in helping him build a firm foundation for his family.

He is the kind of "capitalist offspring" that would make any deal professional proud.

STEVE: *Speaking of offspring, he wanted to be sure you knew the kind of impact you had on him when he sent Daniel and Rachel a touching letter about his experience with you. With your permission, I would like to include that letter as Exhibit 5 to memorialize his inspirational words.*

November 4, 2016

DEAR DANIEL AND RACHEL,

This letter may feel a bit odd to you when you receive it, but it is one that I have felt compelled to write for some time. Your father has had an enormous impact on my career and on me as a person. As many people from NGP have gone off to business school over the years, there have been opportunities for us to write letters of recommendation on their behalf, describing their professional accomplishments and personal qualities. Ken wrote a letter like this for me back in 2005. Well, since Ken has already gone to business school, and I won't be writing a book anytime soon, consider this my letter of recommendation for your Dad, as a leader, a mentor, a person and a friend.

I first met your Dad in February 2004. After meeting with several other members of the NGP team over the previous few months, this was my final interview. The team was in Houston for NAPE and David Hayes let me use his badge to get entrance into the George R. Brown Convention Center. I interviewed with Ken while sitting on the thin carpet floor of the convention center while eating a box lunch. A pretty informal way to meet with the CEO of a private equity firm and begin what has become my career.

You are both at a time in your lives when you will be making decisions about your careers. Some doors will open, and some will close. And perhaps like your Dad, you will find new doors and open them for yourselves. When I was 25 and working 80–100 hour weeks as an investment banking analyst, I was searching for the next best step in my career. And also trying to escape what felt like an unsustainable lifestyle at Deutsche Bank. At the time, I was entirely focused on going to work for TPG or Hicks Muse, two of the largest and most prominent global private equity firms. After a series of exhaustive first round and final round interviews, I was told by each firm that I didn't make the cut. I was so disappointed. Meanwhile, due to no planning of my own, a friend of mine from UT emailed my resume over to his high school buddy's older brother, Billy Quinn, at Natural Gas Partners. At the time, I had never heard of Natural Gas Partners or Ken Hersh. For someone who has spent a lot of my life planning and setting goals, there is a heavy amount of irony that my career was launched through the unplanned gesture of a friend and completely outside of my control.

I joined NGP in August of 2004 as an associate, the lowest level investment professional position. When I joined, we were managing companies from Fund VI (a $370 million fund) and making new investments from Fund VII (a $600 million fund). It was an exciting time in the oil and gas industry, and the firm was having a lot of success. There were things that stuck out to me about the culture your Dad created at NGP. We all ate lunch together, along with our administrative assistants, accountants, junior deal professionals and managing partners. I remember describing to my wife Abbey and my parents the concept of the "NGP family" and how I knew this place was a great fit for me.

Ken also created a culture where it was ok to disagree with others about investment decisions and strategy. I can remember the confidence I felt (after the initial fear wore off!) debating with your Dad. Looking back, it's hard to believe that I felt so comfortable as a 25-year-old, debating with the leader of our firm! But Ken taught us to avoid groupthink. I remember the sign he put up in our conference room, "Creativity dies in rooms with big

continued

conference tables." Most leaders don't encourage people to disagree with them because of their own insecurity. Your Dad has always had the confidence to encourage healthy discourse and the leadership ability to make a decision and lead people forward. I have always admired the way that Ken would comfortably take two sides of the same issue—a skill he probably honed as a debater and one of the reasons my oldest daughter Ellie has just joined the debate team at Parish as a 6th grader!

During our firm strategy offsite in December of 2005, Ken led us in an exercise where we created the NGP Mission Statement. We broke off into groups of four to five people and talked about what we thought NGP stood for and what was most important to each of us as members of the firm. The result was the following mission statement, "NGP will generate superior risk-adjusted investment returns while forming and maintaining the highest quality industry relationships and will conduct its business according to the highest standards of honesty, integrity and fairness." This statement is enclosed in glass and on every person's desk at NGP. I recite it often as it is a great reminder to the 60 employees of the firm of what we are all trying to accomplish each day. And it is a mission I have been proud to serve for the past 12 years.

I was fortunate to join the firm that your Dad helped to build. I remember during my two years back at Stanford for business school realizing just how special NGP was. I was getting to know classmates from all over the world. And I got to hear about my classmates' experiences working for some of those same global private equity firms that I so desperately wanted to join. For the most part, these people weren't satisfied and didn't want to return to their firms after business school. And I realized that NGP had a truly unique blend of attributes. Working alongside intelligent and motivated teammates; working within the extremely interesting and dynamic energy industry; an opportunity to build wealth; working with a group of people who had a strong moral compass and were focused on doing the right thing; the ability to have a reasonable work/life balance; working for a leader who inspired me. Sometimes seeing the grass on the other side can actually make you realize how green it is right where you are standing.

I have always been inspired by your Dad. His work ethic, passion for performance, creativity and leadership qualities inspired my confidence and respect as a business leader. And his natural emotional intelligence and care for people made him a person that I have always respected on a personal level. As I have experienced some of the challenges of helping to lead the firm over the past couple of years, I can really empathize with the role Ken played in leading our firm. I have always been motivated by "pats on the back" and being told that I was doing a good job. As a leader, there is usually no one there to pat you on the back. And that can be lonely. Your Dad sat in that seat for a long time. He helped create opportunity, wealth and a sense of accomplishment for many people around him. And I am not sure that he got many pats on the back along the way. Another motivation for this letter.

We work in an industry where money is a big motivator. Our job is to generate the best risk adjusted returns possible for endowments, family foundations and pensions across the United States and internationally. The work that we do in a small way, helps retired teachers and public employees across the country and fuels the growth of various philanthropies and universities. But often the powerful draw of greed and wealth creation becomes the sole motivator of private equity professionals. Your Dad set a different tone early in the life of NGP. Rather than structuring ownership and compensation focused on benefiting one person, he encouraged broad ownership across the investment team and broader firm. When I joined, even our front office receptionist owned some of the most recent fund. Your Dad has had more success than most people can even dream, and that success was the result of creating one of the best private equity firms in America, with early principles of shared ownership and generosity.

Two years ago we went through a lot of changes at NGP. Several of our partners decided to leave the firm to start their own private equity funds. It was a challenging time. In what was one of the most emotional times in the history of our firm, your Dad handled himself with poise and total class. I remember him addressing several of us with prepared remarks as he talked about NGP's past, present and future and what the firm and his colleagues meant to him. It was an emotional time for me as the people who left were friends, and I was shocked by all of the departures as NGP had experienced nearly no turnover for two decades. Coming out of those departures, I took on the role of one of the managing partners. I was affirmed by your Dad and his confidence that I could take on that role, several years before I really felt ready to do so.

I remember in the summer of 2015 when Ken told me that he was a finalist being considered to be the next Chairman of the Dallas Federal Reserve. I remember feeling proud of Ken and excited for what he could do in that role. But I also felt a profound sense of sadness that he could be leaving NGP. I had looked up to him for so many years and I was just months into my new role as a managing partner. I was not ready for him to leave. Fortunately for me and unfortunately for the Southwest region of the United States, the Fed went in a different direction. Fast forward about a year later and Ken told us that he had been asked by President Bush to serve as the President and CEO of the Bush Center. Again, I was excited for your Dad and thought that the role could be a great fit given his capabilities and genuine interest in politics and world affairs. And while there was still some sadness, it felt like a more natural time for him to take on the next challenge in his career.

We all come across different people in our lives that leave an imprint on who we are. My life has been changed because I have had the opportunity to know and work for your Dad. I met him as a 25-year-old, not too much older than you, Daniel. And I now have four kids of my own. I think it is partially the father in me that makes me want to share this letter with you both. It is also an outlet to express my own feelings and emotions, but writing and sending this letter is mainly to honor your Dad.

Yours Truly,
Chris Carter

Exhibit 5: Letter from Chris Carter to the Hersh children, November 4, 2016

KEN: Thanks for the prod. Maybe my kids will not think I'm so stupid, after all.

STEVE: *Don't count on that!*

CHAPTER 14

I TOOK THE FIRST THING
THAT CAME ALONG

STEVE: *In May of 2016, you were appointed CEO of the George W. Bush Presidential Center in Dallas. That's quite a career change after leading a hugely successful investment firm. What led you to leave the business world for the not-for-profit sector?*

KEN: Well, as I've said earlier, managing a big investment firm became a whole lot less fun. When I was younger and growing the business, it was challenging, for sure. But as a private firm, we were able to chart our course and go. Results spoke for themselves, and we were either rewarded or penalized by the marketplace. We reacted accordingly and moved on. While there was uncertainty all around us, I really felt that we had control over our own destiny.

It was energizing to manage in an environment of uncertainty. In fact, I came to appreciate that a leader's job is simply that—to lead others forward even when it was risky. Clearly, there was a lot of uncertainty in the energy business to navigate.

The juxtaposition of my fiftieth birthday in 2013, the heightened regulatory hassles of the period, and the emerging impatience of our internal team caused some serious introspection. While I still enjoyed what I was doing and I was committed to the firm and our investors, there was a whole lot less joy in doing it.

The Carlyle relationship gave me a good second wind. After our transaction closed in late 2012, I joined the management committee and worked closely with the firm's leadership as an expert in the energy business. Also, the firm was in the beginning stages of its leadership transition. Frequent trips to Washington, D.C., were interesting, and my input was both welcomed and appreciated. In Carlyle, I saw a larger incarnation of what we had built at NGP and had insight into the challenges arising from that complexity.

In hindsight, this plant (me) was being partially repotted. While still deeply engrossed in the day-to-day management of NGP, I found the topics raised by the Carlyle relationship to be intellectually stimulating. Not only did I help the firm think through its expansion in the energy asset management industry around the world, but I also forged a close bond with Glenn Youngkin and others who were addressing the fascinating challenges of planning and executing a smooth handoff of the firm from the founders to the younger partners.

My activities outside of NGP were becoming a major part of my life as well—in particular, my relationship with my alma mater, St. Mark's School of Texas. That relationship has been one of the most significant and rewarding associations of my life—beginning with my twelve years there as a student and continuing through my son Daniel's attendance from first grade through to his high school graduation.

I joined the board of trustees in 1998 and served until 2015. During that time, I chaired most of the committees of the board and ultimately served as president from 2010 through the 2012 academic year. Following my terms as president, I cochaired the head-of-school search committee, which selected the headmaster to follow the iconic Arnold Holtberg, who had led the school for over two decades. My relationship with the school began in 1969 when I entered first grade. Other than my family, no other relationship in my life had this longevity.

Aside from St. Mark's, I was active around the community. In 2010, I had joined a few energy entrepreneurs in purchasing the Texas Rangers baseball team out of bankruptcy and joined its board of directors. Talk about fun! Even though my piece was a small part of the ownership team, getting caught up in the whirl of a professional sports team was intoxicating, especially that year.

We closed the purchase of the team in August of 2010. Ten weeks later, we were in the World Series. Even though we were thrashed by the San Francisco Giants, the fact that we were there a mere couple of months after buying the team was amazing, as was winning the American League pennant over our playoff nemesis, the New York Yankees. Storming the field with Julie and my kids after our Neftali Feliz struck out former Ranger Alex Rodriguez to clinch the pennant and celebrating with the team in the clubhouse were moments I will always remember.

The Rangers went on a tear from that point forward, returning to the World Series in 2011. (I don't want to talk about watching Nelson Cruz muff a fly ball with two outs in the ninth inning of game 6 that cost us that championship. Too soon!) They returned to the playoffs in 2012, 2015, and 2016. Some ownership groups wait a lifetime for a run like that, but we were able to ride that wave at the beginning of our tenure.

In addition, I chaired the team's facilities committee, working through the analysis for and planning of a new indoor stadium, which opened in 2020. I was flexing several intellectual muscles with that one.

Other activities were also heating up. Julie's work in the local arts community and as a mental health advocate was taking off. She became a real voice for mental health, with her unique success story in the recovery process. In addition, we each sat on other community boards around town. While our children were young, our community involvement seemed to revolve around their schools and related causes. Once they were grown, we branched out. Combined, we developed a profile of a family that supported great organizations not only with our money but also with our time. This profile allowed the work of our family foundation to expand, and it enabled us to be involved in some of the more meaningful community outreach. I really feel that, optimally, a community is populated with leaders who take ownership of the civic and cultural institutions as well as support the general welfare of those in need. We found ourselves engrossed in that world. It was immensely satisfying.

As a young professional, I heard elders talk about second careers so often I became almost numb to it. Perhaps we roll our eyes at such musing until it actually happens to us. At any rate, as I entered the rank of elders, it became real for me.

STEVE: *Given the trajectory of your business, it's hard to imagine that something could rival the excitement and satisfaction of your NGP world. How did you come to that realization?*

KEN: My friends helped a lot here. Specifically, my membership in the Young Presidents' Organization offered me a very close peer group. A feature of YPO is each member joining a forum—a small group of members who meet regularly and share each other's life experiences and stories under a strict code of confidentiality. I've joked that a YPO forum is really a book club but with no books. We've been together since the early 2000s, meeting once a month and traveling together at least once and sometimes twice per year. We share experiences and dive deeply into our thoughts, fears, and aspirations.

As part of our regular meetings, we pressed each other on what aspects of our lives were most satisfying and which were chores. I found myself talking about the frustrations of my business and the interesting work I was doing in my extracurricular world. These conversations made it obvious to me which aspects of my full life were the most satisfying. Emotionally, I knew where I was gravitating.

David Albin, who knew me as well as anyone, also weighed in. After many heartfelt conversations about life, happiness, and the future, David pointed out that it was time to go for that second act. "Why manage a fund, Ken?" he pointed out one day. "You *are* a fund."

That hit me squarely between the eyes. I looked at my balance sheet, and it was clear. I had more of my family's net worth invested outside of NGP than inside. David and I had made it our practice to reduce our share of the general partner's equity with each subsequent fund in order to give the younger NGP partners the chance to have a meaningful equity share of the profits. By the time our tenth fund came around, our ability to invest a lot had been crowded out by the rest of the team.

It felt good to point myself in a direction where my NGP activities would dial down over time while my other endeavors and the management of my personal investment portfolio would take on more of my focus.

Then the call came.

STEVE: *What call?*

KEN: A simple call in the spring of 2015 from a local recruiter with one of the large, national executive search firms. Would I be interested in putting my name in consideration for the president's position at the Dallas Federal Reserve Bank? I was taken aback. "I'm an oil and gas private equity guy. Are you sure you're asking the right Ken Hersh?"

The recruiter assured me he had the right Ken Hersh. "Your name came up as someone who could be a good fit," he explained. "The board members who have been following you have seen the extent to which you've developed a strong worldview."

Flattered, I listened. While the timing was not ideal, after discussing the issue with my partners, we concluded that should the position materialize, it would be relatively easy to explain to our NGP team and investors. The simple truth was the recruiter came looking for me, not the other way around.

I took the attitude that if they wanted to draft me to do the job, I would be delighted to take it. I went through the process with the recruiters and the search committee and had several interesting and exhilarating conversations.

Going through the process, though, made me think. This was a position that was completely different from where my career track ordinarily would point. It was validation that I had indeed developed a perspective that could apply to other sectors and, potentially, other organizations. Moreover, it opened my eyes to the fact that my future could easily move beyond the energy industry. Previously, I had thought I would have to do a lot of explaining to justify a transition away from the energy industry, but the Fed's search committee was unfazed.

In June 2015, I learned that the job was offered to the other finalist, Robert Kaplan. He had the ideal background for the position, having had a stellar career on both Wall Street and as a professor at Harvard Business School. I was not the least bit offended by their choice, because their decision made so much sense. A big part of me was relieved, given the difficult message that I would have had to deliver to our investors so soon after closing a new fund.

That is, until the late summer, when the recruiter called me back. Turns out Rob Kaplan had an issue crop up with a family member, momentarily calling into question whether he could relocate to Dallas for the job. The recruiter explained that the bank was up against a deadline, and they pressed me to be in a position to accept the job if he decided he couldn't relocate. I agreed to be their backup in such a case.

This set in motion a series of decisions that would ultimately lead me to where I am today. Immediately, I spoke to David and let him know that the job had resurfaced and that we needed to be in a position for me to take it if the candidate decided he could not. We decided that now was the time to rip the bandage off. Previously, we had added Tony Weber and Chris Carter to the ranks of NGP's managing partners and they had taken on more responsibilities. Now, it was time to step up their internal roles even more. I would either accept the job with the Federal Reserve Bank if it was offered, or I would telegraph that in 2016, I would transition from NGP's CEO and just serve as its chairman.

We held a series of internal meetings to work out the various governance changes that would need to occur and to get the buy-in of the other NGP partners. While that wasn't an easy process, the team worked together and agreed. Tony was a champ in seeing the wisdom in sharing a leadership role with Chris, even though Chris was quite a bit younger. The other senior partners of the firm participated in the discussions as well. The succession plan was now activated. There was no turning back. A week later, the uncertainty ended when Rob announced he was able to accept the position.

Looking back, this was the best of all worlds. I didn't have to make the quick exit that could have upset our investors, but by becoming the chairman at NGP, I could take one step toward that exit while creating a transition to the new leadership of the firm. We convened a conference call of our investors to announce the promotion of Tony and Chris and the introduction of the new chairman title for me. It went over just fine. Given all the time we had devoted to the succession issue during the fundraising process dating back to 2014, this was not news. Everyone took it in stride.

STEVE: *So the stage was set for some kind of Ken Hersh transition. Now what?*

KEN: From that moment forward, I felt an incredible weight had been lifted from my shoulders. Tony and Chris were well prepared and took the helm quickly and smoothly. I was thrilled to let them. My daughter had graduated from high school in

May of 2015 and, as of the fall of 2015, Julie and I were empty nesters. We were in the middle of building out a condominium closer to the center of town, and I started to feel like the future was going to present something fresh.

I should add that I didn't really appreciate the weight that I bore until it was lifted. I started having fun going to the office and contributing to the work at NGP, but I had an eye toward the future. I saw my future fog up again. I got excited as I began to think about the next phase of my life in earnest.

STEVE: *You are also quick to point out that your philanthropic activities played a meaningful role in your thoughts about transition. Let's talk about this important aspect of your life. Did you grow up in a home where there was a belief that the "haves" had a financial responsibility to the larger world?*

KEN: No. There was nothing that obvious in my growing up. I'm not sure if my philanthropy is more out of guilt or obligation. I've already talked about the impact my twelve years at St. Mark's had on me. At the school, everything is named after someone—buildings, fields, rooms, even fountains. So, as a student there, you pick up the idea that this great campus didn't just appear out of thin air. People made it happen, and those people had names. And many of those names were on the walls.

It's kind of like osmosis. Being around that for so many years made me realize that tuition dollars didn't cover it all. The same thing was obvious at our synagogue, where names and appreciation markers were everywhere.

As I became more aware, it was obvious all around town as well. Dallas had city mothers and fathers, almost all of whom were fancy businesspeople or community leaders. Their names were on buildings, freeways, city parks, and other obvious monuments. I think somewhere along the line it dawned on me that I was a beneficiary of a whole lot of philanthropy over many, many years.

For example, the founders of Texas Instruments were responsible for putting so much of the Dallas that I saw on the map. They were the cornerstone donors to St. Mark's School. They were leading philanthropists for the cultural institutions in Dallas. They were political leaders. I am sure there were hundreds of other important aspects of Dallas life for which they were responsible, but I will never know.

There were many business successes in this town. Dallas embraced these corporations and celebrated the success, not just of the corporate leaders but of the impact that such enterprises had on the city. I grew up in a city where the feeling that success happens here was palpable.

Important also, it appeared to me that Jewish leaders were featured prominently around town. Names like Stanley Marcus, Ray Nasher, Mort Meyerson, Ron Steinhart,

Roger Horchow, and the Zale family, to name a few, were household names. Sure, we had country clubs that wouldn't let us in, but heck, we belonged to the Jewish country club when I was growing up, so I did not feel like I was being slighted.

I'm sure that anti-Semitism existed, but the Dallas I grew up in seemed to have exited the blatant, overt discrimination era. Covert discrimination existed, but I never felt its sting. I felt that if I worked hard, due rewards would come. Of course, I am not naive. Despite my experience, it remains much more difficult for people of color in Dallas and everywhere else in this country to escape discrimination—whether blatant or covert.

Never in a million years did I think I'd have money enough to make a difference with my philanthropy. Sure, I did the occasional fundraiser for my synagogue and the annual "Can-paign" at St. Mark's where we gathered canned goods to support local charities, but I was just your average private school kid doing that.

Today, people ask me what motivates my philanthropy, and I don't know what to tell them. Once I started giving money away, the positive feeling that I was making a difference in the community beyond my private enterprise became addictive. Now, when I ask people to support something philanthropically, I tell them, "Don't give until it hurts, but rather, give until it feels *good*." I get so much out of giving it away. I just wish I could do more.

One thing that's quite peculiar is that I consider myself a builder. Yet, in the oil and gas business, I never got a chance to see my product. We would go out and raise this money, invest it, and wire it somewhere. Natural gas that our companies developed traveled underground, got consumed, and our companies got paid. Then someday, if we were lucky, money got wired back to our account. If we ever actually *saw* our oil or gas, it probably meant that there was an environmental issue somewhere. We wanted our product to move around and get consumed practically unnoticed. I did take great pride in the firm we had built and the families that it provided for, but that impact was relatively local. My real estate friends can point at a development and say, "I built that building." As an oil and gas guy, I have a harder time actually pointing to something physical that I have done.

Philanthropy has satisfied that need and become another important part of my life as a builder. Even though it's sometimes frustrating, I've gotten so much joy out of giving that the joy is almost a motivation itself.

STEVE: *You and Julie created a family foundation, the Hersh Foundation, that focuses on three areas: mental health research and mental illness prevention programs, education programs, and North Texas cultural organizations. Why those areas?*

KEN: Our philanthropy reflected our desire to build something. We both believed that a great city should have quality of life for everyone. We also know that much of the cultural scene of a city is not sustainable without donors. In the past, Dallas lost out on corporate relocations when executives felt the city lacked culture. A great city should have great theater, music, and art. We donated to all three.

In addition, we gave generously where our time and our funds are appreciated. Julie was a civic leader of the city's theater scene, and we matched her time with significant financial support. Our family enjoyed incredible experiences at several local schools, and we have paid it forward by being good benefactors of those institutions. And we've also spread our funds around to local community service organizations that serve the less fortunate.

Finally, in large part because of Julie's story, we committed to moving the needle on the diagnosis and treatment of mental illness, along with the strong promotion of mental health.

STEVE: *Do you have a particular philosophy about giving?*

KEN: I am all over the place on this one. At its core, I want our funds to go somewhere constructive that means something to me and our family. I want it to go where it can make a difference and not be squandered. So that leads me to make sure the recipient organization is well run, and mission-driven.

Plus, there are times when I just enjoy making people's days, giving unexpected gifts to people in need or who are relatively underfunded. Sometimes I give anonymously, and sometimes I'm happy to have our names associated with a gift.

STEVE: *When you gave large gifts to your kids' schools you did it quite publicly. It was the first major giving you had done out of your foundation at the time. Why so public?*

KEN: That's quite perceptive. You've done your research.

STEVE: *That's why you pay me the big bucks! Plus, you've got the last edit on this manuscript, so it's not like you're not feeding me the lines.*

KEN: Good point! It was quite intentional. We wanted to send a strong message to Daniel and Rachel. At the time, we were both hard at work building our lives and dealing with the ups and downs of parenthood, a volatile industry profession, and Julie's work to stay healthy. As our children came of age, we really struggled with how to raise them so they didn't feel or act entitled. Sure, we were living a nice lifestyle, and our family was well cared for, but we didn't take our newfound wealth for granted.

We spoke frequently about how to structure both our life and our estate plan so as not to ruin our children's work ethic. I agreed with Warren Buffett's belief that you should leave your kids "enough so that they can do anything, but not so much that they can do nothing."* That always stuck with me. By giving our money publicly and letting people make a big deal about saying thank you, it let our kids see not only that we were not necessarily going to leave it all to them but also that giving it away was as rewarding as making it. We stressed the values of hard work and the adage that "to whom much is given, much is required."

STEVE: *You also get pretty involved in some of the causes you support.*

KEN: Yes. I guess that's in our DNA. From an investment standpoint, my goal was always to align myself with a great operator and then help where I could help, but let the operators operate. In philanthropy, it's a bit different. I always want to give to what works and not have my money go to waste. But there are times when a gift is a gift, and there are low expectations other than to know it was received. Other times, my funds and time go together. Nonprofit organizations that offer rewarding ways for donors to engage seem to be the best run. Sometimes, I like to be active when it comes to my philanthropy, like when I helped both fund and design the energy hall inside the new Perot Museum of Nature and Science. Taking the post at the Bush Center was the ultimate linking of my resources and my time.

STEVE: *How important is it to you from an ego standpoint or a pragmatic standpoint to actually have your name on something?*

KEN: Sometimes I do allow my name to be put out there in recognition, but it isn't a primary motivation for my giving. When we gave money for a building at St. Mark's, we asked that it be named for Robert Hoffman. He was a selfless leader, who had made a huge impact on the school. Sadly, he succumbed to leukemia at age fifty-nine. I always said we lived parallel lives, although I was about fifteen years younger. He had been the editor of the St. Mark's student newspaper, as was I. He went to Harvard (close enough). He was a member of the *Harvard Lampoon* (and part of the group that

---

* Warren Buffett, quoted in Nicolas Vega, "Warren Buffett Is 'Halfway' through Giving Away His Massive Fortune," CNBC, June 23, 2021, https://www.cnbc.com/2021/06/23/why-warren-buffett-isnt-leaving -his-100-billion-dollar-fortune-to-his-kids.html.

started *National Lampoon*). I had worked for *Business Today* magazine while in college, which was a bit more serious. (But I like to think Princeton is always a bit more serious than Harvard!)

Robert came back to Dallas and was an important civic leader, although mostly behind the scenes. He was the CEO of the Coca-Cola bottler here in town. He never put his name on anything. If someone needed something, he was there to help. While his tenure on the St. Mark's board was ending at about the time my stint was beginning, I really got to know him more by chance when we found our families spending spring break at the same resort in Mexico. We had children of similar ages, and we found ourselves poolside or sharing a golf cart for several consecutive years.

When we were asked to make a capital gift to the school, the timing was, sadly, perfect. So I said, "Why don't we call this the Hoffman Center, in honor of Robert?" I went to see his widow, Marguerite, to ask her permission. Through both of our tears, she agreed. Not only was I able to honor a departed friend, Robert, but also, I was able to demonstrate a lesson in philanthropy for our kids and whomever else was watching.

We did the same thing at the St. Alcuin Montessori School (today known as Alcuin School) in town, where our kids went and had a wonderful experience. The Galbraith family had put the sweat equity into that school over a thirty-year period to make it what it was. So I went to our friends Karen Raley and Ted Galbraith and said, "I'd like to put the Galbraith family's name on the new middle school building."

Initially they were stunned. People in Dallas don't seem to do things like that very often. In fact, when I called them to see if I could come over, they were perplexed. They thought their son had done something wrong to our daughter in class and I was coming over as a pissed-off dad. They scolded their son unknowingly and told him to shower and change clothes as I was en route. Clearly, my message to them was a bit more positive. We laughed about it and they let the request sink in. When the building was built, the dedication was all about them.

STEVE: *You've stipulated in your estate plan that monies left to the foundation are to be given entirely away in not more than twenty years. Why do you want your life's earnings to be given all away?*

KEN: I don't want it to be like one of those Mellon-type foundations that go on forever, where the heirs are no longer involved, and they have some executive director and a board that somehow carry on the wishes of a generation long since passed. I want to enjoy giving the money away while I'm still around. Then, the kids will be able to finish the work. I am a firm believer that you can't take it with you—dust to dust, I guess.

I'm affected a bit by an heir of one of the Mellons who I knew as a young adult when he lived in Santa Fe. He was a distant relative of that dynasty. Before his sudden and accidental death, he explained how his relationship with a distant ancestor always added something weird to his life. He lived a nondescript middle-class lifestyle, yet people always wrongly assumed he had quite the trust fund on the side and treated him differently. He wanted to be treated as he was, not as some fancy heir. He was quite distant from the old family wealth being managed as an institutional endowment. I don't want some future descendant of mine to be in that awkward position.

STEVE: *Now that your children are adults, do you feel you've set them up properly?*

KEN: I have two wonderful kids who want to make it on their own. They view our trappings as something they have come to enjoy but that doesn't define them. They appreciate the responsibility that comes with these gifts. They watched their mom and dad continue to work even though they didn't have to, whether it be for profit or for a nonprofit cause.

In 2018, we had our first family meeting where we showed the kids everything. We knew they were mature enough to handle it. We had a PowerPoint presentation that laid out our philosophy and outlined the family's assets and where they were all held. We outlined the entire estate plan, which showed the limited amount that was due to them. It was a good healthy discussion.

Both kids said, "Tell us where you want the foundation money to go."

Wow. My original thought was not to do that; I wanted giving it away to be part of *their* legacy. But they felt that it wasn't their money, and they didn't want to feel irresponsible by giving it to something we may not have wanted.

"It's not our money, Dad," Rachel said. "Tell us where you want it to go."

So we hustled to write a letter to accompany our estate plan, listing organizations from which they can choose. Mission accomplished. These kids should do just fine.

STEVE: *You mentioned investing time as well as money as a motivator for you. Was working at the Bush Center on your mind when you were turning NGP over to the next generation?*

KEN: Not at all. Maybe that's what makes life so interesting. I've never really adhered to some sort of a life plan. In fact, I have spoken at length about the fog of the future and how it excites rather than frightens me.

In the fall of 2015, after I transitioned to NGP's chairman position, I reminded myself of a set of governing principles I'd written several years before and had taped to the wall next to my computer at home. These principles were an attempt by my younger self to remind me of the characteristics to which I was attracted in order to avoid getting sucked into the vortex of activities that drained me.

STEVE: *That is fascinating. Not surprising, but fascinating. What's on the list?*

KEN: Looking at it now, I am reminded of what a glimpse it is into my ultimate wishes. It reads:

- National impact
- Large scope
- Surround myself with top-flight people performing at a high level, and insist that people around them perform at a high level
- Gravitate toward energy enhancers
- Avoid energy sappers
- Protect time
- "Feed" my winners—investments, people, philanthropy
- Heed danger signals
- Be judicious in exposure

STEVE: *I am interested in the energy-enhancers and energy-sappers comment. What did you mean by that?*

KEN: This is a tough one to describe but an easy one to identify. I put people into a couple of different categories according to my reaction to them. There's a particular chemistry that is evident when two people meet. It can be positive, negative, or neutral. As a relationship develops, whether personal or professional, it's pretty easy to see if the energy levels are positive. I feed off that energy, one way or the other.

People who are energy enhancers create a real rush with me. I am excited to see them, excited to share ideas, talk about life, brainstorm, you name it. Time flies when we are together. There's a feeling that we could talk for hours. Conversely, energy sappers are people who make you tired just being around them. They suck the oxygen out of the room and leave me cold. Some describe these folks as emotional vampires.

Interestingly, it doesn't necessarily correlate with a positive or negative attitude. I have tremendous relationships with people who have negative dispositions, but it doesn't faze me. We still push each other, laugh, share stories, and the like. There are also some insanely positive people around who are energy sappers nonetheless. The key is to identify these traits early enough. As I get older, I'm more intentional about surrounding myself with people who feed my intellect and soul while not leaving me as a worn-out sack of shit.

STEVE: *Some might find that rather harsh—or Hersh!*

KEN: Maybe. But it's personal. Someone who saps my energy may feed the energy of someone else. It isn't a judgment on the person as much as it is on whatever circumstance brought us together. At least that's what I tell myself, so I don't look in the mirror and see a total jerk!

STEVE: *Okay, so you had your list. What else did it tell you?*

KEN: It told me to be careful. At age fifty-two, I knew I had a couple of good commitments left in my professional life. I wanted to make sure that whatever I ended up doing next would be fulfilling all the way around. I knew I had a lot to offer; I didn't know where to devote my energy. But I didn't really overthink it because I felt that if I opened my mind to opportunity, something would appear. As I like to say, if you are not in the traffic, there is no way to get hit by a bus.

STEVE: *So when did the Bush Center bus hit you?*

KEN: In November 2015, I went to an event that the Hersh Foundation had underwritten for the George W. Bush Presidential Center as part of the center's Human Freedom and Democracy initiative. At that event, Margaret Spellings, then the president of the Bush Center and President Bush's former secretary of education, pulled me aside. She thanked me for our support and said she had been recruited to become the next president of the University of North Carolina system and would be leaving the center in February of 2016. Truth be told, I was rather annoyed.

STEVE: *Why?*

KEN: I need to give you some history here before answering that. In 2012, our family foundation had committed $1 million to support the Bush Center, agreeing to pay it over a five-year period. They had already raised enough for the building, so we applied our money to programming. At the time, we agreed we'd sit down and review the upcoming program needs and decide where to apply each year's funds. However, we also made it clear that we wanted to support something that continued year after year. I knew as a donor that we could only influence a strategy *before* our check was written. So I was hopeful that our insistence would help guide them to solid long-term programming. "I want to see you build something that will last," I said.

That year, Jim Glassman, the first executive director of the Bush Institute, the think-tank subset of the Bush Center, wanted me to direct our first installment to a certain agenda laying out a prescription for the country to achieve 4 percent annual economic growth. That plan included a commitment to the domestic energy industry. He also invited me to speak at an energy symposium the Institute was hosting. I was happy to hear about the plan and participate.

Later that year, when it came time to decide exactly where our funding would go, I had a meeting with the director of the 4 Percent Growth Project, Amity Shlaes. Amity was hard to say no to. As a decorated author and expert on economic policy and politics, she had a lot of credibility. She got right to the point, noting that the young people in our country were not being schooled on the values of freedom, democracy, and capitalism, yet they'd be the ultimate custodians of our system. This shortcoming in our educational curricula was worrisome to her. That made a lot of sense to me.

Her remedy was to use the activity of high school debate to reinforce these principles. Given my background as a high school debater, I was all ears. She described their intention to create a program where high school students all over the area would spend time preparing for and debating the merits of free markets and capitalism, culminating in a tournament. Our funds could be a major part of ensuring the success of the program, she explained. Aware of my desire to get involved in a hands-on way with our philanthropy, Amity invited me to be a judge at the competition.

This sounded pretty good to me—if it wasn't just a one-year deal. I committed our money over two years, 2012 and 2013. The tournament came off as planned, and it seemed to be well received by those participating.

In 2013, both Jim Glassman and Amity left the Bush Center, subsequent to Margaret Spellings being named the new president and chief executive officer. As a major donor, I was happy to meet with Margaret when she made the rounds to talk about her ideas and goals for the center. She was an experienced policy hand and a no-bullshit kind of operator. She wasn't afraid to talk openly, and we had productive discussions about the value that the Bush Center could bring to an issue and the goals she wanted to pursue. The debate program was not one of them.

While I was slightly annoyed that the program I was supporting was being canceled, I appreciated Margaret's candor and her enthusiasm for two new programs toward which she wanted our dollars dedicated. She envisioned a new Presidential Leadership Scholars program that would be housed at the Bush Center, but comanaged with the Clinton

Foundation, and an initiative to support the values of freedom and democracy around the world. Who could argue with these priorities? Since Margaret had the implicit blessing of President Bush, who was I to say what the Bush Center could and could not do?

When it came time to direct our 2014 gift, we were pleased to push it toward the new Presidential Leadership Scholars program. Late in the year, as I was inclined to do, I again found a way to participate in our philanthropy there by serving on an interview panel during the final stage of the scholars' candidate admissions process.

This was fortunate in that I shared the interview panel with Holly Kuzmich, Margaret's key lieutenant at the Bush Center. Holly had worked for Margaret when she was secretary of education and had then followed her after the Bush administration ended to work in her consulting firm. Holly had worked on Capitol Hill as well as in the White House and in a cabinet office, so she knew the ins and outs of Washington. She was unique in that she didn't have that D.C. insider master-of-the-universe-type persona. She impressed me as sharp, yet humble and knowledgeable without needing to flaunt it. She was comfortable to be around, perceptive, and careful. She wore the Bush style very well, and she was a tough interviewer.

While that leadership program took off in 2015 and quickly found other donors, the Human Freedom and Democracy initiative was more difficult to fund. As a result, Margaret paid me a subsequent visit to persuade me to redirect our 2015 funds toward that project. I guess I had proven to be an easy mark. I always enjoyed my meetings with Margaret, and we seemed to hit it off.

STEVE: *If I'm counting correctly, Margaret was the third person who had redirected your money over a period of only a few years.*

KEN: Yes. And to get back to where this discussion started, now *she* was leaving the center.

STEVE: *Thus, your annoyance.*

KEN: Yes. I'm a patient guy, but my patience is not infinite. I had watched a lot of turnover at the Bush Center, and now, quite possibly, another redirection was coming. I felt like our $1 million was going nowhere. In the car going home from that event, I told Julie about Margaret's impending departure and said, "These guys need to get their act together. The next person they bring in will be the third CEO in a building that is not even three years old."

She could tell I was unhappy. "Quit complaining," she blurted out. "Why don't you just go do it!"

STEVE: *Just out of the blue like that? How did you react?*

KEN: I paused. My eyebrow raised. *Hmmm.* To be honest, I'd thought that, too, as soon as the complaint had come out of my mouth. But I hadn't said anything out of fear my wife would think I had lost it. The rest of the fifteen-minute car ride home was silent. What seemed kind of crazy seemed a lot less crazy by the time we pulled into our driveway. Good thing we didn't live closer to the event, or else life may have taken a different turn.

While that exchange happened in November 2015, I didn't think much of it again until I ran into Mark Langdale, the past president of the Bush Center, on the holiday party circuit that December. I recall casually talking to him about the turnover there and Margaret's departure. Mark was an old friend, and he was the one who solicited us for the original $1 million gift. In that brief conversation, I blurted out that they needed someone like me to infuse a bit of the real world into a pretty political organization—at least that was what it looked like from my vantage point. He chuckled but didn't seem fazed by the suggestion.

STEVE: *Seems like you were testing the waters—without even realizing it.*

KEN: I guess that's right. My subconscious must have been taking the lead. Letting my mind wander about a radical turn in the direction of my career kind of excited me, especially given the industry downturn that NGP was in the midst of navigating.

In early 2016, the industry was caught in the global price war and many of NGP's portfolio companies became collateral damage. The firm had to mark down the carrying value of its portfolio with each passing quarter. This was very painful. In fact, it was so painful that the portfolio values were entering the levels where we, as partners, would have been required to pay back some of the profits that had previously been paid to us. Investors included that clawback term to ensure that the whole fund had to do well before we earned any share of the profits.

In the life of our firm, that provision had never been triggered. Not even close. When we had a fund with early profits, we were confident in making a profits distribution. Well, in the winter of 2016, we were circling the wagons as a team and going through the values of the portfolio with a fine-tooth comb to determine if we needed to start reserving money for such an event.

It was scary, as nobody had that much liquidity on their personal balance sheets, since we were constantly rolling our winnings back into subsequent funds. We were working feverishly to come up with creative ideas on how to manage, and we were able to take some smart remedial actions inside the portfolio to stem the losses. But it was no fun.

At the time, I was serving as chairman of the firm, having turned the reins over to Tony and Chris, so I was not in a position to dictate how to fix the portfolio. It was a tricky time for me. While I was the deepest pocket for the potential clawback liability, I wasn't able to call the shots on how to recover so we didn't have to pay it. I was no longer aligned with my team. Certain team members picked up on that and were quite happy to shun my advice. Certain behaviors really disappointed me. Others were happy to have me in the foxhole with them and work on ideas to boost returns. It was another lesson for me in human nature. Group cohesion is a garden that needs constant tending.

Once again, the relationships that I had maintained and emphasized so much came in handy for the benefit of the entire team. I was able to come up with the idea and help negotiate a merger between our largest portfolio company, Memorial Resources Development Company (MRD), and a large publicly traded independent oil and gas producer.

The Memorial Production Partners company that John Weinzierl had taken public in 2011 had a related party in MRD, which owned its largest asset—an interest in WildHorse Resource Development Corp., another NGP portfolio company managed ably by Jay Graham and Anthony Bahr. Since one company's assets were simply a subset of the others, we were able to take MRD public in 2014 and have Weinzierl manage both entities. Through a series of transactions, we separated Memorial Production from Memorial Resources in early 2016 and Jay Graham became MRD's CEO.

Throughout that spring, while I was working through the Bush Center opportunity, I initiated a conversation with another contact, Jeff Ventura, the CEO of Range Resources, a Fort Worth–based independent oil and gas company. Over lunch, I described the assets of Memorial and introduced Jay and Jeff. Jay took it from there and by mid-May of 2016, the two companies had struck an agreement to merge at an attractive valuation for MRD. This deal was critical in wiping out any clawback liability. The team was happy again.

I, however, did not forget the lessons from that experience. I had outgrown the team I helped shape.

Toward the end of 2015 and into early 2016, everything about the oil and gas business was painful. Given the interpersonal dynamic at NGP, going to the office as chairman was not fun. I let my mind wander about what other professional and personal opportunities might be out there. As the end of my five-year commitment to Carlyle approached, the fog of the future was beginning to excite me more than the present.

STEVE: *So, in December of 2015, you stood there with a 30 percent compounded annual rate of return over twenty-seven years, during which you invested $11.4 billion and returned over $19 billion; you had succeeded as a pioneering investor who took the* *volatility out of a volatile business; you were in your prime and were recognized as a thought leader in the industry; yet you were prepared to walk away entirely. Do I understand that right?*

KEN: Yes, and I was also being quite deliberate in thinking about next steps for my life. I made a list of ideas to consider and people to talk to who had undertaken second-half career moves themselves. For example, I knew through my sitting on the Dean's Council at the Harvard Kennedy School that Harvard had several executive fellowship programs for people like me—middle-aged executives who were in leadership positions but looking for different challenges to tackle. I had a couple of friends who had gone through these programs and raved about the experience.

I would have called my mentor, Richard Rainwater. But he had passed away in the fall of 2015 after a lengthy battle with a rare disease called progressive supranuclear palsy that had left him incapacitated for some time. He was only seventy-one. We can talk more about this later.

In Richard's absence, Ray Chambers had become a surrogate mentor. Ray, who's twenty years older than I, is an acclaimed philanthropist, not to mention the World Health Organization's Ambassador for Global Strategy. He's rightfully regarded as one of the godfathers of the deal business in America. With the former treasury secretary Bill Simon, he formed a buyout firm called Wesray Capital in the early 1980s. William E. Simon was the "Wes" and Ray was, well, the "ray" in the firm's name.

I knew I had some cosmic connection with him because the name of his original firm was about as innovative as Natural Gas Partners. During the 1980s, Wesray was wildly successful, and Ray built a large net worth. Somewhere along the line, he decided to pack it in since, in his words, "the deal business got a whole lot less fun." He left the business and began to focus on his philanthropy and serving causes greater than himself.

Richard Rainwater became close to Ray in the mid-1990s, and Ray was around when we were looking for coinvestors for the Mesa deal. So we had a real business rationale for staying in touch. Thankfully, the Mesa deal worked, so Ray continued to take my calls.

An important aside here if you don't mind. Not only did I enjoy getting to know Ray, but I also really clicked with his top lieutenant, Dave Roy, as part of the process. Dave was a loyal consigliere to Ray across much of his investment portfolio and his life. He was a gentle soul who had a sharp mind, an easy manner, and was the consummate gentleman. I trusted him from the moment we met.

He also enjoyed fly-fishing—a lot! We loved talking about that mutual passion, and through him I met the seller of the New Mexico ranch that we purchased in 2005.

I recharged my soul at that spot each summer. We enjoyed hosting Dave there over the years, and one of the lasting memories I will cherish is fishing with him until well after dark on a September 2015 weekend. It was one of his last weeks of strength and lucidity that he enjoyed before succumbing to pancreatic cancer in 2016.

Anyway, as I began my deliberations about my life's second act, I called Ray Chambers. As always, he had plenty to say, albeit with an admirable economy of words. I hung on every syllable. He recounted the impact that his outreach to thought leaders had had on his personal journey after he left the investment business. He spent time with the Dalai Lama, Deepak Chopra, and even Tony Robbins. He spoke about the need to reach outside your comfort zone to get in touch with your own needs and goals. I was hesitating to start on my own list, but Ray's words inspired me to get going.

"One last thing, Ken," he said quietly but firmly, as we wound up our call. "You will get many opportunities thrown at you. So be ready. But, above all else, do not take the first thing that comes along. Take your time!"

"Of course, Ray," I said reassuringly. "I completely understand. I'm really serious about this process. I'll be patient."

My New Year's resolution for 2016 was to plan my next move. I was motivated. There were some serious reminders all around me that life was short, and I had better enjoy what I was doing. These included Richard's death, Dave Roy's illness, and our youngest's departure for college. In addition, Julie was experiencing a relapse and was about to embark bravely on another series of ECT procedures that would involve both inpatient and outpatient treatments over the coming months.

Just after the first of the year, I placed a call to Mike Meece, President Bush's chief of staff. This was one of the first entries on my list. I had gotten to know Mike over the years, given my interactions at the Bush Center. Among other things, he had helped arrange a private lunch with my old friend Bill Browder and President Bush in October of 2015.

"Mike, I have a crazy idea," I said. "What about me as Margaret's successor? Is this realistic?" Always the enthusiast, he replied, "Ken, I think you'd be fantastic."

I hung up and thought about it some more and put it on my list along with the other calls I had started to make.

STEVE: *According to your timeline, once February rolled around, it appears you got a bit more aggressive in moving the ball forward on the Bush Center opportunity. What happened?*

KEN: My annual trip to Davos happened.

STEVE: *Davos? That is the annual World Economic Forum, right? What does that have to do with the story?*

KEN: Some history is in order. As I mentioned, in 2010, after some urging by Bill Browder, I joined the World Economic Forum and attended its annual meeting in Davos, Switzerland. I'd read a lot about the forum over the years, but I wanted to see it for myself. Recall, too, that at this time, NGP was expanding its footprint globally, having opened up an office in London and taking in investors from around the world after the Barclays transaction of 2006.

The meeting in Davos is not open to everyone. In fact, it is one of the more selective global business gatherings around. It took a year for the World Economic Forum people to sniff me up and down and to qualify NGP and me as appropriate for membership. It is a bit of a process that I initiated in 2009 while living in London. While the rest of the world views this meeting as some sort of global conspiracy, I found it quite the opposite. The attendees were there searching for a venue to discuss all sorts of issues in an open and safe manner, connecting with others around the world facing the same challenges. Like many things in life, those on the outside outnumber those on the inside, so it is ripe for conspiracy theorists to suspect the worst.

Once a member, I became reasonably active in two of their "communities," as they divided them up in Davos. I split my time between the energy community and the asset managers community and was able to participate as a speaker, discussion leader, writer, and listener throughout the conferences over the years. It was a great collection of people and a nice way to participate in a global conversation with so many thought leaders in such a short time. In a week at Davos, I was able to meet and talk with experts, leaders, and audiences that literally would take a decade to replicate. Plus, it was fun and became an annual tradition for me to spend time with Bill Browder.

Bill was a Davos regular, using the forum as a platform for his work in bringing the story of the Russian authorities' persecution of him and the murder of his lawyer, Sergei Magnitsky, to the world. He was serious in his message that Russia's corrupt leadership was at the center of his lawyer's murder. In so doing, he became one of the top social justice advocates in the world.

Bill's attendance at Davos preceded Magnitsky's death. He had been attending for many years before I joined, having found it helpful when he was actively managing his hedge fund. At the time, there was a small collection of hedge fund managers who frequented Davos. They were, to some extent, like fish out of water mingling with corporate CEOs, academics, nonprofit leaders, and government officials from all over the world. Capitalists were welcome at Davos, since someone had to pay the bills, but the big-shot government officials and corporate chiefs seemed to be the conference centerpieces.

Bill hosted a dinner for these fish—er, *managers*—on the forum's opening night every year. He picked a nondescript Italian restaurant a short walk from the main drag in Davos. I was happy to attend at his invitation and was thrilled that some of my old acquaintances were annual attendees. I was not out of place by any stretch among the group of capitalists.

As Bill's Magnitsky saga unfolded over the ensuing years and his feud with Putin and the Russian authorities intensified, the dinner list at Davos expanded. He included his old friends and added a healthy list of new Davos friends, as well as a gaggle of journalists who were anxious to hear his story.

Somewhere along the line, I suggested we expand the dinner list and that I join as a cohost to help share the cost. As I became a Davos veteran and a guest at other people's dinners, it was nice to reciprocate with an invitation of my own. We pooled our guest lists, and it became quite an eclectic gathering—friends from across the business, political, academic, and journalism spectrum. Folks routinely cited this dinner as one of the highlights of their week in Davos. It became an annual tradition.

Now I'll connect this to the Bush Center story. The guest list for our January 2016 dinner included the usual suspects, as well as first-timers David McCormick and Dina Powell. By sheer coincidence, I had met David in California the prior summer through a common friend. An investment manager who'd been a Treasury undersecretary in President George W. Bush's administration, David had Dina Powell as his guest. Dina, who would go on to serve as deputy national security adviser for the first year of the Trump administration (and would later marry David), had also worked in President Bush's administration. She was at this time a senior executive at Goldman Sachs. Both she and David had been in touch with President Bush after his term ended in 2009.

As the dinner wound down, I asked them to stay a bit longer after the crowd had thinned out. Over a glass of wine, I started to describe my conversations with Mike Meece about the Bush Center opportunity.

"What are you waiting for?" David said. Dina concurred. "Ken, I think you'd be perfect. They need someone like you."

I was amazed at how emphatic they were. Given that each was close to the Bush family and understood their priorities and, from a distance, what the Bush Center was trying to achieve, I took their input very seriously. That convinced me to press the issue upon my return.

I phoned Mike Meece again to dive into the possibilities. He was quite helpful in thinking this through. He encouraged me to write something down on paper that he could deliver to President Bush and Don Evans, the former secretary of commerce who was President Bush's best friend and chair of the Bush Center's board.

I warned Mike that I would be an unconventional candidate—particularly if they were going to engage in a process to search from the pool of nonprofit leadership that most recruiters would come up with.

"That's okay," he said. "They need to think outside the box."

If nothing else, my thoughts would represent the input of an active donor. "I'd be prepared to position the Bush Center for the long term," I continued. "We need this platform for the country, but we can't take it for granted. Places like this can wither on the vine if they don't have a strategy to be sustainable."

"Go for it," he said.

So off I went to draft a letter to President Bush telling him what I would do if I oversaw the George W. Bush Presidential Center.

STEVE: *There you go writing presumptuous letters again. How did you approach this, writing a letter to the former leader of the free world in which you were suggesting how the center bearing his name should conduct its business?*

KEN: It helped that I had a relationship with both President Bush and Don Evans that dated back long before their government service began. I considered them friends whom I could address openly and honestly. Plus, I wasn't really looking for a job, so I was somewhat liberated in what I put down on paper. I could take the risk and fire away.

STEVE: *What did you say?*

KEN: My letter to President Bush said, in effect, that the Bush Center had a great opportunity to make a difference in the country provided it was more than just his family office. If it was going to have a lasting impact, it needed to be designed to live beyond his lifetime. If that was a goal he was serious about, I let him know I could bring a set of skills to the table that might help. Mike was helpful in reviewing drafts of the letter before I sent it. A copy of that letter is included here as Exhibit 6.

STEVE: *Before I get to the story of how this came together, I must highlight your end of the letter where you said this could be a fifteen- or twenty-year run. Really? That doesn't sound like you. Did you really mean that? Do you still?*

KEN: You know my pattern by now—I stick with what works. Provided that this post was satisfying, and I was still making a difference, I saw no reason to limit my horizon. However, given my October 2020 health scare, I must say that I have a little more carpe diem in me than I did at the time. We will get into that later.

HERSH FAMILY
— INVESTMENTS —

By Courier

March 2, 2016

The Honorable George Walker Bush
Office of George W. Bush
P.O. Box 259000
Dallas, Texas 75225

Dear President Bush,

I wanted to share a few thoughts regarding the leadership transition at the George W. Bush Presidential Center, and also make the case for you to consider an unconventional candidate like me to succeed Margaret. I would welcome the opportunity to discuss this further in person.

From the outset, I have taken a very active interest in the work of the Center, observing carefully and developing a breadth of perspectives as a major donor, an active program participant, and an admiring friend. I am consistently struck by how closely my own views and those of so many others track the principles you placed at the Center's core. Julie and I have been working to advance many of these same principles through our family foundation; and of course this is why we have been so interested and committed from the word "go".

I know you will replace Margaret with someone of stature and dynamism who has the wisdom to maintain continuity, the vision to create new energy, the thought leadership to draw positive attention, and the organizational leadership skills to build a sustainable, world-class team capable of advancing the Center's core principles for years to come. I hope you will seriously consider my qualifications for the task. I believe my industry profile, my track record in business and connections to donors in Dallas and around the world would make a powerful combination with your great staff and the Center's outstanding programming. Of course, as a demonstration of leadership commitment, I would apply my personal financial resources to amplify the Center's impact even further.

I believe at this point you need an established leader who can connect with the staff, the community, nationwide donors and the broader constituents to make the Center something that people will want to invest in over a long period of time. I also believe you need someone willing to commit for the long haul to a cause larger than self. I would strive to give permanence to this young institution as I have at NGP, where my name was never on the door, even though I was one of the co-founders. I set it up from a capital and personnel standpoint to be able to outlast me. It is now one of the most durable brands in the private investment business in the United States.

The Center has depended enormously in the early going from heavy involvement by you and Mrs. Bush. This is fitting and important, and with luck the two of you will continue this level of personal engagement for many years. But to build endurance, at some point the organization needs to be strong enough to deliver results without you. My goal would be to recruit, retain, and motivate an organization that is mission-driven and designed to outlast the two of you so that the governing principles are advanced well beyond the next 20 years and extend far beyond the city limits of Dallas.

The Towers at Williams Square East · 5221 N. O'Connor Blvd., Suite 1200 · Irving, TX 75039 Telephone: (972) 432-3800 · Facsimile: (972) 432-3801

Anyone watching this primary season can easily see that the need for a strong and lasting keeper of the American ideal has never been more acute. The George W. Bush Presidential Center is uniquely suited to the role; and I believe that, over time, the nation will see the Bush principles not as Republican or Democrat, but rather as central to the American identity. Mr. Trump's antics put that in stark relief.

I am well known and have good relationships with most members of the Center's Board as well as with Holly Kuzmich and Jeff Guy (whom I hired as CFO of the DMA when I was the chair of the finance committee there a number of years ago). I could easily work with them to deliver a seamless transition.

Most importantly, given our long-time friendship and my great admiration of your public service, you and Mrs. Bush can trust that I will **always** represent you well, preserve and enhance your reputation and legacy, and ensure that the Bush Center's activities **always** professionally support your goals.

I am 53 years young and firmly rooted in Dallas. I have been at NGP for 28 years and would anticipate committing to a very long run as I embark on a second career to "give back" what I have been so blessed to receive. If all works out, a **15 to 20 year run** would not be out of the question from my perspective.

Although we have known each other socially for almost 30 years, you may not know the extent of my professional and personal activities over that time - so I took the liberty to outline them in the first attachment. My objectives have always been simple: be excellent, be thoughtful, be fair and have fun.

I have also attached my CV, and hope we can discuss this in more detail, even if only so you can explain how it makes no sense!

Thanks so much; and as always, I value our friendship.

Ken

cc: Don Evans

Exhibit 6: Letter from Ken Hersh to President George W. Bush, March 2, 2016

STEVE: *Okay, then that is a good tease. Let's get back to this story.*

KEN: My first call after sending the letter was to Don Evans. He knew I wasn't really lobbying for the position but rather approaching them as a friend who cared about the success of the place and who had also made a large financial commitment to it.

Don is a consummate gentleman and one of the most pleasant people I know. He's careful and thoughtful. In addition, he's a valuable and protective friend of President and Laura Bush—the type of friend who would put their needs above his own at every step.

When we first spoke, he seemed puzzled. He couldn't quite understand why a guy from the private sector with the kind of success I had had would be interested in running what was, on its face, a nonprofit policy institute. He listened carefully and digested what I had to say. We agreed to keep thinking about it. I wasn't being that aggressive, since it was early in my thought process, not to mention the challenges I was simultaneously navigating at NGP.

Over the course of the month, I had several more conversations with Don Evans and, with his encouragement, I met as many members of the Bush Center board as I could fit into a busy spring schedule. The conversations were fun and instructive, and the board uniformly welcomed my thoughts on how to establish the Bush Center as an important voice for the timeless values that formed the foundations of President Bush's public service. The only meeting left to have was with President Bush and Laura.

On the first weekend of April 2016, I went to their home, and we talked about it.

STEVE: *How was that?*

KEN: Pretty straightforward. I remember sitting upstairs in his art studio/den and discussing it. Laura Bush joined the conversation, as did their cat. As it made its way to the couch I was sitting on, I didn't have the heart to let them know of my cat allergy.

We went back and forth about life and the Bush Center. Then the former president asked me my impressions of the biggest challenges faced by the Bush Center. "My simple answer is a question," I replied. "Is this just your family office? Because if it's just your family office, you don't need me. You'll be able to do your projects, and while you're here, it'll work well. When you're gone or decide to be less active, it will be a great museum with some sort of lecture series. Kind of like most of the other presidential centers around the country."

"Ken, I want this thing to last," he said. "Now, are *you* sure you want to do this?"

"If you're serious about wanting this to live on forever, then that's an interesting strategic challenge," I explained. "How do you take a place that's named for a living person, who everyone wants to come to see and hear from, and establish that institution to live beyond his lifetime? I think it's doable, but it must be managed with that goal in mind while remaining focused on you and your priorities. That is, keep an eye on the present, while we build for a more institutionalized future. I think it would be a fascinating challenge."

After a confirmatory breakfast the next morning with his former chief of staff, Josh Bolten—who coincidentally happened to be in Dallas that weekend for the Bush-Cheney Administration staff reunion at the Bush Center—we agreed I would take the position if asked. The board concurred and it became official. That meeting was in early April, and I took the helm at the end of May, just a week after the Arlington, Texas, city council meeting where our baseball stadium project was approved. I had to tie up that loose end before embarking on a new adventure.

STEVE: *You took it just like that?*

KEN: Yep. But I had to go home and place one quick call—to Ray Chambers, one of my capitalist father figures. "Please don't hate me," I said nervously as soon as he answered.

"Why?" he asked, wondering about the call out of the blue.

"I took the first thing that came along!"

Then, I stammered out an outline of my new job. After a brief silence, during which my heart almost jumped out of my chest, he replied, "Ken, I think this is a wonderful thing for both you and President Bush."

My chest pressure eased. I felt like a little kid getting affirmation from a stand-offish teacher.

"Thanks, Ray," I said. "I'm going to give it a try!"

CHAPTER 15

EVERY PLANT NEEDS
TO BE REPOTTED

STEVE: *Before we get to your tenure as CEO at the Bush Center, I'd like to ask you about your relationship with President George W. Bush prior to taking the job in the spring of 2016. You knew him before he was elected in 2000, correct?*

KEN: Yes. I even knew him before he was elected governor of Texas in 1994—or as I like to say, back when I could call him by his first name. I first met him in 1989 during my early days with Richard Rainwater.

STEVE: *He and Rainwater were friends?*

KEN: Eventually, but business partners first—the business being the Texas Rangers baseball team. I was still at Stanford then, but by chance I was visiting Richard's office when the wheels were set in motion for the purchase of the team.

STEVE: *This I must hear.*

KEN: I was in town from Palo Alto and happened to be sitting across from Richard when the commissioner of Major League Baseball, Peter Ueberroth, called. Richard almost always conducted business over a speakerphone, so I heard everything from the beginning.

"Richard? You want to own a baseball team with George W. Bush, the son of the president?" the commissioner asked. "He needs some more money, and we want him to have more Texans in the group."

As Ueberroth continued to talk, Richard put the speakerphone on mute and turned to me. "Ken, should I buy a baseball team?"

In shock that an investing legend would even care what a twenty-six-year-old visitor had to say, I stammered, "I don't know, Richard. Do you *want* to own a baseball team?"

He furrowed his brow and hit the unmute button on the phone. "Maybe, Peter. Does he know anything about baseball?"

"I don't know, but you should just talk to him and find out."

And that was that. George W. Bush called shortly thereafter. He was in Washington, having moved there from Midland with Laura and their twin girls to help George H. W. Bush with his transition to the presidency. Richard agreed to invest in the purchase with him provided that his (Richard's) dear friend Rusty Rose serve alongside George W. as co–general partners of the team.

The deal was completed in the spring of 1989—prior to the time I joined Rainwater's office after graduation. George W. and family moved to Dallas, and he became a frequent visitor to the office. That's when I first met him. Since he'd been in the oil and gas business during his time in Midland, we had something in common as well as a love of baseball—and, of course, our admiration for Richard. In fact, when an opening came to invest in the general partner of our first Natural Gas Partners fund, George asked to be included as a small investor.

Over the course of the next few years, we would cross paths at baseball games, during his visits to Rainwater's office in Fort Worth, or when I called him for references on people I met in Midland. As I said, he was just "George" back then—a normal friend in his mid-forties who just happened to have a famous father and Secret Service protection. We never were short on things to talk about. Plus, it helped that his investment in our fund was doing incredibly well.

When he ran for governor, we were happy to support his campaign, but I was careful not to be one of those friends who always calls in favors from politicians. I didn't want to compromise him in any way. In fact, I never even went to visit him while he was in Austin.

When he ran for president, I supported him with a donation at the maximum level allowed, but that was it. About the time of his candidacy, the blind trust that had been established to hold his investments while he was governor had to be bought out of our partnership. We reconnected when I'd see him on the occasional rope line for handshakes when he visited Dallas for a campaign stop. I was busy growing my business and didn't really have time to mess with the goings-on in Washington, even though I had a friend in the White House.

STEVE: *During his presidency and post-presidency, until you gave the money for the center, had your worlds collided much?*

KEN: I have to admit that I called his office manager to arrange a private visit in Washington timed before the 2004 election heated up. I didn't want to be the kind of friend who begged a night in the Lincoln bedroom or a gratuitous donor ride on Air Force One. But I knew I might not be this close with a sitting president again, and I didn't want to miss the opportunity to take Julie and my kids to the Oval Office.

We had a great visit one chilly Friday afternoon in January of 2004. We chatted there for an hour and had a memorable behind-the-scenes tour of the White House. Of course, my then-ten-year-old son, Daniel, was much more interested in the fact that the Florida Marlins were in the White House earlier that same day to celebrate their 2003 World Series victory. He was dejected he had just missed meeting Pudge Rodriguez, the Hall of Fame catcher who played a full career for the Texas Rangers before signing with Miami for the year that they just happened to win it all. Here I was thinking I was giving my kids the experience of a lifetime, only to have them be disappointed because they missed seeing a baseball player. Go figure.

When President Bush returned to Dallas in 2009, we had a nice lunch and a few social visits in his office. Remember, the Bush Center did not open until 2013. So he had a private office for himself and his staff. There was another office for the Bush Center team, which was hard at work raising money for the building as well as planning the beginning programs of the Bush Institute. Most of that was outside the public eye. Until, of course, they came around to me as a potential donor. As old friends and supporters, Julie and I were honored to be asked for support by the then-CEO of the Bush Center, Mark Langdale, and proud to contribute to the efforts to build a world-class facility and program in my hometown.

STEVE: *Did you ever have any contact with President George H. W. Bush?*

KEN: Yes. In late 1995, about three years after his term had ended, he called me out of the blue. "My son tells me I could make some money if I invest with you," he said. I was taken aback. I guess George W. had monitored the investment progress of his blind trust after all. Then he explained, "People think I'm the silver-spoon president because of the house in Maine and because we're from the Northeast, but until Barbara's book deal, we didn't have very much extra money. You know, I've been in public service for forty years." He paused in only the way that he could and then chirped proudly, "But now I have a little bit of money, and my son tells me I should invest with you."

STEVE: *How did it feel to get a call from a former president?*

KEN: I thought it was pretty cool, frankly. I didn't know the man but obviously was a fan. The fact that he opened up right away with his personal financial situation was a bit unexpected, but I rolled with it.

STEVE: *And what did you tell him?*

KEN: I said, "Actually, I'm working on a deal right now. I might have something, and it's way bigger than our fund, so we will likely need coinvestors to join in." It was the Mesa deal. He stopped me halfway through my description. "How much do you think I can invest?"

"Well, whatever you'd like to invest," I said. "I think it's going to be quite large."

"Okay, I'll have my money manager call you and get the paperwork in," he said. Then, almost as an afterthought before he hung up, he asked, "Oh, by the way, is there any room for a friend of mine to invest as well?"

I was a bit amused that the former president was now my syndication department. "Sure," I answered quickly. Within the hour after hanging up, I received a call from his mystery friend.

"Ken, this is Colin Powell. President Bush says I can invest with you. Do you think I can invest some money?"

"Are you sure, General Powell?" I answered. "This is sort of a complicated deal, and we are happy to have you, but I want to make sure you understand the timing and the risks. Nothing is guaranteed, you know." I wanted to ensure that he had his eyes wide open. I had this moment of panic that I would be personally responsible for losing the nest eggs of both the former president and the chair of the Joint Chiefs of Staff. I tried to dissuade them.

"I'll be fine, Ken," he said confidently. "I'd like to do it."

As the deal progressed, we kept them on the list and, sure enough, when we closed the transaction in the summer of 1996, they sent us their money and were now in the oil and gas investment business.

After the deal closed, President George H. W. Bush invited me to come see him in Houston. On a couple of occasions, I had wonderful visits with him and Barbara. We also talked on the phone occasionally. He seemed to call out of the blue after there was a big move up or down on the Mesa stock. It was nice to know he was following it. He saw the effort that these deals take once he started tracking it. I remember his commenting how complicated these transactions were. He was such a gentleman, even once he transitioned to the private sector.

One of my nice memories of the Mesa deal is receiving one of the trademark George H. W. Bush typed notes. He sent it in April of 1997, after he called me for an update upon seeing oil prices drop and Mesa stock declining. He wrote:

> Ken, I very much appreciated your bringing me up-to-date on Mesa. I had wondered why the stock dropped a little, but after all, we still have a huge profit. Of course, I am still grateful to Richard, Darla, and you for this. Thank you for your thoughtfulness.

I saw him again in April 2013 at the opening ceremony and private luncheon for the Bush Center's dedication. Under a glaring sun, we shared a warm hello and nice remembrance of our business deal together. He was in a wheelchair and pushing ninety years old, but his memory was sharp as a tack. That was the last time I visited with him. He was a special man and a national treasure.

STEVE: *Okay, back to the Bush Center. When you started as CEO in June of 2016, what did you find, and what were your immediate priorities?*

KEN: First, I found an incredibly motivated team driven by the mission of service and focused on upholding the values that underlie the public service of President and Laura Bush. They believed in the inherent good inside each one of us and maintained such an optimistic vision.

STEVE: *Explain, please.*

KEN: President Bush believed in being a compassionate conservative. In practice, this meant supporting the values of economic and political freedom, less government dependency, and the positive role of the United States around the world. In fact, the word "freedom" is the most prevalent word throughout the entire museum here in Dallas.

The efforts of the team were spread across a series of program areas, each with a dedicated group of professionals working feverishly to make things happen. All the ingredients were there to begin to shape the place for the future. They just needed to coalesce as a unit. Remember, the building opened in 2013 and I took over in 2016, only three years later. It was a Herculean effort to get that center opened and begin the Bush Institute's work all at the same time. My task was relatively straightforward: how to take all the good work of the policy and the public engagement teams and knit it together into a cohesive and impactful strategy.

I had a unique perspective, having seen it through the eyes of a donor. I was unfamiliar with a lot of the work that the Bush Institute was doing, and I was confused as to what the Bush Center even was. This was a problem. Since I was an active donor who was a frequent visitor and participant in the center's programs, if it was confusing to me, just think how it appeared to those less connected. As a result, I set out to make the story and the strategy align and to ensure that all our various constituencies were more engaged with and kept apprised of our work.

STEVE: *You have received lifetime achievement awards for your work in the energy industry and you have been recognized for your community efforts with distinctions like the Anti-Defamation League's Henry Cohn Humanitarian Award. But you never went so far as to earn a paycheck in the nonprofit arena. Was it difficult for you to make the transition from the business world to the not-for-profit world?*

KEN: Not at all. Great businesses start with a great strategy and a team of great people. This is true in both the for-profit and not-for-profit worlds. Frankly, I don't think there is much of a difference at all. The currencies may be different, with for-profit businesses being able to offer financial incentives and disincentives that may not be available for nonprofits. But nonprofits have a lot of other "currencies" to offer—the satisfaction that comes from serving a purpose larger than oneself, for example. If you take type A personalities and put them in the nonprofit setting, guess what happens?

STEVE: *What?*

KEN: They perform at the highest level!

STEVE: *So you approached your new job as you would anything else?*

KEN: You bet. The first thing I did was listen. The senior team there was excellent, and my first job was to let them know I believed in the mission and the team and that I was there, first and foremost, to help build a sustainable future for each of them. This was not a turnaround situation at all. Of course, there were things to tighten up, and the corporate culture was suboptimal, but those are smaller items in the larger scheme of things. The Bush Center had a good amount of momentum, but the long-term strategic direction was lacking. Without the trust of the team, I wouldn't be able to do much of anything. So my near-term objective was pretty clear.

Given that I was a donor and known to several of the employees, after answering the initial question of "Why on earth would he take this job?" I dove in. It became apparent to everyone that this wasn't going to be just a hobby for me. In my all-in style

I made sure to set the example that I was there to work alongside the team to build this place for the future. I wasn't there just to bark orders at people and then watch them work. It's the only way I know how to be. I made it clear that I was there in the foxhole with them all and welcomed any and all of them into my foxhole. While they were a bit incredulous at first, they quickly came to know I was seriously all in.

During the first part of my tenure there, it was apparent we needed to enhance the efficiency of the place and to redouble our efforts to take care of the workforce to reduce staff turnover. Then we could begin to refine the program with an eye toward increasing our impact and making it more sustainable. In this process, I used many of my tried-and-true methods of managing people.

First, I was able to feed the winners quite well. My senior-most colleague, Holly Kuzmich, was an important leader at the center and was serving as interim CEO before I arrived. It was nice I had met her before. I admired her and wanted her to know right away that I looked forward to working with her and that she could trust me. In addition, Brian Cossiboom, the person in charge of operations, was a skilled and loyal executive. He was a White House veteran who'd been involved with just about every brick of the Bush Center. The Bushes were more fortunate than they would ever know to have someone like Brian in their camp. He knew the place inside and out.

Certain members of the team were high performers, always looking for greater challenges and opportunities. I tried to give them all the time I could to mentor them and piled on the opportunities they sought. As I fed the winners, people noticed, and that had the desired effect. Many other team members responded by saying that they wanted to get "fed" as well. Watching people flourish is a phenomenal dynamic, as is watching people have fun at work.

In addition, we simplified the operation and removed the barriers that were hindering people from being the most productive. I increased transparency and enhanced the channels of communication. I tried to make everyone feel part of the center, allowing feedback loops to include virtually all who worked there. We were one team. Why not act like it? Unfortunately, some of those organizational barriers were holdover features from the White House, where hierarchy meant a lot and not everyone had the luxury of being transparent with their work. I knew right away that mentality had to go. We weren't running the country. We were running a policy think tank with public engagement programming attached. It was quite different and needed to be operated as such.

Those efforts paid off. We were able to increase productivity without increasing staff. Consequently, we implemented financial incentives for performance that most nonprofits would never dream of implementing. People felt appreciated again. Sure, there were some yellow lights that didn't turn green, and some people moved on, but, as with any organization, when just a few cultural misfits left, it was amazing how the heartbeat of the place improved. With the positive team culture, we were ready to take on the world. And we have.

STEVE: *How so?*

KEN: A presidential center is a unique platform. There are very few of them in this country, even fewer that have a freestanding institute attached. Less than a handful have a living former president and former first lady around to champion the work. With all that in place, we undertook the bold task of building a sustainable institution that will last forever.

The compassionate conservative values of President Bush resonate in everything we do. We focus on those values toward our mission of ensuring opportunity for all, strengthening our democracy, and advancing free societies around the world. While that mission is quite broad, we've chosen key areas of focus in which to make a difference.

STEVE: *This new world seemed to energize you. Is that a fair read of the situation?*

KEN: As I have said, I believe that every plant needs to be repotted at some point. I felt twenty years younger when I showed up there. The place exuded the confidence of a talented group of young professionals pursuing mission-driven work. I wanted to make sure this talent has a home that's sustainable far into the future.

Our sustainability plan was quite simple yet challenging: Maintain the strong presence of the Bushes and their inspirational voices while, at the same time, build out Bush Institute–branded thought-leadership work, with repeatable and high levels of constituent engagement. And to do all this with a strong financial base.

Ironically, to accomplish this, I had to build separation between the Bush Center and the Bushes. This may seem counterintuitive, but if the success of our work and the attendance at our events and the donations to the place were all reliant on the Bushes' presence, then logic would dictate that, once their presence falls off, all those efforts would be challenged.

STEVE: *That seems like a tall order. Remove the Bushes from the Bush Center?*

KEN: Not remove them at all but, rather, rechannel their presence. I set out with the team to ensure that everything we did benefited from the Bushes' involvement but wasn't *dependent* on them. We had the Bush Institute directors and fellows increase their publishing and speaking. We increased the level of donor engagement and always put on a smart, interesting program worthy of a presidential moniker. Sometimes

President Bush or Laura Bush appeared and spoke; other times they did not. We built our programming content and goals around their beliefs, not around their schedule. Fortunately, however, they have remained very engaged with our work to date.

In essence, we changed the vocabulary of the Bush Center from this being the work of George and Laura Bush to the work *inspired* by them and built on their values. We stopped asking donors to give a gift *to* the Bushes or *because of* the Bushes and, instead, asked them to invest in the *priorities of* the Bushes. We promised to measure all the work we did and assured them that if something wasn't going to produce results, we'd stop it. We stopped having events for the sake of having events, and we were no longer in the donor entertainment business. I wanted our donors to connect with and see our work, so we started building donor events around the presentations of our activities.

STEVE: *Sounds like this worked pretty well.*

KEN: I was gratified that the base of support and our various audiences were ready for this. I was amazed at how many people commented to me that they were wondering what this place was going to look like in the future. They were ready to engage at a deeper level with the various initiatives of the Bush Center. Also, there are so many who were knocking on the door wanting to be a part of what was going on here. By the end of 2021, we had completed a $325 million capital campaign and finished a new long-range strategic plan for the Bush Institute. The future was now solidified.

STEVE: *And President Bush?*

KEN: I hope he's both proud and a little bit relieved that this place is set for the long term. He said he never wanted it to be all about him.

STEVE: *This must make you feel pretty good.*

KEN: I brag that I could have taken this group of people into the private sector and been wildly successful, producing and selling whatever widget we desired. However, none of them would have come with me! This is a mission-driven group of professionals who are service-oriented and committed to the values of the place. It has been a joy to come to the office. This plant was repotted, and it felt great.

STEVE: *You've had the opportunity to get to know President Bush better by working closely with him these last years at the center. What can you say about him?*

KEN: It's so refreshing to be around him because he calls it like he sees it and in a manner that's very respectful and appreciative. He's one of the most painfully truthful persons I've ever met. He didn't lie as president, and he doesn't lie now. I'm always grateful for his candor. What you realize when you talk to people around him is that whether you liked it or not, you knew that he did what he thought was right for the country. He wasn't doing it for money or his personal legacy. His love for and service to the country are real. Those who worked for him would go to the ends of the earth to support him.

I have learned even more about leadership from him. Seeing the chronology of what he did on September 11, 2001, and the week thereafter was telling. Leaders reveal themselves during unscripted moments. September 11 was the ultimate in unscripted moments.

When he got up that morning in Sarasota, Florida, to go for a jog before an event at an elementary school, the last thing on his mind was that his day would involve responding to an attack on the United States and being escorted by fighter jets around the country before returning to Washington, D.C., later that evening.

After 9/11, my friend George was gone. The aw-shucks, self-effacing, folksy guy was still there, but with a gravitas that would never disappear. Some people criticize him for continuing to read a book to a classroom full of kids for nine minutes after Andy Card, his chief of staff, whispered in his ear that America was under attack. I feel just the opposite. His immediate instinct was: *The world is watching me, and the American president does not run.*

That revealed his savvy instinct. He sat there while his team worked in the other room and around the world. There's a wonderful picture of him in the classroom at that moment, with Card whispering into his ear, when the expression on his face says it all: *Dammit, not on my watch.* It was not a scared look. It was the face of determination. From there, his instinct took over as he both consoled the country and reassured the world that freedom would prevail.

STEVE: *And Laura Bush?*

KEN: What can I say? The country has been blessed to have her by his side. She is a shining example of grace and confidence with her own set of priorities. They are a dynamic duo.

CHAPTER 16

SPOONS INSTEAD
OF SHOVELS

STEVE: *You have a perspective as a business executive who's now deeply exposed to those in public service with a unique view of the relationship between the public and private sectors. Can we talk about your view of the role of business in promoting what's called "the social good"? As you know, there's growing debate over whether businesses should produce results beyond the bottom line. In 2019, the Business Roundtable modernized their Statement on the Purpose of a Corporation to say, "If companies fail to recognize that the success of our system is dependent on inclusive long-term growth, many will raise legitimate questions about the role of large employers in our society."**

KEN: I'm familiar with the statement. It reinforces the organization's strong commitment to a free-market system, noting that "businesses play a vital role in the economy by creating jobs, fostering innovation, and providing essential goods and services. Businesses make and sell consumer products; manufacture equipment and vehicles; support the national defense; grow and produce food; provide health care; generate and deliver energy; and offer financial, communications and other services that underpin economic growth." But it goes on to emphasize that businesses now "share a fundamental commitment" to all stakeholders—customers, employees, suppliers, communities, *and* shareholders.

---

* Business Roundtable, "Our Commitment," accessed August 8, 2022, https://opportunity.businessroundtable
.org/ourcommitment/.

STEVE: *Right. And shortly after that, the chairman of the U.S. Chamber of Commerce suggested that companies put a premium on creating good-paying jobs along with making a profit.*

KEN: Yes. As a young capitalist, I learned that maximizing financial returns was a constant I could rely on. The goal was straightforward, but that's no longer a constant.

Making a commitment to a market economy necessitates embracing change. Defining the role of the corporation to serve not only shareholders but all stakeholders is a meaningful and appropriate expression. There is nothing to fear in these changes—the bottom line is well served by broadening the aperture on how success is measured.

Some scoff at this perspective, arguing for the Milton Friedman philosophy that the sole goal should be for a business to maximize its profits, but that's a static view, one that I'd agree with if the goal were to maximize profits for *this year only*. I'd argue that sustaining higher levels of profitability over a long period of time demands that consideration be given to other factors besides just a short-term return.

STEVE: *Such as?*

KEN: Employees are both an input and an output for a healthy business. In addition to great productivity, employee sentiment is a real component of corporate success, especially in a virtual full-employment economy witnessing a changing workforce. Employers don't have the luxury of disregarding the opinions and feelings of their workforce.

Devising solutions aimed at the highest level of employment is not enough, however. If it was, we could issue spoons instead of shovels to do our digging. Who needs speed and productivity if all you want to accomplish is maximum employment? Heck, why not just make all chores more labor-intensive?

The lunacy of that proposition is clear. The value in productive work is as qualitative as it is quantitative. I've always been rewarded by going that extra length to care for those I managed. It was an honor to lead them. I wanted their experience to be as fulfilling as possible. An empowered workforce that believes in the ethics of management and the values of the firm will work harder and stick around longer.

STEVE: *What has changed to spark this evolution?*

KEN: Consumers, for one thing. These days, they consider more than just price when deciding where to shop for a product or service. As a result, market competition demands this kind of approach. In many instances, consumers understand the values they are patronizing when they make a purchase decision. Similarly, companies compete for vendors in a world where supply channels are finely tuned. This heightened level of competition even requires private-sector organizations to consider what matters to the workers at their suppliers.

STEVE: *Can you give a for-instance?*

KEN: Sure. You may remember that in 2020, the employees at Wayfair, the internet furniture marketplace, protested the company's fulfilling an order for a vendor whom the federal government had selected to provide supplies to immigrant detention facilities. Neither Wayfair nor the government contractor was responsible for the federal policy in question, but the vendor's employees protested. Likewise, Google and Amazon employees have balked at their employers' bidding on government contracts during the Trump administration. In each case, their employers had to listen and modify their behavior.

Here's another example. In response to the mass shootings of 2019, including the tragedy in its own store in El Paso, Walmart exercised leadership by taking significant steps on the issue of gun control. The company decided to stop selling ammunition for handguns and some rifle types, as well as terminate the selling of handguns in Alaska (the only state where Walmart sold handguns). The social stance was more important than the profit opportunity for these products.

Of course, those who are anchored to the past will be confused. For years, competition for markets while markets themselves changed demanded that management navigate through uncertainty. The focus was targeted on one common denominator—maximizing return to shareholders. That singular aim helped point everyone in the same direction with an output that could be clearly quantified and measured. Those who could won. Those who could not failed.

Now, there are more considerations. Contributing to the communities in which businesses operate makes good sense. It's important that employees feel good about the community in which they live, work, and play. In a world where an anonymous review on the Glassdoor app can change attitudes toward a company, senior managers need to appreciate that feedback about their organization's reputation can come from anywhere.

In short, a company's brand equity touches employees, vendors, and the communities in which it operates. Aligning these goals is consistent with improving the bottom line.

STEVE: *So it's a balancing act?*

KEN: Exactly. We can't forget that the bottom line remains critical. Without financial success, investors would cease to risk capital and innovation would grind to a halt.

We have seen that in industries that lost their way. Leaders need to ensure that ample consideration is given to all stakeholders, but not to the point of blunting the sharp edge provided by the need to produce a competitive return on invested capital. This is where strong leadership comes into play.

Making trade-offs is inevitable. Knowing *what* to trade against *what* isn't always obvious. Altering a business plan is serious, but it often is inevitable. Apple used to be known for desktop computers, not as a consumer device and entertainment conglomerate. We know how that pivot worked out. Amazon started as a book seller.

Companies need the freedom to adapt when markets change. Imagine what IBM would look like today if it had clung to the mainframe computer-manufacturing business model out of fear of damaging suppliers or its factory workers. Companies like Eastman Kodak that did not adapt ended up as shadows of their former selves, ultimately hurting their employees, vendors, and the community.

STEVE: *You previously quoted former Intel CEO Andy Grove: "Only the paranoid survive." Is it as simple as that?*

KEN: Financial failure, while not ever a desire, is an outcome that always needs to be considered. That fear of failure drives business to respond to the market and innovate. It's the essential ingredient in the creative-destruction equation. When failure happens, the responses are predictable—limit losses, learn from the failure, adjust course, reinvent, and move forward.

This formula has made the U.S. economic machine the envy of the world and translated into remarkable gains in many countries around the world. Capitalism, while not perfect, has produced innovation beyond belief, and these developments have lifted over a billion from the clutches of poverty worldwide.

STEVE: *If this change toward more social responsibility is positive, who needs to drive it?*

KEN: A lot depends on the effectiveness of business leadership. Clinging to a short-term business model that's in the process of becoming antiquated is bad for everyone. At the same time, communities need to appreciate the benefits of the creative destruction process and create a culture of acceptance for that eventuality. By embracing the fact that failure may happen, employees, suppliers, and the entire home community can help businesses adapt and thrive.

By focusing on long-term goals, and communicating them clearly and often, leaders can ensure that all stakeholders pull in the same direction. Rather than fight the urge to innovate, those stakeholders can become partners in the innovation, adapting alongside the company. In fact, they may see change coming first. Leadership should deputize their entire network of stakeholders as a resource in both devising and executing corporate strategy. They're important partners for the long term.

Further, if communication is clear, everyone can hedge. If corporations are not built to earn a competitive rate of return and retain employees for the long term, then vendors and communities would be smart to diversify away from being dependent on those businesses. The days of the old company towns are gone. You can see how cities like Pittsburgh have reinvented themselves, while cities like Detroit have been slower to react. If eyes are wide open, then everyone will develop the capacity to react and plan their individual strategies accordingly.

Playing for short-term survival is not a winning strategy for anyone.

STEVE: *Sounds like you learned that from experience.*

KEN: Traveling to oil-and-gas-dominated towns during both booms and busts put me on the ground to witness these lessons. Eyes and ears are great teachers.

CHAPTER 17

A CLASH BETWEEN
TWO WORLDS

STEVE: *It seems that being at the Bush Center allowed you to synthesize your thinking about leadership and about the challenges facing this country.*

KEN: While I was running a business, I didn't have time to stop and think. Now that I have been able to crystallize my thinking a bit, it's amazing to me what I learned by doing. At NGP, I made many mistakes and tried to learn from my experience. I wish I had always gotten it right, but I didn't. However, I was able to derive real lessons that seem quite transferable to the work of the Bush Center.

Allow me to qualify that: Either they are transferable *or* I am just lazy and I was going to apply them anyway.

In short, real leadership is something altogether different. Often, a leader is defined by geography—the front of the room, the head of the table, a place at the podium, or the top of the organizational chart. True leadership, though, doesn't wait for geography to define it. True leadership is defined by character, the defining mark of which is a desire to serve those being led.

Authentic leadership should not be confused with simply being in charge. This difference can make distinguishing between a leader and real leadership a challenge. Those in charge come in many forms and they may or may not be effective at the helm. It is relatively straightforward to be given authority over something or to take charge, but that may or may not constitute leadership. The person in charge may temporarily occupy a chair that comes with that authority. But instability could emerge, and results could suffer if that authority does not come with a commitment to serving others. Think about an elected official who issues capricious orders while in office, only to have those undone by his or her successor. Elected office is borrowed power, only available to the official until the term expires.

STEVE: *Do you think leadership can be taught?*

KEN: I would say leadership *skills* can be taught, and responsibilities of a position can be conferred. But the character of leadership does not come that easily. Real leadership draws from deeply held principles and simultaneously requires the consent of the led.

What's more, leadership is not necessarily reserved for those who stand out in front of the crowd. Some of history's most notable leaders—Mahatma Gandhi, Dr. Martin Luther King Jr., Mother Teresa, the Dalai Lama, Rosa Parks, and the jailed Nelson Mandela—lacked authority to wield their influence. Yet they led. And they did so with a moral voice that inspired those around them to see their visions of the future, which grew out of a sense of service. As a result, their followers grew.

We particularly need effective global leaders today, given the transitions going on in our society and around the world. A common challenge for all leaders is navigating through uncertainty, and that's truer now than ever before. The pace of change is accelerating so fast that modern leaders are often navigating not just the uncertain but also the unknowable.

STEVE: *Please explain.*

KEN: In the past, rather simple extrapolations of the present could provide a useful approximation of what the future would bring. Today, that may not just be inadequate; it may be helpless. Technological disruption is rapidly changing the way we work, live, and interact. It's even potentially threatening the way we're governed. New paradigms may be unrecognizable.

At the same time, the coming generations are more diverse, more educated, more technologically equipped—and less governable—than perhaps at any time in human history. Combined with the speed of communications and the unleashing of technological advances, the chasm between the older and younger generations is wider than ever.

The institutions governing us were designed to oversee a different world. After an industrial revolution and two devastating world wars, rules of order developed to ensure stability and fairness. The rules of the old order were often established to be slow and to resist the disruptive pace of change—all to ensure that stability. A corporate hierarchy, a governing system of checks and balances, deliberative bodies with rigid rules of order, and multilateral institutional arrangements were built to resist the vagaries of change and to ensure that no malicious force could take over capriciously. In short, they were designed to be slow.

STEVE: *And now?*

KEN: Now, technological and social forces are disrupting those arrangements. By the time traditional rules of order and deliberative bodies reach a conclusion, the problem that they were solving has often become moot. They're constantly putting out yesterday's fires, creating further frustration for those being led.

Our contemporary conditions require adaptive leaders, much like we had after World War II when, paradoxically, many of the old-order institutions were created. Leaders from the nations that had just defeated tyranny didn't have a guidebook to tell them how to create such pillars as the United Nations, the North Atlantic Treaty Organization, or the International Monetary Fund. They established institutions that allowed the post–World War II era to blossom into the most stable and prosperous in modern history. Those leaders did so by drawing on their principles, experiences, and wisdom.

Of course, some now question the readiness of those institutional frameworks to govern a radically different world. Those institutions continue to respond to present challenges like the abuse of human rights in North Korea and the protection of emerging democracies in places like Ukraine. Yet the emerging challenges of a young century call out for a new script and their own institutions to move us forward.

Think about it. The UN Security Council was designed, in part, to prevent Japan and Germany from ever threatening the world order again. Russia and China were given veto power along with the United States. Today, however, Japan and Germany are peaceful and thriving democracies while Russia and China represent emerging threats to global freedom, peace, and prosperity. Clearly the United Nations has lost the credibility and usefulness it had seventy years ago.

STEVE: *Is there a quick fix?*

KEN: No. Those developments will take time and incumbents will fight against change. Thus, adaptive, forward-looking leadership is required. When there is no script on which to rely, leaders can only fall back on their core values and character. They'll be tested. They'll be frustrated. They'll be loved. They'll be ridiculed. Despite those challenges, they can navigate through our uncertain times if they maintain a grounded sense of service.

Effective leaders share attributes that are timeless. First, they are guided by a clear set of core values defined by authenticity. Second, they are not afraid to work with natural and unnatural allies, even crossing traditional divides to meet common objectives. Finally, they're action-oriented people committed to catalyzing positive change.

STEVE: *You've summed this up in a thought piece by framing the world today as a clash between two worlds: the fast world and the slow world. You begin with a great 2018 quotation from the prime minister of Canada, Justin Trudeau: "The pace of change has never been this fast, yet it will never be this slow again."**

KEN: He hit the nail on the head. The fast world is all around us: artificial intelligence, robotics, gene editing, regenerative medicine, cryptocurrencies, and coming soon, quantum computing speeds that are one hundred million times faster than today's semiconductors.

STEVE: *But you also note that at the same time we inhabit a slow world that values truth and accuracy over speed.*

KEN: Right. Some examples of that are our federal government, with its three branches and system of checks and balances; our multilateral institutions like the OECD and the EU; multiparty agreements like NAFTA, now the USMCA; jury trials, which are slow and deliberate truth-finding mechanisms; and the scientific process, with peer review and double-blind studies. All are trying to get to accuracy at the expense of speed.

STEVE: *What is at the core of the conflict?*

KEN: These worlds are different in that they have different views of disruption. In the fast world, disruption has positive connotations—creative destruction, efficiency, wealth creation. In the slow world, disruption has negative connotations relating to the perceived and maybe apparent loss of control. Usually these worlds are far apart, but today they're clashing, and they're clashing without rules of engagement.

STEVE: *Can you give me some examples?*

---

* Justin Trudeau, address at World Economic Forum, Davos, Switzerland, January 23, 2018.

KEN: In our news and politics, the fast world's goal of getting a message out and having it go viral, regardless of whether it's true, is apparent to all of us. Journalists today rush a story to beat the competition, relying on the ability to issue corrections if something is amiss. Of course, once an erroneous story is out, a later correction often fails to undo the damage done.

Also, in our national security, the instruments of war are changing to those of automated drones and cyber warfare. Combatants need not be on the battlefield anymore. Yet there are no rules of engagement for this war. We're used to the Geneva Convention and other laws and treaties on the treatment of prisoners. We're used to treaties, for example, on the use of chemical weapons. But there's no Geneva Convention for artificial intelligence, cyber warfare, or drone warfare.

STEVE: *Do you think how these worlds battle will define the planet over the coming decades?*

KEN: Yes. China and Russia view the old world as superior, and the slow world controls the fast world. There is no doubt who has control over the data and the networks in China and Russia. The Internet 1.0 was a great agent for democracy. Witness the Arab Spring, where one million people went into Tahrir Square in Cairo and Mubarak left office without a shot being fired. However, as the Chinese and Russians are learning, the Internet 2.0 can be transformed into the greatest social engineer in human history, where a small group of people can use it to control enormous populations. China's social credit system is a notorious scorecard enabled by the internet, allowing an authoritarian regime to control its population.

In the United States, we're struggling for an answer. We love the internet. We love the convenience. We love all the things that it has enabled, until we experience how it can threaten us, invade our privacy, or undermine established institutions. Clearly, social media have incredible utility, but we've seen how the sheer scope of Facebook, Google, and Twitter can have adverse consequences as amplifiers of fringe opinion. Do we favor free speech, or do we see these as quasi-utilities that need to be regulated?

This has created a tension around the world that's being sorted out quite differently by different societies. I have a feeling that this tension will not abate as the pace of technological change is outstripping our collective institutions' abilities to even comprehend the extent of its impact.

But at a time when those institutions are at their weakest, we may need them the most, ironically, as the declines in trust elsewhere are notable.

STEVE: *So how do we get out of this situation?*

KEN: Principled leadership being at the helm is our only hope. Having a "true north" set of values is the common denominator in leading amidst the unknowable.

President Bush's behavior on September 11, 2001, is the prime example. The last thing he could have imagined when he woke up that morning was that the United States would've entered a war on terror that continues to this day. But he led through it, defined by his character, with a consistent message that we will not tire, we will not falter, and we will not fail.

Just as the U.S. Treasury bill is the risk-free rate against which all corporate bonds are priced, in many respects, the Office of the President of the United States is the political risk-free rate against which all global actors gauge. If the risk of that office increases, global risks are amplified.

Fortunately, almost all our presidents have understood that the Office of the Presidency is more important than the occupant. Of course, the behavior of Donald Trump was a material deviation from the norm, and we can see the impact that had not only on behaviors of allies and adversaries around the world but also on the soul of America.

STEVE: *This observation echoes your thoughts on how to be a good leader, a servant-leader.*

KEN: We need to recognize that a leader's responsibility is to serve those being led, *all of them*. Our Founding Fathers highlighted that power is derived from the consent of the governed and that micromanaging a large population just isn't possible. As that population is more connected through technology and every fracture is magnified, people will need to be guided, not managed. This world favors a compassionate, conservative philosophy, one that is fiscally conservative and socially tolerant.

STEVE: *Why?*

KEN: Because it has to. The government's resources and capacity are limited. Relying on deliberative bodies that comprise individuals without the collective talent to even comprehend, let alone manage, the forces of change is a bad bet. Moreover, despite the wishes of the progressive movements, the United States cannot run deficits forever. Eventually the debt will come due. We must find market solutions to our problems to serve the most people for the longest time. Having a population dependent on the government for its well-being is not sustainable. Markets, while not perfect, have been the greatest antipoverty program ever. Focusing on expanding opportunity leads to more compassionate outcomes, and socially tolerant because it is *right*.

We now are composed of a population less defined by labels, which is more fragmented, more connected, and more skeptical of institutional arrangements than any in modern history. It can vote with its feet very quickly. This group will only tolerate the moral compass pointing toward the protection of human freedoms. They want competent and fair governance. This is why victimized groups seem so quick to protest in the streets. They want their freedoms. They want to be respected. That's the essence of compassionate conservatism, and that was in the themes introduced by President Bush's words as early as 2000. He saw it early.

Compassionate leadership does not start with government. It actually ends there. It starts at home—at our kitchen tables, on our sidewalks, and in our communities. In the end, our government reflects our values, so that hard work will not be wasted. If we live that philosophy, the politicians will get the drift, or they will be ousted. Seen in this context, party labels are less important over time. Americans can judge leadership.

We have to play the long game with this philosophy. Countries have a collective heartbeat, and the United States is no exception. We've had generational challenges in our past and over a series of cultural and political cycles, we've moved forward. Sometimes we make mistakes, but the country corrects its course. Many times, tragedies happen that spur such corrections. At other times, the collective psyche of the country was unmet by current leaders, and they got ousted. The key is to remain optimistic and retain perspective that Americans will get to the right answer, even though the path won't necessarily be a straight line.

STEVE: *To quote someone I know: We need to be the fastest tortoise in the race.*

KEN: Ha. That person sounds very wise. We need to keep going, stick to the plan, and remain focused on the goal. That philosophy worked in building one of the most durable investment platforms in the country, which put up steady returns over a long period of time that featured an internet boom and bust from 1997 through 2001, two financial crises, and numerous ups and downs of commodity prices. Some traders were able to make considerably higher returns than we did in individual years, but the business graveyard is full of those who didn't. Similarly, the business graveyards are filled with those who chased their dreams in get-rich-quick strategies. Those rabbits sure were cool to watch, but this tortoise just chugged along.

This country is not that different. Since the 1700s, we have made tremendous progress on so many fronts, but we cannot lose sight of the fact that at the age of one hundred, we fought a civil war, and it took another hundred years for both women and minorities to have their civil rights protected by law. Sure, we are a great country, but we did not evolve smoothly. Deplorable events like that of January 6, 2021, demonstrate that we're still working at it. Yet, in the end, we tend to get more right than wrong. We cannot lose sight of the long race we are running.

CHAPTER 18

NORMAN ROCKWELL
WAS A PAINTER

STEVE: *You've shared a number of meaningful Ken-isms up to this point—maxims that genuinely inform a way of looking at or navigating the world. As this is the final section of our conversation, I figured I'd heard them all. But today you sprang a new one on me. One that I might call bittersweet. Lest we keep our readers in suspense, would you mind sharing it with them and the reason it has suddenly become so relevant to this endeavor?*

KEN: Sure. It's this: Norman Rockwell was a painter, and *Leave It to Beaver* was a TV show.

I should explain that this Ken-ism, as you call it, preceded the Washington riots of January 6, 2021, that disgraced our country. When consoling friends and after life's disappointments, I often say, "Life is life. If it is not working out perfectly, it's still your life. We all have joys, sorrows, wins, losses, and ties. Life is a series of learnings along a journey that is by no means perfect."

That seems rather obvious, but the nostalgia that Norman Rockwell so accurately captures in his work is just that—nostalgia. Of course, the harmonious family depicted in the *Leave It to Beaver* TV show was pure fiction.

STEVE: *So we should enjoy the paintings and the reruns but not think reality works that way. Is that your point?*

KEN: Exactly. The truth is, while you may work toward perfection, there's no such thing. Everyone has flaws. Every life has flaws. The chart of every journey has a jagged edge. We all need to take a breath and be slower to pass judgment.

STEVE: *I don't think you've been guilty of any deception along this line. Clearly, you've led a life that many might wish they had—in terms of both accomplishment and wealth—but you've been honest in pulling back the curtain to suggest that your some-what dysfunctional childhood home, your disappointments at the end of your time at NGP, and the 2020 events in your personal life may help many learn the same lesson.*

KEN: I like to think I've been honest.

STEVE: *You have, and I know that's why it's so important to you to share your own experiences of 2020.*

KEN: It is, and I will, but, as I said, my citing the Norman Rockwell/*Leave It to Beaver*-ism precedes 2020. Never more so than in 2015, when my friend and mentor Richard Rainwater passed away at the age of seventy-one. The tragedy actually started several years before, when a horrific disease held the Richard Rainwater I knew hostage.

STEVE: *As I understand it, he was diagnosed with progressive supranuclear palsy, a degenerative disease of the brain, in 2009. And by 2011, a court declared him incapaci-tated and named his son Matthew his legal guardian.*

KEN: This was a cruel irony of fate. Here was this guy who was so full of life, whose stock in trade was his personality. He didn't produce *anything*. He had ideas and a way of relat-ing to people that drew them into his orbit. He'd bring people together in a way no one else could. He didn't just hold meetings. He emceed a circus. He lit up a room, and his enthusiasm was contagious. In the end, he got people to believe they could do anything.

And along comes this almost unheard-of disease, with its primary symptom that of robbing the victim of his or her speech and facial expressions. This robbed Richard of his currency.

STEVE: *How did he handle that?*

KEN: It was hard to tell—he was a prisoner in his own body. Nobody could talk to him directly to get an accurate read. As he deteriorated, his sons Todd and Matthew and his brother Walter, along with the wonderful people in his office, did their best to entertain him, keep him engaged, and provide great social interactions. His team of caregivers made sure he was always comfortable. During this time, there was a steady stream of friends and old colleagues who would make their way to Fort Worth to sit with him for his daily lunch and relish the telling of old stories, no matter how embellished. It was obvious that Richard enjoyed these visits, but the tragedy was not lost on anybody.

STEVE: *And then there was the funeral.*

KEN: His funeral was a real gathering. It included so many friends and associates from his life who made their way to the Broadway Baptist Church near downtown Fort Worth. Just as in life, people *came* to Fort Worth on that sunny day in early October. It was so fitting. It seemed to me that everyone turned out. I was happy to see the nucleus of his 1990s office there. That was the time and place where I recall seeing Richard the happiest—holding court with each of us and the various visitors who came through the office to talk deals. I know Richard would have been happy to see all of us there. Even Rick Scott, then governor of Florida and soon thereafter a U.S. senator, made the trip.

Richard's son Todd had asked me to speak at the service. I gladly accepted the honor on the spot. In planning my remarks, my mind started channeling Richard. Not only did I want to say something memorable in his honor, but also, I felt empowered to do just about anything I wanted—right or wrong, appropriate or not. In the end, I had a risky idea. I would channel my best Richard and try to have his presence really felt at the gathering.

STEVE: *That sounds juicy. What was your "Amazing Grace" moment?*

KEN: You could call it that now, but at the time, I was scared shitless. I took a chance. I prepared my remarks, but, more important, I prepared my outfit.

STEVE: *Your outfit? At a funeral service?*

KEN: Underneath my suit, I put on my gray Stanford Graduate School of Business T-shirt and my black workout shorts in lieu of my traditional white undershirt and boxers. Richard always had a workout room in his office, and this was Richard's ever-present workout outfit that he would have no qualms about wearing around the office, no matter how formal or important the office visitors were. He even held meetings while he was on the treadmill. Many afternoons, he stayed in his workout gear until he went home for the night.

With my undergarments in place, I donned my dark suit and tie and put white sneakers in a brown bag that would crumple up and fit neatly under my armpit. I knew that Richard was not that religious and the downtown Baptist church where the service was held was not the place that so many of his contemporaries would place his final memory. I wanted to provide something that would be vintage Richard. I had to play the part, no matter the cost.

The attendees filed into the huge church and solemnly took their seats in the grandiose main sanctuary while the organ played to set the somber and contemplative mood. I started walking up the center aisle, being ushered to the main pulpit where I would be seated alongside the other speakers. Julie walked with me, but took her seat among the congregation, unaware of my plan. I chose not to tell her in case I chickened out at the last minute.

As I walked up the center aisle, I saw one of my old office colleagues, John Goff, who now has become one of the most successful real estate developers and asset managers in the nation. I stopped to check in with him. He expected me to just say hello and exchange funeral-service pleasantries. But I had a piece of business to do with him. "Hey John," I said, hiding my brown sneaker-filled bag behind my back. "Listen, I may be doing something that I hope is funny. However, I don't know if it will go over well or not, so I need you to cover for me. Just laugh or clap, or something."

He nodded with a gentle grin—his vintage pleasant, yet careful, look. "Of course, Ken. For sure," he replied, easing my nervousness in that moment. So I continued my trek up to the grand pulpit.

STEVE: *Had you cleared your idea with anyone?*

KEN: Not a soul. While I had on my dark suit and tie with my black formal shoes and socks, I knew what I was hiding, but wanted to leave myself an out if I felt that it would go over like a lead balloon. I can't recall the order I was set to speak, but the service, while nice, was missing something vintage Richard. I decided to go for it.

STEVE: *Okay, I'm waiting.*

KEN: When it was my time to talk, I stood up and said, "You know there's something wrong here." I stepped to the side of the lectern, and fully aware of the anticipatory silence that hung over the congregation, I started to undress.

First my jacket, then my tie. I could hear some chatter from the sanctuary. Seconds seemed like hours. Then, I took off my cuff links and undid my belt while I slipped off my shoes. I followed that by stripping off my black socks, exposing the white gym socks that hid underneath. There was an uneasy chitchat starting to build in the crowd, uncertain as to where I was going with this. Then I took off my shirt and quickly followed by dropping my suit pants and stepping one leg out at a time until the pile of clothes at my feet resembled a laundry bag that had somehow been emptied on the stage.

I didn't have time to pull my sneakers out of the brown bag, but I didn't need to. I stood there in front of the throng, in a gray T-shirt, black shorts, and white tube socks as if I was ready to go on a run. Even Julie didn't know what I was planning. I did catch her eye as I was dropping my pants, and I could feel what she was thinking: *What the hell is he doing?*

In my stocking feet, I extended my arms as wide as I could on my five-foot-seven-inch frame and said proudly, "This is how I remember Richard. This is the way Richard would be attending this service!" The congregation erupted in laughter and applause as if to collectively exhale following the somber playing of the "Ave Maria" hymn and the few solemn eulogies that preceded mine.

With the crowd in a mood to hear my remarks, there I stood on the pulpit, comfortable in my shorts and T-shirt, recounting what I believe to have been Richard's magic. He could get people to think big and attempt things they never would have thought they could achieve—like disrobing in front of every dignitary and friend in the city of Fort Worth.

While it was a real risk, I felt I had my downside covered since John Goff said he would have my back. After the service, I went up to him, in relief, and said, "Boy, I'm glad they liked that. I had no idea how it would go over, so knowing you were going to start clapping really gave me some confidence to go for it."

He quickly replied, "That was ballsy, Ken. I'm not really sure I would've done what you did. I'm sure glad it went over well. I'm not sure I would've cheered or laughed had it fallen flat."

"Thanks a lot, pal!" I said somewhat sarcastically, still not knowing if he was flashing his deadpan dry humor or if he really had considered hanging me out to dry. Good thing it didn't matter.

STEVE: *That was in September 2015, a month and a half after you had decided on the timing of your relinquishing the title of CEO of NGP. Do you think there was some connection?*

KEN: Looking back, I think so, even if it was more subconscious at the time. I was clearly feeling liberated as I was starting to think about what the next chapter of my life would bring. So, about a month later, when we attended the Bush Center event at which Margaret Spelling told me she was planning to leave her position as CEO, my mind was open to think about almost anything.

Richard's passing definitely was an end to a chapter of my life. Despite not seeing him consistently for the previous five years, I always knew he was there, and his Fort Worth office was always a place where I'd be welcome. I enjoyed popping in on the amazing team Richard had around him—a team gifted in not only managing his family office but also filling the key role of being ebullient cheerleaders for Richard and his entourage. With his passing, my professional youth passed as well. It represented the closing of a chapter in my life. For the first time, as a fifty-two-year-old, I felt the reality that not everything goes according to plan.

STEVE: *What was your epiphany?*

KEN: Life is short, Norman Rockwell was a painter, and *Leave It to Beaver* was a TV show.

STEVE: *Clearly, you had dealt with extreme volatility in your upbringing and your business career, yet you came through it well. Plus, the trying moments you and your family experienced as you supported Julie in her struggles while you both were busy raising a family made it clear that reality was quite different from the Norman Rockwell nostalgia of a simpler time, or the picture-perfect family depicted on television.*

As we talk about life now, it's apparent that reality has diverged from Norman Rockwell and Leave It to Beaver *even more.*

KEN: 2020 was a doozy in so many ways. However, out of every challenge comes opportunity. Remember the Rainwater investment philosophy: Wherever there is chaos, there is opportunity.

STEVE: *Obviously the biggest international story of 2020 was the COVID pandemic, managed, or not managed, by one of the most divisive presidents in American history. How can you not be depressed when thinking back on this year?*

KEN: I guess I'm confident that this country finds ways to survive. It always has. We have been through pandemics, world wars, global financial crises, and massive social unrest, yet we persevere. Now, that is not to minimize the immense tragedies that each of these dislocations have caused. Human suffering is tragic, especially when it could have been avoided. However, my larger point is that, as a nation, America has an uncanny ability to bounce back.

Early in the pandemic year, I penned an editorial extolling the virtues of the three pillars of American society: the public sector, the private sector, and the philanthropic DNA of the American people. The COVID year put each of these on display, warts and all. Yet what was so amazing was that when our public-sector dysfunction prevented real solutions from being promoted and did so little to bring this country together, our private and philanthropic sectors picked up the slack. Millions of individual acts of kindness all over the country were on display daily, many from the most unassuming places. Front-line essential workers kept our country going, even as our politicians tried their best to shut it down. Our valiant health-care workers and first responders worked tirelessly. Our charities did much to help those with no safety net.

In the end, the capitalist spirit of innovation and investment brought biomedical researchers and large pharmaceutical companies together to both invent a vaccine in record time and mobilize one of the fastest and most comprehensive manufacturing projects the world has seen in a long time. Forget the fact that the original scientific investigators who concocted the vaccine were serial scientific entrepreneurs who'd been working on cures for diseases all over the world. We have to be proud of the system that provided the intellectual capital protection that empowers scientists to discover and investors to fund them. Plus, we cannot ignore an emergency moment in time where the powers that be significantly reduced the regulatory red tape that normally stalls innovation.

STEVE: *There you go defending capitalism again.*

KEN: You're damn right. There were literally hundreds of researchers working on this project, all empowered by the same system and its rule of law. I maintain that an autocratic system cannot create this healthy competition for a solution among the world's greatest minds.

The tragedy is that we could have done so much better and avoided thousands of deaths and human suffering if we had all worked together. But a system that relies on a single body to do the right thing is often disappointed. I will take our crappy performance over that of a dictatorship. The proof is in the pudding. Authoritarian regimes have to resort to stealing the intellectual property of American entrepreneurs because they cannot lead in innovation themselves. That fact is borne out all over the world, but particularly in China and Russia.

STEVE: *The human tragedy here was on a scale we have not seen in a very long time. How can you explain your optimism?*

KEN: In September of 2020, the *Dallas Morning News* editors asked me to contribute to its pre-election Sunday opinion section to discuss how I could be optimistic amid the strident divisions leading up to the November election and the medical and economic tragedy of the global COVID pandemic.

I had my "optimism" column written well ahead of the publication deadline, as I am prone to do, given my study skills dating back to my time at St. Mark's. I had researched the work being done on the virus and the economic innovation that had occurred during the pandemic. I had my facts and figures lined up, with expert sources to substantiate my conclusions. I felt like a real American historical philosopher ready to make the case that America would bounce back.

Then, after finishing the column, I escaped to the mountains with friends for a final trip to our New Mexico ranch prior to its sale, eager to submit the essay upon my return. But instead of submitting the essay, something came over me—the feeling of a herd of elephants sitting on my chest after a brief fainting spell the night before.

I didn't know it at the time, but *I'd had a heart attack.*

Reading my body's signals, I called my doctor on the morning of October 6. Concerned, he asked that I drive to his office at the Baylor Scott and White complex near downtown Dallas. I obeyed. I didn't return home until October 16, and, when I did, I was sporting five new connections in and around my heart. A team of skilled and compassionate caregivers saved my life. Good thing I didn't park in short-term parking!

STEVE: *And then?*

KEN: Bruised but not broken, tired, but not worn down, I followed the well-traveled path of so many who had come before me to regain strength and stamina through a prescribed cardiac rehabilitation program. After twelve weeks, I regained virtually all my strength, lost about fifteen pounds, and have recorded blood pressure and cholesterol levels of someone twenty years my junior. If I keep my shirt on, there are no real signs of my travails, even though the scar I am sporting would make quite the cocktail party conversation.

How blessed I was to have world-class health care and caring medical professionals surround me. This was not a low-tech operation.

STEVE: *I imagine going through something like that—particularly at age fifty-seven when there have been no warning signs—might change the way you look at things.*

KEN: The experience definitely shifted my perspective: During my ten-day ordeal I went on a political cleanse, as my friend Arthur Brooks would describe. Despite my hospital stay occurring about two weeks prior to the presidential election, I watched precisely *zero* minutes of any TV news show and read not a single story about the election or the bickering in Washington. Given what I was going through, the political dysfunction and immaturity seemed even more nonsensical. Thankfully, there was some good baseball to get me through a few painful troughs.

At the same time, I had the opportunity to watch teams of caring professionals working three shifts all over the Baylor complex, focused on getting me home. Seeing First World medical care up close was eye opening. Having the time to digest my own mortality was invaluable.

These health professionals are our nation's essential employees. They are servant-leaders. They should be the role models for our elected officials a couple of thousand miles away. They didn't occupy their time with the shenanigans in Washington. Their focus was on their role in helping me move forward. Their compassionate and positive attitudes shined.

I had to rewrite my column. Our health-care workers were fighting hard through the pandemic, despite the political dysfunction. They hadn't given up. And with people like that working all over this country, America wouldn't give up, either.

Americans are the leading risk-takers and innovators on this planet. We are unafraid to fail, and we have the tenacity to learn from our mistakes, and the resiliency to try again. Our entrepreneurial, immigrant mentality is what helped us persevere, just as it had in challenges throughout our history.

While the situation in 2020 and 2021 was not the same as prior crises—this pandemic has tragically killed hundreds of thousands of Americans, cost millions their jobs, and disrupted the daily lives of millions more—we are still able to apply lessons taught by history.

While we were all caught up in the disaster-news cycle and dire predictions, innovation didn't slow down; it was just out of the headlines. Whole industries were adjusting to new conditions. New technologies were tested. Old ways were discarded. Only with the perspective of time will we be able to appreciate what happened.

Our grief for the tragic loss of life and hardship suffered by so many was real. Over time, the initial pain would lessen, even if the scars would still be with us, but years down the road, we'll have the perspective to understand what was really going on today.

I will also have scars from 2020 that will have healed, leaving the pain a memory. The vision of the wonderful doctors, nurses, and support teams who saved my life are seared in my memory forever. The noise coming out of Washington and the petty problems that seem to occupy a disproportionate amount of time seem trivial to me today.

At the same time, Daniel and Rachel went above and beyond. Each of them sacrificed time early in their professional careers to return home to help me when I needed

it most. They sat with me in the hospital and helped arrange the home for my rehabilitation. They regulated my diet and my phone use to help reduce cholesterol and stress.
I'll never know how it looked from their perspective to see their father weakened and
in dire need of assistance. They made me proud.

While trite, having a run-in with my own mortality did put things in perspective.

STEVE: *So are you going to change your life now?*

KEN: People ask me, "Now what? Are you going quit your job now that you have a
new sense of your mortality?" If I didn't enjoy what I was doing with my time, I guess I
would have that reaction. I feel kind of boring in that I can't really think of something
I'm going to go do just because I had a heart attack.

STEVE: *A bucket list?*

KEN: Not at all. No skydiving for me. I guess I don't really have a bucket list. However, I seem to have developed a new "fuck it" list, trying hard not to sweat the small
stuff. There are places I haven't been that would be nice to go see, but I'm not going to
go out of my way to see them. I've traveled so much my whole life that I'm less interested in running around the globe checking off sights like some sort of scavenger hunt.

While the COVID experience radically changed how we live today and maybe
beyond, there is a silver lining, provided I stay healthy. I experienced my home, my
friends, and my neighborhood. While restaurants were closed, I rediscovered the
kitchen, the dining room table, and backyard patios. This aspect of the experience was
kind of pleasant. Not to take anything away from the human tragedy of the disease,
for those lucky enough to be spared the infection's wrath, there was a bright side to it
if you looked.

STEVE: *There you go again. Do you always find a silver lining in tragedy?*

KEN: I do approach the glass as half full. I never want to be around people who are eternal pessimists, so it makes no sense to be one. As my friend Gerald Turner, the president
of Southern Methodist University, likes to say, "It doesn't cost any more to be optimistic."
Said another way, have you ever wanted to follow someone who was a pessimist?

STEVE: *When you put it that way, it seems rather obvious. You once told me you had
firsthand experience with someone who was dying and was able to stare death down
and maintain an optimistic outlook?*

KEN: Yes. My dear friend Dave Roy, who passed away after a bout with pancreatic cancer in 2016, was a real inspiration. Pancreatic cancer is usually a short-term death sentence, but he fought valiantly while maintaining a wonderfully positive disposition through it all. We enjoyed two different weekends fishing at our New Mexico property while he was in between drug trials and other painful cancer treatments. He was able to enjoy my family in those moments. These memories will be with me forever. His life was dominated by his fight against the disease, but he was still able to approach each day with optimism and a real sense of joy—at least while he had a fly rod in his hand and was casting at trophy-sized trout. He was never bitter.

My heart attack and open-heart surgery hit me at age fifty-seven, so I feel that I have lots of life left to live. While I don't know what my expiration date is, I do know that there will come a time when I won't be able to wade in a river or tie on a fly. Suffice it to say that I have a little more carpe diem in me than I did back in September of 2020.

The good news is I'm spending my days doing work that's intellectually challenging and doing it around people whose company I enjoy. If that were to change, then I wouldn't hesitate to pivot again. In the meantime, my personal investment business has found me wading into the wild world of esports, technology venture capital, and real estate development. These are all new industries to me, so I am learning as I go. I want my time spent on things that excite my mind. This allows me to remain optimistic and forward-looking even if my life experiences volatility.

STEVE: *Speaking of volatility, another unplanned change in your life occurred during the COVID-infested year of 2020.*

KEN: Yes. Julie and I ended our thirty-year marriage—which brings us back to "Norman Rockwell was a painter, and *Leave It to Beaver* was a TV show." From the outside looking in, it may have appeared that Julie and I were a model couple, but over the prior few years it became increasingly clear that we weren't on the same page. She fought heroically to overcome her bouts with depression and, for the most part, was successful. But there was more to our story than her mental illness.

Over the years, our interests diverged, as did the time we spent together. She dove into civic causes and the local theater scene, while I dove into my work and other philanthropic boards. We related well to each other at the surface, but as we aged, our priorities grew to differ. The daily grind of life masked that divergence for the most part, although it would be naive to think that her frequent relapses were unrelated to our growing apart.

Beginning in 2016, she relapsed with greater frequency and, while ECT treatments were effective in getting her back to normal, they did take their toll—on her and on us. Without my even realizing it, I found myself doing things more out of obligation and the need to support her, versus doing things that made me happy. For the most part, my happiness occurred outside of the house. While we had some great moments, I couldn't really relax and be myself at home, out of fear of setting her off or tripping some hidden wire that could cause another relapse. As a result, I stayed at work longer and found time to spend with friends away from Julie. I started this tome during the evenings after she retired for the night.

She did the same. Her time was occupied with theater groups, nonprofit work, book clubs, running groups, a dream group, and a plethora of other friends. She seemed to draw energy from everyone around her except me.

It all came to a head when the COVID lock-in occurred. We had Daniel and Rachel back home from New York, and we were all working from home. We were together twenty-four seven, although we each had our own private space from which to work. Daniel and Rachel had full schedules, as did I, as I tried to ensure that the Bush Center was able to adapt to some real challenges while also navigating dramatic depreciation in the value of our family's portfolio. I wasn't the happiest of campers, even though I tried to keep an even keel. Through it all, however, we were a family. We were able to eat dinner together and take some long walks around our new neighborhood. But, in the end, Julie was more affected by the closures, since her diversions were now unavailable.

I could see the events were taking their toll, and I tried to offset her losses. She had big plans to go to Peru for her sixtieth birthday that had to be canceled. I surprised her with a trip to Los Angeles and Las Vegas to see her favorite entertainer, Leslie Odom Jr., the weekend before COVID shut down travel. On her actual birthday, I planned an impromptu surprise party with friends in a neighborhood park.

As usual, I tried my best. But in this instance, my best wasn't good enough, for whatever reason.

In May, Julie succumbed again to a bout of depression and was, once again, able to recover with the help of a great team of doctors and her willingness to get better. I always admire her for not quitting when I know there's a temptation to do just that. Her recovery time bled into our summer and the time at our ranch in Colorado, where we had planned a family reunion of sorts with her siblings and their families. After another successful sequence of ECT, a more determined Julie showed up at that reunion.

One aspect of her recovery led her to confront me about our relationship and the many ways we had diverged. She was candid in saying that she thought we may not be the best match for this last phase of our lives. She highlighted differences that earlier in our marriage were insignificant, but now had taken on a new scale.

She asked for a separation so that she could go away for a year and travel and see friends and experience people and places that were missing in her life—an "eat, pray, love year" she called it. I did not stop her. Deep down, I knew she spoke the truth.

I didn't do anything *to* her, or her to me. At least I don't think I did. Obviously, in hindsight, I was making choices that caused yellow lights to appear, even if they weren't intentionally lit. We still cared for each other and our children. We were still connected. However, our relationship had become forced. Our communication had become stilted and superficial. We stopped having fun together.

STEVE: *So how did this play out?*

KEN: Our separation began in July of 2020, and we each began to process the meaning of our time apart. It was apparent that we were each better people away from the other.

My heart issue accelerated the conversation. She had to cut short her time with friends to return to Dallas the morning of my surgery. Since she had my medical power of attorney and was still legally my wife, I needed her in the hospital with me. Having not seen her since mid-July, to say it was weird for our next meeting to be in the pre-op room while I was getting an IV and being prepped for surgery would be an understatement. I was conflicted to see her there providing me comfort when we'd been apart and out of close touch for a couple of months. We both knew where our marriage was headed, but the surgery took precedence.

After the surgery, our perspectives clarified, maybe for different reasons. For me, I had a new lease on life, an appreciation that my time on this earth is really finite, and that it was time for me to let go of things that did not bring me joy. For Julie, from my perspective, it appeared that she had grown comfortable being away from me and from Dallas and not being "Mrs. Ken Hersh." She seemed happy and relaxed.

STEVE: *Did you see this coming?*

KEN: It had been brewing for quite some time. I knew that she was a fish out of water when we moved to Dallas, and she wrote about that quite openly in her book. However, our growing family kept us busy and as my career evolved, we were able to do some pretty exciting things as we built a solid community of friends in the city. I was heartened when, a few years back, she started calling Dallas home. That was a real leap for her when she was asked where she was from. She stopped talking about her growing up as a Navy brat, and instead answered that she was from Dallas.

But, as far back as 2000, she expressed doubt about being my partner for life. I read about it in her book. She wrote about my psoriatic arthritis, which, at that time, was not under the control of medicines that would be developed years later. In those days, it was difficult for me to even roll around on the floor with the young Daniel and Rachel. She envisioned taking care of me in my old age or being "trapped on cruise ships and in card games when [her] legs could still scale mountains." She wrote, "I still loved Ken, but squirmed under the weight of our future."*

This was pertinent in ways more than just physical. Julie was always in touch with her feelings, and her book held nothing back about how she felt as my career took off. She explained:

> While I meditated with palms open, *Forbes* magazine featured Ken in an article. We were on different tracks. Ken's route created more wealth, more recognition, more events to attend, and more possessions. He reveled in his business success. I was happy for Ken but felt as if I'd become the caretaker for his spoils. I was the one who dealt with his children, his laundry, his mother, and the giant house of his dreams while he traveled and made brilliant decisions. I felt overshadowed. I wanted to be more than Ken Hersh's wife or the mother of Ken Hersh's children.†

While these words were written about how she felt in the early 2000s, there is no escaping the fact that she never really stopped feeling that way, despite another twenty years of living together, building our family, and enjoying countless adventures.

I read those words in drafts of her book and we talked about her finding her own identity as she dove into her friends and her extracurricular activities. I gave her a ton of space in our relationship and was careful not to ask too much of her unless she agreed. I thought we had made progress in that department, even if it caused me to experience excessive loneliness in our marriage.

Now, with the clarity that we had both achieved, albeit from different experiences, the divorce conversation was inevitable.

STEVE: *Was that a difficult conversation to have?*

KEN: While sad, the conversations we had about splitting up were not as painful as you'd expect. Unraveling thirty years together became emotional along the way, but deep down we knew we would be better off apart. It was not healthy for us to stay together. Of course, there were tears, but there were hugs as well. Regardless of our marital status, we'll always be a part of each other's life.

---

* Julie K. Hersh, *Struck by Living: From Depression to Hope* (Austin, TX: Greenleaf Book Group Press, 2011), 135.
† Hersh, *Struck by Living*, 135. As part of our divorce, Julie K. Hersh changed her name to Julie H. Kosnik; however, her book was published while her last name was still Hersh.

We began our discussions by going over our respective goals and concerns. Two days later, without any lawyers present, we met to talk about how we'd divide things to achieve these goals. It took us about an hour to figure out virtually all of it. We did it nicely because we still wanted to be good parents and grandparents and we couldn't be that if we were at each other's throats. In my opinion, we had too much good history together to deny it ever existed. This process was a testament to our level of mutual respect.

We are two very lucky people. Our relationship just ran its course. There's nothing ugly or wrong about that. We could have tried to force it back together—to try and put a round peg in a square hole—but we both realized doing that would not be optimal. For my physical health now and her mental health, we needed to move on independently.

STEVE: *Why was this so collaborative? I've heard horror stories about wealthy couples splitting up and getting sucked into years of messy litigation.*

KEN: Frankly, she set the tone, and I'll forever be appreciative of her approach. It was a collaborative and cooperative process that concluded in March of 2021.

I'd been deeply involved in helping Julie through her tough times and worked hard not to contribute to relapses. Now that we're apart, I realize I'm no longer responsible for her and that she, in fact, is quite capable of taking care of herself. She has the kids and a great group of friends who support her if she needs them. She is determined and willful and has plenty of life left to live. I'm confident she will be better off away from me.

STEVE: *And you?*

KEN: I'll emphasize again that life is what happens to us while we're busy making other plans. The straight-A student in me is disappointed that my marriage failed. I never wanted to be like my parents. Obviously, I share in the responsibility for that failure, and I'll come to appreciate how much better I could have been as the years go on. Needless to say, I am blessed with wonderful children who make me proud every day of the week. I don't regret my life with Julie one bit.

While my path now won't be neat, clean, and predictable, I will roll with the punch. I'm not afraid of an unscripted future. Once again, I'm energized by not knowing what the future will bring. In many ways, my entire life has been built for this moment. Whether it be writing a cold-call letter, building a successful business amidst massive volatility, taking a chance on the Bush Center post, or enduring the ups and downs of a difficult personal situation, I have learned something and landed squarely on my own two feet.

Yes, Norman Rockwell was a painter, and *Leave It Beaver* was a TV show, but there is nothing wrong with that. Norman Rockwell was a damn good painter who evoked emotions that touched the heart of a nation, and *Leave It to Beaver* was a lot of fun to watch.

Steve, try not to overthink it. Just keep your eyes on the horizon. In life there is just one gear—forward.

STEVE: *Sounds like advice from a speedy tortoise.*

KEN: Exactly.

EPILOGUE

STEVE: *You are a thoughtful guy, so I'm sure this process has crystalized some of your perspective. I'd like to conclude with a sort of study guide for anyone who's taken the time to read your story.*

KEN: Shoot!

STEVE: *Here goes. What are five things you learned about yourself while writing the book?*

KEN:

1. I seem to be comfortable with and almost welcome the unknown. People look at me and think I am an extreme planner, but I don't plan that much and that far out. I have tried to create optionality for the future and then be confident enough to raise my hand when something appears.
2. I always look forward. Mistakes happen, but I try to adjust and move on.
3. I keep coming back to a core group of friends.
4. I cherish the relationships I've made throughout my life.
5. Ready, shoot, aim is not always a bad strategy. Or, to say it differently, take a shot, and call whatever you hit the target.

STEVE: *What are five things you want people to take away after reading this?*

KEN:

1. Keep moving forward. Life has two gears: forward and off. Nothing was ever achieved by idling in neutral.

2. Don't be afraid to put yourself in uncomfortable situations. No muscle was ever strengthened without being stretched.

3. Don't forget to have fun along the way.

4. You cannot be all things to all people. Focus is rewarded.

5. Leaders lead teams by serving them. Nothing is accomplished alone.

STEVE: *If you ruled the world, what are five things you'd do to ensure that we survive and flourish?*

KEN:

1. Give people freedom so that they can have agency to live the lives they want with dignity.

2. Support free and fair markets to ensure people won't become dependent on the government.

3. Ensure quality education for every person that includes reading, writing, history, math, and science, and ensure accountability, so no child is left behind.

4. Return government to the role of ensuring the safety and security of "the commons" and the rule of law, while also sustaining a proper safety net for those unable to find safety and security in the market economy.

5. Build tolerance throughout our populations. We must learn to respect each other and value our individual gifts.

6. I'll add a number six for good measure: Get the Texas Rangers a World Series ring!

STEVE: *Who would you like to interview about leadership and other issues of the day—and why?*

KEN:

1. Benjamin Franklin. I want to know what he was really like. He was a philosopher, an inventor, a motivator, and a doer. Of course, he wasn't a perfect person, either. I just want to understand what made him tick.

2. Mozart and Beethoven. A twofer. I'm not that into classical music, but to meet a couple of prodigies who just "felt" the music would be something to behold.

3. Abraham Lincoln. He clearly was our country's greatest president. Governing during the Civil War, having the courage to end slavery, and, most of all, keeping the country together *after* the Civil War makes his story the one to hear.

4. Tom Landry. He was such a cool coach in a game played on emotion. I want to know how he was able to motivate for excellence and create a winning culture while being such a stoic. Nobody could really be *that* cool. I want to see it for myself.

STEVE: *What should government do to make life better for the coming generations, and what* shouldn't *government do?*

KEN:

1. Understand its own limitations and respect what it cannot do and stay out of those areas.

2. Be fiscally responsible while safeguarding our democracy and the institutions of our democracy.

3. Ensure a system where people are rewarded for their efforts and encouraged to live independently of the government.

4. Remain focused on ensuring that the market economy works and celebrating the combination of freedom, democracy, and capitalism that's lifted more people out of poverty, *with dignity*, than any antipoverty program ever has.

5. Teach our children well.

6. Stay out of the bedroom.

STEVE: *You have two adult children. Assuming they have children, what are five pieces of advice you would give them?*

KEN:

1. Do the right thing.
2. Always care about the world around you; take an active interest in your community.
3. Hug and laugh often.
4. Take what you do very seriously but take yourself a whole lot less seriously.
5. Come visit their grandparents often!

STEVE: *This is your last chance to drive your points home. Go for it!*

KEN:

1. Feed your winners—mediocre ones will step up or step out. Others will get out of the way and let you pass them by and will be content that you did.
2. Yellow lights don't turn green—trust that early warning light.
3. Be uncomfortable—believe in yourself enough to have the confidence to take calculated risks.
4. Raise your hand—you will only be able to get hit by a bus if you're in the traffic.
5. Have a foxhole and welcome people into it—earn and build the trust of those closest to you.
6. If life gives you lemons, make lemonade—things are never as bad as they seem.
7. Be nice and respectful always—demanding doesn't have to be demeaning.
8. Be an optimist. Ask yourself how many people have ever followed a pessimist?
9. Be the fastest tortoise. Slow and steady wins the race, but you have to remain focused to win.
10. Don't be afraid to take your clothes off when delivering a eulogy.

ACKNOWLEDGMENTS

I HAVE WRITTEN HUNDREDS OF pages here recounting stories about events and people who have helped me shape my perspective on life, but that telling did not come together by itself. As a near sixty-year-old, my memory needs to be checked, so I am grateful to my friendly fact-checkers and (courteous) readers who have helped keep me on track. I am also in debt to those who have taught, shaped, and motivated me throughout.

First, Julie H. Kosnik inspired me to pick up my pen. As Julie Hersh, she took the bravest leap of all in telling her story by publishing *Struck by Living*. When your wife writes a book about her life and struggles with depression, there are few secrets left in the household. It was an act of courage and one that has helped so many people come to grips with their depression and find solace in knowing they are not alone. I watched her travel the world talking about her story and being the icebreaker that so many needed to open up about their individual struggles. That is often the first step toward recovery. Julie's book has helped so many. I hope it is a positive step in reducing the stigma around mental illness and that it reinforces the need for positive mental health.

My tale is quite a different animal entirely. I started this exercise with one goal: tell my story to my future grandchildren. As someone who has built a career in the investment business, it is quite hard to point to something and say, "Hey, kids, your grandfather built *that!*" More importantly, in the oil and gas industry, if you ever actually see or smell your product, it's a very bad thing. Other than that pretty blue flame on the stovetop or your water heater pilot light, the actual product that I helped finance is something that should be used and not seen, *ever*.

I would be remiss if I did not name some of the other executives that ran NGP's portfolio companies over my tenure leading the firm. In addition to those named throughout this book, I'd call out Dick Brannon, Jack Brannon, Clinton Koerth, Randy

Stevens, Randy Bruno, Bob Marshall, Mike Grimm, Zane Arrott, Tamy Pollard, Joe Mills, Bill Scarff, Rob Jacobs, Don Gann, Ward Polzin, Tom Isler, Dan Rice, Carl Carter, Embry Canterbury, Kirk Edwards, Maurice Storm, Bryan Sheffield, Greg Laake, Tim Brittain, Mark Hiduke, and John Grier. I learned from each and every one of them over the nearly thirty years in the business. There is another book of stories embedded in this list for sure.

What started out as a professional history morphed into an account of what makes me tick and why—complete with background information for the average reader. This evolution was inspired by Steve Fiffer, my partner in this project. He helped expand the aperture for the project and felt that it could be of value to more than just my future progeny. I think he may have been going on too little sleep when he suggested I restructure it around my significant life lessons and the "Ken-isms" that were peppered throughout our extensive conversations. He also encouraged me to include lessons that future leaders and investors would find helpful. So, if that falls on your deaf ears, please blame Steve. As any good leader understands, it is important to know who to throw under the bus in an emergency!

My friendly set of memory-support personnel started with my work and other professional colleagues. David Albin, John Foster, Dick Covington, Chris Carter, David Hayes, Steve Gardner, Nick Sutton, Ted Gazulis, Phil Smith, Ambassador Robert Jordan, and David Salem each provided good fact-checking as well as thoughtful feedback. I took all their edits to heart. I can't promise that I incorporated all their edits. But I did take them to heart!

Special thanks go to Carol O'Neill and Bill Browder—two of my most respected confidants. Carol and I go back to 1981, and she perhaps knows me as well as anyone. I trust her insights as much as anyone in my life. Bill Browder has been there every step of the way as well. He is the consummate storyteller, and I valued his input. If my story is one-tenth as well told as his, I will have accomplished something.

My personal board of directors also deserves a special mention. My YPO forum-mates—Greg Koonsman, Wade Black, Michael Dardick, Jeff Yarckin, and Mike Karns—have lived with my ups and downs for over a decade. Plus, Robert Alpert, Mike Morgan, Scott Kleberg, John Berg, Bill Davis, and John White have always lent an ear and given me honest feedback along with their friendship.

I also sought out readers who would bring a fresh set of eyes and ears and give me honest feedback. Thanks go to Mike Meece; Zach Clayton; Talmage Boston; Pam Batson; Guy Kerr; Eva Chiang; Bill McKenzie; my sisters, Paula Hersh and Susan Hersh Geller; Samantha Pillsbury; David Rubenstein; Mark Updegrove; and my son, Daniel Hersh. In addition, thanks go to the careful editing eye of Coke Ellington, who brought his career in teaching journalism and writing to bear on the later drafts, as did

Karen Cakebread and the team at Greenleaf Book Group. Tory Tarpley also provided valuable help in creating the finished product.

While they may not have provided detailed edits to this book, my support team in my family office and my wonderful executive assistants have their fingerprints all over my story. People like Randy Chappel, Jim Collet, Rick O'Brien, Andrew Frohman, Jeremy Clark, Matt Shofner, Valerie Dillard, Lauren Minch, Kristi Bernstein, Cameron Smith, Adrianne Morrow, Judy Ingram, J. B. Hayes, Donna Teague, Holly Farmer, and the late Rhonda Houston (plus others I'm sure I'm forgetting) have all been instrumental in keeping me going over the years.

As I reflect on my journey, my relationship with Daniel and Rachel has taken on added importance. They are each unique in their own right, and I am thrilled that our relationships are evolving. They are smart and driven, yet caring. My life would be empty without them. They motivate me to be my best.

Finally, just like every plant needs to be repotted professionally, this plant needed an emotional repotting. Regen Horchow entered my life in late 2020 as my health started to recover and my marriage was ending. She provided me kindness and emotional support during a time when I needed it most. Frequent walks and long conversations were better than therapy for me as we sorted through our respective life transitions during a time of COVID. We approach life in similar ways and see the world similarly. Her gentle, empathetic voice and quality edits were there for me during the past year as this work concluded.

I am fortunate to have found a special person to share this next phase of my life with. As an old acquaintance, she had heard that I was recovering from a heart attack and reached out with a friendly get-well email. That simple gesture served to connect us—a silver lining in an otherwise dreadful situation. Who knows? If I had not had a major health scare, we might not have ever connected. While Julie inspired me to pick up my pen and reflect, Regen inspired me to put it down and go happily into the fog of the future.

Once again, life is a series of historical accidents.

And I sure am lucky to be accident prone.

HOW DID MESA END UP
NEEDING A BAILOUT?

G IVEN MY UNIQUE VANTAGE point and the profile that this transaction had, I would be remiss if I did not offer my analysis as to how the company came to be in such a predicament. The key to understanding the company's circumstances that led to David Batchelder's takeover efforts and our eventual involvement starts with an understanding of Mesa's corporate structure and how T. Boone Pickens was able to manipulate it.

From 1985 through 1991, the company wasn't a company at all. It was actually a publicly traded partnership, more commonly referred to as a master limited partnership, or an MLP. It was called Mesa Limited Partnership. These structures still exist today, but their records of success have been spotty. Partnerships are different from a normal corporation in that they do not pay federal income tax. The taxes (or losses) are "passed through" to every unitholder in the exact proportion that the unitholder owns of the partnership. So a 1 percent unitholder will be allocated 1 percent of the income or losses, as the case may be, and that unitholder has to report that on his or her own tax returns.

There is nothing wrong with the structure, since the unitholder typically enjoys a higher cash-flow yield from these structures than the typical corporate form. In fact, Energy Transfer, which was NGP's biggest success a few years later, was an MLP as well. If the business can afford it, the structure allows distributions to go directly to equity holders and provides a great investment vehicle for them, especially if there were some tax deductions that also flowed through to the individual holders. During the early years, Mesa had distributed in excess of $1 billion to its unitholders. So, for a while at least, they were very happy.

Each MLP has a general partner (GP) who controls the enterprise and limited partners (LPs) who share in the cash flow but have limited governance rights. The GP usually holds a small percentage of ownership in the overall partnership but exercises controls over the whole partnership. The limited partner units are what trade on the public stock exchanges. While there may be a board of directors, the board does not have the same fiduciary obligations as the board of a corporation, since the general partner controls the partnership. Mesa called its board a Board of Advisory. The partnership is really governed by the partnership agreement between the general partner and limited partners.

It's kind of a governance loophole. Of course, when a partnership is formed, the unitholders have to vote in favor of the structure, so their eyes should be wide open as to what they are approving. This contrasts with the governance model of the traditional corporate structure, where shareholders elect the board, the board elects the officers of the company, and the officers carry out the duties of the company, while serving at the pleasure of the board.

At the time, because of generous deductions allowed, most oil and gas deals produced tax losses, yet generated some positive cash distributions. So, from an investor's perspective, a partnership structure was ideal in that you could reduce your taxes with the associated tax loss, yet still get some cash flow from the distributions. Mesa was such a partnership. The general partner, Boone Pickens, had a 2 percent interest and the public unitholders made up the other 98 percent. Those units were traded on the New York Stock Exchange. Boone also owned about 4 percent of the limited partnership units.

Most private oil-drilling deals were done this way, where the operator was the GP, and the investors were the limited partners. The LPs put up the lion's share of the money and then the GP kept total control. That all worked well if the GP was a good manager and created a lot of value for the investors.

In Mesa's case, Boone's game was not to drill wells but rather to make acquisitions. These deals were funded by the partnership issuing debt or equity to raise money for the deal. In the 1980s, they had a nice run because natural gas prices were hanging in there and he was able to amass some decent assets. As long as the unit price increased with each deal, he was able to issue new units to raise the cash needed. Then things went sideways, and their unit price didn't go up. Because the unit price was too low to issue new units to raise money if he wanted to make acquisitions, he had to do so with borrowings.

Early on, Boone identified properties to buy, and since the cost of debt was cheaper than the cost of equity, the name of the game was to max out the amount of the deal you could pay for with borrowed funds and make up the rest with an equity issuance. If the number of units issued was relatively low, the deal would be accretive to the net cash flow per unit of the partnership and the GP could raise the distributions. Then, typically, the unit price would increase, and everyone would be happy. Then, with a higher unit price, the partnership could do a public offering and raise funds to repay the debt, and the whole cycle would start again.

But there was a quirk in the math that caught Boone's eye. Whenever the partnership issued limited partner units, Boone's GP interest, *by contract*, always stayed at 2 percent of the whole. To make it easy to understand, suppose Mesa issued $100 million of units and used that cash to buy a $100 million deal. Then, the public unitholders would immediately have 98 percent of it or, $98 million, and the GP (Boone) would be allocated $2 million of it. Free money for the GP and a 2 percent loss for the limited partners, whenever equity was issued. When Mesa acquired the Amarillo-based Pioneer Corporation for almost $900 million in equity, Boone's GP was able to capture 2 percent of that value essentially for free. The hope was that the deal would be worth more in the future so as to overcome the 2 percent immediate paper loss by a wide margin.

The structure incentivized Boone to keep the unit price up and issue units to pay for just about anything. But it was hard to keep the units trading high when the public holders knew that there would continue to be dilutive offerings in the future. Moreover, since debt was cheaper than issuing dilutive equity, it made more economic sense to use debt whenever possible. But Boone didn't get his 2 percent of a deal that was financed by borrowing the money. He only got his 2 percent when equity was issued.

At least not by contract. So Boone created his own little insider advisory business that "advised" the partnership on every deal and charged a fee on all deals and bank financing that the partnership did. Figuring that the unitholders were better off if the partnership borrowed from the banks rather than suffer dilution, they wouldn't mind if Boone took the same 2 percent in cash that he would've gotten for free if the deal was paid for all with more expensive equity. He must've thought, *Why should I be disadvantaged by helping unitholders use 7 percent debt instead of the 20 percent cost of equity for each deal?*

Boone would win in either case. And just like a broker getting a percentage of the deals, the bigger the deal, the bigger the 2 percent. A billion-dollar deal financed with a billion dollars of debt would net Boone's advisory business a cool $20 million in cash, regardless of whether the deal was worth it. I have no idea what was going through his mind, but everyone had to trust that he was really trying to make the best deal possible and not just earn a higher fee.

During the 1980s, Boone was one of the more aggressive clients of Michael Milken at the investment bank of Drexel Burnham Lambert. Milken promised to raise the money to support Boone's takeover attempts. The formula was pretty straightforward: Boone, through Mesa, would purchase a block of stock of a target company and then, as the saying goes, "get long, then loud." He would hit the airwaves and make the case that the market was undervaluing the company and that the shareholders would be better off selling to him at a higher price. Invariably the stock price would go up and Mesa would make a nice profit on the initial block's purchase, even if the takeover wasn't consummated. In fact, other than the Pioneer deal in 1986, Boone was never successful in taking over another company in this manner, yet Mesa did record large profits for the buying and selling of the stock. In the Pioneer deal, Mesa was the white knight when corporate raider Irwin Jacobs purchased 15 percent of the company and made a cash tender offer.

The unitholders and lenders had to accept the structure and the insider fee arrangements since he was the general partner with total control. If folks didn't like it, they could just sell the units any time they wanted. If banks didn't like it, they didn't have to make him the loan. In fact, Boone even borrowed money to pay the dividend at times, thereby propping up his unit price. Of course, he had a lot of units, so distributions were good cash flow for him personally.

These activities masked what happens when a company takes on too much debt in reliance on a rising commodity price. Mesa was accumulating nice properties, but at increasingly high prices, financed with debt. Despite valiant attempts at operating the assets cheaply, the Mesa unitholders suffered. Ironically, for a champion of shareholder rights, Boone didn't seem to appreciate that his unitholders were suffering the same plight as the shareholders in the companies he targeted. Of course, as one of the largest unitholders, he felt the same pain. And of course, that pain was softened by the fees he was able to extract from the place.

Along the way, in early 1992, it became apparent that the distributions were unsustainable, so it made more sense for the partnership to convert to a corporation with a real board of directors and to be an entity that added value to properties by reinvesting, rather than distributing, the cash flow. However, higher debt levels left over from all those acquisition and partnership distributions, coupled with low natural gas prices, led the company to be short of cash to complete the optimal capital expenditure program. With too little cash to plow back into the business, the company would deteriorate as its assets depleted.

Eventually "Boone Boy" David Batchelder took notice. In 1995, long after the takeover game had ended for Mesa, David Batchelder saw Mesa for what it was—a company with decent assets but with a bad balance sheet and an imperial CEO. As I mentioned before, he advised on Dennis Washington's purchase of a large block of the publicly traded shares to press his case as an equity holder. About the same time, and seemingly independently, another billionaire, Marvin Davis, saw the same thing and also purchased a block of stock.

After a good bit of saber-rattling and dueling lawsuits whereby the new holders threatened to take over the company, Boone and these interlopers reached a standstill agreement. That agreement stated that if Mesa conducted a process to sell itself, sell a major block of assets and retire debt, or enter into a significant equity transaction that would reduce its indebtedness (specifically, an equity infusion of $265 million or greater), then the Batchelder group would stay quiet. If, however, none of those things happened by February 29, 1996, the group would be free to launch a proxy fight at the spring 1996 shareholders' meeting with the aim of taking over the board and gaining control of the company.

As part of an earlier agreement, the Batchelder group was given two seats on the board. And, as part of a larger settlement of the later lawsuits, the company agreed to the Lehman process to sell the company or raise additional equity somehow. This all led up to a hard deadline to strike a deal by February 29, 1996. If that didn't happen, the shareholders could vote to replace Boone, or, worst case, the company would not have had sufficient funds to retire or refinance the major debt maturities on June 30, 1996. Both scenarios had put a gun to Boone's head. He needed a solution, and a face-saving one at that. That set the table for our transaction.

INDEX OF KEN-ISMS

ABOUT THE AUTHORS

Photo by Grant Miller

KEN HERSH'S life has been a series of historical accidents. His story is of a Dallas native who, after graduating from Princeton and Stanford, ventured into the energy industry with no specific training and cofounded and ultimately served as CEO of NGP Energy Capital Management. At NGP, he helped pioneer an investment methodology that enabled NGP to become one of the nation's largest and most successful private investment franchises in the natural resources sector. From 1988 until 2016, under his leadership, NGP invested over $12 billion and achieved a twenty-seven-year compounded rate of return of 30 percent, making it one of the nation's leading investment firms during that period. He and his team succeeded in generating steady returns in one of the most volatile sectors of the economy.

Along the way, he found time to make an impact on his broader community, both locally and nationally, through the efforts of the Hersh Foundation. Ken is known for giving both financial resources and his time to the numerous organizations in which he becomes involved.

As a second act, again with no specific training, he raised his hand in 2016 to assume the leadership of the George W. Bush Presidential Center, where he oversees the organization's operations and public engagement activities, as well as a significant policy institute to support President and Mrs. Bush's priorities of freedom, opportunity, accountability, and compassion. His work to advance its strategic programming and financial stability has ensured that the Bush Center will thrive far into the future.